EMORY UNIVERSITY STUDIES IN LAW AND RELIGION

John Witte Jr., General Editor

BOOKS IN THE SERIES

Faith and Order: The Reconciliation of Law and Religion
Harold J. Berman

Rediscovering the Natural Law in Reformed Theological Ethics
Stephen J. Grabill

The Ten Commandments in History:
Mosaic Paradigms for a Well-Ordered Society
Paul Grimley Kuntz

Theology of Law and Authority in the English Reformation
Joan Lockwood O'Donovan

Power over the Body, Equality in the Family: Rights and
Domestic Relations in Medieval Canon Law
Charles J. Reid Jr.

Political Order and the Plural Structure of Society
James W. Skillen and Rockne M. McCarthy

The Idea of Natural Rights:
Studies on Natural Rights, Natural Law, and Church Law, 1150-1625
Brian Tierney

The Fabric of Hope: An Essay
Glenn Tinder

Religious Human Rights in Global Perspective: Legal Perspectives
Johan D. van der Vyver and John Witte Jr.

Early New England: A Covenanted Society
David A. Weir

Religious Human Rights in Global Perspective: Religious Perspectives
John Witte Jr. and Johan D. van der Vyver

I count it sufficient to have said that nothing may be found in the world so abject or lowly that it gives no witness to God. The poet said, "All things are full of Jove." So long as it endures, whatever is in the world has the power of God hidden under it. If this is discovered through inquiry and knowledge of nature, God will be revealed to us.

Peter Martyr Vermigli, Romans Commentary

Rediscovering the Natural Law in Reformed Theological Ethics

Stephen J. Grabill

William B. Eerdmans Publishing Company
Grand Rapids, Michigan / Cambridge, U.K.

Published 2006 by

Wm. B. Eerdmans Publishing Co.

2140 Oak Industrial Drive N.E., Grand Rapids, Michigan 49505 /

P.O. Box 163, Cambridge CB3 9PU U.K.

Printed in the United States of America

11 10 09 08 07 06   7 6 5 4 3 2 1

Library of Congress Cataloging-in-Publication Data

Grabill, Stephen John.

Rediscovering the natural law in Reformed theological ethics / Stephen J. Grabill.

p.   cm.

Includes bibliographical references and index.

ISBN-10: 0-8028-6313-2 / ISBN-13: 978-0-8028-6313-3 (pbk.: alk. paper)

1. Christianity and law.   2. Natural law — Religious aspects — Christianity.

3. Christian ethics.   4. Natural theology.

5. Reformed Church — Doctrines.   I. Title.

BR115.L28G73 2006

241'.2 — dc22

2006019374

www.eerdmans.com

This volume is dedicated to my parents,
exemplars of faithfulness,
and lifelong teachers of
the Way, the Truth, and the Life

Contents

Acknowledgments

This book, a hybrid of historical and theological resources, is reflective of both the breadth and depth of the faculty at Calvin Theological Seminary — the institution at which I have spent a fair number of years receiving instruction. I express my sincere appreciation to those who served as my dissertation committee, John Bolt, Richard Muller, Calvin Van Reken, and John Hare (of Yale Divinity School), for their guidance, criticism, inspiration, and assistance with all matters concerning the dissertation and its defense. To John Bolt, John Cooper, Ronald Feenstra, Calvin Van Reken, and Richard Muller — Calvin Theological Seminary professors with whom I have had significant interaction over the years — I acknowledge a great debt and even greater trust. I likewise acknowledge the expert research assistance I received from Paul Fields and Lugene Schemper, theological librarians at Hekman Library, Calvin College.

I also wish to express my appreciation to the Acton Institute, where I have been employed throughout the process of writing this book. The Institute provided assistance throughout the dissertation itself and through its subsequent revision into the current form. I thank its president, Father Robert Sirico, and executive director, Kris Mauren, personally for their support of this project. It has also been a delight to work with scholars from such a broad spectrum of fields and so I express my gratitude to my colleagues Samuel Gregg, Jordan Ballor, Kevin Schmiesing, and Gloria Zúñiga. I am grateful for the many intense, informative, and intellectually stimulating conversations we have had on all topics, related to natural law and otherwise. In this respect, I cannot fail to mention a close friend and former colleague, David Sytsma, who has proved to be a competent researcher, analyst, and critic. David has been and, I hope, will continue to be a partner in rediscovering the riches of the classical Christian tradition.

I must also express my gratitude to Professor Russell Hittinger of the University of Tulsa for his encouragement to explore the tradition of natural law within Protestantism, and to Leonard Liggio of the Atlas Economic Research Foundation and Ingrid A. Gregg of the Earhart Foundation for their intellectual affirmation of my project and the dissertation fellowship that provided funding during a portion of its undertaking.

A segment of Chapter Six was presented at the May 2004 conference, "Written on the Heart: The Tradition of Natural Law," sponsored by the Calvin College Seminars in Christian Scholarship and underwritten by Fieldstead & Company. I thank especially J. Budziszewski, the seminar director, and the sixteen participants in the summer seminar, for their intellectual encouragement, vigorous discussion, and ongoing partnerships. A version of Chapter Six also appeared as the article, "Natural Law and the Noetic Effects of Sin: The Faculty of Reason in Francis Turretin's Theological Anthropology," in *Westminster Theological Journal* 67, no. 2 (Fall 2005): 261-79. I thank Westminster Theological Seminary for allowing portions of that article to appear here.

Finally I want to thank my family, without whose support this book would never have become a reality. To my parents, Dr. Daniel and Joan Grabill, I give thanks for their tireless support and encouragement from the very beginning of my education; and to my father my deepest gratitude for instilling in me a profound confidence in and passion for the truth. And to my wife, Rebecca, also a writer, I am thankful for her unfailing support, encouragement, and patience in so many facets and for the entire duration of this project. Finally, I am grateful to my children, Nicholas, Sebastian, and Magdalene, for whom this book, ultimately, is written, that they may attain a knowledge of God far exceeding the miniumum of what has been written on their hearts.

Introduction

The inspiration for this book came from Peter Martyr Vermigli's strategic use of a line from Virgil[1] to encapsulate the apostle Paul's affirmation in Romans 1 that God's eternal power and divinity has been revealed in creation.[2] While evangelicals today (both inside and outside of confessional traditions) may be surprised — even dismayed — by the Italian Reformer's strong affirmation of divine witness through the natural order, the older magisterial Protestant tradition (Lutheran and Reformed) not only inherited but also passed on the doctrines of *lex naturalis* and *cognitio Dei naturalis*, especially the idea of an implanted knowledge of morality, as noncontroversial legacies of patristic and scholastic thought. Yet among twentieth-century Reformed and Lutheran theologians, a cloud of suspicion and hostility has engulfed questions pertaining to natural revelation, natural theology, and natural law, as the celebrated 1934 disputation between Emil Brunner and Karl Barth made clear. Current trends, however, seem to indicate that at least some Protestant intellectuals are beginning to reevaluate their prior philosophical and theological estrangement from the natural-law tradition.

In his latest book, *The First Grace,* Russell Hittinger, the distinguished Roman Catholic natural lawyer and moral philosopher, contends that the renewed interest in natural law among Protestants seems to be occasioned by two phenomena. First, he says, "the political success of evangelical Protestantism has made it necessary to frame an appropriate language for addressing civil politics and law."[3] Second, these same Protestants often "find themselves in dialogue with Catholics, with whom they share many common interests in matters of culture and politics — interests that would seem amenable to natural law discussion."[4] Hittinger also insists, virtually anticipating the argument of this book, "Though Protestants of the sixteenth century questioned more deeply than the scholastics the efficacy of natural law in the human mind, as well as its place in the economy of salvation, the definition of natural law as a higher law retained its vigor in Protestant thought."[5]

This book's aim is to assist contemporary Protestant pastors, denominational officials, theologians, ethicists, public intellectuals, seminarians, graduate students, and general readers to rediscover and rehabilitate natural law and related doctrinal concepts. By way of introduction, then, natural law can be understood as an ancient moral and legal tradition that Christian theologians, jurists, and statesmen have amended, supplemented, and assimilated over time to serve moral, political, legal, and canon law objectives. That tradition, to a large degree, remained unbroken in the theology of the Protestant Reformers and their orthodox sixteenth- and seventeenth-century successors, but sometime after 1750, succumbed to rationalist currents popular among the educated elite of Europe and, by extension, the intellectual descendants of the Reformation. Stated more precisely, the Protestant Reformation carried over, though with some critical modifications, certain theological, philosophical, and legal ideas common to the western Christian church.[6] These common teachings include the idea that God promulgated a natural law that directs and binds human creatures; that this law of nature has been written on every human heart; that conscience and reason serve as natural lights leading people to act in accord with natural law; that the natural law and the Old Law (Decalogue) differ only as means (or conveyors of moral information) but not in fundamental moral content; that while human cognition of the natural moral order was obscured by sin, the natural law still yields sufficient data to assist people in distinguishing between good and evil; that neither knowledge of, nor adherence to, natural law is sufficient for either justification or redemption; and that a natural-law jurisprudence is crucial to maintaining just and well-ordered temporal polities, regardless of whether they are governed by Christian princes or legislatures. Questions pertaining to the efficacy of natural law and its place in the economy of salvation constitute the central concerns of Reformed writers who address the topic of natural law during the period of confessional orthodoxy (ca. 1520 to ca. 1725).

Recovering the Catholicity of Protestant Theological Ethics

While the Protestant Reformers inherited the natural-law tradition from
their late medieval predecessors without serious question, their later heirs
have, more often than not, assumed a critical stance of discontinuity in relation to natural law. In fact, according to one scholar whose views — though
well documented and respected — still typify a minority position in contemporary Protestant historiography, "There is no real discontinuity between the teaching of the Reformers and that of their predecessors with respect to natural law."[7] With the possible exception of Zwingli, writes John T.
McNeill, "Natural law is not one of the issues on which [the Reformers]
bring the Scholastics under criticism."[8] Exploring continuities and discontinuities, developments and divergences between the Reformers and their
successors and even, more generally, between the Reformation, patristic,
and medieval eras in Christian theology sheds light on McNeill's observation about the catholicity of natural-law doctrine. "Where the Reformers
painted with a broad brush," writes Richard Muller, "their orthodox and
scholastic successors strove to fill in the details of the picture. Whereas the
Reformers were intent upon distancing themselves and their theology from
problematic elements in medieval thought and, at the same time, remaining
catholic in the broadest sense of that term, the Protestant orthodox were intent upon establishing systematically the normative, catholic character of
institutionalized Protestantism, at times through the explicit use of those elements in patristic and medieval theology not at odds with the teachings of
the Reformation."[9] Assuming McNeill's conclusion can withstand historical
scrutiny, therefore, it is fair to ask why Protestants have been so critical of
natural law throughout most of the preceding century.

The reasons, while diverse and somewhat broad ranging, encompass
at least three distinct but overlapping sets of issues. Among twentieth-
century Protestant systematic and historical theologians, a primary reason
contributing to the unfavorable assessment of natural law has been the influence of Karl Barth's epistemological criticism of natural theology, his
(along with Emil Brunner's) reinforcement of Calvin as the chief codifier
and lodestar of Reformed doctrine, and his advocacy of a strong version of
divine command theory,[10] each of which will be examined more fully in the
next chapter. Suffice it to say that particularly within the arena of Reformed
theology, the discontinuity thesis was underscored by Barth's acerbic criticism not only of natural theology, but also of any theological formulation
not immediately derivable from Christocentric premises.

A second reason is that natural-law doctrine is thought to originate in, and, therefore, to find its natural seat within, the intellectual milieu of Roman Catholic moral theology. Protestant intellectuals for this reason, then, have typically regarded the natural-law tradition to be doctrinally and philosophically tied to Roman Catholicism, and thus open to the standard Protestant criticisms that Rome does not take either sin or history seriously enough. This viewpoint has been articulated by a number of prominent twentieth-century Protestant theologians and ethicists including such luminaries as Jacques Ellul,[11] Stanley Hauerwas,[12] Carl F. H. Henry,[13] Paul Lehmann,[14] Reinhold Niebuhr,[15] and Helmut Thielicke.[16] Among twentieth-century representatives of the Dutch Reformed tradition, Herman Dooyeweerd,[17] Cornelius Van Til,[18] Gordon Spykman,[19] and G. C. Berkouwer[20] have each been outspoken proponents of this viewpoint, the latter of whom was indelibly shaped by Barthian modes of thought.

A third, more general, reason can be attributed to the anti-scholastic, anti-metaphysical accents of nineteenth-century German liberal theology that continued to exert influence on the Protestant mainstream well into the twentieth century in, for example, Albrecht Ritschl's[21] and Adolf von Harnack's so-called "ethical" theologies.[22] Thus, in commenting on nature and grace in his 1894 rectoral address at Kampen Seminary, Herman Bavinck, one of the chief agents in the Dutch Neo-Calvinist revival in the latter half of the nineteenth century, singled out Ritschl's attempt to separate metaphysics from theology specifically for criticism. "According to the Reformation," wrote Bavinck, "that which is *supra naturam* is not the metaphysical doctrine of Trinity, incarnation, and atonement per se but the *content* of all this — namely, grace. Not as if the Reformers wished to banish metaphysics from theology — the separation of the two proposed by Ritschl is practically speaking not even feasible. But the metaphysical doctrine taken in itself or for its own sake does not yet constitute the content or object of our Christian faith."[23]

As mentioned above, certain promising indications exist that some leading Protestant intellectuals are presently reevaluating the conventional theological taboos associated with the natural-law tradition. To put matters in context: prior to 1990, if a researcher was interested in locating English-language monographs written by Protestants on natural law after 1934, the year of the infamous Barth-Brunner debate, it would be nearly impossible to do so.[24] While a mere handful of dissertations have been written on natural law by Protestant authors,[25] all of which appear after 1960, only one concentrates on the relationship between the natural-law tradition and the

Reformers and Protestant orthodoxy.[26] Even among these, none move much beyond the descriptive task of showing either that a modified tradition of natural law can be found in select theologians or periods of Protestant theology, or conversely, that Protestant theology is unable to assimilate natural law on account of theological hesitations. As might be expected, most of these authors focused on adjudicating the merits of the Barth-Brunner debate,[27] systematically presented the viewpoint of a particular theologian,[28] developed an extended criticism of natural-law theory,[29] or surveyed twentieth-century Protestant viewpoints on the subject.[30] It is important to recognize that the most scholarly and systematic treatments of natural law so far by Protestant analysts have been conducted almost exclusively within a contemporary (or twentieth-century) frame of reference.

My contention is that the contemporaneity of these studies in particular, and the paucity of Protestant treatments of natural law in general, act as contributing factors themselves to the profound gap in historical understanding of the development of Protestant ethics. This gap by its very existence helps to establish historical plausibility for the claim that, particularly among Protestant systematicians and historical theologians, the 1934 debate between Karl Barth and Emil Brunner had two principal consequences. First, from a theological and anthropological point of view, the debate helped to rupture the by then anemic natural-law tradition in Protestant theological ethics by questioning and ultimately denying the epistemological reliability of the post-lapsarian natural human faculties. Second, from a historical point of view, the debate served to reinforce a trend begun already in the nineteenth century to bestow upon John Calvin the misplaced accolade of being *the* chief early codifier of Reformed doctrine.

To address the fundamental inadequacy of the Calvin as chief early codifier position, it is important to acknowledge, first and foremost, that the theology of Protestant orthodoxy, forged in the late sixteenth and seventeenth centuries as a final, dogmatic codification of the Reformation, occupies a seminal — even if, in the minds of many today, a non-normative — position in the history of Protestant thought. "Not only is this scholastic or orthodox theology the historical link that binds us to the Reformation," insists Muller, "it is also the form of theological system in and through which modern Protestantism has received most of its doctrinal principles and definitions. Without detracting at all from the achievement of the great Reformers and the earliest codifiers of the doctrines of the Reformation — writers like Melanchthon, Calvin, and Bullinger — we need to recognize that not they, but rather, subsequent generations of 'orthodox' or 'scholastic' Protestants are responsible for the final form of such doctrinal issues as the definition of theology and the enunciation of its fundamental principles, the fully developed Protestant forms of the doctrine of the Trinity, the crucial christological concept of the two states of Christ, penal substitutionary atonement, and the theme of the covenant of works and the covenant of grace."[31] Such increasing doctrinal complexity and sophistication is also evident in the doctrines of natural revelation, natural theology, and natural law.

If an early Reformer such as Calvin was not the final, or even the chief, formulator of these doctrines, and was not even thought to have held such a position among his esteemed contemporaries,[32] then, from a methodological point of view, it seems highly implausible to assume either radical discontinuity between him and later orthodox successors — the so-called "Calvin against the Calvinists" position — on the one side, or static continuity in the form of reproduction among him, other early Reformers, and later scholastic successors on the other. "The viewpoint of the twentieth century, which has selected Calvin as the chief early codifier, must be set aside," Muller argues, "particularly in those instances when the formative influence toward the development of a specific doctrinal position came not from Calvin but from one of his contemporaries. Orthodoxy must be understood not as a result of or as a defection from the work of a single thinker but as a doctrinal development resting on a fairly diverse theological heritage."[33]

Although the Protestant tradition of natural law atrophied during the years 1934 to 1990,[34] in the last decade of the twentieth century Protestant historians, theologians, and ethicists began to express renewed but cautious interest in natural law. In the judgment of one ethicist there is a clear relationship between the scope of Karl Barth's influence on twentieth-century Protestant ethics and the softening in attitude toward the natural-law tradition that has been occurring in recent years. "As Barth's influence has moderated over the century," states Rufus Black, "there has been a gradual softening in attitude toward natural-law theory — an attitude that was always more open among those beyond the Barthian orbit."[35]

Since 1990 Protestant theologians, historians, and ethicists have become increasingly more interested in the natural-law tradition as a resource for discussing moral issues in the often hostile and religiously pluralistic environment of the public square. Indications of renewed interest in the natural-law tradition can be seen in the work of such scholars as Nigel Biggar,[36] Rufus Black,[37] Carl Braaten,[38] J. Budziszewski (now Roman

Catholic),[39] Michael Cromartie,[40] Jean Bethke Elshtain,[41] Arthur F. Holmes,[42] Paul Helm,[43] Alister McGrath,[44] Susan Schreiner,[45] David VanDrunen,[46] and Daniel Westberg.[47] The privatization of religious belief and the impoverishment of public moral discourse provide the backdrop for the renewed interest in natural law. The natural-law tradition supplies an antidote to these cultural trends because, according to it, there is a universal law to which people of all races, cultures, and religions can have access through their natural reason. Natural law thus provides moral knowledge that all people can grasp without the aid of special or divine revelation. Natural law is particularly advantageous in terms of political discourse and Christian engagement in the public square because it seems to provide a moral vocabulary that can function for both religious and secular interlocutors.

The renewed interest in natural law also seems to derive from a more fundamental concern on the part of Protestant theologians to promote ecumenical agreement on normative moral concerns and to show respect for the common search for truth among Christians and non-Christians in all spheres of intellectual life. This concern to promote ecumenism and to respect the search for truth has been variously expressed by Protestant theologians, characteristically taking form and using language that arises from their particular theological tradition. Contemporary theologians in the Dutch Reformed tradition utilizing a fundamental theological motif such as common grace have moved toward developing public theologies to guide Christian engagement in culture and politics[48] and "theologies of commonness" that describe the relationship of Christian commitment to secular thought.[49] Even so, among contemporary representatives of the Reformed tradition there is a perceived tension between the doctrines of common grace and natural law, ranging from hesitant juxtaposition to fundamental incompatibility.[50]

Reasons for Qualified Protestant Endorsement of the Natural-Law Tradition

Generally speaking, although recent Protestant and Reformed theologians and ethicists have expressed enthusiasm for the revival of the natural-law tradition, they have engaged in a cautious and qualified endorsement of it. There are at least three significant factors that can be isolated to explain this state of affairs. The first two, which are a concern to promote public ecumenism and the desire to avoid tacit acceptance of Roman Catholic pre-suppositions, will be addressed below, while the third, Karl Barth's episte-mological criticism of natural theology, will be taken up in the next chap-ter.

Increased ecumenical engagement by Roman Catholic and Protestant leaders in public intellectual life is one principal factor that has contributed both to the revival of interest in and qualified endorsement of natural law. This factor can be seen in the work of Evangelicals and Catholics Together, an initiative sponsored by Charles Colson and Richard John Neuhaus to promote ecclesial unity,[51] and in the 1996 ecumenical gathering of scholars to discuss natural law, sponsored by the Ethics and Public Policy Center's Evangelical Studies Project.[52] These initiatives accented the importance of reconnecting contemporary Protestant ethics to the older and broader Christian moral tradition. This meant, however, that the subjectivity and the tendency to substantiate arguments by citing isolated Scripture pas-sages, characteristic of many evangelical ethical traditions, would have to recede and be replaced by an ethical theory with greater stability, objectiv-ity, and catholicity.

In this context of ecumenism, moreover, it follows that Protestant in-tellectuals would begin to reappraise the standard theological objections to natural law, even though many still seem to operate under the assumption that natural law cannot be reconciled with the Reformed doctrine of total in-ability. The confusion here stems from an improper demarcation of the scope of total inability. The Reformed doctrine of total inability teaches that, in matters pertaining to justification, people are unable to perform any sav-ing good; however, in nonsalvific matters, some vestiges of natural light re-main such that good and evil are distinguishable and virtue and good works are preferred forms of human behavior. The *Canons of Dort,* a doctrinal stan-dard issued by the Synod of Dort (1618-1619) to resolve a serious contro-versy in the Dutch Reformed churches occasioned by the synergistic teach-ing of Jacob Arminius (1560-1609), states the distinction thus:

> There remain, however, in man since the fall, the glimmerings of natu-ral light, whereby he retains some knowledge of God, of natural things, and of the difference between good and evil, and shows some regard for virtue and for good outward behavior. But so far is this light of nature from being sufficient to bring him to a saving knowledge of God and to true conversion that he is incapable of using it aright even in things natural and civil. Nay further, this light, such as it is, man in various

ways renders wholly polluted, and hinders in unrighteousness, by doing which he becomes inexcusable before God.[53]

The net effect of increased ecumenical engagement has led to a fuller understanding and appreciation of the precedent for natural-law ethics that existed at an earlier stage in the history of Protestant doctrinal development.

A second factor contributing to the hesitant endorsement of natural law is the concern that accepting it requires tacit acceptance of Roman Catholic theological and philosophical presuppositions. Helmut Thielicke, a twentieth-century German Lutheran theologian, has expressed what, in many precincts, are still the standard Protestant objections to natural law. While distancing himself from Karl Barth's rejection of natural law, Thielicke is critical of the static medieval philosophy — Aristotelian Thomism — that he believes to be implicit in the Roman Catholic understanding of natural law. His concern with tacit acceptance led to a certain degree of ambivalence and equivocation in his assessment of natural law, which Carl Braaten, a contemporary American Lutheran theologian, puts as follows: "Natural law came to be seen as a kind of necessary evil, or as an illegitimate child that could not be completely abandoned but whose rights must be severely restricted."[54]

Thielicke is critical of the Roman Catholic doctrine of natural law for two main reasons. In the first place, as he surmises, it holds that the fundamental nature of mankind can be known through natural cognition, that is, apart from the special revelation of God in Jesus Christ. To which he objects, insisting "that man is to be defined as a being in relation,"[55] particularly as a being in relation to God's will as this is "refracted" through the Decalogue. The Decalogue, for him, exposes sin and calls humanity out of its perplexity, doubt, and state of rationalizing sin: "The doctrine of the law must always be viewed against the background of the fall."[56] So, therefore, any attempt to determine the essence of human nature apart from its relation to God's will as expressed through the law is inadequate, for it will invariably substitute mutable and contingent aspects of human nature for the truly constitutive ones. Evidence of this tendency can be found in Aristotle who, claims Thielicke, develops an understanding of human nature on the basis of political relations. "This means that the idea of humanity arises only within a very definite 'political' relation, which is itself conditioned by the contingency of the social order as it existed at that time."[57] To the extent that a Roman Catholic understanding of natural law relies upon this Aristotelian framework, Thielicke believes that it is impossible to develop a view of human nature through natural cognition that is "unchanging and of universal validity."[58] In other words, when human nature is analyzed exclusively within the framework of natural means it is impossible to separate the contingent aspects of cultural, social, political, or economic inputs in the determination of human nature.

His second main objection concerns the variability and contingency seen in the natural-law axiom of *suum cuique,* "to each his own." The issue here has to do with the fact that this principle of justice purports to be a constant and purely formal principle of justice for all ages and places. But, he asks, "of what avail is the constancy of form if the content is always different, varying as it does in accordance with the unending variations in the concept of humanity? Does not the *suum* continually vary according as man is seen as either citizen or slave, either beast of prey or human brother?"[59] The problem of the *suum* parallels that of knowing human nature through natural cognition — namely, the content of the *suum* depends on a view of human nature that is susceptible to constant variation based on differences in gender, age, natural endowments, environmental conditions, and psychological disposition. Once a view of human nature becomes firmly fixed, as it purportedly is in the Roman Catholic doctrine of natural law, a clear definition of the *suum* can then be given. Nevertheless, contends Thielicke, "even in the Roman Catholic doctrine of Christian natural law there can never be anything more than a conditional constancy of the *suum.*"[60] It is important to see that Thielicke is not rejecting the heuristic value of the axiom, but merely the idea that it can be "concretely ascertained and defined by just reading it off from the scale of a given order."[61] His principal objection to the Roman Catholic doctrine of natural law is "that it ascribes a false rank to the *suum cuique,* regarding it as an imperative, the expression of a given and knowable order. The *suum cuique* is thus accorded more than merely heuristic significance. It becomes a symbol of that order of being which we on our part believe, for dogmatic reasons, to be not given and knowable."[62] A subsidiary aim of this book is to reveal that the "dogmatic reasons" Thielicke mentions are in tension with the older Protestant tradition's dogmatic endorsement of the natural-law tradition.

To keep a misleading impression from being formed of Thielicke's view of natural law, it is important to acknowledge that he felt that the matter of ultimate norms, the quest for order, and the impulse toward natural law should be maintained. In fact, he thought that it was a priority of first importance to keep "the question of an order of being" alive, despite the impossibility of demarcating the boundaries of that order. The attempt to determine what is right on the basis of nature or creation is essential for two reasons. The first is that the human quest for absolute laws and immutable orders enable a limit to be placed around human caprice. Thus, insofar as the recognition is made that natural law cannot be grounded in an immutable order of being untainted by sin, natural law can be seen as an "order of preservation" that still functions in the world and provides "ultimate norms" against which to measure human conduct.[63] The second concern expressed by natural law, declares Thielicke, "is a kind of involuntary confession that, living as we do in a world of relativities, the good is something which has to be sought."[64] Thus, insofar as natural law has a heuristic function implicit within it, it acts as a goad to discover ultimate norms or moral truths untouched by historical contingencies.

Nonetheless, reminiscent of Karl Barth's bleak assessment of the postlapsarian natural human faculties, Thielicke holds that it is impossible for people not only to do the good but even to *know* the good: "The good is beyond our knowing not merely because our cognitive function has been reduced, but primarily because this good is not objectively at hand in 'this aeon.'"[65] However, given the realities of life in a fallen world before the eschaton, Christians must not ultimately reject references to natural law because they act as "a kind of symbol in which are expressed both 'recollection' and, if not fear of God, at least something similar, namely, reverence."[66] As a matter of practice, Christians may undertake common political and economic projects with "secular men" since there are parallels in the external, practical form of action between such groups. Nevertheless, the differences between them rest essentially in basic presuppositions, which "can often erupt violently into the sphere of action," leading to the abandonment of common projects.[67]

Is it any wonder, given such reservations and qualifications, that twentieth-century Protestant theologians with similar viewpoints have not made more significant contributions to the renewal of the natural-law tradition in Christian social ethics? In Carl Braaten's judgment, Protestant theologians such as Thielicke "write with an uneasy conscience, as if natural law were forbidden fruit."[68]

Historical Outliers to the Discontinuity Thesis

Despite the fact that the Reformers and Protestant orthodox theologians carried over the natural-law tradition as an uncontroversial legacy of catholic Christianity, many contemporary Protestant theologians and ethicists remain stubbornly suspicious of it as a species of Roman Catholic moral theology. This suspicion, coupled with the influence of Karl Barth's epistemological criticism of natural theology/natural law and the anti-scholastic, anti-metaphysical drift of twentieth-century theology, presents a plausible historical scenario to explain why many contemporary Protestant theologians believe that divine command theory, natural law's main rival in theological ethics, more adequately reflects their fundamental theological commitments. Barth's polemic against natural law was effective in persuading many twentieth-century theologians that the orthodox Protestant theologians of the sixteenth and seventeenth centuries had unwarrantably converted the Reformers' pastorally oriented and exegetically based ethics into the abstract scholastic precepts of natural-law theory. Barth's successful rhetorical strategy had the cumulative effect of undermining the natural-law tradition in Reformed theological ethics[69] and obscuring what actual use a Reformer such as Calvin had made of natural law.

The decline of Reformed natural-law ethics is integrally tied to the theological argument, stemming from Barth's criticism of natural theology, that the fall has disordered natural human faculties to such an extent that apart from Christ it is impossible to obtain genuine knowledge of God — a doctrinal assumption he claimed was implicit in Calvin's teaching on the noetic "incapacity of the natural man."[70] By engaging the thought of several significant but understudied representatives of Reformed orthodoxy spanning the period from the early sixteenth to the late seventeenth century, this book shows that some of the most formative voices in the Reformed tradition taught that the diminished natural human faculties still function sufficiently to reveal the general precepts of the natural moral law. Put in slightly different language, the Reformed tradition affirmed it was possible for people's intellect to *know* the good even if, without divine assistance, it was impossible for their will to be liberated from the bondage of sin to *act* on it.

While it is likely that modern readers may have never given it much thought, the era of Protestant orthodoxy extends for nearly two centuries past the Reformation — a phase in the intellectual development of Protestantism that is approximately three times the length of the Reformation. "Like the Reformation itself," according to Richard Muller, "the era of orthodoxy both drew on and worked to set aside its medieval heritage. Also like the Reformation it both participated in and confronted the shift in European consciousness that belonged to the early modern era."[71] Since two generations of Reformers can be distinguished in the Reformation era (ca. 1517-1565), which historians demonstrate from the dates when major confessions appeared or major theologians died, Muller thinks it is possible to divide the post-Reformation era into five rough periods: early orthodoxy, in two phases (ca. 1565-1618-1640) — one leading up to, the other following, the Synod of Dort; high orthodoxy, likewise in two phases (ca. 1640-1685-1725) — the former developing the orthodoxy of the confessions in much fuller detail both positive and polemical, the latter phase characterized by deconfessionalization and transition; and late orthodoxy (1725-1770). "These periods," it is argued, "correspond with the initial framing and formulation of orthodoxy, the large-scale elaboration of the theology, and the decline of the movement in the eighteenth century."[72]

The representatives treated in upcoming chapters were selected because, corresponding with the period divisions above, they provide a window, albeit a limited one, into the development of natural-law doctrine in Reformed theology up through the era of high orthodoxy. Scholars thus far have made no real effort to ascertain antecedents or applications that such figures as Peter Martyr Vermigli (1499-1562), Jerome Zanchi (1516-1590), Johannes Althusius (1557-1638), or Francis Turretin (1623-1687) made of the natural-law tradition, regardless of how influential or practical their teaching would have been at the time. Each of these persons, along with John Calvin, played a significant and formative role in the larger movement of Reformed orthodoxy, whether as second- or third-generation codifiers of doctrine, as with Martyr, Calvin, and Zanchi, respectively; or as a powerful legal and political consolidator of Reformed ideas at an auspicious time in Protestant history (namely, the Dutch liberation from Spain toward the close of the early orthodox period), as with Althusius; or, finally, as a major formulator of fully developed Reformed doctrine during an era of intraconfessional warfare, as with Turretin. In the conclusion of this book, a brief narrative will be sketched to show how the Barthian discontinuity position was an overreaction to the rationalism of the modern natural-law tradition that first took shape in the seventeenth century but had largely run its course by the late nineteenth century.

A significant consequence of the Barth-Brunner debate, specifically for systematic and historical theologians, was that commentators focused so much attention upon whether Calvin developed a doctrine of natural law that the contributions of his contemporaries and successors were either ignored or dismissed as "scholastic" and "rationalistic." Nevertheless, as research into the period of Reformed orthodoxy has matured during the past thirty years, the former scholarly consensus of it as "dead," "arid," "rigid," "abstract," and "discontinuous with the Reformation" has been overturned in the secondary literature.[73] In nineteenth-century historiography the adjectives *scholastic* and *rationalistic* were used pejoratively to describe "a particular philosophy or as engendering a particular philosophical or theological result. That result, moreover, has been dubbed 'Aristotelian' and, by more than one writer, has been viewed as a form of rationalism that places reason prior to faith and, therefore, philosophy prior to Scripture in the list of criteria or *principia* for theology."[74] The fundamental insight of the new scholarship, in Trueman and Clark's words, is simply that "to describe a theology as scholastic is to make a statement about its method, not its content."[75]

Now, applying the older hermeneutic to the Reformed appropriation of the natural-law tradition, it is apparent that Barthian historiography interpreted the scholastic, Aristotelian, and Thomistic antecedents of the doctrine as *prima facie* evidence of its Roman Catholic pedigree.[76] Following the example of their mentor, Barthian scholars have consistently attempted to portray "pre-Enlightenment Reformed theology, particularly that of John Calvin, as fundamentally a proto-Barthian movement in the history of the church."[77]

A more adequate definition of scholasticism, which rescues the term from its merely pejorative meaning, is "the technical and logical approach to theology as a discipline characteristic of theological systems from the late twelfth through the seventeenth century. . . . [that] is not necessarily allied to any particular philosophical perspective nor . . . represent[ed by] a systematic attachment to or concentration upon any particular doctrine or concept as a key to theological system."[78] Recent scholarship has become increasingly more aware of the continuities — as well as the discontinuities — the Reformers and their successors maintained with the doctrinal and philosophical formulations of the patristic and medieval eras in Christian theology. In assessing doctrinal developments between these eras and Protestant orthodoxy, the methodological challenge "is to examine the course of development, to study the reasons for change, assess the context of each document, and then to make judgments concerning continuity and discontinuity in the light of something more than a facile contrast or juxtaposition."[79]

Since 1990, as we have mentioned, Protestant theologians, historians, and social theorists more frequently appeal to John Calvin than to any other Protestant theologian for assistance in formulating a doctrine of natural law. This phenomenon is most likely attributable to the stubborn persistence among scholars to single out Calvin as the chief early codifier of Reformed doctrine. While this approach is certainly understandable given its commonplace status, the universe of discourse should be widened beyond Calvin to include those Reformers who either preceded him or were contemporaries of his and those later orthodox codifiers of doctrine mentioned above. Though Calvin regularly employs such phrases as *lex naturae, natura dictat, natura docet, naturae ordo, sensus naturae,* and *sensus divinitatis* throughout the commentaries and the 1559 edition of the *Institutes,* it would be mistaken to view his discussion of these concepts as providing systematic treatments of natural theology and natural law. When his treatment of natural law is placed beside that of the medieval tradition, it seems imprecise and unsystematic. The reason for this, relates Schreiner, is that "he neither provided a systematic treatment of natural law nor did he analyze many of the issues commonly discussed by ancient and medieval thinkers. Nonetheless, he took over the traditional terminology and referred (sometimes interchangeably) to the 'ius aequum,' 'lex naturae,' 'lex naturalis,' and 'ius gentium.'"[80] Schreiner's conclusion is that Calvin's discussion of natural law should be seen as an extension of his doctrine of providence. In other words, Calvin uses natural law for what could be labeled the practical purpose of explaining how order is preserved *post-lapsum* in society, law, and morality.

In addition to accenting similarities, this study will also register differences in the development of doctrine among Calvin, Vermigli, Zanchi, Althusius, and Turretin; moreover, it will also demonstrate how each thinker appropriated Thomist and Scotist philosophical perspectives eclectically to formulate his views on natural revelation, natural theology, and natural law. As a precaution to modern readers, however, it should be pointed out that such eclecticism "ought not be understood as an incoherent philosophy, but rather as a philosophy drawn out of a multitude of sources both classical and medieval, modified by a Renaissance reading of texts, and guided by the desire to develop a pattern of rational argument that could serve theology in an ancillary position."[81] Orthodox Reformed theologians after Calvin (d. 1564) especially began to develop the doctrinal foundation for circumscribed uses of natural theology and natural law and, in the process, provided more detailed descriptions of their theological *principia, axiomata,* and *methodus* than their predecessors had even deemed necessary.

Apart from developing the doctrinal foundation for an orthodox use of natural theology, Vermigli, Zanchi, Althusius, and Turretin also developed increasingly sophisticated and comprehensive formulations of natural law that they situated in the wider context of the grand moral tradition with Aristotle, Cicero, Augustine, Aquinas, Scotus, and many others. Each thinker, to varying degrees, exhibited greater continuity (but also discontinuity at points) with the realist wing of the late medieval natural-law tradition (the Thomist and Scotist trajectories) than Protestant commentators have generally acknowledged.[82] The Jesuit historical theologian John Patrick Donnelly supports this judgment, particularly in Vermigli's case: "Does Martyr's scholasticism have affinities to any particular medieval school? Yes. Martyr cannot fairly be called a Thomist, yet his scholasticism stands far closer to Thomism than to any other major school of the Middle Ages. His training was mainly Thomistic; he cites Aquinas far more than any other scholastic except Lombard; he cites more individual works of Thomas than of any other non-patristic theologian; and on innumerable specific points his teaching coincides with that of St. Thomas."[83]

Though Donnelly's principal concern is with Vermigli, Zanchi's and Turretin's affinity to Thomism and Scotism, respectively, are also well known. In this respect, if due appreciation is given to the eclectic nature of the Reformed scholastic appropriation of late medieval philosophical perspectives, then Donnelly's conclusion regarding Reformed scholasticism would apply to this study as well: "The striking thing about the rise of Reformed scholasticism is that its roots in medieval scholasticism run heavily to Thomism [and, one should add, Scotism], hardly at all to nominalism."[84] This conclusion, publicized ironically enough by a devout Jesuit, flatly contradicts the scholarly consensus of a cross-section of prominent twentieth-century Roman Catholic intellectuals (notably without Franciscan representation)[85] who attribute the voluntarist accents of later Protestant theological and ethical systems to nominalist metaphysics rather than to the Reformation's roots, like their Franciscan brethren's, in medieval Augustinianism.[86]

The use of traditional natural-law terminology, concepts, and doctrinal formulae in the theology of Calvin, Vermigli, Zanchi, Althusius, and Turretin indicates significant points of continuity with the realist wing of the late medieval natural-law tradition. The discontinuities with that tradition stem largely from Protestant reaffirmations of Augustinian antipelagianism, fuller treatments of the noetic effects of sin than heretofore existed, and intramural disputes over the interpretation of some key pericopes (such as Rom. 1:18-20; 2:14-15; 3:20, and others), among other factors.[87] Calvin, Vermigli, and the Reformed scholastics all share the conviction that Scripture is the cognitive foundation of theology (*principium cognoscendi*) and that theological and moral arguments can be based on axioms derived from that *principium*.[88] Yet they acknowledge the existence of a natural knowledge of God that arises out of the order of nature and is discernible either in conjunction with or apart from Scripture. This knowledge, however, has no saving efficacy and merely serves to render null and void any rationalization a person may advance for having broken the moral law.

The chapters to follow will move toward consolidating a historical understanding that, in subsequent projects, could be expanded to include a broader array of thinkers, more detailed historical and theological analysis, and the construction of a platform upon which to build a contemporary doctrine of natural law that could be integrated seamlessly into the larger body of Reformed dogmatics. While some Protestant intellectuals are beginning to recognize the utility of natural law as a way of speaking about moral issues in public settings, what remains unexplored is whether it can be successfully integrated into Protestant (and specifically Reformed) theological ethics and anthropology. This book presents a historical case for the former by retrieving an older, preexisting strain of the natural-law tradition that was carried over, refined, and developed further by select sixteenth- and seventeenth-century representatives of the Reformed tradition, while only hinting at an affirmative response to the latter. Those looking for a systematic treatment of natural law in relation to fundamental anthropological topics in Reformed theology will, unfortunately, have to wait for a subsequent volume.

As promised earlier, Chapter One will explore Karl Barth's criticisms of natural theology/natural law, which, given his nearly iconic status among many twentieth-century Protestant systematic and historical theologians, has constituted a significant factor mitigating recent Protestant interest in the natural-law tradition. The argument there is that contemporary Protestant and Reformed theologians generally hold a low view of natural law because the 1934 Barth-Brunner debate obscured the orthodox Reformed understanding of natural revelation, natural theology, and natural law. Barth's strong advocacy of an actualist divine command ethic,[89] coupled with the widespread assumption that Calvin established the parameters for a divine command ethic and therefore rejected the *lex naturalis* to accent the inscrutability of the *voluntas Dei*, has created tension for some contemporary representatives of the Reformed tradition (such as Jacques Ellul, Henry Stob, John Hare, and Richard Mouw) in defining the relationship between common grace and natural law.

As a segue into later chapters, Chapter Two will show how the philosophical and theological debates of the late medieval era indelibly shaped the natural-law tradition that the Reformers and their orthodox successors inherited from earlier antecedents. By the middle of the fourteenth century, it is already possible to differentiate two types of natural-law theories within late medieval scholasticism, each proposing distinct moral ontologies: a realist theory of natural law represented by, among others, Thomas Aquinas and Duns Scotus, and a nominalist theory of natural law represented by, among others, William of Occam and Pierre d'Ailly. The logical first step in determining the continuities and discontinuities between the late medieval era, the Reformation, and Reformed orthodoxy is to ascertain the type of natural-law theory that the representative in question has appropriated. Before that can be done, however, it is necessary to clear away caricatures of nominalism that have become ensconced among later commentators. This will be accomplished by closely analyzing the distinction between God's absolute and ordained power as it pertains to ethics.

Chapters Three through Six will provide detailed analyses of the doctrines of natural revelation, natural theology, and natural law from Reformed representatives in the eras of the Reformation (Calvin and Vermigli), early orthodoxy (Althusius and Zanchi), and high orthodoxy (Turretin). An unfortunate consequence of Barth's wholesale repudiation of natural theology was that, for most of the twentieth century, Protestant *theological* interest waned in the doctrines of natural revelation and natural law given their logical tie to natural theology. To reinvigorate this diminished logical relation and to provide a conceptual structure for analyzing and comparing doctrinal formulations throughout Chapters Three through Six, each representative's work (with the exception of Althusius) will be examined according to the doctrines of natural revelation, natural theology, and natural law. This approach is designed to convey the representative's understanding of the relationship between the aforementioned doctrines and to show that an adequate view of natural law cannot be developed from any theological system without first considering the system's historical context (externally situated) and the relations it establishes among adjacent doctrines (internally situated).

Methodologically, then, Chapters Two through Six will be tied together by showing that the doctrinal formulations of Calvin, Vermigli, Zanchi, Althusius, and Turretin supply the rudimentary theological framework upon which a contemporary Reformed doctrine of natural law could be constructed. Anyone interested in such a project, however, must remain cognizant of two potential methodological pitfalls. First, care must be taken to avoid abstracting doctrines from the previously mentioned figures (or from any other representative of Reformed orthodoxy) without due regard to their original setting and the wider context of their thought, as some nineteenth- and twentieth-century historiographers have tried to do.[90] Second, analysis of the significance of these representatives must not be confined exclusively to their original time and place, as more historicistically oriented analysts might commend, because of the formative influence they have exerted upon the development of the Reformed tradition for nearly half a millennium.

Any attempt to show doctrinal continuity between the Reformed theologians of the sixteenth and seventeenth centuries and those of later centuries must develop a criterion by which to extract a "common doctrinal tradition." That such a common doctrinal tradition is a plausible and pursuable hypothesis is attested in the following passage from Muller's *Post-Reformation Reformed Dogmatics:*

> The contemporary relevance of Protestant orthodox theology arises from the fact that it remains the basis for normative Protestant theology in the present. With little formal and virtually no substantial dogmatic alteration, orthodox or scholastic Reformed theology appears in the works of Charles Hodge, Archibald Alexander Hodge, and Louis Berkhof. Even when major changes in perspective are evident — as in the theology of Emil Brunner, Karl Barth, and Otto Weber — the impact of Protestant orthodoxy remains clear both in terms of the overarching structure of theological system and in terms of its basic definitions. Charles Hodge's *Systematic Theology* draws heavily on Francis Turretin's *Institutio theologiae elencticae* and represents, particularly in its prolegomena, an attempt to recast the systematic insights of orthodoxy in a nineteenth-century mold. Of the other writers, Karl Barth most clearly shows his indebtedness to the orthodox prolegomena — not always in terms of direct appropriation of doctrine, but rather in terms of sensitivity both to the importance of prolegomena and to the issues traditionally raised at this preliminary point in dogmatics.[91]

Such a criterion would help to maintain proper balance between the rigors of historical contextualization and the urgency of contemporary application. One possible criterion could be formulated as follows: A common doctrinal tradition will be evident when a modern theologian either

(1) reiterates the doctrinal formulation and/or conclusion of an earlier theologian without substantial alteration of its principal dogmatic content, or (2) accepts the fundamental doctrinal conclusion of an earlier theologian but alters formal or minor material elements (terminology, relations among subsidiary concepts, and nonessential differences in biblical interpretation) of its formulation and/or application to accommodate new circumstances, philosophical trends, or challenges to the Christian faith.

1

Karl Barth and the Displacement of Natural Law in Contemporary Protestant Theology

The Significance of the Barth-Brunner Debate for Contemporary Protestant Theology

The subject of the natural knowledge of God has generated a considerable amount of sophisticated and polemical argumentation in twentieth-century theological discourse, especially in Calvin studies. Much of the recent concern with Calvin's understanding of the natural knowledge of God is traceable to the 1934 exchange between Karl Barth and Emil Brunner over natural theology.[1] While the already weakened state of natural theology in the Reformed tradition was exacerbated by Barth's assault upon Protestant orthodoxy, it makes sense that during the period of Barthian hegemony (1934-1990) interest in related doctrines such as natural revelation and natural law would likewise atrophy given the logical thread connecting them to natural theology.

As most observers of twentieth-century theology are aware, Barth reacted angrily and decisively to Brunner's prophetic call to action in their 1934 debate. "The task of our theological generation," urged Brunner, "[is] to find the way back to a true *theologia naturalis*."[2] Although Barth had criticized the idea of a point of contact (*Anknüpfungspunkt*) between God and man even as far back as his 1918 *Römerbrief*, it was not until the disputation with Brunner that this criticism was raised to a categorical rejection of every form of natural theology and natural law.[3] He particularly focused the brunt of his criticism on the Roman Catholic doctrine of the *analogia entis* for providing common ground between Christian and pagan theology.[4] The task facing the current generation, insisted Barth, was rather to "learn again to understand revelation as *grace* and grace as *revelation* and therefore turn

away from all 'true' or 'false' *theologia naturalis* by ever making new decisions and being ever controverted anew."[5]

When evaluated by its treatment of Calvin's understanding of the natural knowledge of God, the debate points to serious problems in semantic
ambiguity, *Vorverständnis,* and the misuse of passages to fortify the disputants' predetermined conclusions. Unfortunately, with some notable exceptions to the contrary,[6] the debate, taken together with the cumulative influence of Barthianism upon twentieth-century Calvin studies, set parameters
that would seldom be questioned or adjusted as commentators addressed
whether Calvin sanctioned the use of natural theology,[7] argued over his
precise formulation of the *duplex cognitio Dei,*[8] and debated whether an affirmative understanding of natural law could be developed on the basis of
natural revelation.[9]

Both theologians labored hard to demonstrate that their views more
closely adhered to the teaching of the Reformers, the Reformed confessions, and Scripture. Yet the verdict of history, measured solely by which
viewpoint exerted more influence upon subsequent generations of
Protestant theologians, clearly belongs to Barth. In his 1991 Gifford Lectures James Barr provides a similar and supportive assessment:

> Though many people liked Brunner more, for what was thought to be
> his moderation and his good presentation of ideas, it was Barth who
> seemed to win the day in the end: it was he who came to be esteemed as
> the great theologian of the century, the one who found his way into
> university syllabuses along with Thomas Aquinas and Schleiermacher,
> he who was more and more studied. . . . The sequel, curiously, was that
> the issue of natural theology became less of an issue, came to be less
> talked about. One heard less of it, as if it was no more a question — this
> although a great many people had not been convinced that Barth's ab-
> solute opposition to it was right. Many people doubted it, but did not
> summon up the force for an outright counterattack against him.[10]

Barr's assessment lends credibility to my claim that, during the years from
1934 to 1990, Barth's rejection of natural theology/natural law functioned as
a subtext of sorts in mainstream Protestant criticisms of the natural-law tradition. Moreover, as noted in the Introduction, there are at least two other
sources that contributed to twentieth-century Protestant suspicion of natural
law, and these, along with the criticism of natural law by four prominent representatives of the Reformed tradition, will be examined later in the chapter.

The debate had two unfortunate but significant consequences for Protestant systematic and historical theologians' assessments of the natural-law tradition. First, theologically, it brought into question the legitimate and circumscribed use of natural law in Reformed theological ethics by identifying it as a Thomistic and neo-Protestant doctrine[11] and, therefore, too rationalistic in its formulation of the *imago Dei*, sin, and human reason. As with Brunner, Barth blames the Protestant scholastics of the sixteenth and seventeenth centuries for turning "Calvin into a kind of Jean-Alphonse Turrettini."[12] He criticizes Luther and Calvin for failing to clarify "the problem of the *formal* relation between reason with its interpretation of nature and history on the one hand and the absolute claims of revelation on the other."[13] The crux of this criticism is that the Reformers did not fully appreciate the fact that their dispute with Rome over justification and works righteousness was, at root, a disagreement over the knowledge of God and natural theology. "If we really wish to maintain the Reformers' position over against that of Roman Catholicism and Neo-Protestantism," pled Barth, "we are not in a position today to repeat the statements of Luther and Calvin without at the same time making them more pointed than they themselves did."[14]

Second, historically, and resulting from the preceding theological claim, subsequent discussion of natural law did not examine how Protestant orthodoxy had modified the medieval natural-law tradition it received through the Reformers. The question, instead, was whether John Calvin had either formulated a doctrine of natural law or could be said to have laid the foundation for a doctrine of natural law.[15] As a result, twentieth-century theological discussion of the place of natural law in Reformed ethics has largely overlooked any precedent it may have had in Reformed orthodoxy or in the late medieval era, which has left many contemporary theologians without a sound basis to resist adopting the widely publicized objections to natural theology/natural law. To the extent that Protestant and Reformed ethicists endorse Barth's fundamental theological and philosophical presuppositions, they have tended to advocate a divine command ethic saddled with the concomitant problems of actualism[16] and occasionalism[17] that are evident in Barth's theology.

In the pamphlet *Natur und Gnade*, Brunner had advocated what he called "a Christian natural theology."[18] His intention was to assert that the *imago Dei* had not been completely disintegrated as a consequence of humanity's fall into sin. Relics of the image were still observable and thus formed a point of contact for the gospel. Moreover, to demonstrate the feasibility of his view, Brunner appealed to Calvin for historical as well as theological support. In this respect, he insisted, "Calvin considers this remnant of the *imago Dei* to be of great importance," to which he added: "One might almost say that it is one of the pillars supporting his theology."[19]

Barth's angry and uncharitable response in his pamphlet, *Nein! Antwort an Emil Brunner,* challenged Brunner's appeal to Calvin on theological grounds. Zahrnt recalls that Barth criticized Brunner's viewpoint "as unbiblical, Thomistic-Catholic, anti-Reformation, and tainted by the Protestantism of the Enlightenment."[20] Barth's energetic repudiation of natural theology is, at least, somewhat more understandable given his firsthand exposure to "the *'deutschen Christen'* fortifying themselves with an appeal to natural theology."[21] In response to Brunner, Barth appealed to passages in Calvin that *appeared* to point to Christ as the *exclusive* epistemological point of entry into the knowledge of God. Barth characterized Calvin's position to teach that a knowledge of the "One true" God may be accessed only through the instrumentality of Scripture as illumined by the Holy Spirit. From which he drew the following conclusion: "The possibility of a real knowledge by natural man of the true God, derived from creation, is, according to Calvin, a possibility in principle, but not in fact, not a possibility to be realized by us. One might call it an objective possibility, created by God, but not a subjective possibility, open to man. Between what is possible in principle and what is possible in fact there inexorably lies the fall."[22]

In a series of lectures that were originally delivered as the 1937-1938 Gifford Lectures, and published under the title *The Knowledge of God and the Service of God according to the Teaching of the Reformation,* Barth vigorously denounced natural theology. He began by declaring that both the Reformation and the teaching of its churches stand in direct antithesis to the pagan teaching of natural theology. As one might anticipate, Barth acknowledges that the Reformers "occasionally made a guarded and conditional use of the possibility of 'Natural Theology' (as Calvin did, for example, in the first chapters of the *Institutes*)."[23] However, he emphatically denies that this conditional use in any way alters the fundamental Reformation conviction "that the revival of the gospel by Luther and Calvin consisted in their desire to see both the church and human salvation founded on the Word of God *alone,* on God's *revelation in Jesus Christ,* as it is attested in the Scripture, and on faith in that Word."[24]

Yet, even after the attempted revision of Calvin, Barth was still unnerved by the "historical form" of the Reformers' teaching on natural theology, and so it became necessary to develop an explanation of what they actually intended to teach. He stated his rationale accordingly:

> This is the reason why their teaching — if we disregard the fact that in
> its historical form it is not absolutely free from certain elements of
> "Natural Theology" — is the clear antithesis to that form of teaching
> that declares that man himself possesses the capacity and the power to
> inform himself about God, the world and man. From the point of view
> of Reformed teaching what could be more impossible than this task,
> undertaken by all "Natural Theology"?[25]

Barth concluded from reading select portions of the *Institutes* (e.g., 1.6.1;
1.10.3) that humanity's post-lapsarian knowledge of God was *nothing more
than* idolatry and superstition.[26] As he understood Calvin, natural theology
only served the negative function of reminding fallen human beings of their
inexcusability before God and of establishing God's wrath against them.[27]

For many mid-century theologians, the Barth-Brunner debate solidi-
fied the trend to enshrine the doctrine of revelation as the centerpiece of
Protestant theological systems, and in so doing it assumed the status of a
watershed event in the twentieth-century interpretation of Calvin's doctrine of the knowledge of God. Approximately two decades after the altercation, Edward Dowey Jr.'s[28] and T. H. L. Parker's[29] monographs both appeared and reinforced the historical and theological parameters originally
laid down in 1934. Willis, however, thinks it is improper to view these
scholars as strict partisans of either theological perspective, though he does
acknowledge that even a cursory reading of the monographs reveals that
"in their interpretations of Calvin one [Dowey] is more receptive to the insights of Brunner and the other [Parker] to those of Barth."[30]

One of the primary features distinguishing Dowey and Parker relates
to the selection of issues they raise concerning how to ascertain the "foundational ordering principle" that Calvin utilized in structuring the 1559
edition of the *Institutes*. Dowey argues that this structure, not to mention
the very foundation of Calvin's entire theological corpus, is built upon a
twofold, not a fourfold, division. The first of the two divisions, the revelation of God as Creator, is the more general and inclusive category, which in
turn provides the setting within which the latter, the revelation of God as
Redeemer, is to be grasped.[31] According to Dowey's analysis, the root ordering principle of the 1559 *Institutes* is the *duplex cognitio Domini*, not the
structure of the Apostles' Creed.[32]

Dowey impresses upon his readers that Calvin's formulation of the *duplex cognitio Dei* cannot be equated with the traditional distinction between
general and special revelation — that is, with the revelation of God in cre-

ation and in Scripture. As a matter of fact, according to Dowey, Calvin understood the twofold nature of the knowledge of God to be permeable and dynamic, meaning that the first element, the general revelation of God in creation, was able to cross the border into the realm of special revelation.[33] Thus he observes that for Calvin, "The knowledge of the Creator has two sources: creation and the 'general doctrine' of Scripture; and the knowledge of the Redeemer has one source, Christ."[34] Willis reads Dowey as arguing that "the structure of Calvin's *Institutes* conforms to Calvin's conception of the *duplex cognitio Dei*, according to which the *duplex cognitio* is not the one supplied by nature on the one hand and revelation on the other but is supplied by our knowledge of God the Redeemer, known only through the Scriptures, and of God the Creator, known through Scripture and the world."[35] It would be more accurate to state that knowledge of God the Creator has two sources for Calvin: creation and the general doctrine of Scripture; while knowledge of God the Redeemer has one source: not Christ per se, but Christ as revealed in Scripture. As it turns out, then, Willis's reading of Dowey is closer to the truth than Dowey's reading of Calvin.

Parker, on the other hand, following Barth's interpretation, reduces Calvin's epistemological problem of the *knowledge* of God to that of the event of God's self-disclosure in special *revelation*. In contrast to Dowey, Parker denies vociferously that Calvin patterned the *Institutes* after the *duplex* scheme, but instead asserts that the *Institutes* reflects the structure of the correlative knowledge of God and of ourself.[36] According to Parker, after opening Book 1 with the sentence about the sum of our wisdom, Calvin develops the concept of *revelation*, not knowledge, in the subsequent chapters.[37] Parker's debt to Barth is apparent in the following citations:

> Even apart from any idea of sin, God is incomprehensible in His transcendence and voluntary hiddenness, and therefore is unknown to man unless He makes Himself known to him. The presupposition of man's knowledge of God is the self-revelation of God; and the presupposition of the self-revelation of God is His incomprehensibility.[38]

Furthermore,

> Revelation implies not only the impossibility of knowledge without it but also the will of God to be known and His ability to make Himself known, as well as the capability of man to receive revelation (even if this capability is caused by revelation itself).[39]

Based on these passages, it seems that Parker's Barthianism threatens to override the objectivity of his historical and theological analysis.

Until a relatively short time ago, scholars sought to decipher the key principle or theme *(Centraldogmen)* that functioned as the unifying center to Calvin's entire system of theology. Although recent scholarly opinion has flatly rejected the central dogma thesis,[40] traces of it can still be found in commentators. After appraising various proposals advanced in the search for the core principle of Calvin's theological system, D. Brent Laytham concluded that such a unifying theme could not be found and thus claimed, insofar as his own study was concerned, the knowledge of God would not be introduced under that rubric.[41] In the end, unfortunately, Laytham followed Dowey and Parker in holding that the knowledge of God existed not only as a basic theme for Calvin, but that it also functioned as an "interpretive key" to the structure of the 1559 edition of the *Institutes*.[42] While it is disputable whether Laytham ever truly escaped the central dogma thesis, there is no doubt that T. F. Torrance did not. For Torrance insists that Calvin, by his very application of the *duplex* distinction, was instrumental in making "the difficult transition from the medieval mode of thinking in theology to the modern mode."[43]

On a subtler level, however, Laytham and Dowey diverge sharply from Parker in acknowledging the importance of development in Calvin's structuring of the *Institutes*. Beginning in 1536 and continuing through 1559, the argument is that Calvin employed a traditional catechetical structure: Decalogue, Apostles' Creed, Lord's Prayer, and Sacraments. According to Benoît, in the 1559 edition, Calvin altered this plan to follow the format, relatively speaking, of the Apostles' Creed.[44] Furthermore, Dowey adds, Calvin accords greater structural emphasis to the *duplex* scheme in 1559 than he had in any of the earlier editions. Thus, as a result, by closely observing the ordering of the material in the 1539 edition a clear distinction emerges, Dowey contends, "between the knowledge of God as Creator and of God as Redeemer, even within the Scriptural revelation."[45] Yet he also concedes that the succeeding chapters of Book 1 show that Calvin did not strictly adhere to the *duplex cognitio Domini* in the ordering of the system,[46] which ultimately leads Dowey to the presumptuous conclusion that he understood better the implications of Calvin's ordering principle than Calvin himself.

Richard Muller criticizes Parker and Dowey for taking the 1559 *Institutes* as the primary gauge of Calvin's thought and for neglecting an examination of his ordering or reordering of topics in the intervening editions between 1536 and 1559. Most of the detailed efforts to understand Calvin's thought processes and intentions, states Muller, "have been focused on either the origins of his work in the 1536 *Institutes* or the final form of his work in the 1559 Latin and 1560 French *Institutes*. There have been but few examinations of the intervening editions from 1539 to 1557, and there have been virtually no concentrated analyses of the form and content of the great transition from the first edition of 1536 to the edition of 1539 and those that immediately followed it."[47] At the risk of truncating a complex discussion, Muller thinks that Calvin's comment, in his 1559 letter to the reader about not feeling satisfied with the order of the *Institutes* until the present edition, should not be taken to mean that "all previous arrangements and relationships had been discarded or that he had successfully established either the four principal creedal topics or the 'twofold knowledge of God' as the sole overarching organizational structure. What he probably meant was that, in 1559, the creedal model already resident within the *Institutes* had, for the first time, been successfully integrated with the remaining elements of the catechetical model, and, above all, with the basic outline of the Pauline *loci* [sin, law, grace, the people of God and the call of the Gentiles, predestination, good works, civil authority, Christian liberty, and the problem of offense or 'scandal'] drawn from Melanchthon's *Dispositio* and *Loci communes*."[48]

The implication of Muller's analysis for the *duplex* pattern of organization is that "Even in 1559, the dominant ordering principle is the Pauline order as inaugurated in 1539. . . . The initial division of subject into the knowledge of God and knowledge of self, certainly accounts for the initial chapters of Book 1, but, if the Pauline *ordo* is also seen as present, this initial division accounts for the entirety of Book 1 of the *Institutes,* understood as the basic argument of Romans: the relationship of God to humanity, the character of the human predicament, and the fact that humanity is left 'without excuse' in the presence of the revelation of God in nature."[49] In Muller's judgment, "the *duplex cognitio* accounts for the movement from Book 1 to Book 2 of the *Institutes,* particularly when Dowey's understanding of the term is set aside in favor of a view that recognizes the beginning of the knowledge of God the Redeemer in the right understanding of sin — and, moreover, subsumes the *duplex cognitio* under the Pauline *ordo*. The *duplex cognitio,* in other words, makes sense as a way of describing the movement from Paul's initial description of humanity, in the presence of the Creator and nature bereft of the saving revelation of God's grace in Christ to the series of *loci* concerned with the work of salvation."[50] With this brief narrative as backdrop to recent discussions in Calvin studies that were spawned, to a large extent, by the 1934 debate, it makes sense now to move into an examination of Barth's more mature theological objections to natural theology and the natural-law tradition.

Karl Barth's Criticism of Natural Theology and the Natural-Law Tradition

Although Barth slightly moderated his stance on natural theology and the natural-law tradition toward the end of his life, there is no line by which to measure the degree and importance of these changes because he was reluctant to state what they were in unequivocal terms. Paul Henry sheds important light on Barth's change of mind and his early overreaction to nineteenth-century liberalism: "It is unfortunate that what little commentary does exist pertaining to Barth's social ethics often fails to take this [change] into account. The closest Barth comes to actually admitting the fact that there have been some important changes in his thought occurs when he himself reflects on his earliest writings, which were highly critical of the rationalistic strain in nineteenth-century liberalism. Of these earlier writings, Barth states that he overreacted to the situation: 'What should really have been only a sad and friendly smile was a derisive laugh.'"[51]

While this modification must be acknowledged in Barth's thinking, and too seldom has been, it is also equally important to distinguish between what remained constant and what was softened to avoid driving an artificial wedge between the earlier and later periods of his thought. The theological reasoning and biblical hermeneutics that Barth developed early on for rejecting natural theology remained intact throughout all phases of his career, whereas the relative degree of importance assigned to the structures of human existence, society, ethics, and natural moral norms changed slightly during the later period. Moreover, Barth's concern to show that his understanding of natural theology and natural law more closely resembled the "true spirit of the Reformation" without the so-called "rationalist tendencies" of Protestant orthodoxy also remained consistent throughout his long career. The change in Barth's viewpoint, in my judgment, requires the analyst to give less priority to his statements in the 1934 debate and the 1937-1938 Gifford Lectures and more to the *Church Dogmatics* and the shorter political tracts written during World War II.[52]

Barth's fundamental theological criticism of natural theology and natural law is that these doctrines set up an independent, normative source of revelation knowable apart from the self-revelation of Jesus Christ. Variants of this criticism can be found in nearly every major locus in which Barth examines theological issues that relate to these doctrines. But this criticism is seen preeminently in his discussion of the epistemological consequences of sin and, more specifically, in his treatment of the knowledge of sin, the impossibility of a natural knowledge of God, and the question of the remaining relics of the *imago Dei*.

With respect to the knowledge of sin, Barth thinks it is impossible for a person to know through introspection that he is sinful and thus at odds with God, his neighbor, and himself: "Within the sphere of the self-knowledge not enlightened and instructed by the Word of God there is no place for anything worthy of the name of a 'knowledge of sin.'"[53] This, however, is entirely apart from whether a person may recognize that he is limited, deficient, and imperfect. According to Barth, "Access to the knowledge that he is a sinner is lacking to man because he is a sinner."[54] With respect to this point, Barth presupposes that all serious theology has taken its knowledge of sin from the Word of God and, in turn, sought to base it solely on this Word. Any attempt to ascertain one's knowledge of sin apart from Jesus Christ is doomed to failure because the natural man "sees and thinks and knows crookedly even in relation to his crookedness. . . . Crooked even in the knowledge of his crookedness, he can only oppose the Word of God which enlightens and instructs him concerning his crookedness."[55] Barth laments that the older theologians thought it was possible for knowledge of sin to be derived on the basis of "the knowledge of God in His basic relationship to man — as distinct from His presence, action, and revelation in Jesus Christ."[56]

This position opens an avenue for the knowledge of God "by the law that is revealed to man by nature and generally (through the mediation of conscience)."[57] Barth contends that such a position presupposes it is possible to separate the knowledge of God revealed through the law and the knowledge of God revealed through the self-revelation of the Word. While such a distinction may be "useful to stir up a sense of the infinitely qualitative difference between God and man,"[58] he warns that it is not a "harmless fiction" because in it the real God is dishonored and his real law is emptied of content. "The man of sin has every reason to divide the living God in His living Word, regarding Him as God, and His Word as the Law which is given to him, only in the form of this abstraction."[59] Barth holds that unless the fall is viewed only through Jesus Christ as the substance and center of

Scripture, there will be no way to prevent supplementary (and sometimes fundamental) material from being taken over from philosophy, reason, or a combination of these with Scripture.[60] "There is no other book which witnesses to Jesus Christ apart from Holy Scripture. This decides the fact that only in Holy Scripture do we have to do with the one and the whole Word and revelation of God. But if we do not see this, it is inevitable that the question of other sources of revelation should be put, and that sooner or later it should be given a positive answer."[61]

To the extent, then, that we presume to know what "the Law and sin are 'by nature' and therefore (because the Law of God is written on the heart) of ourselves," writes Barth, "to that extent our knowledge will not in fact be the knowledge of faith."[62] Instead, it will be knowledge of an immediate nature that has been drawn from self-reflection and not mediated by the Word and Spirit of God. Under such circumstances, in his judgment, there neither will be, nor can be, any knowledge of the real demand of God and real sin of man. A general philosophy of religion, life, or existence will be substituted in place of the power of the resurrection, the forgiveness of sins, and the righteousness purchased by Jesus Christ. Barth views the natural-law doctrine of Reformed orthodoxy to be evidence of such a substitution: "Once we begin to toy with the *lex naturae* as the inner *lex aeterna* we are well on the way to this. And once the reversal has taken place — as it did in Protestant theology at the turn of the seventeenth century — there can be no stopping on this way."[63]

His primary reason for rejecting the natural-law tradition in Reformed theological ethics is because it presents a false and complacent picture of man the sinner as already at peace with God, his neighbor, and himself:

> At bottom, man is quite able to cope with himself even as the man of sin. He always was. And the supposed *lex naturae* in his own heart certainly will not prevent him but invite and demand that he should see it this way. In so far as this law is in our own hearts it gives us the competence, in so far as it is eternal it gives us the authority, and in so far as we ourselves are the men of sin we have the need and the desire and the self-confidence, to arrange and deal with ourselves as the men we are in this very comfortable way.[64]

Accepting the idea of the law written on the heart, contends Barth, will introduce two sources of revelation and lead inevitably, as it supposedly did for the Protestant scholastics, to compromise formal fidelity to the Bible and the self-revelation of Jesus Christ with pure rationalism.[65] The temptation to compromise begins where "we think we have to create the message of sin from some other source than that of the message of Jesus Christ." "This," declares Barth, "forces us to ask for an independent normative concept, and to move forward to the construction of it, and we fall at once into the whole arbitrary process."[66] The knowledge of human sin is enclosed exclusively and comprehensively in the knowledge of God's atoning work in Jesus Christ. "The knowledge of human sin is acquired in and with the acquiring of this knowledge: not anywhere else, not as separated from it in any respect or to any degree, but strictly and accurately and fully in it. . . . It is irrelevant and superfluous to seek for a normative concept by which to measure sin, to construct such a concept from biblical or extra-biblical materials. . . . it is misleading and futile to do so. It is indeed a form of sin."[67]

A further epistemological effect of sin is that direct discernment of the original relation of man to God has been taken away by the fall. Classically, relates Barth, natural theologians have sought to analyze humanity on the basis of a divine revelation from creation as the introduction to a *theologia vera* grounded in a special revelation. Muller provides a precise statement of the idea that Barth is describing, but as it actually appeared in Reformed orthodox theology:

> Although a contrast is frequently made, sometimes even in the scholastic systems themselves, between *theologia naturalis* and *theologia revelata* (or *theologia revelata sive supernaturalis*), it should already be clear that the contrast is imprecise insofar as natural theology is a form of revealed theology. The precise distinction is between *revelatio naturalis* and *revelatio supernaturalis* and the forms of theology resting upon these revelations, *theologia naturalis* and *theologia supernaturalis,* the former being conceived according to the natural powers of acquisition belonging to the mind, the latter according to a graciously infused power bestowed on the mind by God. Natural theology arises out of the order of nature, whereas supernatural theology, transcending the powers of nature, belongs to the order of grace — but both arise as revealed knowledge, not as a matter of mere human discovery.[68]

For Barth, regardless of these conventional distinctions, natural theology is possible only for Roman Catholic theology, since it presupposes God's manifestation in humanity is directly discernible by us. "This direct discernment of the original relation of God to man, the discernment of the creation of man which is also the revelation of God, has, however, been taken from us by the fall, at least according to Reformation ideas of the extent of sin, and it is restored to us only in the Gospel, in *revelatio specialis*."[69]

This restoration in *revelatio specialis* is such that, while God's revelation in proclamation and Scripture is certainly an aspect of the restored state of affairs, it cannot be isolated from the singular event of God's self-revelation in the Word. The danger, as Barth sees it, comes in isolating Scripture and proclamation from God's giving of himself in revelation, which cannot be known as a general truth or function as the basis of theology or ethics. Nonetheless, he does not rule out the possibility of a highly restricted theological anthropology. Such an anthropology will eliminate the possibility of moving from man to God, and "will consist simply in a depiction first of the original *status integritatis* which is indicated in the Word of God itself and manifested in Jesus Christ and then of the *status corruptionis* which now obtains."[70] For Barth, knowledge moves in only one direction, from above to below, "For we do not even know we are created merely from being created but only from the Word of God, from which we cannot deduce any independent, generally true insights that are different from God's Word and hence lead up to it."[71] To understand God "from man," insists Barth, "can only mean from man of the lost *status integritatis* and hence from man of the present *status corruptionis*."[72] To understand God in this way, claims Barth, is "either an impossibility or something one can do only in the form of Christology and not of anthropology (not even a Christology translated into anthropology). There is a way from Christology to anthropology, but there is no way from anthropology to Christology."[73]

The uniqueness of the knowledge of God, for him, is such that it cannot be measured by the requirements for knowledge of other objects or by a general epistemology but only in terms of its own object. Since understanding God "from man" entails humanity of the present *status corruptionis*, and furthermore, since Barth categorically denies that sinful humanity retains any capacity for the Word of God, it follows that no *Anknüpfungspunkt*, no relics of the *imago Dei,* remain in people after the fall. He develops this position unflinchingly:

> In this sense, as a possibility that is proper to man *qua* creature, the image of God is not just, as it is said, destroyed apart from a few relics; it is totally annihilated. What remains of the image of God even in sinful

man is *recta natura,* to which as such a *rectitudo* cannot be ascribed even *potentialiter.* No matter how it may be with his humanity and personality, man has completely lost the capacity for God. Hence we fail to see how there comes into view here any common basis of discussion for philosophical and theological anthropology, any occasion for the common exhibition of at least the possibility of inquiring about God. The image of God in man of which we must speak here and which forms the real point of contact for God's Word is the *rectitudo* that through Christ is raised up from real death and thus restored or created anew, and which is real as man's possibility for the Word of God. The reconciliation of man with God in Christ also includes, or already begins with, the restitution of the lost point of contact. Hence this point of contact is not real outside faith; it is real only in faith.[74]

For Barth, it is only possible to speak of the *Anknüpfungspunkt* theologically on the basis of faith and not philosophically on the basis of the *analogia entis.* In faith man conforms to God — that is, becomes capable of receiving God's Word and conforming his own decision to the decision God has made about him in the Word. However, according to Barth, Christ's indwelling must never be converted into an anthropological statement. Grace revives the possibility to hear God's Word but not "as a natural capacity in man — it is grace after all that comes to sinners, to incapable men — but as a capacity of the incapable, as a miracle that cannot be interpreted anthropologically, nevertheless as a real capacity which is already actualized in faith . . . whose existence can only be stated, since in becoming an event it already showed itself to be a possibility even before any question about it could arise."[75]

The doctrine of the *analogia entis,* more than any other, draws Barth's severest criticism. He attributes to it the fundamental error of Roman Catholicism and all systems of natural theology. "I can see no third alternative between that exploitation of the *analogia entis* which is legitimate only on the basis of Roman Catholicism, between the greatness and misery of a so-called natural knowledge of God in the sense of *Vaticanum,* and a Protestant theology which draws from its own source, which stands on its own feet, and which is finally liberated from this secular misery. Hence I have no option but to say No at this point. I regard the *analogia entis* as the invention of Antichrist, and I believe that because of it it is impossible ever to become a Roman Catholic, all other reasons for not doing so being to my mind short-sighted and trivial."[76]

Theological Ethics as an Ethic of Divine Command

Barth develops his understanding of theological ethics on the basis of the preceding discussion of the epistemological consequences of the fall. As a result, he is critical of any attempt to wed theological ethics, which is concerned with whether humans will obey the command of their Maker and Ruler when it is put to them, and philosophical ethics, which attempts to discern the good in human action. The fundamental ethical question, in Barth's mind, concerns what constitutes the rightness of the modes of action that remain constant and normative. "What is the true and genuine continuity in all the so-called continuities of human action? . . . This is — roughly — the ethical question, and — roughly again — the answering of it is what is generally called 'ethics'. . . . Our contention is, however, that the dogmatics of the Christian Church, and basically the Christian doctrine of God, is ethics."[77] If dogmatics is ethics, this means it must be a *divine* ethic that is primarily concerned with "the good of the command issued to Jesus Christ and fulfilled by Him." "There can be no question of any other good in addition to this," insists Barth. "Other apparent goods are good only in dependence on this good."[78] Thus, for him, the Christian doctrine of God is a doctrine of God's command, which means that theological ethics must reject the possibility of carrying out a general moral inquiry that is independent of the grace and command of God. The starting point of theological ethics is "that all ethical truth is enclosed in the command of the grace of God — no matter whether this is understood as rational or historical, secular or religious, ecclesiastical or universal ethico-social truth."[79]

Barth criticizes the Roman Catholic understanding of the relationship between theological and philosophical ethics precisely because, in his judgment, it unwarrantably coordinates moral philosophy with moral theology. What separates Barth's view from the Roman Catholic one are basic differences in the doctrines of God, humanity, sin, and grace, which are not merely of a formal but also of a material nature. According to him, the Roman Catholic view "rests on the fundamental conception of the harmony, rooted in the concept of being, between nature and supernature, nature and grace, reason and revelation, man and God. The order of obligation is built on the order of being, ethics on metaphysics, which forms the common presupposition of philosophy and theology."[80] Elsewhere, he insists, "If obligation is grounded in being, this undoubtedly means that it is not grounded in itself, but ontically subordinated to another, and noetically to be derived from this other."[81] According to this view, declares Barth, the fall does not alter humanity's capability of obtaining true knowledge of God apart from grace due to the relic of our original relation by creation to God. He, of course, finds this viewpoint to be thoroughly unacceptable. As an ethical theory that derives obligation from being, it weakens and destroys obligation as such. "If there is a divinely ordered obligation, how can it be grounded for us except in itself? Does not its command have to be one and the same as the divine act of commanding; indeed, as the divine commanding itself? How can we look beyond this to an underlying divine being, and if we do, have we taken it seriously as an obligation?"[82] Barth's fundamental criticism of Roman Catholic ethics is that it permits a separation to occur between God's being and his act. It is only by God's act of grace, the event in which God meets us and gives us his command, that humanity can have fellowship with God.

Grace, for Barth, must never be understood as that which only serves to kindle a previously existing natural light of reason in ethics. "The Protestant axiom behind which we cannot let ourselves be pushed," he declares, "is either full, total, and exclusive grace or it is not divine but at best a demonic power and wisdom."[83] In light of the sole efficacy and sufficiency of grace, it follows that Barth's understanding of the fall cannot allow room for any remaining relation to be maintained between God and humanity on the basis of creation or the *imago Dei*: "We cannot accept a purely relative, quantitative, and factual significance of the fall for the capacity of man in relation to God."[84] In Barth's estimation, it is due to their radically different understandings of grace that Protestant and Roman Catholic ethics diverge from one another. Roman Catholicism, as Barth sees it, is distracted by a misplaced optimism due to its doctrine of the *analogia entis*. "The central task of the Protestant irenic and polemic in relation to Roman Catholic theology is to recall it from this distraction to its proper business, the Christian theme. For in this distraction it is particularly incapable of establishing the concept of the divine command, and therefore of introducing serious theological ethics."[85] In another place Barth refers to this distraction as an aberration, but now in relation to the early church. "It was again an aberration when the early church from at least the second half of the first century began to seek and find the sources of Christian morality and moral teaching in both reason *and* revelation and consequently in both Cicero, etc., *and* the Gospels."[86]

The distinguishing mark of Protestant ethics, as Barth puts it, consists in its exclusive reliance upon the divine command delivered through the self-revelation of God in Jesus Christ. In two short publications, written in 1941 and 1946, Barth argued that adopting natural law would entail a loss of Christian distinctiveness and would lead to an acceptance of Nazism. In his 1946 essay, "The Christian Community and the Civil Community," he contended that Christian decisions in the political sphere utilize no idea, system, or program but instead refer to a direction and a line that must be recognized in all circumstances. This line, however, cannot be defined by appealing to natural law:

> To base its policy on "natural law" would mean that the Christian community was adopting the ways of the civil community, which does not take its bearings from the Christian center and is still living in a state of ignorance. The Christian community would be adopting the methods, in other words, of the pagan State. It would not be acting as a Christian community in the State at all; it would no longer be the salt and the light of the wider circle of which Christ is the center. It would not only be declaring its solidarity with the civil community: it would be putting itself on a par with it and withholding from it the very things it lacks most. It would certainly not be doing it any service in that way. For the thing the civil community lacks (in its neutrality toward the Word and Spirit of God) is a firmer and clearer motivation for political decisions than the so-called natural law can provide.[87]

When the Christian community bases its political decisions on natural law, it does not mean that God cannot make good come from evil; but rather, for Barth, that the Christian community is sharing in the illusions and confusions of the ignorant, neutral, pagan civil community. While the Christian community is called to share in the natural, secular, and profane tasks of the civil community, says Barth, "the norm by which it should be guided is anything but natural: it is the only norm which it can believe in and accept as a spiritual norm, and is derived from the clear law of its own faith, not from the obscure workings of a system outside itself: it is from knowledge of this norm that it will make its decisions in the political sphere."[88]

When the Christian community relies upon its spiritual norm it is free to support the civil community, but this does not mean that the Christian community expects the state gradually to become the kingdom of God. Thus, as Barth relates, "The state as such, the neutral, pagan, ignorant state knows nothing of the kingdom of God. It knows at best of the various ideals based on natural law. The Christian community within the state does know about the kingdom of God, however, and it brings it to man's attention."[89] The state is not destined to become the kingdom of God, but it is based on a divine ordinance that "is intended for the 'world not yet re-deemed' in which sin and the danger of chaos have to be taken into account with the utmost seriousness and in which the rule of Jesus Christ, though in fact already established, is still hidden."[90] Like the state, the Christian community also exists in the "world not yet redeemed." Even at its best, the Christian community cannot be identified with the kingdom of God. When the Christian community attempts to redeem the state, Barth thinks it has confused the kingdom of God with the ideal of natural law.

Far more serious than merely sharing in the illusions and confusion of the civil community, in his letter to Great Britain written in April 1941, Barth warned his Christian brethren in England that opposing Hitler on the basis of natural law would ultimately lead to a compromise with him. It is impossible, he declared, "to make any impression on the evil genius of the new Germany by seeking to refute it on the ground of natural law, by con-fronting its evil and dionysian doctrine of man and society with a humane and apollinistic one."[91] Resistance to Hitler will be built on a really sure foundation, insists Barth, "only when we resist him unequivocally in the name of peculiarly Christian truth, unequivocally in the name of Jesus Christ."[92] According to Barth, all arguments based on natural law are "Janus-headed." "They do not lead to the light of clear decisions, but to the misty twilight in which all cats become grey. They lead to — Munich. Ev-erything depends on our having unambiguous reason for our opposition to Hitler, a reason which makes it impossible to land again in Munich."[93] For him, the choice is stark: Jesus Christ or natural law? There is no common middle ground between these two alternatives upon which a decision to oppose Hitler can be anchored: "Is it still too soon," he asks, "to urge on you more earnestly today than ever before that Christian decisions as weighty and firm and lasting as they must be in this present crisis can be made only in the name of Jesus Christ, and not in the name of any human ideal?"[94] Grounding political obligations on natural law will lead inevita-bly, so Barth thinks, to a division between the political and Christian spheres of existence and, in the end, to a crisis of faith for Christians.

Contemporary Reformed Critics
of the Natural-Law Tradition

One major obstacle for twentieth-century Reformed theologians and ethicists in their assessment of the natural-law tradition has been to overcome the widely misunderstood relationship between the theology of the Reformers and the theology of post-Reformation orthodoxy. The older scholarship tended to describe this relationship in terms that set Calvin against his orthodox successors.[95] As a rhetorical strategy, this tendency is evident already in the 1934 debate when Barth blames orthodoxy for turning Calvin "into a kind of Jean-Alphonse Turrettini."[96] The fundamental problem with setting Calvin against his successors is that it seems "as if Calvin were the only source of post-Reformation Reformed theology and as if the theology of the mid-seventeenth century ought for some reason to be measured against and judged by the theology of the mid-sixteenth century."[97] The Barth-Brunner debate, in the end, came down to the issue of whether natural theology and natural law arose from the "true" teaching and spirit of Calvin's theology or whether it was attributable to a Thomistic and rationalistic distortion that began in Protestant orthodoxy and culminated in Neo-Protestant modernism. As a result, we have seen that subsequent generations of scholars were encouraged to line up behind Barth or Brunner without first assessing Calvin's continuity or discontinuity with his medieval predecessors or his Reformed contemporaries.

A second hindrance to Protestant endorsement of the natural-law tradition is the widespread supposition that it is doctrinally and philosophically wedded to Roman Catholic moral theology. Carl F. H. Henry, Stanley Hauerwas, Paul Lehmann, Reinhold Niebuhr, and Helmut Thielicke, leading Protestant voices representing a variety of ecclesiastical affiliations, are united in their opposition to natural law and in their assessment of it as essentially Roman Catholic. In the Dutch Reformed tradition very similar criticisms have been expressed by Herman Dooyeweerd and G. C. Berkouwer, a devotee of Barthianism for much of his long career at the Free University of Amsterdam, and is reiterated at points in Henry Stob's and Richard Mouw's treatments of natural law.

A third hurdle for Reformed theologians and ethicists to surmount is the belief that divine command theory is the most theologically consistent option for a Reformed ethic. Among some practitioners this supposition is embodied in the assumption that Calvin established the theological parameters of a divine command ethic by rejecting the *lex naturalis* to accent the inscrutability of the *voluntas Dei*. More than anything else, the supposition of Calvin's precedent of a divine command ethic and the voluntarist accents of his theology have created tension for contemporary representatives of the Reformed tradition in defining the relationship between the doctrines of common grace and natural law. This tension ranges from hesitant juxtaposition in some to fundamental incompatibility in others. A survey of Jacques Ellul's, Henry Stob's, John Hare's, and Richard Mouw's thought reveals that their criticism of the natural-law tradition stems largely from various combinations of the above.

Jacques Ellul

Jacques Ellul, the twentieth-century French Reformed jurist and social analyst, in one of his earliest publications, *The Theological Foundation of Law*, insists that Protestants should not utilize the natural-law tradition to any extent. Ellul characterizes the relationship between common grace and natural law as one of fundamental incompatibility. His primary reason for rejecting any use of the natural-law tradition in Reformed ethics centers on his explicit acceptance of Barth's theological argument for rejecting natural theology.[98]

Ellul's Barthian presuppositions emerge clearly in his discussion of justice, including legal justice, where he asserts that the person of Jesus Christ is the meaning and ground of justice. The righteousness of God, in Ellul's judgment, cannot countenance any implicit connection between itself and human justice because God's righteousness, unlike human justice, is grounded in itself, independent, and dynamic. When human justice and divine righteousness are correlated, it is too easy for us to think of God's righteousness "as a kind of a higher court of appeal on which to pin our hope" when human institutions fail.[99] However, when God effects justice, according to Ellul, he encompasses all dimensions of justice in his action, because apart from his will there is no such thing as justice existing eternally on its own.

> How many theologians have, in one way or another, claimed that justice exists by itself, that it has a content of its own, or that it is an attribute of God. All this is erroneous from the biblical point of view. There is no justice apart from God, as there is no measure of his will, nor any cause prior to him. There is no content of justice, because, as we shall see, justice is expressed in judgment. There is no attribute of God, because God is righteousness. This really means that the measure of justice is the will of God. Justice is what is in accordance with the will of God.[100]

Barthian actualism and Christocentrism are apparent in Ellul's understanding of justice insofar as, for him, there is no justice apart from God's judgment, the judgment being understood as "the present and concrete act of God."[101]

Since God's will is, for Ellul, ultimately what makes something just, he remains consistent when he speaks of law as an act of God. This is nowhere more apparent than in God's declaration of Jesus Christ as righteous in his substitutionary death upon the cross: "Either all justice is founded, realized, and qualified by the Son of God, or there is nothing. We could not appeal to anything, not even to the absolute righteousness of God!"[102] The implication of this statement for the Thomistic natural-law tradition is obvious: Since law and justice come into existence only by God's judgment, any realist understanding of justice or law as abstract, universal, objective, or grounded in eternal law has been radically undercut. Ellul states his position with unmistakable clarity: "Law is entirely Christocentric. For this reason we must reject the Thomist doctrine of natural law with its formal connection between *lex aeterna* and *lex naturalis*. *Lex aeterna* rules the world yet cannot be rationally known. It belongs to the realm of faith. *Lex naturalis* is that part of *lex aeterna* that is accessible to human reason, while for us the will of God expresses itself within and not outside a relationship. Furthermore, the relationship between *lex aeterna* and *lex naturalis* is established without any necessary reference to the lordship of Christ."[103]

According to Ellul, the doctrine of natural law teaches that the fall did not cause a complete separation of humanity from God. Some versions of natural law hold that humanity retains a measure of free will, while other versions insist that humanity has a capacity for knowing and doing the good. In Ellul's estimation, however, the fall entailed a complete and utter break between God and humanity, resulting in humanity's spiritual and physical death. Though God still preserves human life, he cautions that this does not mean that any relic of our original creation has been preserved. Humanity has been radically despoiled by sin.

As a result of this total devastation the *imago Dei* was annihilated, thus leaving no foundation upon which to construct a doctrine of natural law; "The fact that man is created in God's image in no way implies that the *imago Dei* remains strong enough after the fall to generate in man an understanding of justice and law."[104] Some try to sidestep this issue, says Ellul, by appealing to Romans 2:14 to marshal support for natural law with the concept of the law written upon the human heart. According to him, the phrase "by nature" in Romans 2:14 could mean that God's law, which the Holy Spirit writes upon the heart of the believer, *becomes* natural law. Thus, from his perspective, "It is meaningless to say that it is not natural law since it is the law of God. Either this law is revealed and thus not written upon the hearts of the Gentiles, or it has become natural, inasmuch as God has embedded it in nature."[105] Once God's law is identified with a nature in which his law is embedded, Ellul is concerned that the philosophical and historical criticisms of natural law, which he takes to be persuasive, will also apply to the law of God. So to avert a potential identification of divine law with natural law, he, like Barth, opts for the more extreme measure of closing off any possible correlation between them by teaching that the *imago Dei* was completely destroyed. More important still, given his understanding of law as an act of God realized in Jesus Christ, Ellul thinks that the law written upon the heart understood as natural law cannot legitimately be called the law of God since no necessary connection is claimed between it and Jesus Christ.

Ellul's Barthian-style actualism becomes evident in a brief discussion he provides of the foundation of law. What God creates, he also reveals: "The content of creation, inasmuch as it concerns us, has been sufficiently made known to us by God."[106] Not only, claims Ellul, does Scripture nowhere mention natural law; natural law seems to present the idea that while God originally created the universe with its laws, he then left it to function on its own. For him, this is equivalent to the eighteenth-century deistic watchmaker idea, in which God sets up the natural law of justice and then leaves the universe to run on its own accord. To this viewpoint he takes exception:

> I cannot believe that this is the real meaning of creation. God creates continually. The world is created by him ever anew. It only survives because God acts. The laws of creation are laws only because God applies them. He is a "God of order." There exists no set principle as a natural source of life. God continually brings to life what, in itself, is but nothingness. There can, therefore, be no original juridical principle.[107]

Justice, for him, is nothing more than conformity with the actual and eternal will of God. Natural law, by contrast, is the philosophers' idea of creation and has been given a "Christian" interpretation that adulterates God's word by human reason. God's law cannot provide the foundation to natural law because anything that corresponds to human reason, as is alleged for natural law, has been drawn into the cosmic consequences of the fall: "Nothing entitles us to say that law is just because it is natural, since nature is 'subjected to futility,' which is the very opposite of justice according to our summary of the biblical teachings about justice."[108] In the end, though Ellul never acknowledges a formal debt to Barth, Barth's influence upon him is evident from start to finish.

Henry Stob

Henry Stob, late professor of moral theology at Calvin Theological Seminary and a highly regarded Reformed ethicist, was also critical of the natural-law tradition in theological ethics. However, Stob's criticism seems to derive from two different sides — the one philosophical, the other theological. From the philosophical vantage point, unlike Ellul, it is clear that Stob has been influenced by the reformational philosophy of the *Wijsbegeerte der Wetsidee*'s criticism of Roman Catholic dualism and its corresponding scholastic ground-motive. He studied under Vollenhoven and Dooyeweerd at the Vrije Universiteit for the 1938-1939 term and, upon returning home, was appointed professor of philosophy at Calvin College, the post through which he functioned as the principal mediator of the *Wijsbegeerte der Wetsidee* to the Calvin College community of the 1940s and early 1950s.[109] Yet from the theological vantage point, it is possible to detect the influence of a Barthian-style actualism in his mature criticism of natural-law ethics, most likely filtered through the anti-scholastic and Christocentric theology of G. C. Berkouwer that was popular in Christian Reformed circles during the 1960s and 1970s.[110] "When I read what Barth had to say," recounts Stob in his memoirs of his student days at Hartford Theological Seminary, "my spirits rose. I sensed that here was a man who, affirming a transcendent God and a veritable supernatural revelation, expressed my own deepest sentiments and afforded me a contemporary reference point from which to engage my mentors and fellow students in relevant discussion. . . . I can fairly say that it was Karl Barth who, even in his Kierkegaardian existentialist phase, helped to establish me more firmly in the Reformed faith."[111]

Interestingly, Stob affirms two points that historically have been associated with the tradition of natural-law ethics. First, he attests that the moral law under which human beings reside is the law of God, which is authoritatively articulated in the Decalogue, and that the moral law is unitary, which means it applies equally to all. Second, he acknowledges that there is a natural and universal awareness of this law such that no person can plead ignorance when breaking it.[112] Nevertheless, Stob questions whether humankind, "apart from a special disclosure of God's will in the form of a personal address, has, or can have, an *adequate* knowledge of the single moral law under which it resides."[113] Formally, enough of the moral law is knowable by natural cognition to leave people without excuse for their trespasses. Materially, even, enough is known to enable people to distinguish between right and wrong, to maintain equitable and decent relations with one another, and to establish a just civil society.

For Stob, however, the more important theological issue "is whether those outside the fellowship of Christ can know more than this, whether in particular they can know enough to enable them to elaborate an ethic that reflects with fidelity the will of God for our lives."[114] Roman Catholics reply in the affirmative, while Calvinists reply in the negative, even though, as Stob recognizes, on this matter Calvin sometimes seems to ally himself more with Roman Catholics.[115]

In Stob's judgment, there are three principal "mistakes" underlying the tradition of natural-law ethics. The first of these so-called mistakes "is a philosophical dualism that unwarrantably separates nature and grace."[116] In traditional Roman Catholic teaching, as Stob summarizes, nature and grace are described as "two distinct and independent magnitudes" whose relationship "never goes beyond external juxtaposition." He describes the mechanism of the nature-grace relationship as follows: "Grace, when operative, does 'perfect' nature, but it does so only by addition, not by penetration. Therefore, any 'whole' that nature and grace may constitute becomes not a true unity, but a sum."[117] In the case of Adam's fellowship with God, then, his human nature was combined with "superadded" grace such that the fall "effected not the inner spoliation of his human nature but merely the external subtraction of the *superadditum,* leaving his nature deprived but basically unimpaired."[118] Given this conceptual framework, it makes sense that sinful human beings would be able through exercising their reason to discern the moral law and, as a result, to develop systems of natural morality.

However, as Stob relates, this view may be mistaken, principally because it separates what is "a real unity, with an inner concentration point in our heart."[119] His criticism here reiterates a perduring theme in Herman Dooyeweerd's criticism of the so-called scholastic ground-motive: "Instead of *reformation* [the church fathers] sought accommodation; they sought to adapt pagan thought to divine revelation of the Word. This adaptation laid the basis for *scholasticism,* which up to the present impedes the development of a truly reformational direction in Christian life and thought."[120]

If this criticism of scholasticism and the nature/grace distinction is adequate, and there is reason to believe that it is not,[121] then it would follow that the whole structure of natural-law ethics is questionable and indeed untenable as Stob thinks it is. The adequacy of this criticism from the perspective of Reformed orthodoxy will be revisited in succeeding chapters.

The second so-called mistake of the natural-law tradition is that it leads to the view that the moral law is an objective datum that can be severed from the Lawgiver and possessed exclusively by the human mind. Stob's focus on the doctrine of revelation and his inclination to formulate the doctrine in actualistic terms becomes apparent in his explanation of this mistake:

> The law, in [the Thomistic] view, becomes less a mode of revelation to be listened to in existential fear than a property to be pocketed. But when we regard him who, choosing to manifest his will in the form of the law, remains sovereign in his disclosures, it becomes plain that we are not to think of the law as "existing in the mind" in any literal sense. Indeed, the moral law as such can hardly be said to *be* any "where." The law is "posited" by God; it holds for humanity, but it does not "exist" in some place or region, for it is nothing other than a fixed divine "determination." It cannot be said, therefore, to be literally "written on the heart" or "engraved on the consciousness of men." These are metaphors that figuratively express the fact that the law is "present" to our conscience, that we know the law with a certain degree of immediacy.[122]

As with Ellul's denial of a straightforward reading of Romans 2:14, Stob likewise feels compelled to provide an alternative and actualistic interpretation of the passage. If there is no immediately accessible law deposited in the heart of the believer, how much more is the nonbeliever dependent upon the divine will to *posit* the awareness of such on his consciousness. For Stob, there is no moral law "in" the nonbeliever either in terms of "common notions" or an implanted practical knowledge of morality that is possessed, controlled, or discerned apart from God's sovereign self-disclosure. "There is presented to [nonbelievers] a manifestation of the law that, under favorable conditions, their conscience can comprehend, but there is no law actually 'written on their heart.' The law is always above and beyond them, and only so much of it as God has revealed to them is available for their perception."[123]

The third so-called mistake of the natural-law tradition is that it leads to the view that natural revelation is sufficient to reveal the moral law and that the special revelation of God in Jesus Christ can ultimately be set aside. Stob's point that whatever is revealed outside of Scripture, Christ, and the prophets "enters into the unredeemed consciousness in a dim and distorted form" is also unanimously attested by Reformed orthodoxy.[124] Still, to conclude from this that nonbelievers' blindness, ignorance, and rebellion nullify the awareness of the moral law is to swing the pendulum too far in the other direction. In Stob's words, "It is not intellectual imbecility that characterizes the unregenerate; the whole imposing edifice of science contradicts that. What characterizes them is moral obtuseness, what Jesus called 'hypocrisy.'"[125] He contends that nonbelievers do not have an adequate knowledge of the moral law because there is a limited disclosure of that knowledge in nature and because of their subjective inability to get even that limited disclosure into clear enough focus. His concern is to thwart a natural ethics that presumes to dispense with the revelation of God in Christ. This revelation is indispensable "not only for the proper articulation of religious duties and the acquisition of theological virtues but for the definition and cultivation of all the virtues and for the illumination and establishment of even the meanest duty in the most mundane situation. Without God's special redemptive disclosure, his will for our being and conduct in each and every area of life remains in a significant sense 'unknown.'"[126]

Henry Stob's understanding of the relationship between the natural-law tradition and the doctrine of common grace has had significant influence on such philosophers and ethicists in the Dutch Reformed tradition as Richard Mouw, Lewis Smedes, and Nicholas Wolterstorff. His view can be characterized as one of antithetical incompatibility.[127] His fundamental contention is that pagan ethics, though illuminating and useful to the Christian, ultimately misapprehends the moral law and fails to provide reliable moral guidance. Ontologically, knowledge of God and awareness of the moral law do exist in the world, but noetically this knowledge is held down in unrighteousness and suppressed by human wickedness. The noetic differences between believer and nonbeliever are seen in terms of a basic antithesis "in the stance and vision of the unregenerate, a fault that distorts whatever reality they apprehend, the distortion being greater at the center than on the periphery."[128] By saying this, however, Stob does not mean to imply that nonbelievers know nothing about God or have not made important contributions to ethics. His claim is merely that given the fault running between Christian and non-Christian thought, the ethical contributions of nonbelievers function more as "ancillary services" to Christian ethics[129] that believers can and ought to put to good use. So, for Stob, common grace is God's work of preserving order and saving the "unthankful and recalcitrant from the worst consequences of their folly, and which, without drawing them into the divine fellowship, does enable them, by various endowments, to perform those human tasks that are serviceable, beyond their knowing or intent, to the ends of Christ's kingdom."[130]

John Hare

John Hare, professor of philosophical theology at Yale Divinity School, is also critical of the natural-law tradition. Instead of relying upon divine self-disclosures or Barthian formulations of the doctrine of revelation, Hare develops a version of divine command ethics on the basis of a perceived historical connection between John Calvin and Duns Scotus. In his estimation, "Calvin is closer . . . to Scotus than to Thomas Aquinas. This is not surprising," he says, "since Scotus was in general more influential than Aquinas in the two hundred years after Scotus's death."[131] While there is some merit to this historical argument, the more significant issues concern whether Scotus's ethical theory may be legitimately classified as a divine command ethic and the methodological pitfall, mentioned earlier, of supposing Calvin to be the chief early codifier of Reformed doctrine.

One way to avert the methodological problem is to assess how other Reformers appropriated medieval doctrinal and philosophical formulations. The question of whether Calvin is closer to Scotus or Aquinas is less important for the development of Reformed ethics than whether Calvin's fellow Reformers and orthodox successors believed the natural-law tradition to be consonant with their doctrinal and theological commitments. Unfortunately, Hare does not address this question, but he does seem to view Calvin, on the one hand, as the chief early codifier of Reformed theology and to classify Scotus, on the other, as a divine command theorist. He thinks that the project of "describing and modifying [Scotus's] account, which . . . is the best version we have of a divine command theory . . . is especially promising for Calvinists, because of the connection between Scotus and Calvin."[132] From a meta-ethical vantage point, Richard Cross,[133] Allan Wolter,[134] and Hannes Möhle,[135] each accomplished Scotus scholars in their own right, would challenge Hare's classification of Scotus as a divine command theorist, as would Muller *et al.*, from an historical-theological vantage point, the view of Calvin as chief early codifier of Reformed theology that Hare also seems to espouse.

Cross, for example, states plainly what his objection would be to Hare's classification of Scotus: "It is sometimes thought that Scotus' voluntarism extends to his ethics too, and that he accepts some sort of divine command theory. I shall argue that, although Scotus's theory shares some important characteristics with divine command theories, it should not properly be seen as such a theory. Scotus's theory is not open to an objection that is fatal for divine command theories, and thus might prove appealing to those who share the sorts of motivations that lead to acceptance of a divine command ethic."[136] The fatal objection, in Cross's allusion, concerns the ground of the obligation to obey God. "What is the origin of the obligation to obey God? It cannot be a divine command," insists Cross, "since the theory is then circular; it cannot, however, be anything other than a divine command, since on the theory no obligations derive from anything other than a divine command. The divine command theory also makes it difficult to give anything other than the thinnest account of God's goodness."[137]

For purposes of our discussion here, however, it is less important to assess Hare's case for a connection between Calvin and Scotus or even to assess the accuracy of his characterization of Scotus as a divine command theorist,[138] but it is germane to examine his criticism of natural-law doctrine, which he develops from an interpretation of Scotus's ethics.

According to Hare, the fall has disordered our natural inclinations to such an extent that "we cannot use them as an authoritative source of guidance for how we must and must not live."[139] Divine command theory, which he defines as "the theory that what makes something obligatory for us is that God commands it," sees moral obligations as an expression of God's will that is recapitulated in human moral decisionmaking:[140] "The move from the good to the obligatory, or from attraction to constraint, comes because after the fall our perception of the good is splintered and disordered. We need to be held back from some of our pursuits, and we need to trust that this constraint is consistent with our good."[141] In *God's Call* Hare does not provide a full theological explanation for why the post-lapsarian natural human faculties are unable to provide an "authoritative source of guidance" for right living; in fact, there is no discussion of Scotus's view of reason or the relics of the *imago Dei*. The closest Hare comes to addressing these issues can be seen in his treatment of Scotus's doctrine of the two affections: the affection for justice and the affection for advantage.[142] After the fall, writes Hare, we are born with an *inordinate* affection for advantage — with the inclination toward our own advantage *above everything else* — that constantly threatens to trump the affection for justice — the inclination toward intrinsic goods for their own sake.[143]

In *Why Bother Being Good?* Hare asserts that the demands of morality are too high for unredeemed humanity "given the natural capacities we are born with,"[144] which is what creates the problem of the moral gap, a problem he has grappled with elsewhere.[145] Yet in this book he provides no theological justification for why this is so. Simply stated, the moral gap arises from the tension between the natural inclination to put the good of oneself above the good of the whole. Given the fact that we, in the first place, tend to be drawn more toward our own good and that we, in the second place, are finite creatures, writes Hare, "we feel the magnetic pull of the good in a very fragmentary and incomplete way. We need some kind of procedure for checking at least provisionally whether the good we feel drawn to is consistent with the flourishing of everyone (and everything) as a whole."[146]

Because the fall has disordered the proper relations originally inhering between the soul's component parts (intellect, will, affections), Hare rightly calls attention to an "important difference between what God created human nature to be and what it is after the fall."[147] However, to conclude from the disparity between pre- and post-lapsarian anthropology — as Hare seems to do — that natural human capacities are incapable of yielding reliable moral knowledge or that persons are no longer oriented toward good in any meaningful ethical sense is to draw an overly pessimistic and theologically unwarranted conclusion.[148] If the affection for justice survives in unredeemed humanity *post-lapsum,* as Hare claims, then, at the very least, his position must be distinguished from Barth's and Ellul's, who each claim that the *imago Dei* was annihilated in the fall, thus leaving no basis upon which to appeal to any rudimentary knowledge of morality or justice.

It is possible, as will be seen in the cases of John Calvin, Peter Martyr Vermigli, Jerome Zanchi, Johannes Althusius, and Francis Turretin, to acknowledge the truth of humanity's inordinate affection for advantage but to conclude that the diminished natural human faculties still function sufficiently to reveal the general precepts of the natural moral law — which, although minimal, yields a fuller account of morality for the unregenerate than does Hare's rendering of the affection for justice.

Richard Mouw

Richard Mouw, professor of Christian philosophy and president of Fuller Theological Seminary, has modified his view of the natural-law tradition in some important respects between the publication of *The God Who Commands* (1990) and *He Shines in All That's Fair* (2001). In the earlier book Mouw follows David Little's[149] characterization of Calvin's thought as voluntarist and emphasizes how Calvinist voluntarism attempted to distance itself from Thomism. He also acknowledges the plausibility of Dooyeweerd's narrative of how the medieval church, to use his own words, "had prepared the way for a cultural capitulation to secularism by granting legitimacy to natural reason, functioning apart from the acceptance of divine revelation."[150] In the later book, however, he is more receptive to the natural-law tradition but not without some "Calvinist misgivings."[151] Where natural law is addressed there, his goal is to understand better the relation between it and common grace, which, for him, can be characterized as hesitant juxtaposition.

In *The God Who Commands* Mouw builds on Little's thesis that Calvin employs the notion of "new order" as the organizing theme of his political thought. Little's argument is that Calvin departed from the concept of order in Stoicism, humanism, and medieval Catholicism because it was too static. In describing Calvin's alternative concept of moral and political order, Little, "rightly" in Mouw's estimation, "makes much of the strong *voluntarism* in Calvin's thought."[152] Proper political obedience for Calvin, as Mouw cites Little, is directed toward "the 'free will' of God as the source of order," and the human response of obedience is itself a voluntary one that "mirrors God's freedom."[153] The actualist motif in Mouw's thought begins to emerge here. According to Mouw, the "emphasis on the naked will-to-will character of the central divine-human encounter is necessary for seeing clearly how Calvin was distancing himself from the sort of medieval account associated with, for example, Thomism."[154] The differences between the Thomist and Calvinist visions are framed as follows:

> While Calvinist voluntarism featured a revelatory encounter in which a naked divine will issued legal commands to a naked human will, the Thomist preferred a picture in which both the divine and human wills were already immersed in law prior to the presentation of the biblical imperatives: the revealed legislation in the Scriptures, that which comprises the *lex divina,* is itself a specification of the primary law, the *lex*

aeterna, which is God's own everlasting normative point of reference; and the biblical laws are in turn understood by human beings in light of the *lex naturalis* to which they have extrabiblical noetic access.[155]

Calvin's voluntarism led him, in Mouw's judgment, "to focus on the revealed legislation of the Scriptures as a free and direct address from sovereign divine will to defenseless human will."[156] Instead of viewing Scripture as a form of "free and direct address," for Calvin (as for Aquinas), the *lex divina* (i.e., the Decalogue) and the *lex naturalis* reveal the same moral ontology, the primary difference between them being ease of epistemological access to the moral law. After the fall, the moral law is more quickly discerned by reading the Decalogue than by constructing rational arguments on the basis of experience and logic as with the natural law.

Mouw's project in *He Shines in All That's Fair* is to answer the question, "What is it that Christians can assume they have in common with people who have not experienced the saving grace that draws a sinner into a restored relationship with God?"[157] A large part of the answer to that question hinges on how one understands and applies the doctrine of common grace. The concern here is not so much with the way that Mouw defines and applies common grace to the present cultural situation, but with the way that he understands the doctrine vis-à-vis the natural-law tradition.[158] The Christian tradition offers many significant strategies for promoting commonness, according to Mouw; in fact, "One obvious place to look is the 'natural law' tradition, and it is gratifying to see how Christians from several traditions — particularly Roman Catholics and evangelicals — are engaged in dialogue about how natural law themes can be appropriated for our contemporary context."[159] Although Mouw thinks that one need not choose between natural law and common grace as competing doctrinal strategies, he juxtaposes them because common grace embodies sensitivities — so-called "Calvinist ones" — that are not present in other ways of addressing the issue of commonness.

The element of mystery is an important aspect of Mouw's definition of common grace and may indicate that common grace is best understood as an aspect of the doctrine of providence. While Mouw is convinced that such a thing as common grace exists, he is not very clear in his own mind about what it is. "We stand here," he is convinced, "before a mystery."[160] "Properly understood, common grace theology is an attempt to preserve an area of mystery regarding God's dealings with humankind. In an important sense, an acknowledgement of common grace is arrived at by a 'way of negation'; it is something we are left with after having gone through a process of elimination."[161] Contemporary Calvinists, it is true, have not endorsed with much enthusiasm any of the major alternative views of commonness in the Christian tradition. "Outside of the Calvinist tradition," states Mouw, "the major alternative views — general revelation, natural law, and natural theology, for example — have commanded considerable respect and been put to extensive use in establishing patterns of commonality. But we Calvinists have generally approached these explanatory schemes with many misgivings."[162]

Conclusion

Despite Ellul's, Stob's, Hare's, and Mouw's protestations to the contrary, the argument of this book is that historically, in fact, Calvinists have made good use of the natural-law tradition, but that it ceased to exist in twentieth-century Protestant theological ethics for a variety of reasons, not the least of which can be attributed to Karl Barth's epistemological criticism of natural theology, the identification of natural law as a doctrinal and philosophical component of Roman Catholic moral theology, and a regnant anti-metaphysical bias among contemporary theologians. Moreover, as a corollary effect, one reason why it may be difficult to develop a more rigorous formulation of common grace is that in the older scholastic systems the idea of common grace was expressed through the doctrine of general providence. This is true for Calvin and illustrated well in the use he makes of the bridle metaphor throughout the *Institutes* and commentaries, as Schreiner has shown.[163] Common grace may be difficult to grasp by itself and to understand in relation to natural law precisely because it is a synthetic term that has been severed from its proper doctrinal locations in prolegomena, theology proper, and anthropology. The concepts of common grace and antithesis do not function well outside of these circumscribed areas where the relationship between them and the related doctrines of natural revelation, natural theology, and natural law is not logically established.

Furthermore, as this chapter has amply documented, twentieth-century Reformed theologians and ethicists have been powerfully attracted to voluntarism, divine command theories of ethics, and Barthian-style actualism, which they believed to be consonant with a view of the *voluntas Dei* that was thought to have been codified in the theology of John Calvin and the Reformed confessions. However, as we will see in subsequent chapters, an orthodox Reformed view of divine omnipotence vis-à-vis the precepts of morality not only is reconcilable with the natural-law tradition but also was profitably used by Calvin, Vermigli, Zanchi, Althusius, and Turretin as the preferred system of ethics.

2

Development of the Natural-Law Tradition through the High Middle Ages

Caricatures of Nominalism and the Problem of "Protestant Voluntarism"

Anthony Quinton's criticism of Duns Scotus's ethics is applied to most theological accounts of moral obligation: "Things are good because God wills them and not vice versa, so moral truth is not accessible to the natural reason."[1] The type of theological voluntarism that Quinton ascribes to Scotus — a moral ontology emanating from the divine will as the sole origin of all order of essences and moral laws and impervious to rational investigation — is an apt summary of Karl Barth's divine command ethic, even if it is a gross mischaracterization of Scotus's natural-law ethic. But mischaracterizations of this sort abound in late modernity. For example, Christian ethicist Arthur Holmes thinks that nominalism laid the philosophical foundation for such contemporary ethical theories as emotivism, relativism, and consequentialism[2] — a viewpoint that is even shared by a variety of Christian scholars outside the discipline of ethics.[3] Another, widely discussed critique of nominalism, arising from within the academic mainstream, occurs in the work of the German intellectual historian Hans Blumenberg.[4] Likely unaware of the implications that the late medieval dialectic of *potentia Dei absoluta/ordinata* had for understanding God's action in history, Blumenberg thought that nominalism, which he characterized as accenting radical divine freedom and unconstrained power, was implicitly at odds with the modern view of human agency in its stress on human self-realization, self-assertion, and self-exploration. An omnipotent God bounded by no one or no thing, so he reasoned, threatened to run roughshod over legitimate human achievements.[5]

A popular Roman Catholic criticism of nominalism, particularly among Dominicans and heirs of Leo XIII's revival of Thomism (but not among Franciscans), is that "nominalism represents decadent scholasticism, even a theology no longer authentically Catholic."[6] This narrative line, attributable to Heinrich Denifle and Joseph Lortz, attempts to undercut the catholicity of Luther's doctrinal reforms (i.e., his medieval Augustinian roots in the *via moderna*[7]) by suggesting that the Occamist milieu at the universities of Erfurt and Wittenberg (à la Gabriel Biel and Jodocus Trutvetter as mediators of "decadent" nominalism) accounts for his insufficient literacy in the "orthodox" theology of Thomas Aquinas, which, consequently, facilitated his fall into schism and heresy. According to this hypothesis Luther's ignorance of Thomism, which Denifle and Lortz take to be scholasticism in its highest form, left him open to the reform theologies of Wyclif and Hus and what later would become the Protestant doctrinal corrections.[8] The Denifle-Lortz thesis has been subjected to close scrutiny by a number of scholars, specifically on the question of Luther's familiarity with Thomas and late medieval Thomism, and found to be historically untenable.[9] This is not to say, however, the association of Protestant theology with late medieval nominalism is not understandably reinforced at times by the Reformers' favorable appropriation of the medieval Augustinianism of such right-wing nominalists as Thomas Bradwardine, Gregory of Rimini, and Gabriel Biel, on the one hand, and their strong reactions to the Pelagianism of such left-wing nominalists as Robert Holcot, Adam Wodeham, Nicolas de Autrecourt, and Jean de Mirecourt, on the other.[10]

The supposition that Protestant theology and nominalist metaphysics are fundamentally wedded, a derivative of the Denifle-Lortz thesis, resurfaces in some Roman Catholic accounts of Protestant ethics. The Protestant Reformers, according to one analyst, took "the voluntarist or Ockhamist line on the precepts of morality, while the Catholic writers tended towards the objectivist or intellectualist view."[11] Such a facile contrast is difficult to sustain not only between the historical development of Protestant and Roman Catholic ethics in general but also, and more importantly, in the identification of voluntarism (i.e., a priority accorded either to the divine or the human will over the intellect) with nominalism (i.e., Occamism).[12] The most influential voluntarist in the late medieval era, and indeed for almost two hundred years after his death, is John Duns Scotus (d. 1308), and Scotus is a philosophical realist and not a nominalist.[13] According to Michael Bertram Crowe, "the voluntarism in much Reform theology presented an uncongenial setting for anything like the classical thirteenth century concept of a natural law."[14] In fact, he asserts, within Protestantism as a whole "the natural law was disparaged in favor of the Bible as the expression of the legislative will of God."[15] While this caricature of Protestant ethics may more accurately describe sixteenth-century Anabaptist theology, it breaks down when applied to Vermigli, Zanchi, Althusius, and Turretin as will be seen in the course of subsequent chapters.

Based on the alleged identification of voluntarism with nominalism, the claim is often made that "Protestant voluntarism" promoted a view of God as an arbitrary and unaccountable sovereign, which then undercut confidence in the reliability of the natural moral order and led, in turn, to the idea of the divine right of kings in the seventeenth century. A. P. d'Entrèves and Heinrich Rommen, each influential Roman Catholic intellectuals in their own right, consider Reformed theologians to be among the worst offenders in this respect, largely because of the importance ascribed to the divine will in the so-called "Calvinist dogma of predestination." D'Entrèves insists that Protestant voluntarism is the reason why natural law was disparaged "in favor of the divine law of the Bible on the one hand, and, on the other, of the positive law of the State conceived as ultimately grounded upon the will of God."[16] Rommen, following the same line of reasoning, completes the interpretive circle in d'Entrèves's intimation: "The so-called Reformers had drawn the ultimate conclusions from Occamism with respect to theology. Contemptuous of reason, they had arrived at a pregnant voluntarism in theology as well as at the doctrine of *natura deleta*, of nature as destroyed by original sin. . . . The absolute power of God in Occam's doctrine became at the hands of Thomas Hobbes the absolute sovereignty of the king."[17] In the end, therefore, Protestant voluntarism is thought to lead to the position that ethical values can have no other foundation but the will of God that imposes them. "The notion of God as an unlimited and arbitrary power," states d'Entrèves, "implied the reduction of all moral laws to inscrutable manifestations of divine omnipotence."[18]

History shows, however, that instead of increasing the sovereign's power, the Saint Bartholomew's massacre of 1572 actually set events in motion that would gradually lead to the emergence of the democratic constitutional state.[19] In resisting the absolutist regimes of France, Spain, and Scotland, late sixteenth- and seventeenth-century Protestant, particularly Reformed, theologians and jurists actually fomented the rise of modern constitutionalism[20] and the role of voluntary associations in contributing to the foundation of a vibrant, peaceful, and juridically organized civil society.[21]

While there are many different facets to the caricature of nominalism and its association with so-called Protestant voluntarism, in each case there is a failure to apprehend sufficiently some of its more subtle historical, philosophical, or theological nuances. The last three decades have witnessed a resurgence of interest in nominalism and a shift in the scholarly consensus surrounding it. So before examining Calvin's formulation of the *duplex cognitio Dei* and his appropriation of natural law in Chapter Three, it is necessary to investigate first what effect the medieval debates had on the development of the natural-law tradition.

Types of Natural-Law Theories

One way to begin this discussion is to address an ambiguity that is present in most contemporary treatments of natural law.[22] While it is customary to speak of the "classical and Christian" natural-law tradition before the twelfth century in its Greek, Stoic, or Roman phases of development, during the later Middle Ages (ca. 1150 to ca. 1500) two streams of natural-law theories emerge within the Christian moral tradition. By the middle of the fourteenth century, it is already possible to differentiate two types of natural-law theories within late medieval scholasticism, each proposing distinct moral ontologies: a realist theory of natural law, represented by — among others — Thomas Aquinas and Duns Scotus, and a nominalist theory of natural law, represented by — among others — William of Occam and Pierre d'Ailly.[23] Thus, given the scope and importance of these developments, it is simply improper to speak of any *single* "classical and Christian," or even "medieval" natural-law tradition that could be juxtaposed to the "modern" (i.e., Enlightenment) tradition of natural law.[24]

It is possible to illustrate the basic differences between these theories through simple contrast and to arrive at some surprising discoveries. First and most important, the opposite of a realist natural-law theory is not necessarily a divine command theory, as many analysts following Otto von Gierke and Karl Barth have supposed it to be, but rather a nominalist natural-law theory. What adds a layer of complication to this observation is that realists and nominalists alike shared many fundamental theological starting points, even when they differed on key philosophical and methodological points. For example, the belief that God reveals himself in nature as well as through Scripture was a commonplace that Thomas Aquinas, Duns Scotus, William of Occam, and the scholastic tradition in general, took for granted. "That is why for Scotus, as well as for Occam who followed him," states Wolter, "the substantive content of the natural law is ba-

sically the same as it was for the generality of the scholastics. It is only in
their interpretation of why and how it binds that we discover a significant
difference. It is a 'law' and to that extent 'obliges' inasmuch as it represents
an expression of God's will in man's regard."[25]

Furthermore, on the question of the *ultimate* origin of moral obligation, namely, the divine will, Aquinas, Scotus, and Occam also maintain
general agreement. The disagreements in the scholastic tradition arise where
some, such as Aquinas, following Augustine and the divine ideas tradition,
derive the *proximate* ground of moral obligation by linking the *lex naturalis*
with the *lex aeterna,* while others, such as Scotus and Occam, sever that link
to accent God's "synchronic contingency" with respect to the orders of nature, grace, and morality.[26] Like Scotus and Occam, Aquinas held that the
divine will initially generates the moral obligation to do and pursue that
which is good and avoid what is evil.[27] Etienne Gilson, a principal agent in
the neo-scholastic revival of Thomas Aquinas, comments of his teaching
that "the understanding and the will reciprocally include and move each
other,"[28] a recognition that seems to diminish some of the stereotyped differences between realists and nominalists, intellectualists and voluntarists.

On the basis of these qualifications it is possible to hold, as both realist
mediating and nominalist theories of natural law attest, that what makes
something *ultimately* obligatory is that God commands it. The divine command, in these formulations, typically occurs through the instrumentality of
God's ordained power (i.e., the natural moral order established at creation,
where his will is expressed concerning moral imperatives), but which may
have been created other than it was had God chosen to actualize the total
possibilities initially open to him *(potentia absoluta)* differently than he did.

Accepting the view that moral obligation ultimately originates from
the divine will, therefore, does not entail a strong divine command formulation of the *proximate* ground of moral obligation (i.e., the *content* of ethics), where God's command is both necessary and sufficient for an action to
have moral value. Hence, there is no contradiction between holding to a
natural-law formulation of the content of ethics and an account of human
moral obligation that originates ultimately from God's command. In fact,
realist and nominalist natural law theorists were agreed that the faculty of
right reason,[29] which can be defined as a natural power of the human intellect by which human beings assent to self-evident first principles, was capable of apprehending as good those things to which the rational creature
already has a natural inclination. Contemporary proponents of a strong divine command theory, such as Karl Barth, reject any variant of natural-law

theory because of its more optimistic estimation of the post-lapsarian natural human faculties.

Given this analysis, the logical first step in determining the continuities and discontinuities between the Protestant Reformers and their medieval predecessors and scholastic successors is to ascertain the type of natural-law theory that a theologian may have appropriated. Only after obtaining a reasonable assessment of antecedents in a theologian's formulation of the *lex naturalis, synderesis,* or *recta ratio,* is it possible to discern what elements have been modified and why. Maintaining awareness of the different types of natural-law theories is doubly important for anyone interested in the ethics of Reformed orthodoxy because so little has been written on this subject[30] and because commentators, such as Oakley,[31] have focused on developments only in select Protestant figures (for example, Luther, Zwingli, Calvin, Ames, Grotius, Locke, and Hobbes).

From the 1880s until the 1960s, Otto von Gierke's distinction between realist and nominalist theories of natural law served as the *locus classicus* on the subject for intellectual historians and theologians.[32] Ironically, given Ernst Troeltsch's respect for and frequent citation of Gierke's scholarship, he does not follow Gierke's precedent of distinguishing between realist and nominalist theories of natural law. Troeltsch, rather, classifies natural law according to the principal epochs of redemptive history: the "pure natural law of the primitive state" (in the conflicting senses of Eden and early Christianity), the "relative natural law of the fallen state," and the "Christian theory of natural law." Troeltsch sees elements of each epoch as more or less dominant in various periods, movements, or persons in the sociopolitical history of the Christian Church.[33]

However, by the late 1960s, several significant treatments of nominalism had already appeared that would expose historical and philosophical shortcomings in Gierke's influential analysis of the nominalist theory of natural law.[34] More recently, Oakley has shown that Gierke based his analysis of the scholastic authors in that footnote, "not (or so I would judge) on his own independent analysis of their texts, but rather on the somewhat tendentious characterizations of their views to be found in the *De Legibus ac Deo Legislatore* of Francisco Suárez (d. 1617). In that summation, Suárez had contrived to assimilate Aquinas's much more intellectualistic position to his own more juridical one, improperly ascribing thereby to the earlier Thomists the distinctly Suárezian teaching that the binding force of the natural law, though not its content, was to be ascribed to its legislation by the divine will."[35] Nonetheless, for all of its problems, Gierke's presentation of the two types of natural-law theories is still a useful place from which to launch our analysis. He provides a better rudimentary framework than Troeltsch for understanding nominalist natural-law theories, even though his analysis itself is not fully adequate. Troeltsch, unfortunately, broad-brushes nominalism much like Crowe, d'Entrèves, and Rommen.[36]

Gierke described the foundation of the older view, which he considered to be the realist theory of natural law developed by Hugh of Saint Victor, as "an intellectual act independent of Will — as a mere *lex indicativa,* in which God was not lawgiver but a teacher working by means of Reason — in short, as the dictate of Reason as to what is right, grounded in the Being of God but unalterable even by him."[37] The opposite view, "proceeding from pure Nominalism," as he put it, "saw in the Law of Nature a mere divine Command, which was right and binding merely because God was the law-giver. So Ockham, Gerson, d'Ailly."[38] Gierke's sentence seems to indicate that the nominalist theory of natural law derives not only its idea of moral obligation *but also* its proximate ground (and quite possibly even its content) from the divine command — which, if so, logically raises the possibility that God may, at any moment, alter or suspend the ordained moral order to suit his wishes. Since Gierke describes the realist theory of natural law as a dictate of divine reason — entirely independent of the divine will — that not even God himself can alter, it is reasonable to suppose that he thought the opposite view — the nominalist theory of natural law — to espouse an understanding of divine omnipotence that set the *potentia absoluta* over against the *potentia ordinata.* He does acknowledge, however, that the prevailing view of the medieval era sought to steer a middle course between the two sides but leaned mostly toward the realist theory. It is here, contrary to what one may expect, that Aquinas is placed.

The mediating view, as Gierke portrayed it, "regarded the substance of Natural Law as a judgment touching what was right, a judgment necessarily flowing from the Divine Being and unalterably determined by that Nature of Things which is comprised in God; howbeit, the binding force of this Law, but only its binding force, was traced to God's Will. Thus, Aquinas, Caietanus, Soto, Suárez."[39] Just as Gierke mischaracterized the two powers distinction by setting the *potentia absoluta* over against the *potentia ordinata,* his use of the phrase *unalterably determined* in conjunction with the mediating view misreads Aquinas's understanding of the relationship between the divine will and eternal law.[40] *Unalterably determined* seems to imply for the mediating view, what it did for the older realist view, namely, that the divine will is subordinate to eternal law (i.e., the divine intellect in its movement of all things to their due end). However, in Aquinas's case, such subordination would be unlikely given his strong view of divine simplicity.[41]

Gierke includes Aquinas among those subscribing to a mediating view because, as a realist, Aquinas "derived the content of the Law of Nature from the Reason that is immanent in the Being of God and is directly determined by that *Natura Rerum* which is comprised in God Himself," but in so-called nominalist fashion, "traced the binding force of this Law to God's Will."[42] Even though, quite rightly, Aquinas is thought to have developed a realist theory of natural law, it is more precise to state that, in his view, what ultimately makes something obligatory is God's command.[43] However, for Aquinas, the divine command does not supply either the first precept of law, namely, "Good is to be done and pursued, and evil is to be avoided," the self-evidence of natural-law precepts, or the proper conclusions of practical reason. Thus, given what the divine command does not supply, it follows that Aquinas's theory should be properly classified, as Gierke contends, within the category of realist mediating views.

Oakley correctly points out that Gierke, and, by implication, Crowe, d'Entrèves, and Rommen, offer no documentation for the caricature of the nominalist theory of natural law as grounded in a series of possibly arbitrary divine commands.[44] In 1932, the intellectual historian Max Shephard challenged Gierke's interpretation of nominalism by showing that in Occam's linking of natural law and natural reason he "held to the time-honored ancient and medieval tradition of eternal, immutable principles of nature, discoverable by the use of reason."[45] Shephard concluded that "no really essential difference exists between Occam and Aquinas on this point, and that it is on the whole erroneous to extend the nominalistic-realistic schism to embrace their respective theories of natural law."[46] Shephard's conclusion, although moving in the right direction, still fails to appreciate sufficiently the real differences between the medieval theories of natural law and their connection to the doctrine of divine omnipotence.

The Dialectic of Divine Power and the *Via Moderna* in Ethics

In 1277, shortly after Aquinas's death, Stephen Tempier, Bishop of Paris, issued a condemnation of 219 propositions, several of which were in direct response to Aquinas's theology and natural philosophy. Article 147, for example, condemned the view that the impossible cannot be performed by God. "The condemnation of this article did not cause," as Heiko Oberman points out, "but rather legitimized and supported the late medieval appeal to God's *potentia absoluta* by such eminent schoolmen as Duns Scotus, William of Ockham, Peter Aureole, Jean Buridan, Nicolas of Oreseme, Gregory of Rimini, Pierre d'Ailly, Marsilius of Inghen, and Gabriel Biel."[47] It should be repeated here not only that Scotus was a philosophical realist but also that his understanding of revelation and the two powers distinction differs in important respects from Occam's.[48]

Aquinas assumed the primacy of reason to will not only in human beings but also in God, thus enabling him to construe the natural moral law and the physical laws of nature as the external manifestations of an indwelling and immanent reason. It is in this sense, therefore, that he spoke of an eternal law ordering to their appropriate ends all created beings, rational and irrational, and defined it as "nothing else than the type of divine wisdom as directing all actions and movements."[49] The advantage of Aquinas's theory, as Oakley surmises, was "that it enabled [him] to regard the whole of being — including the realm of natural causation as well as that of man's moral endeavors — as in its own fashion subject to the dictates of the same law. The disadvantage, however, is that that subjection to law could well be seen to extend to God himself, thus threatening his freedom and omnipotence, since the eternal law is nothing other than one aspect of the divine reason, and in God reason is prior to will."[50]

Tempier's condemnations of 1277 should be interpreted against the backdrop of mounting concern with Greek-Arab necessitarianism that was believed to have made inroads into Christian theology through Aquinas's embrace of Aristotle. In an effort, therefore, to vindicate God's freedom and omnipotence, Scotus and Occam forged a new way that reversed the priority Aquinas had given to the divine intellect over the divine will and developed the accompanying conceptual structures to ground the order of the world in the deliverance of an inscrutable divine will. Oakley describes well the ramifications of 1277 for the advent of the *via moderna:*

> The inclination now was to take the divine omnipotence as the fundamental principle, to accord to the divine will the primacy in God's workings *ad extra,* and to understand the order of the created world (both the moral order governing human behavior and the natural order governing the behavior of irrational beings) no longer as a participation in a divine reason that is in some measure transparent to the hu-

man intellect, but rather as the deliverance of an inscrutable divine will. The hallowed doctrine of the divine ideas came now under challenge, and with it the epistemological realism and the whole metaphysics of essences in which it was embedded, as well as the affiliated understanding of the universe as an intelligible organism penetrable by *a priori* reasoning precisely because it was itself ordered and sustained by an indwelling and immanent reason. The tendency, therefore, was to set God over against the world he had created and which was constantly dependent upon him, to view it now as an aggregate of particular entities linked solely by external relations, comprehensible . . . each in isolation from the others, and, as a result, open to investigation only by some form of empirical endeavor.[51]

With this excursus as background, an analysis can now be made of the distinction between God's absolute and ordained power as it pertains to the natural-law tradition.[52]

Contrary to the Denifle-Lortz thesis, Oberman argues that the new emphasis on the *potentia absoluta* can only be understood in relation to its dialectical complement, the *potentia Dei ordinata*. As stated above, there is a tendency among those critical of nominalism to set the *potentia absoluta* over against the *potentia ordinata*, thereby making it appear as if the nominalist view of God was that of a whimsical and capricious tyrant. In this light, one of Oberman's main contributions has been to show that the distinction between God's absolute and ordinary power is not properly understood unless it is presented as "dialectics."[53] He admonishes commentators to "beware of taking it for granted that a particular philosophy forced Biel or any other nominalist to particular theological conclusions, a view that is implied, for example, in the widespread thesis that the philosophy of nominalism corrupted its theology. If any corruption took place, theology itself or some exterior force may be primarily responsible."[54] The understanding of the distinction that emerges from Oberman's careful study of the period is, what God has actually chosen to do *de potentia ordinata* in creation and redemption, he very well could have chosen to decide differently *de potentia absoluta*.[55]

There is some disagreement among the leading scholars of nominalism — William Courtenay, Francis Oakley, and Heiko Oberman — concerning the precise meaning of the distinction. Courtenay and Oberman think "the distinction meant that according to absolute power God, inasmuch as he is omnipotent, has the *ability* to do many things that he does not *will* to do, has never done, nor ever will do."[56] By viewing God's power in this way, proponents of this interpretation argue that thirteenth-century theologians were able to acknowledge "an area of initial possibility for divine action, limited only by the principle of contradiction, out of which the things God did do or is going to do were chosen."[57] As a result, they insist that the distinction should be seen in theological terms, as it was for Aquinas,[58] with the intention of simultaneously upholding the law of contradiction and of affirming God's freedom (i.e., that God did not act out of necessity, that he could have done things other than those he chose to do).

In this understanding of the distinction, it is still possible to argue that the present order, the order God established at creation, cannot be identified with his goodness, justice, or wisdom, because these perfections could have found expression in another universe. "The distinction is deceptive for the modern reader," relates Courtenay, "because it seems to be talking about possibilities and avenues for divine action when in fact it is making a statement about the non-necessity of the created order."[59] Contingency is the best one-word summary of the nominalist program, which for Oberman "is understood in two directions, embracing both the vertical relation God-world-man and the horizontal relation world-man-future."[60] This is a crucial point that warrants repeating: The dialectic of the two powers was not intended to present a theory of divine action but to affirm the contingent nature of the created order. This understanding of the distinction is captured well in the following quotation:

> *Potentia absoluta* referred to the total possibilities *initially* open to God, some of which were realized by creating the established order; the unrealized possibilities are now only hypothetically possible. . . . *Potentia ordinata,* on the other hand, is the total ordained will of God, the complete plan of God for his creation. The ordained power is not identical with the particular ordinances that God has willed, for those ordinances are only the most common way through which the ordained will of God is expressed.[61]

If *potentia ordinata* denotes "the total ordained will of God, the complete plan of God for his creation," as Courtenay suggests, then it would seem that there are two equally plausible interpretations of this power. Since everything that happens reflects God's ordination, it would be possible on the one hand to distinguish, as Courtenay and Oberman do, between the ordained power and the laws by which the established order normally operates, and on the other to identify them, as Oakley does, so that the *potentia absoluta* is understood as God's ability to transcend and dispense with the laws of the established order, if necessary.

Oakley follows d'Ailly and Suárez in acknowledging that the expression *potentia ordinata* could be (and in fact was) used in both ways and, also, in preferring the second to the first interpretation. "It was used," he states, "to denote both the ordination whereby God has externally willed that certain things are to be done and the ordinary power by which he acts in accord with the order — natural, moral, salvational — that he has in fact established and ordained and apart from which he can act only *de potentia absoluta*."[62] As an historical reference point, for example, Aquinas and Occam favored the first interpretation, while d'Ailly, Scotus, Suárez, Luther, and Sir Thomas More favored the second. In Oakley's judgment, it is the second interpretation "that alone made sense of the theological analogy drawn by jurists when they distinguished between the ordained or ordinary power of the pope (or emperor or king), whereby he was bound by the provisions of the established law, and the absolute power, whereby he transcended those provisions and could dispense with them."[63]

Recently, however, Oakley has challenged Courtenay's essentially conservative rendering of the two powers distinction whereby any reading of the *potentia absoluta* that took it to denote a presently active or operationalized divine power — such that God might in fact intervene to change or contradict the order of things which, by his ordained power, he had established — was considered to be straightforward "historiographic error."[64] The research of Eugenio Randi and Katherine Tachau (a former student of Courtenay's) has shown that good precedent exists for Oakley's interpretation of the distinction in the early thirteenth century. As Tachau demonstrates, far from being a later medieval development, "the tendency [among theologians] to interpret *potentia absoluta* as a type of action rather than a neutral sphere of unconditioned possibility had its roots in the same [early thirteenth century] generation as the formulators" of the classical definition.[65] Moreover, drawing from Randi's observations in a pair of articles,[66] Oakley observes "no more than a century later that same tendency had come to be widely prevalent among the disciples of Scotus and among such 'nominalist' figures as Robert Holcot and Adam Wodeham."[67] It is little wonder, then, that by 1375-1376, when Pierre d'Ailly came to comment on Lombard's *Sentences* in Paris, both understandings of the distinction — Oakley's and Courtenay's — were so well-established that he felt it necessary to allude to both.[68]

Regardless of which interpretation they might favor, Courtenay, Oakley, and Oberman agree that it was not the intention of the nominalist theologians to suggest that God is prone to act in an arbitrary or despotic way. "If God has freely chosen the established order, he *has* so chosen," contends Oakley, "and while like an absolute monarch he can dispense with or act apart from the laws he has decreed, he has nonetheless bound himself by his promise and will remain faithful to the covenant that, of his kindness and mercy, he has instituted with man."[69] Each of these commentators insists that the biblical motif of covenant plays a prominent and indispensable role in the way that late medieval nominalists portray God's relationship to the created order.[70] A firm scholarly consensus now exists that the basic intention of the distinction is that "it marks the voluntary self-limitation of the omnipotent God and hence the non-necessary contingent nature of the established order of creation and redemption."[71]

To sum up, it can be argued that a better grasp of the subtleties in the two powers distinction demonstrates how nominalist theologians could develop a non-necessary theory of natural law that was still reliable, binding, and, for some, even immutable.[72] Courtenay supports this judgment: "The ethical system that prevails is not a necessary system, which God was forced to adopt, but a chosen system, one of several God might have chosen to institute, had he so desired. Having chosen this one, however, it is binding and God will not arbitrarily or capriciously interrupt the present order to institute a new morality."[73] Nominalist theories of natural law, moreover, should not be anachronistically construed as leading to relativism[74] or legal positivism[75] simply because God is no longer bound by an unalterable metaphysic of essences — or even, for that matter, because of a new stress on the divine will, the divine freedom, or the text of Scripture. Interestingly, Occam and Biel, two quintessential nominalists, both believe "that the ethical system reflects the wisdom and intellect of God as well as his will (these being one and the same), and the voluntary nature of the present moral order (voluntary only for God, not for man) does not prevent God from having his own reasons for choosing the present order, even if man cannot know them."[76]

John Calvin and the Dialectic of the Two Powers

To set the stage for the next chapter, it is important to have a clear idea of Calvin's view of the two powers distinction. Several scholars have recently explored Calvin's view of the two powers distinction in the broader context of his relationship to medieval scholasticism.[77] Each one, to varying degrees, analyzes Calvin's treatment of the distinction not only in relation to his encounter with Scotist and nominalist theology, but also "against a background of recent reappraisal of Scotism and nominalism, in which a theme of divine transcendence has been emphasized at the same time that the claim (found in older scholarship) that the language of *potentia absoluta* indicated an utterly arbitrary God."[78] Yet, as Calvin's antipathy toward the excesses of the "Sorbonne doctors" indicates, ". . . the Reformer also distanced himself at crucial points from the older theology and rejected not only interpretations or abuses of scholastic distinctions but some of the distinctions themselves."[79] The two powers distinction is one of the more prominent scholastic distinctions that Calvin seems to reject entirely.[80]

When Calvin takes up the issue of God's absolute power in the *Institutes* (3.23.2), the immediate context is predestination, specifically in response to the objection leveled against it in his commentary on Romans 9 — whether the doctrine of election makes God a tyrant. Steinmetz thinks that Calvin's response is in line with Scotus.[81] "God's will is so much the highest rule of righteousness that whatever he wills, by the very fact that he wills it, must be considered righteous," states Calvin. "When, therefore, one asks why God has so done, we must reply: because he has willed it. But if you proceed further to ask why he so willed, you are seeking something greater and higher than God's will, which cannot be found."[82] Calvin's response is characteristic of the anti-speculative position of the early Reformation, especially when he writes, "it is very wicked merely to investigate the causes of God's will. . . . [W]hen . . . one asks why God has so done, we must reply: because he has willed it."[83] But, as Steinmetz observes, when Calvin is asked to name this exalted will of God, this "cause of causes," this "law of all laws," he shrinks back from calling it God's absolute will.[84] Thus, states Calvin, "we do not advocate the fiction of 'absolute might'; because this is profane, it ought rightly to be hateful to us. We fancy no lawless god who is a law unto himself."[85] This quotation, of course, presents formidable difficulties for those interpreters who still hearken back to the problem of Protestant voluntarism mentioned at the outset of the chapter.

How, then, should Calvin be taken? To whom and to what is he responding? Is this passage (3.23.2) a rejection of scholastic theology as such or, alternatively, a rejection of an excess of one strand of scholastic thought that defined the divine transcendence as *ex lex* (beyond the law)? From an investigation of Calvin's sermons and commentary on Job, Muller concludes:

. . . Calvin is clearly attacking not scholasticism in general but a specific excess of late medieval nominalist speculation concerning the limits of divine transcendence and the *potentia absoluta*. What is notable
here is not only the specification of "Sorbonistes," and the association
of their theology with a notion of God as *ex lex* (not characteristic of
the theology of the great scholastics of earlier times), but also the fact
that Calvin opposes this particular "scholastic" or Sorbonnistic teaching with equally "scholastic" assumptions concerning the divine simplicity and the essential identity of the divine attributes. It is also the
case that Calvin can argue that God sometimes overrules secondary
causes and the order of nature, a point resembling one of the implications of the *potentia absoluta/ordinata* distinction, again indicating a
considerable degree of specification in what, superficially, might appear
to be a general denunciation of scholastic theology.[86]

In Oberman's appraisal, the whole "extra" dimension of Calvin's theology — that is, the ways in which the concept of the *extra calvinisticum* is
applied to various *loci* (*extra ecclesiam, extra carnem, and extra legem*) —
exhibits how the Reformer "stands in a scholastic tradition which, rooted
in St. Augustine, was unfolded by Johannes Duns Scotus and became the
central theme in late medieval theology, expressed as God's commitment to
the established order, *de potentia ordinata*."[87] He thinks that Calvin retains
the basic structure of the *potentia ordinata* as it was developed in late medieval nominalism, namely, as the realm of God's free but dependable commitment. Yet, as we have seen, when it comes to the *potentia absoluta*, Calvin diverges precipitously from the nominalist tradition.

> Whereas the *potentia absoluta* served in late medieval theology to show
> that there is no *necessitas rei* and hence no *necessitas dei* for commit-
> ments *de potentia ordinata*, with Calvin the *potentia absoluta* does not
> indicate what God could have done but what he actually does. For Cal-
> vin the *potentia* (or *voluntas*) *absoluta* is not the realm of the *Deus ex lex*
> but of God's rule *etiam extra legem*; it is the *ius mundi regendi nobis
> incognitum*.[88]

Thus, for Calvin, God's rule according to the law and his rule beyond the
law are "both to the same extent an expression of his very being, his power
and justice."[89] In light of the Scotistic accent of Calvin's concern to uphold
the reliability of God's commitment to his expressed will, *de potentia*

ordinata, there is no *prima facie* reason to suppose that in ethics Calvin would likewise diverge from the rudimentary structure of Scotus's natural-law theory. But the question remains for the next chapter: is this supposition reasonable?

3

John Calvin and the
Natural Knowledge of God the Creator

Beginning here and extending over the next three chapters, our focus will shift from analyzing the modern and medieval milieus to providing detailed analyses of the doctrines of natural revelation, natural theology, and natural law in select representatives from the Reformation, early orthodoxy, and high orthodoxy. As described more fully in Chapter One, an unfortunate consequence of Karl Barth's repudiation of natural theology was that, for most of the twentieth century, Protestant *theological* interest waned in the doctrines of natural revelation and natural law given their logical tie to natural theology. So, as part of an effort to reinvigorate that logical relation and to establish a conceptual structure for analyzing doctrinal formulations in the remainder of the book, each representative's work will be examined according to the categories of natural revelation, natural theology, and natural law.

Calvin's Complex Appropriation
of the Medieval Natural-Law Tradition

Put simply, John Calvin not only adopts a modified doctrine of natural law from medieval antecedents but also utilizes the doctrine of the twofold knowledge of God (*duplex cognitio Dei*) to ground natural law (*lex naturalis*) in the natural knowledge of God the Creator. His doctrine of the natural knowledge of God is founded on two principal sources: creation and the natural means by which God is known in Scripture. Consequently, the Barthian discontinuity thesis, which asserts that Calvin rejects any and all forms of natural law, not only misreads Calvin's own statements but also overlooks the way his contemporaries and successors appropriate this doctrinal point. By contrast, it can be argued that Calvin, at least in principle, leaves open the formal possibility of developing a systematic doctrine of natural law founded on the natural knowledge of God the Creator, even though that possibility remains materially unfulfilled in his mature statement of doctrine. Barth disagrees that such a formal possibility even exists in the first place, not to mention whether such a doctrine could be developed materially on the basis of Calvin's theology.[1]

An intimation of that formal possibility can be seen, however, in Calvin's treatment of Augustine's distinction between humanity's destroyed supernatural and corrupted natural endowments.[2] Following Augustine's logic, Calvin distinguishes between "heavenly" and "earthly" sorts of intelligence, each of which is able to function competently within its proper sphere.[3] The pure knowledge of God, the nature of true righteousness, and the mysteries of the heavenly kingdom are associated with the former sort, while governance, household management, mechanical skills, and the liberal arts, including the discipline of ethics, are associated with the latter sort.[4] Calvin made extensive use of the scholastic natural-law tradition to organize earthly, particularly civil, affairs because he believed that reason's "natural light" still shone brightly enough to illumine the dictates of God's will for right and orderly conduct: "God provided man's soul with a mind, by which to distinguish good from evil, right from wrong; and, with the light of reason as guide, to distinguish what should be followed from what should be avoided."[5] In fact, he insisted that the seed of political order universally implanted in all persons was "ample proof that in the arrangement of this life no man is without the light of reason."[6]

Moreover, he employs the *duplex* distinction to demonstrate that the universally imprinted nonsalvific knowledge of God the Creator, which is sometimes designated as *prolepseis* or "a preconception of God" in the commentaries on Jonah,[7] John,[8] Acts,[9] and Romans,[10] is a constitutive aspect of the human mind and thus justly holds people accountable for their implicit moral sense and their awareness of God's existence. Even so, the primary purpose of the natural knowledge of God differs in respect to natural theology as it does to natural law. With respect to natural theology, its primary purpose is to affirm humanity's universal awareness of divinity (*sensus divinitatis*),[11] whereas with respect to natural law it is to affirm human *culpability* for actions that violate the moral law.[12] The natural apprehension of the moral law, revealed through the intellectual habit of conscience (*synderesis*) and the law written on the heart (*lex naturalis*), which are

closely identified for Calvin, averts any possible escape from moral culpability under the pretense of ignorance. But that natural apprehension also
suggests affirmatively, when taken together with "the general grace of God"
toward all[13] and the desire implanted in humanity to search for truth, that
reason is sufficient to apprehend moral precepts related to civil, social, and
economic order (i.e., second table precepts) since sparks of its original in-
tegrity still gleam through fallen human nature.[14] Yet, because reason is
"choked with dense ignorance"[15] and fails to see beyond the blindness of
its own concupiscence,[16] it is insufficient to apprehend precepts related to
true faith, true worship, and God's perfect righteousness (i.e., first table
precepts).

Inasmuch as it is even possible to differentiate the principal components of Calvin's natural-law doctrine, his discussion of the purpose of natural law — to render humanity inexcusable — seems to assume a commonly held understanding (among the various schools of late medieval
theology) of the nature and authority of moral obligation. Yet as several
commentators have observed, Calvin's emphasis upon the divine will as the
ground of the moral law[17] and the origin of human moral obligation[18]
likely points to elements of late medieval Augustinian and Scotistic
thought that recur — whether occasionally by direct, self-conscious reiter-
ation or typically by indirect, tacit mediation through secondary channels
— in his doctrinal formulation.[19] Although definite parallels exist between
Calvin's teaching and such late medieval scholastics as Gregory of Rimini
and John Major, documenting them precisely and charting their trajectory
in and through Calvin's thought is fraught with difficulty and ambiguity.[20]
Nonetheless, if select streams of medieval influence can be isolated to some
extent, as medieval Augustinianism and Scotism have been, then it may be
possible to discern hints of a preference for the realist natural-law tradition
in Calvin's criticism of "the doctors of the Sorbonne" — which, at the very
least, would likely have made the realist tradition a more attractive option
in his mind, especially when judged over against late medieval nominalist
perspectives on the limits of divine transcendence and the abuses of ecclesiastical and political authority stemming from a presently operationalized
view of the *potentia absoluta*.

It should be remembered — even in light of the relative significance
assigned to the faculties of intellect and will in the created[21] and fallen
states, the former of which is reflected in his admonition to "discern good
by right reason"[22] — that Calvin is not interested in providing either a
philosophically coherent account of the faculties in the fall or a discussion

of the nominally good but not salvifically meritorious acts of pagans and the unregenerate. Reformed epistemologist Dewey Hoitenga, however, is interested in both of these latter possibilities. According to Hoitenga, there is an overt "logical inconsistency" in Calvin's view of the will.[23] In the fore-word to Hoitenga's book, Richard Muller seems to lend support to Hoitenga's observation that the central issue with Calvin's view turns on Calvin's movement from a philosophical-intellectualist understanding of the intellect and will in the created state to a soteriological-voluntarist understanding of the will in the fallen state, where the will, not the intellect, is explicitly identified as the chief seat of the power of sin. But, as it turns out, Muller wonders whether philosophical consistency and logical rigor, as op-posed to "the context of debate in which Calvin lived and worked and his assumption of the non-meritorious nature of any and all good works,"[24] are the real issues underlying the "apparent" discrepancy in Calvin's view of the will. In fact, Anthony Lane has pointed out that Calvin's own state-ments do not quite work the way Hoitenga wants them to.[25] For the discus-sion here, it is enough to observe that Calvin's more negative assessment of the post-lapsarian will than the post-lapsarian intellect (2.2.26-27), when combined with his view of the pre-lapsarian priority of the intellect over the will (1.15.7), makes it viable to suppose that he would be inclined to-ward the realist stream of the natural-law tradition.[26]

Following the scholastic tradition in general, Calvin describes the conscience as an intellectual habit that grasps and acts upon the precepts of the moral law, either apprehending them inwardly from the law written on the heart (*lex naturalis*) or outwardly from the written law (Deca-logue). While both sources may function as legitimate means for discern-ing the content of morality, Calvin prefers the written law because it pro-vides "a clearer witness of what was too obscure in the natural law."[27] Commenting on Psalm 119:52, "When I think of your ordinances from of old, I take comfort, O Lord," Calvin teaches that the *lex divina* is a republication — although in a more particularized form — of the same moral content underlying the broader and logically prior *lex naturalis*.[28] "Why does [the Psalmist] say that the law of God has been from everlast-ing? This may to some extent be accounted for from the righteousness here mentioned not being of recent growth, but truly everlasting, because the written law is just an attestation of the law of nature, through means of which God recalls to our memory that which he has previously engraved on our hearts."[29]

In attributing greater weight to the post-lapsarian conscience[30] over the pre-lapsarian reason[31] as the hallmark of his natural-law doctrine, Calvin may be attempting to modify the realist tradition to accord more fully with Reformation teaching on the epistemological consequences of sin and the opaqueness associated with the natural knowledge of God. Although he affirmed that natural revelation provided an ongoing reliable and culpable knowledge of God, he was also concerned to show, contrary to Roman Catholic teaching on merit and good works, that it has no saving efficacy and should not be thought to teach "ought" implies "can."[32] In any event, while it is an open question whether Calvin knew enough of any medieval tradition to see himself as modifying philosophical realism in particular, it is certainly true of his theological anthropology that intellectualism (indicating priority of the intellect) and voluntarism (indicating priority of the will) do not necessarily correspond to realism and nominalism respectively — and Calvin, certainly, whether he was a realist philosophically, was a voluntarist *post-lapsum*.[33]

Duplex Cognitio Dei in the Thought of Pierre Viret (1511-1571)

"Two basic models for understanding the relationship between natural and supernatural, nonsaving and saving knowledge of God were developed by second-generation Reformers," recounts Muller. "From Calvin, Viret, and the editor of Vermigli's *Loci communes,* Robert Masson, comes a discussion of the twofold knowledge of God; from Musculus comes a similar model, substantially in agreement with Calvin and Viret, of a threefold knowledge of God."[34] As part of a larger consideration of Calvin's doctrine of natural revelation, it is appropriate to examine the differences between Calvin's and Viret's formulations of the *duplex cognitio Dei.*

Most commentators — with Muller being the principal exception — do not typically address the question of antecedent influences in Calvin's development of the *duplex cognitio Dei,* and, as a result, their investigation is confined to showing how the distinction evolves to its definitive form in the 1559 *Institutes.* The need for such an investigation of antecedents is heightened because some scholars seek to drive a wedge between Calvin and his scholastic forerunners and successors. For example, as we saw earlier, T. F. Torrance attributes to Calvin the honor of having single-handedly made the "difficult transition" between medieval and modern theology, and to have outstripped his contemporaries by centuries "with the result that they tended to fall back upon an old Aristotelian framework, modified by Renaissance humanism, in order to interpret him."[35] In contrast to Torrance's sweeping generalization, use of a sounder historiographical method leads to a different conclusion:

> Although the phrase *duplex cognitio Dei* is probably original to Calvin and was first used as a structural principle in the final edition of the *Institutes,* the basis of the concept was the Augustinian piety held in common by the theologians of reform. Earlier than 1559 Calvin stated the problem of a twofold knowledge of God as a corollary of his exegesis of the Gospel of John. A very clear statement of the *duplex cognitio Dei* also occurs contemporaneously with the last editions of the *Institutes* in Pierre Viret's exposition of the Creed.[36]

In 1531, Viret joined William Farel as a Swiss Reformer and soon became an influential preacher and expositor of Christian doctrine. Viret was instrumental in consolidating the burgeoning Reformation in the city of Geneva, and Viret and Calvin were familiar with each other's writings.

According to Viret, human beings are creatures who seek after their own highest good instinctually, but without God's assistance they are only able to attain a "shadow" of that goodness.[37] Humanity's highest good is not found either in Epicurean pleasure (voluptuousness), which he takes to be self-evident, or in Stoic virtue, because the Stoics never really understood "what the true virtue was that might lead to highest goodness, and only with great pain did they attain the shadow and could not find the right way to lead them for they always left a man to himself."[38] If the search to obtain the highest good is to yield fruit, mankind must "go beyond himself."[39] Even many pagans and heathens know this much on the basis of the "natural light given them by God,"[40] declares Viret. Yet because the human appetite is insatiable and will not be content until it possesses all that it desires, even then it will not be satisfied: "For man cannot have all, except he has God to whom all things pertain and [are] his own, in which only he may be satisfied and perfect according to the testimony of the prophet."[41]

Knowledge of God, in Viret's formulation, comes in two basic varieties. The first, the unfaithful sort, is exemplified in the behavior of demons, for they acknowledge God but "fear him as an evil doer fears his judge."[42] The second, the faithful sort, is seen among true believers who also fear God but "as a good child fears his father."[43] Faithful knowledge is obtainable only by believing through Jesus Christ that God is a merciful father and a gracious savior. Apart from Christ, Viret contends, God can only be known as a "cruel tyrant" because, being unfaithful and unresponsive to God's love, "the evil conscience feels itself culpable of his judgment."[44] In contrast to Calvin, then, Viret presents the twofold knowledge of God in terms of Judge and Redeemer, rather than as Creator and Redeemer:

> . . . it is impossible that any should have the true knowledge of God, such as is required to come unto this sovereign goodness, but he that hath [God] in contemplation, not in himself and in his majesty, nor in any other habit than in this human flesh that he hath put on by his son Jesus Christ, in which he hath declared his goodness, love, mercy, and favor toward man; and it is not possible that he that knoweth otherwise should love him; if he love him not, he cannot willingly honor him nor yet promptly and readily obey him because the knowledge he has is too imperfect, for it is the true knowledge that moves and induces man to honor him.[45]

This difference between Calvin and Viret became important particularly as it had corollary effects on their respective views of natural theology.

Like many commentators today, Viret makes a simple bifurcation between non-saving and saving, unfaithful and faithful, natural and revealed theology. This means that he believes those "who attempt to reach God through creatures or through themselves encounter not the highest good but rather a judge of sin and, indeed, a 'cruel tyrant.'"[46] Moreover, building on these premises, it follows that Viret would be hesitant to examine the divine attributes philosophically, if for no other reason than that this procedure can have no ultimate soteriological value.[47] For him, as for Reformed orthodoxy in general, saving knowledge of God cannot arise from the light of nature but only from faith in God's good will toward us through Jesus Christ.[48] Muller argues that Viret's fundamental contribution to the development of the *duplex cognitio Dei,* his "parallel language of the knowledge of God as judge and tyrant[,] had its impact on orthodoxy — but his simple bifurcation was less influential than Calvin's distinction between knowledge of God as Creator and knowledge of God as Redeemer, with its implication, spelled out at length in the argument of book one of the *Institutes,* that knowledge of God as Creator, albeit a natural knowledge, was available both as a false, pagan theology and as a true, Christian theology clarified by the 'spectacles' of Scripture."[49]

Analysis of the *Duplex Cognitio Dei* in Calvin

To recap our findings so far, it may be said that Calvin, instead of denying the existence of a legitimate natural revelation of God outside of Christ, insists rather on its inefficacy with respect to justification and on its distinct epistemological status from God's supernatural revelation in Christ and the Scriptures: "God is manifest as Creator both in the workmanship of the universe and in 'the general teaching of Scripture' but as Redeemer only in Christ. Although Calvin speaks of a twofold knowledge of God, he points to three forms taken by that knowledge — a corrupt, partial, and extrabiblical knowledge of God as Creator, a biblical knowledge of God as Creator, and a knowledge of God in Christ as Redeemer."[50] If this analysis is correct, then the Barthian interpretation of the *duplex cognitio Dei* as *only* serving to remind fallen humanity of its inexcusability before God fundamentally misinterpreted Calvin's formulation of the concept. To prove this conclusion, it is necessary to examine Calvin's mature statement of the *duplex cognitio Dei* in the 1559 *Institutes,* with subsequent references to passages in the commentaries in which he makes additions or expansions upon his initial remarks.

Calvin opens Book 1 by making several significant observations regarding the nature of our knowledge of God. For one, he defines in part a requisite condition for attaining the true knowledge of God. We know God not when we merely understand intellectually that there is some God, but when we grasp what it is right for us to understand of him, what is proper to his glory — what, in short, it is beneficial to know concerning him, "For, properly speaking, we cannot say that God is known where there is no religion or piety."[51] Later in the same section, Calvin proposes a concise but rich understanding of piety as "that reverence joined with love of God that the knowledge of his benefits induces."[52]

What Calvin has in mind here is not a rationalistic knowledge of God, as in the deduction of proofs in logical demonstration, but a discursive, rhetorically determined form of exposition. "It is probable that Calvin's choice of a discursive, rhetorically determined form of exposition for the *Institutes* generally led him to use rhetorical rather than demonstrative arguments: he therefore presses the Ciceronian point of the universal belief in God, the rhetorical argument *e consensu gentium.*"[53] Calvin's appeal to the terrors of the guilty conscience, the *sensus divinitatis*, the order and workmanship of the world, and the "preposterousness" of human beings regarding themselves as the source of their existence each indicate a rhetorical or hortatory use of proofs for God's existence: "If, then, the *Institutes* does not contain demonstrations of the existence of God, it certainly contains arguments to the point, several of which relate to the traditional proofs. Both these less logically stated forms of the logical proofs and Calvin's rhetorical and hortatory arguments find, moreover, precise parallels in the Reformed orthodox systems, in which rhetorical arguments stand alongside the logical proofs and in which the logical proofs often take on rhetorical rather than purely demonstrative forms."[54]

Is it not the case, for Calvin, that only regenerate people can attain genuine knowledge of God? After all, as he says, God is not known where there is no true religion or piety. Calvin tackles this question differently depending upon the angle from which it is approached. If considered from the vantage point of a broad, natural, or intuitive sense of the divine (*sensus divinitatis*), Calvin would certainly respond negatively. "There is," he asserts, "within the human mind, and indeed by natural instinct, an awareness of divinity."[55] He elaborates further: "To prevent anyone from taking refuge in the pretense of ignorance, God himself has implanted in all men a certain understanding of his divine majesty."[56] Moreover, Calvin also speaks of a "seed of religion" (*semen religionis*), sown in all men, which remains — though uncultivated — in even the most degenerate sorts of people.[57] Or, again, in other passages, Calvin declares without ambiguity that there is "a sense of deity inscribed in the hearts of all,"[58] that men's minds have been "imbued with a firm conviction about God, from which the inclination toward religion springs as from a seed,"[59] which simply cannot be "effaced from their minds."[60]

Nonetheless, with a narrower focus, Calvin is quick to recognize that "all degenerate from the true knowledge of him."[61] In fact, he emphasizes quite forcefully that the result of vanity being mixed up with pride can be detected in the fact that, "in seeking God, miserable men do not rise above themselves as they should, but measure him by the yardstick of their own carnal stupidity, and neglect sound investigation." They therefore imagine God "as they have fashioned him in their own presumption."[62] Accordingly, they "plunge headlong into ruin," "wantonly bring darkness upon themselves," "become fools in their empty and perverse haughtiness,"[63] and being "immersed in their own errors, are struck blind in such a dazzling theatre."[64]

In light of the preceding, it is important to distinguish just what Calvin has and has not argued. As Egil Grislis has meticulously demonstrated through his research, Calvin is "prepared to acknowledge the continuous and positive dynamic role that is played by nature in bringing the existence of God to the attention of sinful humanity."[65] But the twin problems of atheism and idolatry are the two most serious objections that can be leveled against Calvin regarding the clarity of the natural revelation of God in conscience (*sensus divinitatis*).

Atheists, in Calvin's view, despite the appearance of "effacing" God's existence from their minds, graphically portray that humans cannot blot out or eradicate their "natural disposition" to worship deity. "If, indeed, there were some in the past, and today not a few appear, who deny that God exists, yet willy-nilly they from time to time feel an inkling of what they desire not to believe."[66] The premier example of an atheist who strove to deny God's existence but wound up affirming it was Gaius Caligula. Here is the case of one who had "unbridled contempt for deity" during moments of ease, but when any sign of God's wrath began to appear, he trembled miserably and "shuddered at the God whom he professedly sought to despise."[67] And so it happens, relates Calvin, that in the very process of denying God's existence, atheists tacitly acknowledge his presence:

> Indeed, they seek out every subterfuge to hide themselves from the Lord's presence, and to efface it again from their minds. But in spite of themselves they are always entrapped. Although it may sometimes seem to vanish for a moment, it returns at once and rushes in with new force. If for these there is any respite from anxiety of conscience, it is not much different from the sleep of drunken or frenzied persons, who do not rest peacefully even while sleeping because they are continually troubled with dire and dreadful dreams.[68]

So on the one hand, Calvin affirms unequivocally the fact of a universal natural knowledge of God implanted in all. Yet on the other, he also insists that this natural knowledge of God has been irrevocably distorted and abused by sinful humanity. For Calvin, it seems that natural revelation can only be drawn on reliably by the regenerate — albeit still not salvifically.

The problem with idolaters, however, is not that they disavow God's existence, but that they latch onto superstitions or simply revolt from his sovereign rule. In either manifestation, the result is attributable to the same root cause: namely, that the natural knowledge of God through conscience becomes fundamentally scarred and epistemologically ambivalent. Calvin eloquently describes the situation thus: "Yet after we rashly grasp a conception of some sort of divinity, straightway we fall back into the ravings or evil imaginings of our flesh, and corrupt by our vanity the pure truth of God."[69] He continues this analysis by noting that the form of idolatry varies between persons, "because each one of us privately forges his own particular error; yet we are very much alike in that, one and all, we forsake the one true God for prodigious trifles."[70] Nonetheless, Grislis judiciously concludes, "Such a situation does not, of course, mean that mankind has now so far departed from God as no longer to have any natural knowledge of Him."[71]

The situation is similar with respect to the natural revelation of God in the design of the human body as it is with respect to creation. Even though, as a result of the fall, it is not possible to attain a fully adequate knowledge of God through his external works, Calvin vigorously asserted that a minimal knowledge of God is, in fact, available for all to share. He writes regarding the revelation of God through creation: "There are innumerable evidences both in heaven and on earth that declare his wonderful wisdom; not only those more recondite matters for the closer observation of which astronomy, medicine, and all natural science are intended, but also those that thrust themselves upon the sight of even the most untutored and ignorant persons."[72] In commenting on Acts 17:27, "That they should seek God," Calvin pursues a similar line of argumentation: "For God has not given obscure hints of his glory in the handiwork of the world, but has engraved such plain marks everywhere, that they can be known also by touch by the blind. From that we gather that men are not only blind but stupid, when they are helped by such very clear proofs, but derive no benefit from them."[73]

Calvin, likewise, registers his fascination and awe-struck wonder at the intricacy of the human body. He declares, "[O]ne must have the greatest keenness in order to weigh, with Galen's skill, its articulation, symmetry, beauty, and use."[74] In fact, he does not hesitate to employ the classical category of "microcosm" in referring to humanity: "Certain philosophers, accordingly, long ago not ineptly called man a microcosm because he is a rare example of God's power, goodness, and wisdom, and contains within himself enough miracles to occupy our minds, if only we are not irked at paying attention to them."[75]

Nevertheless, Calvin acknowledges without hesitation or ambiguity that *post-lapsum* the natural revelation of God in conscience and the created order has been obfuscated, and thus is impotent in itself to bring people to a true and saving knowledge of God. Accordingly, he observes, "In this ruin of mankind no one now experiences God either as Father or as Author of salvation, or favorable in any way, until Christ the Mediator comes forward to reconcile him to us."[76] But how is the true knowledge of God attained? "No one," says Calvin, "can get even the slightest taste of right and sound doctrine unless he be a pupil of Scripture."[77] Or, speaking from a different but complementary perspective, "[H]owever fitting it may be for man seriously to turn his eyes to contemplate God's works, since he has been placed in this most glorious theatre to be a spectator of them, it is fitting that he prick up his ears to the Word, the better to profit."[78] Notice that on the one hand Calvin repeatedly affirms that humans can know God salvifically only through Jesus Christ as found in Scripture, while on the other he repeatedly denies the claim that without Christ there is no valid knowledge of God whatsoever.

The main difficulty attending the natural knowledge of God, in Calvin's mind, is not its nonexistence but its lack of clarity. "It appears that if men were taught only by nature, they would hold to nothing certain or solid or clear-cut, but would be so tied to confused principles as to worship an unknown god."[79] Contrary to the consensus among Barthians, the key question for Calvin in the debate over the natural knowledge of God pertains to its post-lapsarian status as an ongoing reliable and culpable *knowledge* of God. Calvin does not frame the issue in terms of the *ontology of revelation* — that is, whether all objective traces of the Creator have been removed from the created order — but from the standpoint of the *epistemological consequences of sin.* Calvin argues that God is revealed in nature but that humans misperceive this revelation because of sin, which ultimately leads them to suppress, distort, and abuse the knowledge God has placed at their disposal. But, as we will see in the next chapter in relation to Peter Martyr Vermigli, Calvin's emphasis on the epistemological consequences of sin is exaggerated, and thus slightly far afield of the very Augustinian tradition he is attempting to uphold.

It should be clear from the preceding analysis that Calvin holds to the existence of an objectively knowable, and ultimately culpable, knowledge of God that may be perceived by anyone. But what function does the natural revelation of God play in Calvin's theological method? And what means does he use to integrate the two aspects of the *duplex cognitio Dei (cognitio Dei creatoris et redemptoris)* into a unified act of knowing?

Already at the outset of the *Institutes,* Calvin accents the thematic importance of knowledge by distinguishing broadly between two parts to human wisdom. "Nearly all the wisdom we possess, that is to say, true and sound wisdom, consists of two parts: the knowledge of God and of ourselves."[80] A few pages later in chapter 2, and first fully developed only in

1559,[81] Calvin inserts his well-known statement of the two primary orders of the knowledge of God:

> First, as much in the fashioning of the universe as in the general teaching of Scripture the Lord shows himself to be simply the Creator. Then in the face of Christ he shows himself the Redeemer. Of the resulting twofold knowledge of God (*duplex cognitio Dei*) we shall now discuss the first aspect; the second will be dealt with in its proper place.[82]

Methodologically speaking, Calvin utilized the *duplex* scheme to identify the theme of the entire first book of the *Institutes* as the knowledge of God the Creator, which he then distinguished from the knowledge of God the Redeemer that began in Book 2, chapter 6. That Calvin was fully conscious of the scope of his statement can be ascertained by listing a number of references to it, which were arguably included in the 1559 edition to keep the *duplex* scheme before the mind of the reader. The following citations show that Calvin's methodological repetitions of the *duplex cognitio* are basically expressions of the more foundational Creator/Redeemer distinction.

To keep his appeal to Scripture in 1.6.1 from being misunderstood as a shift of subject from natural to redemptive revelation, Calvin states plainly what he is doing. At this juncture he leaves the revelation of God in creation and begins to speak of Scripture, and particularly of the Word of God coming to the patriarchs. Yet he reminds his readers:

> I am not yet speaking of the proper doctrine of faith whereby they had been illumined unto the hope of eternal life. For, that they might pass from death to life, it was necessary to recognize God not only as Creator but also as Redeemer, for undoubtedly they arrived at both from the Word. First in order came that kind of knowledge by which one is permitted to grasp who that God is who founded and governs the universe. Then that other inner knowledge was added, which alone quickens dead souls whereby God is known not only as the Founder of the universe and the sole Author and Ruler of all that is made, but also in the person of the Mediator as the Redeemer. But because we have not yet come to the fall of the world and the corruption of nature, I shall now forego discussion of the remedy.[83]

Again, at 1.10.1, Calvin, who is comparing the revelation of God in creation with that in Scripture, reminds his readers that although God acted as the Redeemer in adopting Abraham, "We, however, are still concerned with that knowledge that stops at the creation of the world, and does not mount up to Christ the Mediator."[84]

In the chapter on the Trinity, Calvin reminds readers again that he is now writing only of the "Eternal Word," the second person of the Trinity, and not yet of the person of the Mediator, "Further, I do not yet touch upon the person of the Mediator, but postpone it until we reach the treatment of redemption. Despite this, because it ought to be agreed among all that Christ is that Word endued with flesh, the testimonies affirming Christ's deity are suitably included here."[85] Consequently, it should be clear from these citations that Calvin's "separate treatment of the two species of knowledge" makes a crucial "transition," as Edward Dowey refers to it,[86] from the *cognitio Dei creatoris* to the *cognitio Dei redemptoris,* beginning in 2.6.1:

> Therefore, since we are fallen from life into death, the whole knowledge of God the Creator that we have discussed would be useless unless faith also followed, setting forth for us God our Father in Christ. The natural order was that the frame of the universe should be the school in which we were to learn piety, and from it pass over to eternal life and felicity. But after man's rebellion, our eyes — wherever they turn — encounter God's curse.[87]

Calvin viewed the knowledge of God the Creator as belonging both to the order of nature and to the general teaching of Scripture. So, far from denying that the pagan philosophers (or even the common folk) have received an elementary and useful knowledge of God as Creator from natural revelation, Calvin showed that because of sin they failed to move from that knowledge to true religion, and thus, in the end, their gifts rendered them yet more inexcusable. Commenting on the phrase in Romans 1:20, "That they may be without excuse," he writes: "We must, therefore, make this distinction, that the manifestation of God by which he makes his glory known among his creatures is sufficiently clear as far as its own light is concerned. It is, however, inadequate on account of our blindness. But we are not so blind that we can plead ignorance without being convicted of perversity."[88]

Accordingly, scriptural revelation was necessary to attain even a true knowledge of God the Creator, not to mention that apart from it there can be no knowledge of God as Redeemer. A pivotal implication of Calvin's use of the *duplex* concept in Book 1, is, as Muller explains,

> . . . that knowledge of God as Creator, albeit a natural knowledge, was available both as a false, pagan theology and as a true, Christian theology clarified by the "spectacles" of Scripture. God is manifest as Creator both in the workmanship of the universe and in "the general teaching of Scripture" but as Redeemer only in Christ. Although Calvin speaks of a twofold knowledge of God, he points to three forms taken by that knowledge — a corrupt, partial, and extrabiblical knowledge of God as Creator, a biblical knowledge of God as Creator, and a knowledge of God in Christ as Redeemer.[89]

Calvin repeatedly affirms that humans know God salvifically only through the person of the Mediator. Likewise, it has been shown that Calvin even goes so far as to say that apart from Christ there is a legitimate, nonsaving knowledge of God. But, since all people have this knowledge at their disposal, it has the twofold effect of rendering them without excuse and leading to their ultimate condemnation. Remember that natural theology, in Barth's interpretation of Calvin, only served the negative function of reminding fallen human beings of their inexcusability before God and of establishing God's wrath against them.[90] Nevertheless, for Calvin, the nonsaving, natural knowledge of God still functions competently in the earthly spheres of law, society, politics, economics, and ethics — which, as we saw in Chapter One, Barth flatly denies.

Is Barth's estimation of all natural theology to be false, pagan, and idolatrous true to Calvin? No! What Calvin consistently argues is that false, pagan natural theology exists but that it has distorted God's natural revelation into various forms of person-specific idolatry. As one commentator has put it, "Calvin must argue in this way because he assumes the existence of natural revelation which *in se* is a true knowledge of God. If natural theology were impossible, idolatrous man would not be left without excuse."[91] The import of Calvin's argument appears to be that, while fallen human beings know that God exists, they misperceive, suppress, distort, deny, and abuse the true knowledge God has given them through the fabric of creation. It is precisely because of the human tendency to corrupt the natural knowledge of God that Calvin insists upon the epistemological necessity of the "spectacles of Scripture" to gather up the confused (natural) knowledge of God in our minds, disperse our dullness, and clearly show us the true God.[92] Yet, for all of Calvin's epistemological hesitations, he ascribes both positive and negative functions to the role of God's natural revelation in his mature theological system. The positive function concerns the universally implanted awareness of divinity and morality and the usefulness this has to preserve order in a fallen world, while the negative function concerns the establishment of human inexcusability for breaking the moral law. (A parallel discussion of these points occurs in the threefold use of the law within Puritan theology).[93]

To round off our analysis of Calvin's doctrine of the knowledge of God, a brief investigation must be made of the means by which he integrates the two aspects of the *duplex cognitio Dei (cognitio Dei creatoris et redemptoris)* into a unified act of knowing. Willis has argued that the concept of the *extra calvinisticum* performs three valuable functions in Calvin's doctrine of the knowledge of God. It serves, first, "to bind closely together the two aspects of the *duplex cognitio Dei (cognitio Dei creatoris et redemptoris),*" second, "to emphasize the basic unity of the act of knowing in this twofold fashion," and third, "above all to emphasize the unity of the God thus known."[94] Another way of stating these functions is that Calvin's use of the concept underscores the trinitarian character of our knowledge of God. Willis's comments clearly and insightfully delineate just how the *extra calvinisticum* operates with respect to the *duplex cognitio Dei:*

> It does so by helping Calvin to insist on the Christological character of our knowledge of God without either making the Father and the Spirit subordinate in revelation or sacrificing the decisive role that the revelation of God in the flesh has for Christian theology. In this way it serves as a constant reminder that creation, redemption, and sanctification are the interpenetrating spheres forming the context that is presupposed by the Church's knowledge and service of God.[95]

The relevance of Willis's insight to the concept of the *duplex cognitio Dei* arises in response to the Barthian claim that apart from Christ there is no factual possibility whatsoever for attaining knowledge of God. Barth's problem is that he collapses all special revelation into Christ and argues Christ alone as revelation, whereas Calvin, as we have seen, maintains *both* special revelation apart from Christ *and* general revelation. What Calvin stresses instead is that because God has fully revealed his *redemptive* plan only in Jesus Christ it is both "unnecessary" and "ungrateful" to seek knowledge of God *extra Christum*. Willis adds an important clarification to Calvin's stipulation of *extra Christum:* "Calvin's doctrine of the knowledge of God is exclusively Christological only in the sense that a saving knowledge of God is available through Christ alone, who as the Eternal Son of

God cannot be isolated from or known without his manifestation in the flesh, but who is not restricted to that flesh."[96] In Calvin's words, "Those, therefore, who do not rest satisfied with Christ alone, do injury to God in two ways, for besides detracting from the glory of God, by desiring something above his perfection, they are also ungrateful, inasmuch as they seek elsewhere what they already have in Christ."[97] This is an entirely different point, however, from arguing that God does not reveal himself elsewhere in nature, conscience, or providence.

Calvin's use of the *duplex cognitio Dei,* which yields the knowledge of the one God in his twofold revelation as Creator and Redeemer, is the mechanism that enables Calvin to integrate his "separate treatment of the two species of knowledge" into a unified act of knowing. In sharp contrast to the Barthian discontinuity thesis, Willis aptly remarks: "The two facets of our knowledge of God are not *creatoris et Christi* but *creatoris et redemptoris,* because for Calvin Christ is not only the redemptive Word of God but also the creative Word of God, just as the Spirit is not only regenerative but also creative. And, equally important, Calvin for the same reasons does not envisage a *cognitio redemptoris* that does not presuppose the *cognitio creatoris.*"[98]

Duplex Cognitio Dei and the Doctrine of Natural Law

Given that Calvin assigns both positive and negative functions to the natural knowledge of God the Creator in his mature statement of doctrine, the way is now clear to examine his understanding of the nature and purpose of natural law. While there are scattered references to natural law throughout the commentaries and sermons, in the *Institutes* itself there are only a few passages where the subject of natural law is raised explicitly. As shown in Chapter One, the widespread influence of the Barth-Brunner debate in Calvin studies set parameters that have remained relatively unchallenged until the last few years. The general consensus was that Calvin's use of natural law only served a negative function — that is, it merely rendered people inexcusable for breaking the moral law.

More recent commentators maintain, however, that Calvin also espoused an affirmative use of natural law, particularly with respect to civil, social, and economic affairs, though some of them diminish this insight by incorrectly formulating how his view was discontinuous with the older tradition.[99] The deficiency in these commentators' methodologies arises from their misidentification of the type of natural-law theory he assumes, which results in the absence of a proper template by which to gauge his modifications to the medieval natural-law tradition. They also fail to differentiate adequately between the principal components of the view he seems to present in the *Institutes*. Based on the categorization of natural-law theories described in Chapter Two, it can be argued that Calvin works within the parameters of a realist mediating theory of natural law, most likely in the line of Duns Scotus and the *via moderna*.[100] If this is accurate, then it will be possible to find that Calvin, like Scotus (and, interestingly enough, like Aquinas), roots human moral obligation ultimately in the divine will but formulates the content of ethics on the twofold basis of rationally apprehensible and revealed moral precepts. The remainder of the chapter will attempt to establish the feasibility of this conclusion through an analysis of several key passages in the *Institutes* and the commentary on Romans.

In the *Institutes* Calvin first raises the subject of natural law explicitly in Book 2, chapter 2. The immediate context of paragraph 22, where the reference appears, is an analysis of reason's ability to discern spiritual matters, particularly whether it has the capability of ordering a person's life to accord with the rule of God's law.

> There remains the third aspect of spiritual insight, that of knowing the rule for the right conduct of life. This we correctly call the "knowledge of the works of righteousness." The human mind sometimes seems more acute in this than in higher things. For the apostle testifies: "When Gentiles, who do not have the law, do the works of the law, they are a law to themselves . . . and show that the work of the law is written on their hearts, while their conscience also bears witness, and their thoughts accuse them among themselves or excuse them before God's judgment" (Rom. 2:14-15). If the Gentiles by nature have law righteousness engraved upon their minds, we surely cannot say they are utterly blind as to the conduct of life.[101]

Here Calvin makes the point that a sufficiently clear and immediately apprehended knowledge of right and wrong has been engraved on the human mind. The nature of this "law righteousness," as he labels it, is such that it yields universally accessible knowledge, which in turn supplies a rule to guide right conduct.[102]

In the very next paragraph, Calvin moves away from describing the nature of law righteousness to a discussion of why humanity has been endowed with such knowledge. Calvin subsumes this discussion under the general rubric of the purpose of natural law. It is only because the conscience stands in place of the written law that Gentiles, who do not have the Decalogue, can be justly obligated to obey it.

> There is nothing more common than for a man to be sufficiently instructed in a right standard of conduct by natural law (of which the apostle is here speaking). Let us consider, however, for what purpose men have been endowed with this knowledge of the law. How far it can lead them toward the goal of reason and truth will then immediately appear. This is also clear from Paul's words, if we note their context. He had just before said that those who sinned in the law are judged through the law; they who sinned without the law perish without the law. Because it might seem absurd that the Gentiles perish without any preceding judgment, Paul immediately adds that for them conscience stands in place of law; this is sufficient reason for their just condemnation. The purpose of natural law, therefore, is to render man inexcusable. This would not be a bad definition: natural law is that apprehension of the conscience that distinguishes sufficiently between just and unjust, and which deprives men of the excuse of ignorance, while it proves them guilty by their own testimony.[103]

For Calvin, then, all people are culpable for breaking the moral law because their conscience, operating in conjunction with the knowledge of that law etched in the mind, dismisses any ground for rationalization based on ignorance of the written law's demands. In short, people are obligated to act in accord with the written law because of the engraved knowledge of what it requires of them.

The second *Institutes* passage addressing natural law occurs at the beginning of Book 2, chapter 8, and largely reinforces what was said concerning its nature and purpose in 2.2.22. Here Calvin asserts that the natural law and the written law, in a broad sense, teach essentially the same general moral precepts. The advantage of the written law, however, is that it more clearly depicts God's will with respect to human moral obligations.

> Now that inward law, which we have above [2.2.22] described as written, even engraved, upon the hearts of all, in a sense asserts the very same things that are to be learned from the two Tables. For our conscience does not allow us to sleep a perpetual insensible sleep without

being an inner witness and monitor of what we owe God, without holding before us the difference between good and evil and thus accusing us when we fail in our duty. But man is so shrouded in the darkness of errors that he hardly begins to grasp through this natural law what worship is acceptable to God. Surely he is far removed from a true estimate of it. Besides this, he is so puffed up with haughtiness and ambition, and so blinded by self-love, that he is as yet unable to look upon himself and, as it were, to descend within himself, that he may humble and abase himself and confess his own miserable condition. Accordingly (because it is necessary both for our dullness and for our arrogance), the Lord has provided us with a written law to give us a clearer witness of what was too obscure in the natural law, shake off our listlessness, and strike more vigorously our mind and memory.[104]

Calvin refers to conscience not only in terms of the purpose of natural law, namely, to render people inexcusable by depriving them of the excuse of ignorance, but also as an "inner witness and monitor" of the difference between good and evil and of that which is owed to God.

It would be mistaken to interpret Calvin's use of the qualifier *in a sense* in 2.8.1 to mean necessarily that the Decalogue and the natural law are either synonymous or coterminous with one another. Taken at face value, the first sentence in the citation affirms that the natural law and the written law are equally legitimate *means for accessing* the same basic content of morality. In this respect, therefore, Calvin seems to follow Aquinas's distinction in question 94, article 6 between general precepts known to all, which are written in men's hearts and also ascertainable from the Decalogue, and secondary, more detailed precepts known only to the wise, which are conclusions that follow closely from first principles, that is, the general precepts. Calvin's point here is to state that general precepts can be known either through the law written on the heart or through the Decalogue.

The sentence ("Now that inward law, which we have above described as written, even engraved upon the hearts of all, in a sense asserts the very same things that are to be learned from the two Tables") does not, however, insist that *all* natural-law precepts (particularly those of a secondary or a tertiary nature) must be reducible to a logical correlate in the Decalogue, as R. S. Clark assumes.[105] On the contrary, Steinmetz asserts, for the Reformers "the validity of the Ten Commandments rests not only on the authority of Moses but on the conformity of the commandments to the principles of natural law, that is, to the will of God as it can be known by human reason. The law of Moses is nothing more than the *Sachsenspiegel* of the Jews. It is a law-code for a particular people, embodying universal principles of natural law, but adapted to the historical situation of ancient Israel."[106] Calvin is silent on this issue, whereas Aquinas has a great deal to say.[107]

Aquinas thinks that all moral precepts (including those revealed in the Decalogue) belong to the law of nature, but not all in the same way (some precepts are known immediately to be done or avoided, some are known only after careful consideration and must be inculcated by the wise, and some can only be known on the basis of divine instruction). Clark, like Klempa[108] and Stob,[109] makes the identification of the natural law and the Decalogue into a litmus test of discontinuity between Calvin and Aquinas. "Turning to Calvin's epistemology and definition of natural law it will become evident that the most notable difference between Thomas and Calvin is that the latter defined natural law primarily in terms of the Decalogue and Thomas did not."[110] Later on, Clark elaborates further on the idea he stated previously: "Far from being a conduit of the Classical or Thomistic view of the *lex naturalis* Calvin made a very sophisticated revision of the concept of natural law by removing it from the Stoic and Thomistic corpus of 'self-evident' truths and identifying it with the content of the Law revealed in the Garden and at Sinai and in the Sermon on the Mount."[111]

In fact, the principal difference between Aquinas and Calvin may relate more to Calvin's *epistemological* modifications to the realist theory of natural law, which he shares with both Aquinas and Scotus, than to a fundamental difference in moral content as mediated by either the *lex naturalis* or the *lex divina*. Calvin, in distinction to Aquinas and Scotus, attributes greater priority to the post-lapsarian conscience than to the pre-lapsarian reason as the defining characteristic of his doctrine of natural law. Yet, Clark assumes that Calvin held to an exclusively Scotistic formulation of natural law.[112] He bases this judgment largely on the historical likelihood, reinforced by Alister McGrath and Thomas F. Torrance, that while in Paris, Calvin read and was influenced by John Major's Scotist commentary on Lombard's *Sententiae*.[113] Historian Alexandre Ganoczy, however, has shown that it is highly unlikely that Calvin had either any direct contact with Major or even a proper initiation into Major's theology while he was in Paris.[114]

The final *Institutes* passage in which explicit mention is made of natural law occurs in Book 4, chapter 20. Immediately preceding the passage where natural law is referenced, Calvin relates that all laws can be distinguished according to the type of constitution in which they appear and the equity on which they are founded.[115] His goal in developing this distinction is to show that equity, which is tied to the moral law by means of natural law and conscience, is the condition that legitimizes any given law and functions as the ultimate good of every law:

> It is a fact that the law of God that we call the moral law is nothing else than a testimony of natural law and of that conscience which God has engraved upon the minds of men. Consequently, the entire scheme of this equity of which we are now speaking has been prescribed in it. Hence, this equity alone must be the goal and rule and limit of all laws.[116]

In this statement, which remained unaltered from the 1536 edition of the *Institutes,* Calvin condenses what he already stated in previous passages with respect to the law of God, the moral law, natural law, conscience, and equity.

It should be apparent from this survey of passages that Calvin leaves much unstated about natural law in comparison to his medieval predecessors' and Reformed successors' treatments of the subject, as will be seen in subsequent chapters.[117] Even a cursory comparison of Calvin with both Aquinas and Scotus reveals that the former, unlike the latter two, never intended to formulate a systematic doctrine of natural law. The same could also be said of Luther — namely, that he too never set out to formulate a systematic treatment of natural law, yet employed natural law extensively in the realms of law, politics, economics, and ethics.[118] In both cases, then, the Reformers maintain relative continuity with the scholastic natural-law tradition but engage polemically the disputed theological questions of the day.

As a case in point, Calvin does not attempt to resolve systematically any of the following disputed questions of the late medieval debate in ethics: the relationship of eternal law to divine omnipotence, the relationship of eternal law to natural law, the relationship of primary to secondary and tertiary precepts, and the dispensability of second table precepts — and in some cases even first table precepts. Broadly put, Calvin follows the realist tradition (most likely in its Scotistic trajectory, especially given the conspicuous absence of reference to the *lex aeterna*) in its affirmation of the ontological status of moral knowledge, meaning that moral precepts are objective, universal, and stable, but differs with it epistemologically, meaning in the degree to which unaided reason can adequately apprehend precepts of the natural moral law. All of this is just to say that Calvin's use of natural law pertains to its post-lapsarian status as an ongoing reliable, culpable, but nonsaving knowledge of God's will for human moral conduct.

As stated earlier, Calvin's understanding of the faculties of intellect and will in both their pre- and post-lapsarian states, taken together with the importance attributed to conscience as an intellectual habit that grasps and acts upon the precepts of the moral law, places his discussion squarely within the scholastic natural-law tradition, and, as we have argued, quite possibly even in the realist trajectory of that tradition. In Helm's judgment, one cannot fail to be struck by a number of "evident similarities and equally evident dissimilarities" between, for example, Aquinas's and Calvin's views of natural law. Helm is not suggesting that there is a causal link between their views, nor is he denying the existence of such a link. Rather his claim is "that Calvin was, in general, a contented occupant of a general climate of thought of which Aquinas was a distinguished member, but also someone who did not hesitate to depart from elements in this climate of thought when he judged this to be necessary."[119] One of the most significant ways in which Calvin departed from the "Thomistic climate of thought" was, as Chenevière[120] has shown, by emphasizing conscience (where Aquinas and Scotus had emphasized reason) as the hallmark of his natural-law doctrine. Backus concurs with Chenevière's judgment and argues that conscience for Calvin yields a "superior form of *scientia*" and "acts as mediator between man and God — enabling man to submit his wrongdoings to God's justice."[121]

According to Backus, a critical difference between Aquinas and Calvin turns on the manner in which each understands the *lex aeterna*. Because Aquinas defines natural moral law as participation of the law of God in every rational creature, all creatures thus derive an inclination to those actions and ends that are proper to their nature. "This is particularly important as it implies that to Aquinas the term *natural law* applies in its strict sense not to the natural tendencies and inclinations of man on which his reason reflects but to the precepts that his reason enunciates as a result of this reflection. This metaphysical definition of natural law, which allows human reason a certain amount of autonomy in the moral realm, is absent from Calvin's work. Needless to say, it implies that Aquinas cannot define conscience as simply the mediator between God and man. *Conscientia* in his system is the human act of applying moral principles to particular actions and is to be distinguished from *synderesis*, which is the habitual knowledge of primary moral principles."[122]

Calvin's accent on conscience suggests that he may have sought to modify the realist natural-law tradition to bring it more fully into line with

Reformation teaching on the epistemological consequences of sin. The faculty of conscience enables him to overcome the fundamental epistemological problem attending all forms of natural revelation, namely, that humans misperceive natural revelation because of sin and thus suppress, distort, and abuse the knowledge God has placed at their disposal, because conscience, far more than merely distinguishing between right and wrong, carries an immediate awareness of divine judgment for wrongdoing that compels people to acknowledge their guilt. Calvin's acceptance of the broad outline of scholastic natural-law doctrine and his epistemological modifications to it become evident in his definition of natural law. Since conscience plays a prominent role not only in Calvin's definition of natural law but also in every other passage where natural law is mentioned, it is necessary to take a closer look at it before investigating Vermigli's formulation in Chapter Four.

Calvin teaches that natural law is discovered by the use of reason and conscience working in tandem. In 2.2.22, as we have seen, he defines natural law as "that apprehension of the conscience that distinguishes sufficiently between just and unjust, and which deprives men of the excuse of ignorance, while it proves them guilty by their own testimony."[123] Unfortunately, Chenevière overstates his essentially correct insight by severing the symbiotic connection between conscience and reason. In his view, Calvin broke the bonds that attached the knowledge of natural law to reason and rested it upon conscience, which he understood in conventionally modern terms as a subjective faculty that had no need for reason to authenticate its prescriptions and prohibitions.[124] That Calvin never intended to sever the connection between reason and conscience can be seen from his definition of the faculty in the following passage:

> We must take our definition from the etymology of the word. When men grasp the conception of things with the mind and the understanding they are said "to know," from which the word "knowledge" is derived. In like manner, when men have an awareness of divine judgment adjoined to them as a witness which does not hide their sins but arraigns them as guilty before the judgment seat — this awareness is called "conscience." It is a certain mean between God and man, for it does not allow man to suppress within himself what he knows, but pursues him to the point of making him acknowledge his guilt. This is what Paul means when he teaches that conscience testifies to men, while their thoughts accuse or excuse them in God's judgment. A sim-

ple awareness could repose in man, bottled up, as it were. Therefore, this feeling, which draws men to God's judgment, is like a keeper assigned to man, that watches and observes all his secrets so that nothing may remain buried in darkness. Hence, that ancient proverb: conscience is a thousand witnesses.[125]

In this definition, it should be noticed that Calvin closely associates conscience with knowledge on the one hand, and intellect on the other.

A distinctive quality of conscience is that it functions as a means for obtaining various sorts of knowledge. In the definition of natural law, Calvin speaks of conscience as being capable of making sufficient distinctions between justice and injustice. Yet conscience does much more than merely provide a natural knowledge of right and wrong; it also serves as "a thousand witnesses" to divine judgment for morally culpable actions that otherwise "may remain buried in darkness." Thus, commenting on Romans 2:15, "They show that what the law requires is written on their hearts, to which their own conscience also bears witness," Calvin states that the testimony of conscience is equivalent to "a thousand witnesses" and the "strongest pressure" that could be brought to bear upon the apostle Paul's audience:

> Men are sustained and comforted by their consciousness of good actions, but inwardly harassed and tormented when conscious of having done evil — hence the pagan aphorism that a good conscience is the largest theater, but a bad one the worst of executioners, and torments the godly with more ferocity than any furies can do.[126]

From this passage, Calvin concludes there is a certain natural knowledge of the moral law, which is "that one action is good and worthy of being followed, while another is to be shunned with horror."[127] His formulation here bears a striking resemblance to Aquinas's statement of the first precept of law in *Summa theologica,* I-II, question 94, article 2.[128]

Calvin's association of conscience with intellect more so than will is revealed in his commentary on Romans 2:14-16. After relating that the Gentiles have "imprinted on their hearts a discrimination and judgment, by which they distinguish between justice and injustice," Calvin adds immediately that Paul did not mean to imply that the awareness was engraved on their will so that they pursued it diligently. Instead, he interpreted the apostle to mean the Gentiles were "so mastered by the power of truth as not to be able to disapprove of it."[129] From this Calvin concludes, "There is no basis for deducing the power of the will from the present passage, as if Paul had said that the keeping of the law is within our power, for he does not speak of our power to fulfill the law, but of our knowledge of it."[130] He addresses at length the anthropological issue of the post-lapsarian will's bondage to sin and its dire need for liberation by the Holy Spirit in the debate with Albert Pighius.[131]

From that same passage Calvin develops two important points related to conscience and natural law. In the first place, appealing to the Greek notion of *prolepseis,* he demonstrates that God implanted in the consciences of pagan nations an understanding of right and wrong, justice and injustice, sufficient to offset any mitigating excuse for sin. If *synderesis* can be defined as "a natural disposition of the human mind by which the basic principles of behavior are apprehended . . . without inquiry,"[132] then in his use of *prolepseis* to establish a fundamental perception of justice and injustice in the consciences of all human beings it is clear that Calvin has something like *synderesis* in mind in the following quotation: "There is no nation so opposed to everything that is human that it does not keep within the confines of some laws. . . . Therefore they have a law, without the law; for although they do not have the written law of Moses, they are by no means completely lacking in the knowledge of right and justice."[133] Another phrase that Calvin uses to point to *synderesis* is "the natural light of righteousness,"[134] which he claims the Gentiles in fact possessed.

The second point comes directly on the heels of the first. Without the deontic knowledge of first principles afforded by *synderesis,* it would not otherwise be possible for people to distinguish between actual cases of vice and virtue *(conscientia).*[135] Not only is conscience an accuser, "a thousand witnesses," in relation to actual wrongs committed, it is also, as Backus rightly shows, "a mediator between man and God" through which human wrongdoings are directly arraigned by God's justice.[136] "God's judgment," which is actualized at present and in part through conscience *(conscientia),* writes Calvin, "informs those who willfully conceal themselves in the hideaways of their moral insensibility that those innermost thoughts, which are at present entirely hidden in the depths of their hearts, will then be brought to light."[137] It is precisely through Calvin's emphasis upon the immediacy of conscience to convict for actual sins committed and even for sins contemplated *(conscientia)* on the basis of the proleptic knowledge of right and wrong *(synderesis)* that he overcomes the fundamental epistemological problems attending all forms of natural revelation, namely, the tendency to rationalize, to excuse oneself, to suppress guilt, and to obfuscate facts.

The most developed aspect of Calvin's natural-law doctrine in the *Institutes* is its purpose, which, incidentally, is the very context in which his definition of natural law as an apprehension of conscience is introduced. The intent, it seems, of Calvin's discussion of the purpose of natural law — to render humanity inexcusable — is to present an explanation for the origin of human moral obligation. Since knowledge of the moral law, which is rooted in God's will and apprehended through conscience (*synderesis*), is a constitutive aspect of the human mind, people are justly held accountable for their inner awareness of the obedience they owe to God (*conscientia*). Yet, Calvin prefers that awareness of moral obligation be generated on the basis of the written law rather than the natural law, because the former is clearer and less susceptible to corruption.[138] Even conscience, when its moral apprehension is applied to particular cases, can be easily deceived. Calvin thinks the intellect is seldom deceived in general definitions but is much more susceptible to deception in particular circumstances. Take, for example, the cases of murder and adultery: "In reply to the general question, every man will affirm that murder is evil. But he who is plotting the death of an enemy contemplates murder as something good. The adulterer will condemn adultery in general, but will privately flatter himself in his own adultery."[139] Since the intellect, like the natural law, only provides knowledge of general precepts, therein lies its inherent tendency to excuse, rationalize, or suppress what is known to be true.

Conclusion

While Calvin neither constructs nor sanctions a robust natural theology, he certainly does not deny the formal possibility of developing subsidiary doctrines of natural theology and natural law on the basis of God's reliable but obfuscated natural revelation within creation, design of the human body, and conscience. Despite the human fall into sin, with all of its attendant epistemological frustrations and ambivalences, Calvin still considers humanity's corrupted natural endowments to function competently in matters related to the earthly sphere (such as politics, economics, and ethics). The human conscience continues to provide knowledge of moral precepts; the created order continues to reflect God's wisdom, goodness, and power; and God continues to nourish civic virtues among the unregenerate. Calvin's legacy to future generations of Reformed theologians concerned with the relation of the natural to the supernatural lies principally in his formulation of the *duplex cognitio Dei*. Although Calvin himself never developed a systematic doctrine of natural law, the Reformer Peter Martyr Vermigli, an older contemporary, formulated a more sophisticated doctrine of natural law on the basis of a modified Thomist understanding of the natural knowledge of God, as we will see in the next chapter.

$\backsim$ 4 $\backsim$

Peter Martyr Vermigli and the
Natural Knowledge of God the Creator

The Modern Renaissance in Vermigli Studies

Although Pietro Martire Vermigli (1499-1562) was arguably one of the most respected and erudite Reformed theologians of the sixteenth century, after the year 1700 his influence was eclipsed by such luminaries as John Calvin (1509-1564), Heinrich Bullinger (1504-1575), and Theodore Beza (1519-1605). Yet in the sixteenth century, his eminence was widely acknowledged, most strikingly in poems written on the occasion of his death by many leading Reformed scholars and colleagues. These poems were reprinted as tributes to his life and work in the 1583 edition of Robert Masson's *Loci communes* and elsewhere. French Reformed historian Jacques-August de Thou quotes a passage from Joseph Scaliger, a highly regarded sixteenth-century philologist and contemporary of Calvin and Peter Martyr, in which he remarks that they are "the two most excellent theologians of our times."[1] If printing frequency is any indicator of latent interest in an author's work, Donnelly reports there to have been approximately 110 separate printings of Vermigli's various writings during the years 1550 to 1650.[2] The question remains, nonetheless, if his theology generated this much interest well into the seventeenth century, why was his contribution relatively neglected until the 1950s?

According to Donnelly, it is possible to adduce three primary reasons to explain this state of affairs.[3] First of all, unlike Calvin, Bullinger, and Beza, Vermigli never assumed leadership of a local church, which would have lent institutional weight and scope to his activities and teachings. He spent his mature years as a professor either preparing lectures or becoming embroiled in disputation with the Roman Catholics Richard Smith on celibacy, Stephen Gardiner on the eucharist, and Albert Pighius on free will, predestination, and original sin, and the Lutheran Johann Brenz on the two natures of Christ. The influence that he did exert was mainly through his published commentaries and the legacy of his teaching carried on through the work of famous students and disciples (including John Jewel, Edwin Sandys, Jerome Zanchi, Zacharias Ursinus, and Caspar Olevianus). Second, after leaving Italy permanently in 1542 and living abroad as an exile, he was forced to move every five years on average to escape his pursuers. As a result, his institutional gravitas was in a state of near constant flux. "Even though Martyr flits across the ecclesiastical history of Germany, England, France, and Switzerland," writes Donnelly, "he was an Italian in the last analysis."[4] In the end, this meant that his reputation was too closely associated with the abortive attempt to reform religious life in Italy. While the Italian Reformation had made great strides in the 1530s and 1540s, the Inquisition had all but squelched it by 1555. Finally, since there was no strong Italian Protestant church to cultivate Vermigli's memory as a founding father in the aftermath of the Inquisition, he was principally remembered in terms of his associations with such international Reformed churchmen as Archbishop Cranmer, Calvin, Bullinger, and Beza.

Prior to 1950, scholars focused more on rendering an account of Vermigli's life and associations than on his development of doctrine. The first and fullest biographical account was an expanded funeral oration by Josiah Simler, Martyr's confidant, disciple, and successor as professor of Old Testament at Zurich.[5] Although Beza and Martyr were friends, Beza's profile of his life in the *Icones* seems to be based in large measure on Simler's oration.[6] Other early accounts of Vermigli's life published between the years 1562 and 1809 can be found in the writings of John Sleidan,[7] John Strype,[8] the Capuchin priest Nöel Taillepied,[9] and Anthony à Wood.[10] During the nineteenth century three biographical sketches appeared, the first written by Friedrich Christoph Schlosser in 1809[11] and the other two by Charles Schmidt in 1834[12] and 1858[13] respectively. From the publication of Schmidt's second monograph to the contemporary resurgence of interest in the 1950s, the only literature to appear on Vermigli was a few scattered chapters and articles,[14] some encyclopedia entries,[15] an inventory of his library,[16] and one long, three-part article.[17]

After 1950, however, an awakening began to take place in Reformation studies of the formative influence Vermigli exerted as a Reformer and intellectual leader in the middle decades of the sixteenth century. Scholars took unprecedented interest in chronicling Vermigli's life and assessing his doctrinal contributions. Gordon Huelin led the way in 1954 by authoring the first English-language dissertation on Vermigli.[18] Three years later Joseph McLelland's pivotal study of Vermigli's sacramental theology appeared in print.[19] A decade later Philip McNair's meticulous survey of Vermigli's pre-exilic life in Italy was released.[20] The 1970s witnessed the publication of significant historical and doctrinal monographs by Klaus Sturm,[21] Salvatore Corda,[22] Marvin Walter Anderson,[23] and John Patrick Donnelly, S.J.[24] In 1980 Robert Kingdon released a selection of Martyr's key political texts[25] and Joseph McLelland published the proceedings from the 1977 conference at McGill University on the "Cultural Impact of Italian Reformers."[26] But the most significant boon to modern Vermigli studies was the inauguration of *The Peter Martyr Library* in October 1994, a massive effort from an array of international scholars and institutions to translate his major writings into English.[27] The *Corpus Reformatorum Italicorum*, which was launched in 1968 to compile the source documents of the Italian Reformers and to evaluate their contributions, has also led to a fuller understanding of Vermigli's role as an early codifier of Reformed doctrine.

Peter Martyr Vermigli's Contribution
to the Development of Reformed Theological Ethics

While scholars have only just begun to appreciate Vermigli's influence as a principal shaper of Reformed theology, the main lines of investigation thus far have focused on reconstructing his intellectual biography and assessing his thought on key doctrinal topics. As already mentioned, the historical studies by Huelin, McNair, and Anderson constitute a solid core of rich and well-documented modern research into Vermigli's life, writings, and disputations. Scholars have also addressed matters pertaining to his residence in England,[28] his participation in the Colloquy of Poissy,[29] his correspondence with Bullinger and Calvin,[30] and his role in the Italian Reformation[31] and European reform[32] generally. Intellectual historians have also sought to locate his thought in the history of ideas, so portraits have been presented of him as a Florentine humanist[33] on the one hand, and as the key transitional figure in the rise of Reformed scholasticism[34] on the other.

Not surprisingly, given Martyr's celebrated disputations with Richard Smith, Stephen Gardiner, and Albert Pighius, modern Reformation scholars have demonstrated keen interest in his ecclesiology and soteriology. In addition to the studies mentioned earlier by McLelland and Corda on Martyr's sacramental theology, several articles have been written on topics pertaining to his ecclesiology.[35] Joseph McLelland[36] and Frank A. James III[37] have devoted considerable attention to Vermigli's soteriology, particularly to his formulation of the doctrines of predestination and justification. As a logical consequence of probing Martyr's development of distinctive Reformed doctrines, scholars have paid limited but increasing attention to his biblical and philological scholarship.[38] Marvin Anderson's research in the 1970s set the standard for categorizing and assessing Vermigli's extensive biblical and exegetical literature,[39] specifically on 1 Corinthians[40] and Romans.[41] Daniel John Shute[42] and John L. Thompson[43] have focused recently upon Martyr's use of the rabbis and the survival of allegorical argumentation in his Old Testament exegesis.

While much attention has been paid to Vermigli's ecclesiology and soteriology, no serious interest has been taken yet in his ethics. With the exception of a single exploratory essay by Donnelly,[44] no systematic study has been made of Martyr's prolegomena in relation to his ethics.[45] This is a striking lacuna not only because his treatment of natural theology and natural law is far more extensive than Calvin's, but also because his analysis of the Decalogue stretches to ten chapters in the *Loci communes*, while Calvin's is confined to one in the *Institutes*. The situation is similar with respect to political questions. Although Robert Kingdon[46] and Marvin Anderson[47] have done significant work on aspects of Vermigli's political thought, given the volume of available material, many topics remain uninvestigated. Whereas Calvin's treatment of political questions is limited to the final chapter of the *Institutes,* the *Loci communes* concludes with eight chapters that address a broad range of social and political questions — namely captives and spoils of war, duels, nobility, slavery, debts, monopolies, rebellions, and the toleration or removal of tyrants.

The purpose of this chapter is to define the doctrinal parameters of Vermigli's understanding of natural revelation, natural theology, and natural law. By approaching the topic in this way it will be easier to ascertain how he orders relations among those *loci* on the one side, and to discern what is distinctive about his formulation in relation to Calvin's on the other. Though he never wrote a treatise on the proper relation of philosophy and theology and the role of reason in theology, Vermigli affirms without hesitation that natural knowledge makes an important contribution to Christian doctrine. True philosophy can rise from knowledge of creatures to knowledge of God's everlasting power and divinity; however, such knowledge has inherent limitations and boundaries beyond which it cannot proceed. To the extent that natural knowledge illuminates revealed knowledge, Martyr held that classical literature and philosophy, especially Aristotle's *Ethics, Politics,* and *Rhetoric,* was of great assistance to theologians in developing and defending orthodox Christian doctrine.

Based upon a close analysis of the relevant passages from his commentary on Romans 1 and 2, the *locus classicus* of biblical texts pertaining to natural revelation, natural theology, and natural law, it is evident that Martyr's formulation (unlike Calvin's) of the knowledge of God can be characterized as broadly Thomistic with a strong Augustinian accent. "Calvin, of course, has been argued to evidence Scotist inclinations," according to Richard Muller, "but the problem of documenting their source and extent is notorious. Vermigli, by contrast, leaned more clearly on Thomist models, typically with a strong Augustinian accent."[48] As Muller observes elsewhere, "It was the Thomist-trained Vermigli, though, who of all the early Reformed codifiers of doctrine, produced the most extended treatment of the problem of the natural knowledge of God in relation to theology."[49] But Vermigli is also critical of Thomism; and, in particular, of the *analogia entis.* He insists that no matter how clearly God may be inferred from nature, apart from faith, such knowledge only serves to tighten the noose of culpability for sin.

When Robert Masson organized Vermigli's *scholia*[50] into the 1576 edition of the *Loci communes,* the epistemological nuances between him and Calvin were obscured because Masson patterned the *Loci communes* after the 1559 *Institutes* with only minor modifications.[51] Nevertheless, even in light of their divergent formulations, Calvin and Vermigli articulate essentially the same position concerning the objectivity of the natural knowledge of God and the impossibility of pleading ignorance vis-à-vis the *lex naturalis,* the *sensus divinitatis,* and the habit of conscience *(synderesis).*

The fundamental differences between Calvin and Vermigli have to do with the latter's more extensive and disciplined use of natural theology/natural law, which makes sense given the degree to which he, as a formally trained theologian, was shaped by teachers who were rooted in the *via antiqua* and the extent of the noetic impairment of the natural faculties brought about by sin, which will be addressed later in the chapter. Donnelly, though certainly aware of these differences between the Reformers, nevertheless states that he "knows of no passage in which Martyr, in contrast to Calvin, speaks of a moral natural law."[52] This erroneous judgment may stem from the method Donnelly employs to analyze Vermigli's thought.

Marvin Anderson has criticized Donnelly's method for not according sufficient weight to the patristic and humanist dimensions of Martyr's work. According to Anderson, Donnelly customarily cites the *scholia* as printed in the commentaries but often so in isolation from their larger exegetical context. As a result, since Vermigli never devoted *scholia* in any commentary to natural law or ethics per se, it is likely that Donnelly's "decision not to use the exegetical corpus which exceeds in sheer volume the compilation of *loci* in the *Common places* could be misleading in the end, i.e., if one uses his monograph [*Calvinism and Scholasticism*] to view Martyr as a tidy-minded pioneer who returned Calvinism to a scholastic mentality."[53] Quite apart from the view of scholasticism that Anderson's comment implies, his criticism of Donnelly's method may serve to explain why Donnelly failed to recognize the substantive use Martyr made of natural law.

For Vermigli, all knowledge is either revealed or acquired, corresponding in the first instance to theology and in the second to philosophy. Knowledge of God, as he comments on Romans 1:19, "For what is known of God is manifest among them," implies two distinct species of knowledge that parallel the more fundamental categories of revealed and acquired knowledge. The first species is more restrictive and consists of knowledge pertaining to God that is apprehended only on the basis of special revelation, namely, justification, forgiveness in Christ, and the resurrection of the body. The second species concerns knowledge pertaining to God that is open to all persons and apprehended through natural means.

With respect to the second species, Vermigli presents two possible explanations to describe its origin. In the first case, knowledge of God can arise through the natural course of reflecting upon the effects of the Creator. The idea here is that "the workmanship of the world" clearly exhibits God's almighty power and wisdom. In the second case, knowledge of God can be generated from certain information (or "anticipations") that the Creator naturally implanted in the human mind.[54] Given this ineradicable data, people are "led to conceive noble and exalted opinions about the divine nature," and consequently endeavor to align their moral and religious behavior to the knowledge that such information yields. Martyr labels the first explanation as contemplative, which is fundamental to the natural theology of Romans 1, and the second as practical, which grounds the natural moral law of Romans 2.[55] Like Calvin, he held to the existence of a universally imprinted nonsalvific knowledge of God — insinuated into the very fabric of the human mind — that justly holds people accountable for their innate moral consciousness and awareness of divinity. While Vermigli acknowledges reason's post-lapsarian limitations, he is more sanguine than

Calvin regarding its ability to grasp the precepts of the natural law through sense experience, moral intuition, and dialectics.

Natural Revelation and Natural Theology as Forms of a Contemplative Knowledge of God

In the introduction to his unfinished and posthumously published commentary on the *Nicomachean Ethics*,[56] Vermigli lays out the philosophical structure grounding his view of natural or acquired knowledge. The distinction he draws between revealed and acquired knowledge on the one hand and contemplation and practice on the other was operative already in his exegesis of Romans 1 and 2, as will become apparent throughout the remainder of the chapter.

Prolegomena to a Doctrine of Natural Revelation

Following Aquinas's *duplex notitia* distinction (*S.T.* I-I, 1, 1), Vermigli divides all knowledge into two principal categories: "All our knowledge is either revealed or acquired. In the first case it is theology, in the other philosophy."[57] Anticipating objections by philosophers who might claim that wisdom (*sophia*) is the knowledge of everything that exists, he contends that the word *philosophia* is a compound term. Assuming, as the philosophers would, that wisdom consists only of firm and certain knowledge, Vermigli insists that philosophy cannot include knowledge of everything that exists, since it is unable to know particulars, accidents, or contingencies on account of their impermanent nature. He also rejects the argument that philosophy is the knowledge of things that are both divine and human. His objection here stems from the great differences and varieties between the divine and human realms as seen, for example, in the cases of celestial bodies, constellations, elements, minerals, plants, and animals. Those who argue along this line, writes Vermigli, "ascribe heaven to God because it is eternal, saying that lesser things are unsuitable for human beings, since they are corruptible. But where will they place mathematics?"[58] In an effort to underscore both its importance and its status as acquired knowledge, philosophy is defined as "a capacity given by God to human minds, developed through effort and exercise, by which all existing things are perceived as surely and logically as possible, to enable us to attain happiness."[59] Philosophy, for Vermigli, is a praiseworthy discipline because it illustrates that God "endowed our minds with light, and planted the seeds from which the principles of all knowledge arose."[60]

As a species of acquired knowledge, Martyr follows Aristotle's classic distinction and divides philosophy into branches corresponding with contemplation and practice. Contemplation is concerned with observation and classification, while practice does what is known. In addition, contemplative knowledge stands as an end in itself; practical knowledge (like wisdom) leads toward a goal beyond itself — which is why theology is said to be both. Each branch of philosophy is differentiated from the other on the basis of its end. Thus, "theory rests in the very contemplation of things, since it cannot create them," while "practice observes, but only insofar as it may express what it knows in action."[61] In human anthropology, then, there are two basic operations: first thinking and then acting. Vermigli contends this order is reflected even in God, who not only understands himself as being perfectly happy, but also creates by his providence and rules what he has created. Human happiness similarly is considered to be twofold: "The one we may call action, of which Aristotle writes in book 1. The other, far more perfect and admirable, is contemplation, which he discusses in book 10. Thus it is obvious that man may approach to a small degree the likeness of God, if this is accomplished through such double felicity."[62]

Contrary to Aristotle, Vermigli holds that the faculties of intellect and will do not correspond with contemplation and practice respectively. Rather, he argues, intellect and will are operative in each category of knowledge but to varying extents depending on the nature of that faculty's object. According to him, "[S]ciences are distinguished by their objects."[63] Objects of the intellect have God and nature as their cause, and so pertain to the contemplative genus, since such objects cannot be created through human volition. Objects of the will, on the other hand, rely on human choices as their cause, and so pertain to the genus of practice, since human beings are able to will and to choose them.[64]

With the severing of Aristotle's parallelism between the categories of knowledge and the faculties of the soul, the way was cleared for Martyr to clarify the sense in which theology is practical. "A science is called practical not because it is accompanied by some action but because the very same object is attained that was known beforehand."[65] To illustrate this point, Vermigli considers the mixed results that a pure contemplation of heaven and nature yields. "When we contemplate nature and heaven, even if worship and the love of God follow, we cannot call such knowledge active, since what we contemplate is not something produced. No one can create heaven and nature, so that all the results of such contemplation are said to happen by accident."[66] It is no guarantee that simply contemplating nature indicates a favorable disposition to love or cherish God; in fact, it is quite possible to contemplate the Creator's handiwork and simultaneously remain alienated from him. It is for this reason, as Donnelly observes, that Martyr, following Aquinas (*S.T.* I-I, 1, 4), "reverses the primacy that the Greeks gave to the speculative over the practical intellect."[67] The goal of such contemplation, according to Vermigli, ought to be that the works resulting from speculative knowledge, and theology itself, "seek to know God more and more so that in heaven we can look closely at him face to face."[68]

At the close of each chapter in his commentary on the *Nicomachean Ethics,* Martyr endeavored to show the extent to which the philosopher's thought either diverged or accorded with Scripture on a given point. Toward the end of the preface to the commentary, Vermigli urges that the Aristotelian distinction between practice and contemplation is also reflected in Scripture. "The things in which we believe and which are contained in the articles of faith pertain to contemplation since we perceive them but do not create them."[69] Whereas the laws, deliberations, and exhortations of Scripture pertain to practice, because the human ability to act and to choose are critical aspects of this genus of knowledge. The main difference between Aristotle and Scripture arises in how the relationship between practice and contemplation is ordered. For Aristotle, "action precedes contemplation because, as it is said, we can contemplate neither God nor nature by human powers unless our emotions are first at rest."[70] For Scripture, however, "speculation comes first, since we must first believe and be justified through faith. Afterwards, good works follow, which occur more abundantly the more frequently we are renewed by the Holy Spirit."[71]

The apostle Paul writes according to the method of Scripture, says Vermigli, for he first deals with doctrinal topics and only subsequently takes up moral instruction and principles for living. Martyr acknowledges that Scripture's description of the relation between contemplation and practice is contrary to what might be expected: Reason teaches that righteous deeds must be done to warrant justification. But Vermigli, likely assuming a *tertius usus legis,* insists Scripture reverses the natural expectation: "[F]irst we believe, and afterwards are justified, then the powers of our minds are restored by the Spirit and by grace, and finally just and honest deeds follow."[72] The primary difference between philosophy and Scripture concerning contemplation and practice turns on the basis of their respective goals or ends. The goal of philosophy is to reach happiness in this life by the exercise of human power, while the goal of Christian devotion "is that the image in which we are created in righteousness and holiness of truth be renewed in us, so that we grow daily in the knowledge of God until we are led to see him as he is, with face uncovered."[73]

Since the distinction between contemplation and practice serves such an important purpose in Vermigli's exegesis of Romans 1 and 2, it is worth showing how it relates to the conscience before moving on to his analysis of Romans 1. To avoid confusion, it should be recognized that the distinction is not between two different faculties but rather, as Donnelly observes, "between two sets of objects with which the same mind deals."[74]

According to Martyr, speculative philosophy breaks down into three parts in relation to its objects: metaphysics, physics, and mathematics. Metaphysics treats of objects such as God and the intelligences (such as angels and demons) that are separated from matter. Physics deals with objects that are so closely connected with matter they cannot be defined apart from it. Mathematics deals with objects that cannot exist without matter but can be defined and understood without it. While intellect and will are operative in each category of knowledge, as mentioned above, the intellect is predominantly ordered to contemplation while the will is predominantly ordered to practice.

Like Aquinas and Calvin, Martyr follows the scholastic tradition in defining conscience as the action of the practical intellect by which behavior is either vindicated or reproached. According to Donnelly, "Martyr sees conscience as working syllogistically: *synderesis* (man's innate knowledge of moral first principles) provides the major of the moral syllogism: adultery is wrong. Conscience then adds the minor: what you are about to do is adultery, and draws the conclusion in reproaching us. Whoever acts against his conscience sins."[75] By placing contemplation and practice in a complementary relationship, Martyr affirmed the importance of the intellect and will not only in terms of philosophy and anthropology but also in terms of theology and ethics.

Contemplative Knowledge of God in Martyr's Exegesis of Romans 1:18-20

Vermigli's exegesis of the first chapter of Paul's epistle to the Romans provides the most comprehensive statement of his view concerning what can be known of God on the basis of natural revelation. His understanding of natural theology is developed primarily in conjunction with his exegesis of Romans 1:18-20. To afford a more coherent presentation of Martyr's natural theology, Masson divided sections of Vermigli's commentaries into thematic *loci,* which he then systematically arranged to correspond to the outline of topics in Calvin's *Institutes.* The first edition of the *Loci communes* was published in 1576 and the *Common places,* its English translation, appeared in 1583. However, in selecting passages from the Romans commentary to include in the *Loci communes* under the heading of the natural knowledge of God, Masson deleted portions of the text that, in his judgment, were too closely tied to the pericopes from which they were drawn. Since this excised material conveys significant theological reflection in the context of Martyr's exegesis of the first two chapters of Romans, priority will be given to the commentary, with key citations being cross-referenced to their counterparts in the *Common places.*

Commenting on Romans 1:19, "For what is known of God is manifest among them," Martyr thinks the Greek conveys the sense, "What may be known of God." By using these words, he believes the apostle meant to teach two distinct ideas: First, that many divine mysteries cannot be reached by natural means; and second, that God's existence can be ascertained naturally through reflection on his philosophical attributes of everlasting power and divinity. In the first instance, Martyr held that divine mysteries "such as that God would justify us freely, forgive our sins through Christ crucified, and restore these very bodies of ours to eternal happiness" were not taught by nature.[76] Therefore, when Paul declares in verse 19, "what can be known of God is made manifest in them," he is responding to the statement from verse 18 of what kind of truth pagans withheld in unrighteousness. The truth withheld "was the knowledge of things divine that they attained by a natural light."[77]

In the second instance pertaining to the knowledge of God's existence from his philosophical attributes, Vermigli insists that pagans knew of God's almighty power "by the composition of the world." "They also knew," he states, "by the beauty, appearance, and variety of things that such great power was ordered by the highest providence and wisdom. Moreover, the suitability and utility of created things taught them the divine majesty, which consists principally in doing good to all."[78] Such natural knowledge of divinity was a gift God bestowed on humanity universally; but especially so to the wise who abused it. Instead of acknowledging God through appropriate worship and adoration, pagan philosophers converted that gift into the worship of images made of rocks and wood. Because of the intentional nature of their distortion and the clarity of the knowledge afforded them by the light of nature, Vermigli affirms the propriety of God's wrath against them.

By stating "It was manifest in them," and not "it was manifest in all," Martyr insists Scripture distinguishes wise men and philosophers from the crude and ignorant masses. It is important to affirm he is not arguing that Scripture teaches two different forms of natural revelation, but only that there is a difference in the capacities of philosophers and common people to discern the truth about God from nature. In fact, Vermigli seems to hold there are even higher and lower standards of culpability associated with a person's capacity to intuit the truth about God from creation: "Everything was not known to all alike; but it happened through the fault of these philosophers: they should have proclaimed what they knew to the people openly and forcefully. They failed to do what prophets and apostles did, but with proud mind kept these matters to themselves and in a sense hid them lest they be understood by all."[79]

Martyr castigates the philosophers for intentionally defiling the revelation they knew to be pure. In effect, he says, they reasoned as follows: "Since it is improper for common folk to worship the highest divinity that is present everywhere (for they cannot comprehend it), it is better to divide it and assign it to images, heavenly signs, and other creatures."[80] The philosophers, to their credit, acknowledged God is separate from corporeal matter, and so ought to be worshipped in mind and spirit. But it was thought the masses were so uninformed in comparison to them that a less incorporeal form of worship must be introduced. This led the philosophers to introduce external rites and ceremonies devised from their own heads, the origin of all forms of idolatry, so that those who performed the rites might think they had fulfilled their duty to honor God. However, according to Vermigli, the faulty reasoning of the philosophers had the opposite effect: It corrupted what people could discern from creation in its purity and encouraged them to be unfaithful to the truth they already knew. While likening the philosophers' corruption of God's natural revelation to an inconsiderate pupil who neglects the diligent teaching of a schoolmaster, Martyr provides an apt statement of the promise and peril of natural theology: "For [God] continually holds open the book of creation before our eyes; he is always illuminating and calling us; but we regularly turn our minds away from his teaching, and are busy elsewhere."[81]

Addressing the phrase in 1:20, "For God has revealed to them,"

Vermigli declares the apostle teaches all truth comes from God and is not invented by humanity. But Martyr acknowledges there are two divergent opinions concerning the means by which all truth descends from God. The first holds that all truth comes from God because he is the Creator of the things by which truth is perceived. This position implies that material objects are the principal bearers of divine truth: God first created the raw materials of creation and then fashioned them into objects that convey information about him. When the information carried by the objects is adequately represented to the mind, then the truth about God is known. The second (which Vermigli prefers) holds "that God has planted *prolepseis* in our minds, that is, anticipations and notions through which we are led to conceive noble and exalted opinions about the divine nature."[82] Commenting on Romans 2:14, "When Gentiles, who do not possess the law, do by nature what the law requires, these, though not having the law, are a law to themselves," Calvin also opts for the second position but does not develop it to the same extent as Vermigli does: "Since, therefore, all nations are disposed to make laws for themselves of their own accord, and without being instructed to do so, it is beyond all doubt that they have certain ideas of justice and rectitude, which the Greeks refer to as *prolepseis,* and which are implanted by nature in the hearts of men. Therefore they have a law, without the law; for although they do not have the written law of Moses, they are by no means completely lacking in the knowledge of right and justice."[83]

The advantage of the second position, from Vermigli's perspective, is that ideas of God naturally engrafted in our minds "are daily confirmed and refined by the observation of created things."[84] Arguing in the same vein elsewhere, Vermigli asserts, Paul "speaks of that truth that is naturally engrafted in us, as well as what we obtain by our own study. Both [ways] teach us the highest things concerning God, nor can the injustice we commit blot it out of our minds. Yet the scholars of the Academy tried to teach the same thing, when they contended that nothing can be determined by us with certainty."[85] He is critical particularly of the Epicureans, who "try to delete from our minds those things concerning God imprinted in us by natural preconception. But [they] could not achieve what they sought. Whether they wish it or not, these truths still remain in men's minds, although tragically held down in wickedness."[86] An unfortunate disadvantage of natural theology, however, is that some fail to acknowledge God as the author of such truth and credit philosophers with having invented the notion of *prolepseis.* Philosophers such as Plato and Aristotle, in Vermigli's estimation, ought to be viewed as agents or instruments of God's truth but not as authors of it.[87]

In clarifying how philosophers can be agents of God's truth, Martyr provides an important rudimentary sketch of the epistemological structure of the natural knowledge of God derived from creation. First of all, he observes that philosophers speak much as an Israelite might, saying that the truths of the law were known not through God but through Moses, who was simply God's messenger and mediator. Vermigli responds to this idea as follows: "Although God is a nature so separated from matter that he cannot be perceived by the senses, he regularly declares himself by signs and what may be called sensible words."[88] The signs or effects or visible traces of himself that God leaves in creation are described as "creatures." Thus, when natural philosophers diligently study these creatures, they are led to knowledge of God on account of the wonderful properties and qualities of nature. Consequently, knowing well the order of causes and effects, and clearly perceiving the impossibility of an infinite regress, philosophers reason there must be a first cause, and so conclude that God exists.

Although Martyr commends Plato, Aristotle, and Galen for their skillful articulation of God's revelation in creation, he cautions that Scripture must not be neglected, for it too describes a similar source of natural knowledge. "Christ sends us to the birds of the air, to the lilies and grass of the field, that we might acknowledge the singular providence of God in preserving those things that he created. Solomon commends the ant to us for imitation on account of its foresight, by which it prepares in the summer what it will need in the winter."[89] Furthermore, consider David's testimony in Psalm 19:1, "The heavens declare the glory of God," and the dialogue of the book of Job. "For the speakers [Job] introduces were heathen, so that the subject is handled by natural reasons alone."[90] A natural knowledge of God's existence is possible, contends Vermigli, because creation reveals to all the eternal power and divinity of God.

Human beings themselves, even more so than the natural order, are a self-attesting source of knowledge that reveals God. As a result of being made in God's image and likeness, human beings resemble their Creator most of all in regard to the soul, writes Martyr, "where the foresight of things to come is reflected — justice, wisdom, and many other most noble habits; also the knowledge of what is right and honest, and what is wrong and unclean."[91] Since the soul is not a self-generating and self-sustaining entity, it follows that it depends on God for its existence and thus ought to acknowledge him as its chief and principal author. From the injunction to acknowledge God as the Creator and Sustainer, Vermigli concludes that "God foresees everything that is done, and is a just judge of our deeds, to whom honest things are as pleasing as evil are displeasing."[92] At this point, he responds to Cicero (*Nature of the Gods,* Book 3) who thought it was improper to attribute to God what is merely excellent in ourselves. Martyr so strongly thought human nature revealed God's eternal power and divinity that, he insisted, "whatever is perfect and absolute in us" should not be withheld from the divine nature.[93]

As a faculty of the soul, the conscience functions as a proleptic source of information about God. It reveals God in its natural disposition to deplore evil and to encourage good.

> Paul teaches us all this when he says: "The wicked hold down the truth of God in unrighteousness." The truth strives as much as it can to break forth into action, but is hindered by lust. At the beginning of the *Ethics* it is written: the better part of the soul always encourages and exhorts to better things. For God and nature have so framed us that we wish to express what we know in deeds. When this does not happen we are reproved by our own judgment. Here are the marvelous powers of conscience, which can never be completely at rest when faced with the most serious offenses.[94]

Since this knowledge is engrafted in us by nature, insists Vermigli, "we are taught the divine judgment to come, a condemnation that so terrifies our mind that sometimes it courts madness; on the other side, it rejoices through hope of a judgment of acceptance and reward from that tribunal."[95] In summarizing his understanding of natural revelation, Martyr states, "I count it sufficient to have said that nothing may be found in the world so abject or lowly that it gives no witness to God. The poet [Virgil] said, 'All things are full of Jove.' So long as it endures, whatever is in the world has the power of God hidden under it. If this is discovered through inquiry and knowledge of nature, God will be revealed to us."[96]

At this juncture, an important difference emerges between Calvin and Martyr in the way each understands the epistemological effects of the fall on natural revelation. In a seminal essay, "Calvin and the Natural Knowledge of God,"[97] David Steinmetz first examines Augustine's interpretation of Romans 1:18-32 and then shows how theologians in the early period of the Reformation largely reiterate but also amend that interpretation. Augustine argued that the import of Paul's teaching was that wise Gentiles knew God the Creator through creation but abused that knowledge through pride. Moreover, as Steinmetz shows, the late medieval exegetical tradition that Denis the Carthusian represents, which recurs in the exegesis of Philip Melanchthon, Heinrich Bullinger, and Martin Bucer, "points to a general consensus on the meaning of Romans 1 that incorporates Augustine's point in a more complex and nuanced vision. All agree that there is a general knowledge of God from creation that is accessible to human reason apart from grace. This knowledge rests in part on inferences drawn from observation of the created order (Denis, Melanchthon, Bullinger, Bucer) and in part on an innate knowledge implanted in the human mind by God (Denis, Melanchthon, Bucer)."[98]

Calvin's exegesis of Romans 1, nevertheless, diverges from the Protestant commentators above by shifting the discussion toward the knowing subject and the noetic effects of sin. As Steinmetz explains, "Calvin repeats Paul's argument that pagans naturally know there is a God but 'suppress or obscure' his 'true knowledge.' While the natural order demonstrates the existence of God, it reveals, not God's essence, but knowledge accommodated to the limited capacity of human beings to comprehend God. Calvin calls this a revelation of God's glory, which he defines as 'whatever ought to induce and excite us to glorify God.' Calvin insists that all works of God 'clearly demonstrate their Creator.'"[99] It is precisely here, however, that Calvin breaks with the exegetical tradition since Augustine "by distinguishing sharply between what is offered to natural reason and what is received."[100] On the one hand, Calvin wants to insist that "the manifestation of God by which He makes His glory known among his creatures is sufficiently clear as far as its own light is concerned."[101] On the other hand, he wants to point to the fact of culpable human blindness.[102] "The difficulty," as Steinmetz surmises, "is not with what is shown to fallen human reason through the natural order; the difficulty is with human misperception because of sin. The metaphor of blindness . . . is too strong. If blind, then ignorant; if ignorant, then not culpable. The earlier exegetical tradition did not have this problem because it admitted that natural reason knows both that God exists and that God is just, powerful, and providential. Such knowledge is not saving, but it is nevertheless authentic."[103]

Vermigli is just one theologian, culled from an impressive list of Calvin's contemporaries (such as Martin Luther, Huldrych Zwingli, Johannes Oecolampadius, Wolfgang Musculus, and Andreas Hyperius, to mention only a few) who dissent from Calvin's exegesis of Romans 1. "In the judgment of Calvin's contemporaries, Paul does not stress an acute noetic impairment because of sin or distinguish sharply between what is revealed in nature and what is perceived by fallen human reason. . . . The point that Paul makes is not how little the Gentiles knew, but, considering the circumstances, how much they did know and how little use they made of it. By stressing the damage human reason has incurred through sin, Calvin makes the argument for the moral responsibility of the pagans all the more difficult to sustain."[104] Martyr, by contrast, argues that God is revealed in nature, and that this revelation, however limited and inadequate, is real knowledge and "perceived by fallen human beings, who, precisely because of their sinfulness, proceed to suppress, distort, deny, ignore, forget, and abuse what they know."[105]

After examining Scripture passages that could be taken to deny any knowledge of God to the wicked, Vermigli distinguishes two principal kinds of knowledge of God.[106] It is possible that Martyr's distinction was inspired in part by Aquinas's affirmation in the commentary on Romans 1:19-20 that natural law is ineffective in leading human beings to the good.[107] The first, labeled "effectual" knowledge of God, is indicative of a spiritual transformation that has taken place in the mind and is now expressed in deeds. Regarding such knowledge, Martyr claims that truth obtained by faith is more likely to proceed to action than truth perceived by nature. Why?

> Surely this does not happen because one truth by itself and taken on its own is stronger than another. Truth has the same nature on both sides; the difference arises from the ways and means by which it is perceived. Natural strength is corrupt, weakened and defiled through sin, so that the truth that it grasps has no effect. But faith has joined with it the divine inspiration and power of the Holy Spirit so that it apprehends truth effectively. Hence the difference consists in the faculty by which truth is apprehended. This should not be taken to deny that more than we know through nature is revealed to us by the Scriptures, the New as well as the Old Testament. But we have drawn a comparison between the same truth when known by nature and when perceived by faith.[108]

In tandem with Martyr's explanation above, Rogers summarizes Aquinas's position to be that "natural law moves human beings not one step closer to right action — unless it is restored by grace. Only the New Law, the Holy Spirit indwelling in the heart, rectifies nature."[109] By itself, therefore, natural law "proves feckless, except by the Spirit."[110]

To avert any possibility of remaining unresponsive to God's call, Vermigli recommends that whenever any truth is attained through observation or study "to ask ourselves immediately why God calls us through that truth which he presents to our mind."[111] Lest his view of truth be considered naïve or optimistic, Martyr cautions, "[T]hose who boast of Christ and yet live wickedly, in the end surpass all others however evil, in corruption and vileness. The truth is in a sense held captive within those who understand it but do not express it in deed and in life. It is bound and tied with chains of evil lusts that break out of the lower parts of our spirit, darkening the mind and enclosing familiar truth in a dim prison. God illuminates it in our minds, but through evil lusts it is quite overshadowed."[112]

The second, labeled "frigid" knowledge of God, consists of an intellectual assent to God's existence, but beyond that has no noticeable effect on a person's life. With respect to this kind of knowledge, he writes, "Since knowing God in this way brings no results, Scripture rejects it so much that not once does it give it the name of divine knowledge, but insists that God does not know the wicked because this is the way they are."[113] Given that true knowledge of God will entail a change in one's actions, it makes sense that Martyr would use the occasion of Paul's phrase in 1:20, "So they are without excuse," to explore the ways in which natural revelation removes any excuse of knowing how to act toward God and neighbor.

In the first place, Vermigli contends that God did not reveal such natural knowledge for the sole purpose of establishing his wrath against the Gentiles, as Karl Barth asserts.[114] The fact of their inexcusability is due first and foremost to a culpable lack of action on their part. Recognizing that such a viewpoint seemed to yield too much latitude to the will in soteriological matters, he clarifies the sense in which all people are responsible for what they know and do (and fail to do). "If it is true that by our own strength and free will we cannot even fulfill the law that we know how will such people be said to be inexcusable? If what we say is true, they might easily be excused, because they knew this law by a natural light but lacked the strength to fulfill what they knew; therefore, they do not seem inexcusable."[115] Vermigli responds to this problem by pointing out that the apostle in 1:20 deals only with the excuse from ignorance.[116] He holds that Paul limited his treatment here to ignorance because his readers would not have acknowledged any deficiency in their ability to choose the good. Since they would not have pled any lack of strength, all that remained to excuse them was ignorance. But, as Martyr alleges, the apostle anticipates this response and brands them inexcusable on the grounds of their own judgment. "To admit that they were too weak while knowing what they should do would have proved Paul's point. Knowledge of natural law did not make them better, because even if the law is known it cannot change us nor give us strength to act rightly; therefore, we must run to Christ. Because [Paul] knew that the Gentiles did not seek that excuse, he rejected what he saw as an obvious objection, that is, ignorance."[117]

What if, for the sake of argument, the Gentiles conceded the apostle's case against the excuse of ignorance? Would the excuse from infirmity (lack of power) be open to them, regardless of how reluctant they may be to invoke it? Vermigli thinks not, for though the will was impaired by the fall into sin, it maintains partial freedom "in relation to those good things that are subject to the senses and do not exceed human capacity."[118] The fact that the will was weakened in the first place is directly attributable to culpable human choices made in the Garden of Eden. Thus, he asserts, Gentiles "could not have been excusable since they did not even do the little that lay within their power, namely the outward acts of which they were aware. For we are not so destitute of strength through sin that we cannot do much by outward works; in this respect they showed themselves worst of all."[119] It is important to recognize that the ability to conform to the law externally (that is, in civil, ethical, or economic matters) does not mean that the law's internal (or motive) requirements have been satisfied. "The law does not require of us mere externals, indeed that is the least concern; above all it requires good inward motives, that we should love God with all our heart, with all our soul, and with all our strength."[120]

For these reasons, therefore, the Gentiles were without any viable excuse. Yet, when it is remembered that in sinning no person acts against his will, the case for inexcusability is even stronger. From this line of reasoning, Vermigli concludes, "We should not think that God gave [the Gentiles] this excellent natural knowledge in order to render them without excuse. That arose through their own fault, although divine providence made full use of their depravity to illustrate God's glory and righteousness."[121]

Natural Law as the Form of a Practical Knowledge of God

To frame his exegesis of Romans 2, Vermigli reiterates his earlier division of acquired knowledge into two branches, contemplation and practice, at the outset of the chapter. Contemplation, the knowledge of God derived from the observation of created things, is foundational to the natural theology the apostle articulates throughout Romans 1. Although such knowledge is apparent both from the handiwork of creation and from being engrafted in the human mind, corrupted human beings still fall prey to idolatry, and so are justly punished for their shameful distortions of God's revelation. The second type of knowledge, practice, being concerned primarily with right conduct, anticipates the establishment of justice and equity in human affairs by appealing to the divinely implanted knowledge of right and wrong. But even just laws can be abused by the powerful to punish certain sins in others, and yet "wink at the same sins in themselves."[122] According to Vermigli, the apostle uses the category of practical knowledge throughout Romans 2 to show that such persons will not escape God's judgment, even if they happen to circumvent human judgment in the meantime.[123] Martyr insists that Paul's intent in Romans 2 is to use the engrafted knowledge of morality to abolish any excuse that may be advanced to justify immoral conduct.

The first issue addressed in relation to Romans 2:14 concerns the fact that even though the Gentiles did not have the Decalogue, they did "by nature" the things contained in it. In Vermigli's judgment, the phrase *by nature* should not be construed in such a way as to exclude divine revelation or assistance vis-à-vis the requirements of morality. Since all truth originates in God, he thinks the term *nature* ought to be interpreted "to signify that knowledge, which is grafted in the minds of men. Even as in the eyes of the body, God has planted the power of seeing."[124] At this point in his exposition, Martyr insists the apostle is "only speaking of certain outward honest and upright actions, which as touching civil righteousness might by nature be performed by men."[125] That the post-lapsarian will maintains partial freedom to act in accord with the implanted knowledge of morality is evident from Vermigli's essay on free will, where he asserts in relation to Romans 2:14, "no nation is so savage or barbarous that it is not touched by some sense of right, justice, and honesty. . . . We might say instead that by this freedom our works may agree with the civil or economic law, which has regard to outward acts and is not much concerned with the will."[126]

The fact that pagans had the capacity to act in accordance with the Mosaic law should not be taken to mean that they kept the law entirely or even that their partial obedience somehow justified them. All that can be said is that they performed adequately in relation to certain external strictures of the law. "The light of nature," declares Vermigli, enabled them "to discern between honesty and dishonesty, between right and wrong. So if we look upon the life and manners of Cato, Atticus, Socrates, and Aristides, we shall see that in justice and civil comeliness they far excelled a great many Christians and Jews. Therefore they cannot excuse themselves for not having had a law."[127]

At this stage in his argument, however, Vermigli acknowledges that Ambrose and Augustine would both take issue with his interpretation, so out of respect for these venerable authorities, he restates their viewpoints in order to identify the crux of the disagreement. According to Ambrose, when Paul writes in 2:14 that the Gentiles do by nature what the law requires, the apostle has in mind "the full and absolute accomplishment of the law."[128] But seeing it is impossible for any unbeliever to keep the law fully, since Christ is the end of the law, Ambrose declares that "Paul is speaking here of such Gentiles, as were now converted to the Gospel, and believed in Christ."[129] Therefore, he was referring to believing Gentiles, and not humanity at large, when it was stated in 2:14 that the Gentiles not having the Decalogue still do what it requires.

Augustine expresses the same opinion in *De Spiritu & littera ad Marcellinum;* namely, "the Gentiles" refers to those Christians in Rome that were converted from among the pagans. But, unlike Ambrose, Augustine employs that idea to typify the differences between the Old and New Testaments: "[F]or he herein puts the difference between the Old and New Testaments, namely, that in the Old Testament the law was described in outward tables, but in the New Testament it should be written in the hearts and bowels of men, according to the prophecy of Jeremiah 31."[130] On the basis of this interpretation, Augustine contends the apostle's reference to the Gentiles' instinctive ("by nature") fulfillment of the law could only pertain to that inward law of the New Testament prophesied by Jeremiah. Since the phrase *by nature* seemed to provide counterevidence for Augustine's interpretation of 2:14, the Bishop of Hippo felt compelled to formulate a defense, which Vermigli restates as follows: "And because [Augustine] saw that this was against him, where it is said, 'by nature,' he says, that by that word the law of Moses is excluded but not the grace and spirit of Christ, by which, nature is not overthrown but restored to its old estate; wherefore his idea is that the Gentiles fulfill the law by nature, being reformed by the Spirit and grace."[131]

He regards Ambrose's exposition as weak because it fails to account for the fact that many before Christ may have believed in God, been justified, and observed the things contained in the law. To lend support to his case, Vermigli recalls the following examples from Scripture: Job, although living before Christ, trusted God and walked in righteousness; Daniel's preaching to the king of Babylon and the resultant conversion of many Chaldeans; and Jonah's ministry to the Ninevites that steered them toward the truth. "Seeing that all these attained salvation," he asserts, "undoubtedly they looked for the Mediator to come, and by that means endeavored to perform those things that pertained to the law."[132]

Vermigli criticizes Augustine's interpretation along similar lines as Ambrose's. While the New Testament certainly teaches that the Holy Spirit illuminates the law of God written on the heart, why should it be assumed that this did not occur prior to Christ's coming? Martyr observes that the Old Testament prophets, being endowed with the "faith of Christ" and the Holy Spirit, possessed the law engraved not only in stone but also in their hearts. "And although they lived before the Son of God took on flesh, yet inasmuch as they believed in him, they pertained unto the Gospel."[133] Vermigli argues that the New Testament is not so named because it is new, but rather because it was "published abroad in the latter days and then publicly received."[134] Although God's truth was not publicly professed among the Gentiles before the preaching of the apostles, it still flourished among many pagans in whose hearts the law of God was sealed — so much so, in fact, that apart from the Decalogue they were rightly instructed to frame their actions to the precepts of God.[135] In a fascinating remark, Martyr points out that in chapter 7 of *De Spiritu & littera ad Marcellinum,* Augustine makes the same argument as he does regarding "certain excellent actions of the pagans, which were notwithstanding ungodly."[136] These excellent works, when considered strictly according to their nature, remain sinful, "but inasmuch as they agree with the things that God commands in the law, cannot be condemned by the judgment of man. But that they were wicked before God, therefore is not to be doubted, because they were not referred to the right end."[137] In sum, therefore, Augustine seems to come full circle, stating that the work of the law is written in the hearts of infidels because "the lineaments of the first estate still abide."[138]

From the discussion of Ambrose's and Augustine's views, Vermigli distinguishes two principal uses for why knowledge of the moral law was implanted in the human mind. The first, corresponding with a "frigid" knowledge of God, exists to nullify any excuse by providing objective and universally accessible knowledge of the moral law and the judgment to come. The second, corresponding with an "effectual" knowledge of God, exists to increase human "readiness" and "strength" to do that which is known to be just and honest. It is the second use, as Vermigli insists, that prods humanity to pursue true righteousness and that serves to renew

God's image in us. "The image of God, in which man was created, is not ut-terly blotted out but obfuscated in the fall, and for that reason is in need of renewal by God. So natural knowledge is not fully quenched in our minds, but much of it still remains, which Paul now touches upon."[139] While the apostle affirms pagans have the work of the law written on their hearts in the first sense, Martyr thinks they are missing the second sense, which is why true righteousness could not be attained from what they did or knew.

According to Vermigli, Paul uses the proleptic knowledge of morality in the second sense to create a readiness within pagans to act according to the dictates of right reason. Once this readiness to act has been "stirred up" by the Holy Spirit, a person is then poised to act effectively *on the basis of the implanted knowledge of justice and morality*. Apprehensive that his posi-tion could be identified with Chrysostom's libertarian freedom of the will, Vermigli clarifies the sense in which human beings are free to choose the good. *Pre-lapsum* humans were free (*autoarche*) to eschew vice and embrace virtue, whereas *post-lapsum* that capacity has been diminished but not obliterated. As Martyr explains, "forasmuch as without Christ we can do nothing of ourselves, even by our own strength we cannot so much as think any good thing, much less do any good thing. Unless peradventure [Chrysostom] understands this as touching the knowledge of justice and uprightness in general, of which we are now speaking. For the very same father in another place more than once announces that we have altogether need of the grace of God."[140]

As the practical form of the knowledge of God, Martyr's understand-ing of the purpose of natural law emerges at the end of his exegesis of Romans 2:14-16. There it is argued that God cannot be justly accused of veiling his moral will because it has been imprinted on the hearts of all. Ac-cording to Vermigli, the natural knowledge of God, described in terms of the law written on the heart, is useful for responding to those who seek to undermine God's providence by implying that humanity had no knowledge of right and wrong prior to Christ's advent. Martyr's response to such impi-ous critics is straightforward: The observation of created things and the law written on the heart provide both a publicly accessible and culpable knowl-edge of God's will to guide right conduct, "For as touching knowledge [mankind] had enough, whether we understand that which pertains to contemplation or that which is directed to working and doing. Therefore, before the coming of Christ they complained unjustly that they were for-saken, as though they lacked knowledge or thought they lacked sufficient strength."[141]

Conclusion

As with Calvin, it would be improper to regard Martyr as having elaborated systematic doctrines of natural theology and natural law. Yet it can be argued that his formal training in the *via antiqua* and the medieval Augustinian traditions enabled him to develop a more internally consistent and sophisticated understanding of these doctrines than was possible for Calvin. Moreover, Martyr's more optimistic appraisal of the post-lapsarian natural human faculties in all likelihood allowed him to make greater use of the natural-law tradition in the exegesis of Romans 1 and 2. As will be seen in the next chapter, Johannes Althusius, syndic of Emden (1604-1638) and the first systematic Reformed political theorist, like Calvin and Vermigli worked within the realist natural-law tradition (the Thomistic and Scotistic trajectories) to provide a firm ethico-theological foundation upon which to construct his theory of politics.

5

Natural Law in the Thought
of Johannes Althusius

Johannes Althusius:
Jurist, Political Theorist, Syndic of Emden

Until Otto von Gierke's (1841-1921) revival of Johannes Althusius (1557-1638) in the 1880s, few political theorists, and even fewer theologians, had any substantive appreciation for Althusius's contribution to the Western political canon. This modern veil of ignorance stands in marked contrast to the seventeenth-century milieu, in which rank and file Calvinists not only knew of the *Politica,* but also drew inspiration from the courage and piety of the syndic of Emden's blueprint of a holy commonwealth. One possible explanation for the rather slow reception of Althusius among twentieth-century scholars, at least until recently, is that prior to Frederick Carney's 1964 translation there had been no published translation of a substantial portion of the *Politica* in any vernacular language.[1] Another contributing factor, however, is less benign: Althusius was the focus of a maelstrom of criticism from all sides by seventeenth-century polemicists. From the mid-seventeenth century onward, he was routinely attacked by Hermann Conring, Naamann Bensen, Peter Gartz, Johann Heinrich Boecler, and Ulrich Huber who insisted that the *Politica* was "a book worthy of the flames," "the most noxious fruit of Monarchomachism," "the dogma of popular sovereignty a product of Presbyterian error," and its author "the seditious architect of disorder."[2]

It should hardly be surprising that the *Politica* would occasion such searing indictments, for it vigorously defended the local autonomies of the old plural order of guilds, estates, and cities against the rise of territorial absolutism, and against those early apologists of the modern unitary nation state such as Jean Bodin (1520-1596) and Thomas Hobbes (1588-1679). Furthermore, in later editions of the *Politica,* Althusius urged readers to follow closely the logic of the arguments presented therein, for they provided theoretical justification for the Dutch revolt from Spain. That much is clear from the dedication of the book (second and third editions) to the Estates of Frisia, which he praised for their role in resisting the king of Spain and in fearlessly proclaiming the right of sovereignty "to reside in the association of the multitude and the people of the individual provinces."[3] Needless to say, the *Politica* was one of the most widely read, and by some the most despised, book of its day.

Even though Althusius had already begun to establish a scholarly reputation with his first (*Jurisprudentia Romana,* 1586) and second (*Civilis Conversationis Libri Duo,* 1601) books, it was the *Politica* (1603) that seems to have been instrumental in securing for him an attractive offer to become syndic of Emden in Friesland. Althusius assumed his duties in 1604 and led the city's legal and political affairs without interruption until his death in 1638. During his lengthy term of service, he published two new and enlarged editions of the *Politica* (1610 and 1614), and also wrote the *Dicaeologica* (1617), an immense work that sought to construct a single comprehensive juridical system by collating the Decalogue, Jewish law, Roman law, and various streams of European customary law.[4] In 1617 Althusius was elected elder of the church of Emden, a position he held until his death twenty-one years later. "There is a sense in which [Althusius's] two functions of syndic and elder, coupled with capacities for leadership and hard work," observes Carney, "enabled him to coordinate the civil and ecclesiastical jurisdictions of the city, and thus to exercise somewhat the same kind of influence in Emden as Calvin did in Geneva."[5]

The Modern, Interdisciplinary Renaissance in Althusius Studies

As mentioned above, the modern resurgence of interest in Althusius began with the nineteenth-century German jurist and historian Otto von Gierke.[6] Gierke recovered Althusius from two centuries of relative obscurity and attributed to the *Politica* the distinction of making one of the pivotal contributions to Western political thought. He saw in Althusius a seminal thinker who was enabled by an exceptional education in law, theology, politics, and history to develop a political theory that served as a capstone of medieval social thought and a precursor to modern political ideas.[7] The chief feature of this theory, Gierke thought, was its federalist structure, which he understood to result from an admixture of contractual and natural-law principles. Althusius's main contribution, in Gierke's words, was "to give logical unity to the federal ideas that simmered in the ecclesiastical and political circles in which he lived, and to construct an audacious system of thought in which they all found their place."[8] Gierke believed, however, that he could discern deist and rationalist elements in Althusius's system that arose from his supposed sequestering of religious belief from political theory.[9]

The renewal of interest in Althusius was given further impetus by the work of Carl Joachim Friedrich,[10] who, as Carney states, "in 1932 not only republished the largest part of the 1614 edition of the *Politica* in its original language, but also provided for it an introduction that considerably advanced our knowledge of Althusius's life as well as his thought."[11] Friedrich, contrary to Gierke, focused attention on the concept of the symbiotic association as the foundation of Althusius's political theory, and on his religious beliefs as the interpretive key to understanding the concept of symbiosis. Nonetheless, like Gierke, Friedrich conceded that Althusius seemed to be drifting toward deism — though, in his judgment, the move was attributable to "the rigid determinism of the dogma of predestination" as it came to expression in his new science of politics.[12] Friedrich self-consciously read Althusius through the interpretive lens provided by Max Weber, and so concluded that Althusius's alleged biological naturalism (sym*bio*sis) and determinism were rooted in his Calvinist concept of God,[13] that stressing the emotional bonds among persons living in groups led to his formulation of a theory of the corporate state (akin to the collectivist states of Italy and Russia in the 1930s),[14] and that utilitarianism had come to maturity in his version of secularized Calvinism.[15] Despite the evident differences in their appraisals of Althusius, Friedrich shared with Gierke a very high estimate of Althusius's importance — so much so, in fact, that Friedrich considered him to be "the most profound political thinker between Bodin and Hobbes."[16]

In addition to Gierke and Friedrich, the two scholars most responsible for reestablishing Althusius's reputation after a three-hundred-year hiatus, there is a broad array of twentieth-century scholars from various disciplinary backgrounds who have devoted considerable attention to his thought. As might be expected, political theorists and historians have been in the vanguard of scholars assessing the importance of Althusius's contribution to the development of the Western political tradition. The older generation of political historians, such as A. J.[17] and R. W. Carlyle,[18] William Archibald Dunning,[19] and John Neville Figgis,[20] all acknowledge a debt of gratitude to Gierke for reviving interest in Althusius, and largely follow his lead in viewing Althusius as an early proponent of social contract as the foundation of an ordered and authoritative political society.[21] A. P. d'Entrèves[22] in particular subscribes to Friedrich's version of the Weber thesis — that Althusius's political theory was an attempt to develop the implications of a deterministic doctrine of predestination for the natural order — and, on that basis, concludes that Calvinist nominalism led inexorably to Hobbesian voluntarism.[23]

By mid-century, scholars were already skeptical of Gierke's and Friedrich's assessments of the relationship of Althusius's religious beliefs to his political theory and sought to address a broader range of topics in Althusian scholarship. Pierre Mesnard[24] and Frederick Carney,[25] for example, provided extensive analyses of Althusius's constitutionalism, focusing on the institutional foundation of his political theory in the associations of civil society. Stanley Parry addressed the issue of the relation of political norms to processes in Althusius. He suggested Althusius's concern with symbiosis is actually a search to find a means for obtaining participation by the people in decisions rulers conceive to be the demands of natural law.[26]

In the 1950s and 1960s Ernst Reibstein,[27] Peter Joachen Winters,[28] Erik Wolf,[29] and Eckhard Feuerherdt[30] focused scholarly attention on the antecedents, application, and role of the natural-law tradition in Althusius's thought. Reibstein and Winters in particular disagreed over the extent to which Althusius worked within the natural-law tradition and the way he related it to the moral precepts of the Decalogue. Reibstein argued Althusius first became acquainted with the natural-law tradition of the Spanish school of Salamanca through Diego Covarruvias' and Fernando Vásquez's writings on Roman law jurisprudence. He contends Althusius's early conflict with the Herborn theological faculty already evidences his inclination toward a "natural-law interpretation of the Bible"[31] by reducing the commands of the Decalogue to the precepts of natural law. So, when Althusius appeals to profane examples in the *Politica* to illustrate his theory, Reibstein thinks he intentionally employs the humanistic natural-law methodology of the Spanish school with only minor modifications.

Winters responds to Reibstein with a Barthian-style argument claiming precisely the opposite. According to him, Althusius developed a "biblical or Christological interpretation of natural law"[32] since, for Althusius, it was not possible to speak either of the Decalogue or the *lex naturalis* except through Christ, the One who is the very fulfillment of the moral law. For this reason, then, Winters insists Althusius does not appeal to an abstract ontology to ground his formulation of natural law, but rather to God's sovereign will and the revelation of his justice ascertained through Scripture alone. Unfortunately, neither Reibstein nor Winters look to antecedents in the Reformed tradition (other than Calvin) to assist in tracing the development of Althusius's doctrine of natural law.[33]

In the early 1970s, scholars began making a concerted effort to probe the theological (covenantal) and political (federalist) dimensions of Althusius's thought. Building on the work of P. S. Gerbrandy,[34] neo-Calvinist James Skillen[35] sought "to discover the place of Althusius in the development of Dutch Calvinist political thought," and in so doing challenged Gierke's and Friedrich's understanding of Althusius's religious beliefs and discerned the importance of the concept of symbiotic communities for later Dutch Calvinist political thinkers. Skillen comments that neither Groen van Prinsterer nor Abraham Kuyper display "any direct knowledge of Althusius's writings, yet the most important twentieth-century political thinker from those circles, Herman Dooyeweerd, recognizes in Althusius the kernel of truth that lies at the heart of his own covenantal political perspective."[36] Dooyeweerd praises Althusius for being the first to take account of "internal structural principles in his theory of human symbiosis" but thinks this insight put him "in opposition to the entire medieval-Aristotelian tradition."[37] Unfortunately, Skillen accepts Dooyeweerd's judgment that Althusius developed his doctrine of symbiosis and understanding of common law (that is, natural law) and proper law (that is, positive or customary law) along non-Aristotelian, non-scholastic lines.

Skillen is concerned to rebut Friedrich's claim that Althusius, as an Aristotelian, is merely using the concept of symbiosis to develop the Graeco-Roman tradition of state absolutism.[38] However, instead of acknowledging Althusius's obvious debt to Aristotle and the ways in which Althusius's thought is either continuous or discontinuous with Aristotle's, Skillen juxtaposes Dooyeweerd's anti-ecclesial, anti-scholastic mentality to Friedrich's position as mutually exclusive alternatives. "If Friedrich is correct, then there is no conception in Althusius of an internal difference of nature, or independence, of the various human associations. If Dooyeweerd is correct, then we will discover in Althusius a definite limit to the state according to its peculiar nature — a limit which is determined, at least in part, by the peculiar natures (and laws) of other human association which will not permit the state to 'devour' the entire community."[39] Thus, Skillen feels compelled to assent to Dooyeweerd's viewpoint that Althusius had not yet fully separated himself from "the old Roman Catholic culture with its scholastic thinking" to discover "God's order for the creation (including human social life) not the order which the church had sought to impose upon it."[40] As a result of accepting Dooyeweerd's analysis, Skillen is unable to appreciate fully the extent to which Althusius employs the natural-law tradition as it had developed in the work of John Calvin, Peter Martyr Vermigli, and Jerome Zanchi, and also the precise relations Althusius establishes between the concepts of *lex moralis, lex naturalis, lex communis, lex propria,* and *lex divina.*[41]

Contemporary theologians and political theorists such as J. Wayne Baker, Alain de Benoist, Daniel Elazar, Ken Endo, Thomas Hueglin, Fabrizio Lomonaco, Charles McCoy, and Patrick Riley, who are each interested in reinvigorating federalist political structures, have devoted extensive scholarly attention to Althusius's role as a codifier and theorist of European confederal political arrangements of the late sixteenth and early seventeenth centuries. While each of these scholars would add important qualifications to the following statement by Elazar, they would all agree that "The federal theology that [Reformed Protestantism] articulated . . . stimulated the renewed political application of the covenant idea, which was given expression first by political theologians and then by political philosophers such as Althusius and in the next century was secularized by Hobbes, Locke, and Spinoza."[42] Each of the aforementioned scholars has approached the matter of Althusius's contribution to the development of federalism from different but complementary perspectives.[43]

J. Wayne Baker,[44] Fabrizio Lomonaco,[45] and Charles McCoy,[46] for example, focus on the relation of Reformed covenantal theology to federal theories of government in the post-Reformation era of England, Germany, the Netherlands, Switzerland, and France. They are interested in showing that Althusius's federal political philosophy arose out of the political and theological climate of the time. According to Baker and McCoy, federal political models "were widely practiced, especially in areas influenced by the Reformed tradition coming from Zurich and Bullinger. Althusius could draw, therefore, on many actual examples of operating federal polities as well as scholarly treatises of the past and present on government."[47] Furthermore, McCoy insists covenant is the "root metaphor" by which Althusius understands human society. In fact, he thinks the concept of covenant (*pactum*) is what ties together the various streams of Greek, Roman, biblical, and sixteenth-century polities from which Althusius draws.[48]

During his lifetime, Jewish scholar Daniel Elazar was at the forefront of the twentieth-century interdisciplinary and ecumenical interest in assessing Althusius's contribution to the development of federalism. Throughout publications spanning more than three decades, Elazar argued the arduous road to modern democracy began with the Protestant Reformation's revival of the biblical-covenantal tradition of politics.[49] In his introductory essay to Carney's translation of the *Politica*, Elazar contended exponents of Reformed Protestantism developed a theology and politics that set the Western world on the road to popular self-government, emphasizing liberty and equality: "Only at the end of the first century of the Reformation did a political philosopher emerge out of the Reformed tradition to build a systematic political philosophy out of the Reformed experience by synthesizing the political experience of the Holy Roman Empire with the political ideas of the covenant theology of Reformed Protestantism."[50] Elazar's main concern with the *religious* foundation of federalism centers in its origin in the covenantal structure of the Old Testament. Indeed, the argument could be made that Elazar's legacy consists of having shown how the covenantal basis of Judaism was reiterated in Reformed Protestantism and later expressed in the federalist principles of the American polity.[51]

By focusing on the constitutional dimensions of Althusius's federalism, contemporary political theorists such as Michael Behnen,[52] Alain de Benoist,[53] Ken Endo,[54] Thomas Hueglin,[55] and Patrick Riley[56] have provided nuanced assessments of Althusius's political theory as a form of medieval corporatism and modern constitutionalism on the one hand, and argued that his doctrine of subsidiarity can be seen as more or less consonant with modern federal (territorial) and confederal (non-territorial) polities on the other. Hueglin, in particular, has been a vigorous proponent of the confederal tradition of political thought Althusius represents:

> The classical canon of political thought has remained committed to the idea of state power as an independent variable of societal organization. Given the pluralization of power among political, economic, and social actors in the modern polity, the continued adherence to that canon amounts to nothing less than "studying the wrong authors." Althusius reminds us not only that there is an alternative tradition of political thought that emphasizes the horizontal over the vertical in political life. His conceptualization of politics also serves as a reminder that the

sovereign territorial state is but an episode in the history of political civilization. . . .[57]

Recent publications sponsored by the Johannes Althusius Gesellschaft have also investigated such topics as consensus and consociation in early modern federalism and the concept of subsidiarity in church, state, and society.[58]

While interest in Althusian federalism continues to accelerate among the current generation of political theorists, scholarly examination of the seventeenth-century context of Althusius's thought, particularly with respect to the classical, historical, and theological dimensions of his thought, has largely subsided.[59] Yet, ironically enough, at precisely the same time, scholars in religion, law, and ethics are attempting to rehabilitate older streams of jurisprudential and political thought from within their particular theological traditions.[60]

Althusius and the Use of Ramist Logic

Unlike previous chapters, where attention was placed upon showing the logical connection between a theologian's formulation of the doctrines of natural revelation, natural theology, and natural law, the approach in this chapter must be amended in recognition of the fact that Althusius, as a political scientist utilizing the methods of Ramist logic, sought to demarcate strictly the *Politica*'s subject matter to minimize the importation of "elements that are improper and alien to political doctrine."[61] He states the matter thus: "It is necessary to keep constantly in view the natural and true goal and form of each art, and to attend most carefully to them, that we not exceed the limits justice lays down for each art and thereby reap another's harvest. We should make sure that we render to each science its due and not claim for our own what is alien to it."[62] In the case of political science, the principal subject matter is indicated by the discipline's purpose. The purpose of political science is "that association, human society, and social life may be established and conserved for our good by useful, appropriate, and necessary means. Therefore, if there is some precept that does not contribute to this purpose, it should be rejected as heteronomous."[63]

As one who rigorously employed Peter Ramus's (1515-1572) logical method,[64] Althusius routinely criticized philosophers, jurists, and theologians who blurred the boundaries between the disciplines of political science, ethics, theology, and jurisprudence. However, in the second and third editions of the *Politica,* he acknowledges that the principles of the Decalogue "inasmuch as they naturally infuse a living spirit into the association and symbiotic life that we propound, uphold the social life and deeds for which we aim, and constitute and prescribe a way, rule, guiding light, and limit of human society."[65] Therefore, "If one were to remove them from politics, one would ruin political life; indeed, one would ruin all symbiosis and social life among human beings. For what is human life without the piety of the first table and without the justice of the second?"[66] The purpose of this chapter is to investigate the relations Althusius establishes between the concepts of *lex moralis, lex naturalis, lex communis, lex propria,* and *lex divina,* and to show that his formulation and employment of the realist natural-law tradition is consistent with Reformed orthodoxy but is particularly indebted to Jerome Zanchi's analysis of the types of law.

Question of Sources in Ascertaining Althusius's Natural Knowledge of Morality

To determine accurately Althusius's doctrine of natural law and the way he employs it throughout the *Politica,* it is necessary to raise the issue of what sources Althusius referenced to ground moral claims. Did he adhere to a single or multiple source(s) of authority to provide a stable and objective foundation for morality in constructing his political theory? While very few commentators have expressed any sustained interest in this matter, Frederick Carney has examined in considerable depth the relationship Althusius established between the *lex divina* and the *lex naturalis* by surveying every passage in the *Politica* where the subject of natural law is mentioned.[67]

Carney raises the issue of Althusius's ultimate source of authority to respond definitively to Gierke's contention that "Althusius . . . deduces his system in a rational way from a purely secular concept of society."[68] Another way of stating Carney's concern is to point out that Gierke, Friedrich, d'Entrèves, and others in that line of interpretation think Althusius's development of the concept of symbiosis is derived more from philosophical than from theological considerations, or from an already secularized doctrine of natural law than from the Bible as understood through the Reformed theological tradition. Thus, Carney's strategy in responding to Gierke and the others is to show that Althusius's concept of society is normed by Scripture, and that natural law serves as a "handmaiden" to an essentially biblical concept. "In the final analysis," insists Carney, "Althusius did not adhere to two different logical sources of authority, but only to one. This one source was the Word of God, to which he appealed indirectly in the secular order through the concept of symbiosis, and directly in the ecclesiastical order through biblical exegesis."[69]

After surveying all of the natural-law passages in the *Politica*, Carney concludes they tend to support Friedrich's observation that "the significance of the law of nature for Althusius's system is rather problematical."[70] Carney contends Althusius does not use natural law nearly as much as biblical law (that is, divine law or the Decalogue). "For every reference to the former, there are three or four to the latter. Even the citations of natural-law authors and writings are not as frequent as those pertaining to biblical law."[71] Furthermore, he continues,

> While the content of the Decalogue is thrice explicated in the *Politica* (chaps. 7, 10, 11), at no point is there a specific analysis of the content envisaged for natural law. It is left in the uncomfortable position of being a concept in search of meaning. It affirms, of course, the existence of a boundary upon human caprice, and suggests that good ought to be pursued and evil shunned. But these statements are only formal. For its true meaning, natural law in the *Politica* is largely dependent upon the Decalogue, as understood within the larger context of the Word of God.[72]

To summarize, then, Carney's argument is that Althusius's treatment of natural law in the *Politica* is largely dependent upon the Decalogue to provide moral content, for without a foundation in the written law, the natural law would be devoid of specifiable content. He concludes his survey of the natural-law passages: "The normative meaning that symbiosis conveys can, to a limited extent, be expressed in natural-law terms. But for a fuller meaning recourse must be had to the Word of God. Moreover, even to the extent that natural law informs the meaning of symbiosis in the *Politica*, the Word of God in turn largely informs the meaning of natural law."[73]

Carney is correct to raise the question of the source(s) of authority for moral knowledge in the *Politica*, but his claim that natural law is dependent upon the Decalogue misconstrues the nature of the relationship Althusius believes to inhere between these two types of law. Like Reibstein and Winters, Carney misses the fundamental relationship Althusius establishes between the Decalogue and the natural law, in part because he sees them as two separate *and* juxtaposed sources of law,[74] and also because he does not look to antecedents in the Reformed tradition (beyond Calvin who, as we saw in Chapter Four, tends to accentuate the noetic effects of sin) to illuminate Althusius's doctrine of natural law.[75] Had he done so in the latter case, he would have surely given a more prominent place to Jerome Zanchi's analysis of the types of law.[76] By viewing Althusius's natural-law doctrine as a further elaboration and application of Zanchi's conceptual framework, it can be shown that Carney's understanding of the relationship between the Decalogue and the natural law ought to be reversed. In fact, for Althusius, like Reformed orthodoxy in general, the moral law of the Decalogue is simply a renewed and re-enforced form of the logically prior *lex naturalis,* the universal knowledge of morality God originally implanted in the mind at creation, but which after the fall has become obscure and difficult to discern with precision and reliability. Consequently, before examining the precise relationships Althusius establishes between the various types of law in the *Politica* and the *Dicaeologica,* it is necessary to lay some preliminary groundwork by taking a close look at Zanchi's understanding of the types of law and the relationships they maintain with one another.[77]

Antecedent to Althusius:
Jerome Zanchi (1516-1590) on the Types of Law

It should be mentioned at the outset that Carney is readily aware of the fact that Zanchi's understanding of law exerted singular influence upon Althusius. It was Zanchi's categorization and demarcation of the types of law, relates Carney, which more than any other treatment contributed to "Althusius's understanding of the relation of the Decalogue to natural law, and of both to the proper laws of various nations."[78] In chapter 21 of the *Politica,* Althusius discusses the topic of political prudence in the administration of the commonwealth. He thought magistrates should administer commonwealths on the basis of prudence, which involves knowledge both of law and of the changing and contingent circumstances to which the law is applied. "The discussion of law at this point," observes Carney, "is an extended treatment of the relation of the Decalogue to natural law, and of the role of these two together as common law [natural law] in the formulation of proper law for particular societies."[79]

In the same chapter, Althusius himself credits Zanchi with the view

that "The Decalogue has been prescribed for all people *to the extent that it
agrees with and explains the common law of nature for all peoples.* It has also
been renewed and confirmed by Christ our king. Jerome Zanchi says that
this is the common judgment of theologians."[80] In this paraphrase of
Zanchi's position Althusius summarizes the standard (namely, "common
judgment") Reformed orthodox view of the relationship between the moral
law, the natural law, and the Decalogue, which Zacharias Ursinus (1534-
1583), Zanchi's colleague at Heidelberg, elaborates in his commentary on
the *Heidelberg Catechism:*

> We must also observe, in passing along, the difference that exists be-
> tween the moral law, the natural law, and the Decalogue. *The Decalogue*
> contains the sum of the moral laws that are scattered throughout the
> Scriptures of the Old and New Testaments. *The natural, and moral law*
> were the same in man before the fall, when his nature was pure and
> holy. Since the fall, however, which resulted in the corruption and de-
> pravity of our nature, a considerable part of the natural law has become
> obscured and lost by reason of sin, so that there is only a small portion
> concerning the obedience which we owe to God still left in the human
> mind. It is for this reason that God repeated, and declared to the church
> the entire doctrine and true sense of his law, as contained in the
> Decalogue. The Decalogue is, therefore, the renewal and re-enforcing
> of the natural law, which is only a part of the Decalogue. This distinc-
> tion, therefore, which we have made between the several parts of the
> divine law must be retained, both on account of the difference itself, so
> that the force and true sense of these laws may be understood, and that
> we may also have a correct knowledge and understanding of the abro-
> gation and use of the law.[81]

A few paragraphs later, Althusius states his agreement with Zanchi's two
principal reasons for the establishment of proper law as presented in his
Operum theologicorum. Examining Zanchi's treatment of the law in general
will bring to light several key phrases, concepts, and distinctions Althusius
either fully maintains or slightly alters in his presentation of natural-law
doctrine in the *Politica* and the *Dicaeologica.*

Zanchi's contribution to the development of the Protestant natural-
law tradition is immense,[82] as can be seen from the sophistication with
which he treats the various forms of law and the facility with which he employs the scholastic method. Chapter 10, "On the Law in General," in the

fourth volume of his *Operum*,[83] serves as an introduction to Zanchi's equivalent treatise to Aquinas's treatise on law in the *Summa theologica*.[84] In the
fourth volume of his *Operum*, Zanchi devotes just over eight hundred Latin
pages (chapters 10-28) to an exposition of the law in all its parts.[85] John
Patrick Donnelly, S.J., considers him to be the best example of what he labels a "Calvinist Thomist," identifying a writer that was Calvinistic in
terms of theology but Thomistic in terms of philosophy and methodology.[86] To give some impression of Zanchi's relationship to Thomism, on the
one hand, and to the scope of his theological system, on the other, Donnelly makes the following insightful observation:

> Zanchi clearly planned a great Protestant "summa" modeled after the
> *Summa theologiae* of Saint Thomas. The first four volumes of the
> *Operum theologicorum,* which appeared under separate titles as Zanchi
> finished them at Heidelberg, cover the same material at twice the
> length as the *Pars prima* and *Prima secundae* of Saint Thomas. Even
> though Zanchi was unable to finish his "summa" after he left Heidel-
> berg, it remains without rival for thoroughness and synthetic power in
> sixteenth-century Calvinism.[87]

In reading Zanchi's chapter on law, one is immediately impressed not only
by his frequent references to Aquinas, to Roman law, to common law (that
is, natural law), and to proper law (that is, customary law) but also by the
importance that he places upon law in general.

Building on the apostle Paul's teaching that knowledge of sin comes
primarily through the law (Rom. 3:20), Zanchi begins his treatment of law
by distinguishing its two chief functions. In the first place, law teaches human beings what should be done or what should be avoided, and, in the
second place, it prods and obligates human beings to do what should be
done and to avoid what should be avoided. But law has other uses beyond
the two just mentioned; it can also reward and punish.

Regarding the definition of law, Zanchi observes that the Hebrew
word *torah* means "teaching," which is especially appropriate, for, as he
says, the law of God "teaches what truly good, fair, and just things ought to
be done and what truly evil things ought to be avoided."[88] The Italian word
for law, *áligando,* has the connotation of a binding obligation; thus human
beings are bound by laws to do some things and to avoid others. Others,
however, substitute the word *bond* for law, as in Psalm 2, which reads, "Let
us burst their bonds asunder and let us cast their cords from us." The most

important function of law in light of the preceding semantic field, contends Zanchi, is the binding obligation it places upon persons. "Law separates those things that are truly good, right, and just from those that are evil, shameful, and unjust, and teaches that we should do the one but avoid the other."[89] The fact that law is a teacher, relates Zanchi, is "essential to the concept of law itself. Every teaching makes something known to us, but it does not necessarily obligate anyone to do anything."[90]

But what is it exactly that law commands us to do? Following Justinian, Zanchi replies it is to do justice, which means to give fairly to all what they deserve. "God's law simply requires in its first and second tablet that we render to God what is owed to him alone and that we do not refuse to our neighbors what they deserve."[91] Any action that rejects or contradicts this requirement, Zanchi considers to be sin. This leads quite naturally into the primary goal of all good laws, which is first and foremost the glory of God, and then secondarily the good of one's neighbor understood both privately and publicly. "If the basis for law is, in fact, fairness; namely, that all people get what they deserve, then nothing is more fair than that God receives all honor and glory in the highest and that our neighbors receive what benefits their health and happiness of mind and body."[92] That all actions should be oriented to advancing God's glory and honor arises from the implicit teleology of law; however, the secondary goal of law — to work for the good of one's neighbor — follows from the primary one and carries with it the promise of future life for those who obey the law. "When [the law] commands first and foremost that we love our neighbor as we love ourselves, it teaches that whatever we do to our neighbor we ought to do in such a way that we benefit our neighbors and advance their well-being. If that is not possible, we should at least be concerned with the common good of the church and the human race."[93]

After clarifying the function, the foundation, and the goal of all good laws, Zanchi argues God must be seen as the primary (but not necessarily proximate) origin and source of good laws. The primary origin of all good laws, he writes, is the revealed will of God, which teaches and commands what should be done and what should be avoided. God endows princes and magistrates with the authority to enact laws but those laws must not be in opposition either to the will, the wisdom, or the prescribed arrangement of God. Therefore, if human laws represent the will of human beings established by reason and common sense, then the will of God must be acknowledged as the ultimate source of all laws.[94] Moreover, if human wisdom and all good things are lights from the Father above, as Scripture affirms, then all good laws must ultimately participate in the divine wisdom, even though their moral content may be proximately derived from right reason.[95]

Like Aquinas and Scotus, Zanchi attests that "divine will is not separate from divine wisdom."[96] Following in step with the Augustinian *via antiqua* tradition, Zanchi explains how it is that all laws descend from the eternal law of God. "If you admit that the earth is governed by Divine Providence, then you must agree that the just laws, by which every kingdom, province, home, and community is governed, come necessarily from God. Augustine and later, Aquinas, concluded that at first an eternal law dwelt in God who is the most perfect embodiment of reason, and by this reason, God rules the world and thus is the reason for all things that happen. Then, they argue, this reason was imparted to human beings and by it we rule our own activities, and from it flow out our laws."[97] From this analysis, then, it should be clear that Zanchi accepts the metaphysical and epistemological parameters of the realist natural-law tradition but, as a Reformed moral theologian, emphasizes the advancement of God's glory and honor as the underlying teleological orientation of law and morality.

In the end, therefore, Zanchi defines law as "the divine and eternal revelation of God's will, through which he teaches what he wishes human beings to do and avoid, and by which he warns that it be done or avoided for his own glory and for the good of the human race both in private and most of all in public."[98] God has customarily revealed his will concerning what people should and should not do in various ways, but in different eras of redemptive history he has used alternative means to reveal his will. To some, he reveals his will without words; to others through words — some spoken, some written. Zanchi provides the following lengthy description of the ways in which God has revealed his will throughout redemptive history:

> To his church, at first, he made it known verbally himself as he did to Adam and the patriarchs; at other times he did so through others, whether angels, miracles, or through ordinary persons, as through Adam to his children or through the preaching of the prophets and apostles. Later he spoke in books and writings through Moses, the prophets, and the apostles. In fact, it was never his habit to speak to nations himself but only through outsiders or those within these nations who have been divinely inspired. Often, he stirs up scholars and teachers for this purpose as he did through the laws of Solon, Lycurgus, Romulus, and Numa, or through missionaries such as Jonah to the

Ninevites, other prophets to other nations, and the apostles to the entire world.[99]

It is important to keep in mind the differences between *people* to whom God's will was revealed and the *methods* God used to reveal his will, insists Zanchi, for "the primary classification of law arises with it; that is, into the laws of nature, nations, and God, in other words, into natural law, human laws, and divine laws."[100]

In this chapter we will focus upon Zanchi's understanding of the relationship between natural law and divine law, for the simple reason that Althusius assimilates most of this teaching into his doctrine of natural law. Zanchi begins his analysis of natural law with the observation that canon lawyers and theologians restrict their idea of natural law to human nature, defining it as "the law common to all nations and that is obeyed everywhere by natural instinct, not by any statute."[101] Civil lawyers also employ this definition for the law of nations, because all people employ these laws and are led by them. Examples of such laws, in Zanchi's estimation, include ones that pertain to God, public worship, religion, obedience to superiors and the state, and self-defense with respect to oneself, one's family, and the state. Thus what civil lawyers include in the law of nations — namely, human affairs — theologians and canon lawyers classify as natural law. Nonetheless, according to Zanchi, the apostle Paul in Romans 2:14-15 seems to indicate that natural law is principally concerned with human affairs: "Gentiles, who do not possess the law (i.e., Scripture), do instinctively what the law requires. . . . They show that what the law requires is written on their hearts." To which he responds: "Surely, the requirements of divine law and Scripture have not been 'written on the hearts' of the other animals. For this reason, Isidore defines natural law as this: 'That which is common for all people.'"[102] So, contrary to Aquinas, Zanchi wants to limit use of the term *natural law* to that which pertains to human beings, thereby excluding its extension to the animal kingdom or to things that lack intellect (such as physical regularities in nature).

He distinguishes three levels to natural law, in the following order.[103] On the first and most basic level, natural law teaches that people may protect themselves against violence or injury, which is instinctive in all things, even in trees and plants. "From this instinct," remarks Zanchi, "comes the idea included in the laws of nations that it is permitted to repel force with force."[104] On the second level, natural law teaches that human beings may not only protect themselves but also advance their race through the procreation and education of children; this level is shared with animals as well. "Because of this impulse," observes Zanchi, "civil lawyers include marriage, reproduction, and rearing children under natural law."[105] On the third level, natural law applies only to human beings, because they "recognize their inclination to God and worship him as they do good to those with whom they live, and they know justice and honesty and turn to them naturally."[106]

To maintain a proper formulation of natural law, Zanchi thinks the doctrine must be placed within a redemptive-historical context, both to circumvent later confusions and to understand correctly the quotes by Damascene, Aquinas, Augustine, and various patristic authorities he will cite throughout the section on natural law. Before sin entered the world, natural law was perfectly instilled in human beings; "Divine will and the precepts for doing some things and avoiding others had been co-created with Adam when the image of God was breathed into him. Thus, before sin, this spark of reason had been perfectly placed inside human beings."[107] After the fall, however, "natural law was almost entirely blotted out as was any law that looks to God and the worship of him or to our neighbors and the just and fair relationship with them."[108] Not only was the so-called "narrow" image of God in true justice, righteousness, and holiness lost in Adam's free choice to disobey, but Zanchi believes all people became completely blind in their minds and totally depraved in their hearts, and the first level of natural law (i.e., natural instinct) became fundamentally warped.[109] So for example, instead of assuming a merely defensive posture with respect to their legitimate instinct to self-preservation, *post-lapsum* people assume an aggressive stance vis-à-vis injustices perpetrated upon them, and therefore rush headlong into violence under the guise of self-preservation.

Concerning the second level mentioned above, Zanchi insists distortion has taken place there as well. Whereas before the fall the human race was advanced uprightly through marriage, procreation, and child rearing, after the fall human beings do not know how to do without some sin or vice what animals still do blamelessly. Thus, writes Zanchi, "the first and second levels of natural law (according to Thomas's division) have become extremely corrupt in human beings; the third was almost entirely destroyed after the fall — so much so that if we should ever see a sliver of this aspect of natural law again in a human being, we must believe it was written in that person's soul a second time in its entirety by God himself, as Paul says in Romans."[110] In this quotation, Zanchi is alluding to his disagreement with the Thomistic natural-law tradition over the interpretation of Romans

2:14-15. When the apostle Paul declares in 2:15 that the moral law has been written on the heart, Zanchi contends the passage is teaching that natural law originates not from the corrupt nature of human beings but from God himself, who, as is stated a few pages later, "because of his own goodness, inscribed it anew in the minds and hearts of human beings after the fall, enough to preserve the common good and to convict people of sin."[111] "Natural law" is not so called, then, because it was passed down to us from Adam naturally — for by nature human beings are now blind and depraved — but rather because God has "reinscribed" general, natural principles of worship, goodness, fairness, and honesty into humanity at large. For Zanchi, natural law cannot be identified with either "a relic of the original image of God" or some "essential part of human nature" but with the *knowledge* of morality that has been "restored by God because of his goodness and grafted anew in our hearts."[112]

After surveying various definitions of natural law advanced by classical authors and theological authorities, Zanchi presents his own lengthy definition.

> Natural law is the will of God, and consequently, the divine rule and principle for knowing what to do and what not to do. It is, namely, the knowledge of what is good or bad, fair or unfair, upright or shameful, that was inscribed upon the hearts of all people by God himself also after the fall. For this reason, we are all universally taught what activities should be pursued and what should be avoided; that is, to do one thing and to avoid another, and we know that we are obligated and pushed to act for the glory of God, our own good, and the welfare of our neighbor both in private and in public. In addition, we know that if we do what should be avoided or avoid what we should do, we are condemned; but if we do the opposite, we are defended and absolved.[113]

It is important to recognize, among other things, that Zanchi's definition distinguishes natural law from other types of law in two primary ways. First, it draws attention to the fact that natural law has been inscribed on the hearts of all people by God himself. Second, it shows that natural law has also been "impressed and inscribed anew" upon the hearts of all people also after the fall. Given the corruption of nature and human nature that took place in the fall, Zanchi contends the foundation of natural law cannot come from these sources but must come from God. "Natural law, however, being a principle of reason, is a good, divine, and spiritual thing.

Thus, it must come from somewhere besides nature; that is, it must, as I have demonstrated, come from God."[114] Furthermore, he argues, if natural law came either from nature or from human nature, "then it would exist equally in all people; for those things that are shared by all people naturally exist equally in all people."[115] However, experience shows some people are wiser, more devoted to justice and honesty, and more zealous for God; although, interestingly enough, Zanchi thinks one would never find people who deny that God exists and who could not distinguish between right and wrong. Consequently, his definition emphasizes that natural law does not arise from natural instinct but is rather a gift of God. Those within the Augustinian tradition, Zanchi remarks, "call it natural law as the apostle Paul does because the principles of justice and honesty have been inscribed on our hearts by God and those little sparks of heavenly light (as Cicero calls them) appear inside of us as innate and natural."[116]

In light of the definition, Zanchi discerns three principal functions of natural law that correspond with the highest goods to which the natural law is already oriented. First, natural law is a "trait shared with all other living things that we protect and save ourselves. This includes eating, drinking, sleeping, resting, moving, using medicine, clothes, et cetera. This produces these laws: A healthy lifestyle is praised while an unhealthy one is rejected; it is permitted to drive off force with force, et cetera."[117] Second, natural law is a "trait shared with all animals, that we endeavor to propagate our species, that we take time for having and rearing children, and the other things related to it; that is, that we pay attention to domestic affairs."[118] Third, natural law is a "trait applying to all human beings, that we know and worship God and that we maintain a community among human beings."[119] The third aspect of natural law is customarily divided into two headings, just as the Decalogue is divided into two tablets: The first pertains to the knowledge and worship of God (piety), while the second pertains to loving our neighbor (justice). The conceptual framework Zanchi establishes in his analysis of natural law's third function is what becomes the foundation of Althusius's natural-law doctrine in the *Politica*, seen particularly in Althusius's acknowledgment that the principles of the Decalogue prescribe a way, rule, guiding light, and limit to human society.[120]

The first heading of natural law's third function articulates a natural theology for the worship and love of God on the basis of an incipient natural knowledge of God. As proof, Zanchi cites Romans 1:19: "What is known of God is manifest among them." But, on what basis, is such knowledge known? His answer: "From God who imparts this knowledge into their hearts."[121] But how has God shown it to people? From the book of nature, as the apostle relates in Romans 1:20: "Ever since the creation of the world his eternal power and divine nature, invisible though they are, have been understood and seen through the things he has made." From this initial principle, writes Zanchi, "the Gentiles passed down many things about the knowledge and worship of God."[122] Because of the natural knowledge of God the Gentiles were given, the apostle Paul relates they were rightly accused and condemned internally through their conscience and externally through the law, for even among the pagans "those who were touched by no religion were considered criminals."[123]

The second heading of natural law's third function seems to suggest a consociational understanding of social relations, as Althusius's concept of symbiosis develops. Zanchi describes the guiding idea behind the second heading as follows: "Maintain fellowship and goodwill among human beings; that is, do not do to another what you do not want done to yourself and vice versa."[124] Common human experience shows that friendship must be cultivated with one's peers and that something should not be done to another that one would not also want done to oneself. For this reason, Zanchi holds nature itself teaches that no one should be affected by injury; so, to the degree that being unkind, quarrelsome, disloyal, or hurtful poisons human fellowship and undermines social concord, it is a sin against nature. Christ confirmed this heading of natural law, Zanchi contends, when he reduced all of the commands of the second tablet to the love of one's neighbor.[125] Thus, he writes, "we see confirmed by Christ what God had written in the hearts of even the Gentiles. In fact, it had also been a law among the Gentiles — the words of Emperor Severus were heard and inscribed everywhere: 'Do not do to another what you do not wish to be done to yourself.' From this second element of natural law, other laws are derived that are written in the hearts of nearly every human being: Live justly; do not hurt another person. Give to each person his due, stay loyal."[126]

Before delving into Althusius's understanding of the relations between various types of law, it is important to address the fact that the two headings under natural law's third function are not equally inscribed on the hearts of all people. In the first instance, concerning the worship of God, Zanchi reiterates Cicero's maxim that no race is so barbaric, no philosophy so savage as to deny that God exists. Yet, he points out that pagan philosophers were divided over whether God should be worshipped only with the heart because he is spirit or whether he should be worshipped through idols and public rituals because he is corporeal. In the second instance, concerning the fellowship of human beings, Zanchi observes that all people are not equally aware of what follows from the principle. Consider, for example, the Spartans, who praised acts of thievery, while the Romans punished them severely. From this example, and many others, Zanchi adduces, "it is clear that natural law has not been written in every person's heart equally, but more in some and less in others."[127]

Furthermore, in the same vein, it is also clear that natural law has been implanted and instilled more effectively in some and less effectively in others; in the hearts of the elect natural law "is always more fully and effectively written as the Lord promised in Jeremiah (31:31-34)."[128] Zanchi treats this idea more fully in the section "On the Law of the Spirit," under the category of Divine Laws:

> Natural law teaches only what must be pursued, what must be avoided, and warns and pushes people to whatever that may be. Still, it does so in such a way that it does not exhibit the power to establish or implement itself; it simply allows us to see what is naturally better and to follow the approved and better path. The law of the Spirit [which is simply the will of God impressed on our hearts through the power of the Holy Spirit], however, not only teaches but lives and effectively moves us to obedience to God.[129]

But regardless of the effectiveness with which the natural law has been written on one's heart, its first principles remain constant even if the conclusions and applications derived from them are sometimes obscured by human sinfulness.

Althusius's Understanding of the Relations Between Various Types of Law

As mentioned earlier, Althusius devotes all of chapter 21 in the *Politica* to a discussion of the role of prudence in guiding the magistrate's administration of the commonwealth. Althusius argued that magistrates ought to administer commonwealths on the basis of prudence, which involves knowledge both of law and of the changing and contingent circumstances to which law is to be applied. Given his task in chapter 21, it makes sense that one would encounter there Althusius's fullest (but by no means exclusive) account of various types of law and the relationships among them. So, it is fitting to begin our examination of Althusius's natural-law doctrine with chapter 21 of the *Politica,* and make reference to other relevant passages in the *Politica* and the *Dicaeologica*[130] where the topic is also discussed.

Althusius frames his discussion of law by observing three things that are "properly and unavoidably" to be learned and known by the supreme magistrate in the administration of the commonwealth: "First is the rule of living and administering; the second is the nature of the people; and the third is the nature of rule *(regnum).*"[131] His description of the magistrate's first function is reminiscent of Zanchi's definition of natural law: "The rule of living, obeying, and administering is the will of God alone, which is the way of life, and the law of things to be done and to be omitted. . . . Thus the administration and government of a commonwealth is nothing other than the execution of law. Therefore, this law alone prescribes not only the order of administering for the magistrate, but also the rule of living for all subjects. . . ."[132] The rule of living and administering, which, as Althusius remarks, "is solely God's will for men manifested in his law, is called law in the general sense that it is a precept for doing those things that pertain to living a pious, holy, just, and suitable life. That is to say, it pertains to the duties that are to be performed toward God and one's neighbor, and to the love of God and one's neighbor. . . ."[133] From his identification of the moral precepts of the Decalogue with the first precept of law (viz., "Do and pursue that which is good and avoid what is evil") that undergirds law in general, Althusius concludes laws act like fences, walls, guards, or boundaries to guide people along the appointed way for achieving wisdom, happiness, and peace.[134]

After describing the foundation and the function of law in general, he distinguishes between two species of law: common and proper.[135] In the *Politica,* he states that common law *(jus commune),* which is a synonym for natural law *(jus naturale),* "has been naturally implanted in all men. 'Whatever can be known about God has been manifested to men, because God has made it manifest to them' [Rom. 1:19]. As to knowledge *(notitia)* and inclination *(inclinatio),* God discloses and prescribes the reason and means for worshipping him and loving one's neighbor, and urges us to them. 'For there was reason derived from the nature of the universe,' Cicero says, 'urging men to do right and recalling them from wrong-doing, and this reason did not first become law at the time it was written down, but at its origin.' It is commonly called the moral law *(lex moralis).*"[136]

In the *Dicaeologica,* Althusius identifies common and natural law as synonymous: "A law is natural and common if common sense *(recta ratio*

communis) correctly produces it for the necessity and utility of human social life. It is then called natural law *(jus naturale)*."[137] Then, a few paragraphs later, he addresses the practice of using these terms interchangeably
to refer to natural law.

> Some distinguish common law *(jus commune)* from natural law *(jus
> naturale)* or the law of nations *(jus gentium)*. . . . Others, in fact, more
> correctly call each natural. . . . Natural law applies to human beings
> alone, and anything called a law of nations is often called natural law
> by Christ himself. . . . What they call natural law is called αναποδεικτως
> [undemonstrated first principles], which simple logic teaches people as
> human and animal instinct does . . . to live a holy and pious life. . . .
> Thus by some it is called the law of reason *(jus rationalis)* . . . even
> though it itself is not inborn but only εννοιαι [a thought in the mind,
> notion, or concept], the perception of it or rather the ability to recog-
> nize that this law is implanted by nature. It is also called natural law
> *(lex naturae),* . . . or natural justice *(naturalis aequitas),* . . . because
> wild animals sometimes imitate it and are said to have some images of
> it [in their behavior].[138]

Conscience (in the sense of *synderesis)* is another term Althusius employs to refer to the knowledge of the moral law that has been universally
imprinted by God within the human race. Such knowledge has two principal functions: first, by it people come to know and understand law; second,
by it people come to know of the means to be employed or avoided for
maintaining obedience to law. "By this innate inclination, or secret impulse
of nature," contends Althusius, "man is urged to perform what he understands to be just, and to avoid what he knows to be wicked."[139] In the
Dicaeologica he provides a fuller description of the nature and purpose of
that "secret impulse of nature."

> Therefore, a law is common if it has been inscribed by nature or God
> directly onto people's hearts in order that they are moved by it to do
> and avoid what is appropriate for maintaining the public good of hu-
> man society, to convict of sin those who injure others, and to excuse
> the innocent. . . . Thus the idea and natural instinct of this law exists in
> human beings. By it people recognize what is right, and they are
> pushed by this hidden natural instinct to do or avoid what they recog-
> nize to be just or unjust.[140]

To support this assertion, Althusius appeals to various texts of Scripture, namely, Romans 1:19-21, 32; 2:15-17; 7:15-18, 22-23; and 1 Corinthians 5:1-3 and 11:14. As he states in the *Politica,* common law sets forth for all people "the general theory and practice of love, both for God and for one's neighbor."[141] Referring to the knowledge of morality written on the heart by God and the role of conscience (in the sense of *conscientia*) in pushing people toward goodness and away from evil, Althusius affirms in the *Dicaeologica* that God "teaches and inscribes on human hearts general principles of goodness, fairness, evil, and sin and obligates, prods, and incites all people to do good and avoid evil. He also convicts those who ignore these things through their own consciences and excuses those who do them (Rom. 2:15-16; 7:15-18, 22-23). Therefore, he pushes them to good and calls them away from evil. If they should follow his lead to goodness, he excuses them. If not, he condemns them."[142]

While Althusius attests that the natural knowledge of morality has been incontrovertibly and indelibly imprinted in human consciousness, he nonetheless affirms with Calvin, Vermigli, and Zanchi that "law is not inscribed equally on the hearts of all. The knowledge of it is communicated more abundantly to some and more sparingly to others, according to the will and judgment of God."[143] Furthermore, given the unevenness of knowledge of the moral law among people, Althusius infers that God does not move all persons to obedience to this law in the same manner and to an equal degree; "Some men exert themselves more strongly, others less so, in their desire for it."[144]

After establishing that all people have been sufficiently equipped with an intuitive awareness of the moral law in terms of knowledge and inclination, Althusius turns to a discussion of the Decalogue. What is interesting here is that he assumes and builds on the parameters Zanchi laid down earlier in his treatment of the relationship between the Decalogue and natural law. For Zanchi, recall that the third function of natural law is conventionally divided into two headings, just as the Decalogue is divided into two tablets with the first pertaining to the worship of God and the second pertaining to the love of our neighbor. Thus, according to Althusius, Christ set forth two headings to the common (natural) law: "The first heading pertains to the performance of our duty immediately to God, and the second to what is owed to our neighbor."[145]

At crucial junctures in the *Politica,* such as 7.7-12 and 21.22-28, Althusius explains how the precepts of the Decalogue arise out of common law and inform his theory of symbiotic relations. For example, in 21.24-28,

he distinguishes between affirmative and negative precepts of the Decalogue. Affirmative precepts concern the performance of duties owed to God
and one's neighbor, while negative precepts concern prohibited things that
ought to be avoided entirely. First table precepts pertaining to God are, in
Althusius's words, "always, absolutely, and without distinction binding
upon all, to such a degree that the second table of the Decalogue ought to
yield precedence to the first table as to a superior law."[146] Moreover, first table precepts "can never be set aside or relaxed, and not even God himself is
able to reject them."[147] Now, second table precepts pertaining to one's
neighbor can be distinguished as either proper or common. Proper duties
are comprehended by the fifth precept, which treats those things inferiors
are expected to perform toward superiors, and vice versa. Common duties,
which are to be performed toward everyone, are treated in the remaining
precepts. According to Althusius, God sometimes relaxes the restrictions of
the fifth, sixth, and eighth precepts, but that power of dispensation has not
been granted to human beings.[148]

Like Zanchi, but contrary to Carney, Reibstein, and Winters, Althusius
holds that the moral precepts of the Decalogue are derivative from the logically prior *lex naturalis,* that is, the universal knowledge of morality God implanted in the human mind at creation. He states, "The Decalogue has been
prescribed for all people *to the extent that it agrees with and explains the common law of nature for all peoples.* It has also been renewed and confirmed by
Christ our king. Jerome Zanchi says that this is the common judgment of
theologians."[149] Although he makes only passing reference to Zanchi in the
citation, it is clear from the development of his argument that Althusius
adopts the conceptual structure Zanchi lays out in his so-called treatise on
law. Not only does Althusius affirm with Zanchi that the Ten Commandments are a species of natural law because they define and describe the same
general precepts of the natural law; in the *Dicaeologica* he states, "Natural
law applies to human beings alone, and anything called a law of nations often is called natural law by Christ himself."[150]

So how does Althusius conceive the relationship between the
Decalogue and the natural law? To answer this question it is necessary to
see what Zanchi had to say concerning the Mosaic law because, on the one
hand, Althusius credits him with expressing what was the "common judgment" of Reformed theologians and, on the other, because Althusius only
articulates indirectly and somewhat cryptically how he understands the
written and the unwritten laws to relate to one another. Zanchi makes two
pertinent observations on this matter. The first observation is that the Mo-

saic law (that is, the written law) was given to the Jews alone and not to the Gentiles. If this is so, asks Zanchi, "Why, then, do the nations obey many of the things laid out in the Mosaic law?" He replies, "They learned them from natural law, although some also borrowed ideas from Mosaic law as Justin Martyr proved about Plato, and Eusebius demonstrates concerning Caesariensus."[151]

A second observation bearing on the relationship between the Decalogue and the natural law concerns the imputation of guilt for violating laws only for which people are, properly speaking, held accountable. So, in the case of the Ten Commandments, the apostle Paul does not accuse the Gentiles of violating the Mosaic law (Rom. 2:14: "Gentiles, who do not possess the law . . . are a law to themselves") as he does the Jews. "He, instead, condemns them for violating natural law. Why is this? Because a law speaks only to those who are under it."[152] It is for the following reasons, then, that Zanchi insists Jews at the time of the apostles sinned when they sought to subject Gentile converts to the Mosaic law. First, Gentiles had never been obligated by Mosaic law, and it did not apply to them. Second, Christ himself had freed even the Jews from the guilt of violating the Mosaic law. "How great is the iniquity, then, if Christians want to subject people today, Gentiles and magistrates, to Judaic law? As long as those laws were handed down to the Israelites, they did not apply to the Gentiles. It is only when they coincide with natural law and were confirmed by Christ himself that they apply to all people."[153] Christ's reaffirmation of the Decalogue in the Sermon on the Mount is a clear application of the moral law to the Gentiles not only as it came to expression in the written law of the Old Testament but also in the unwritten law inscribed on the human heart.

The second species of law Althusius distinguishes is proper law *(lex propria)*, which is "the law that is drawn up and established by the magistrate on the basis of common law *(lex communis)* and according to the nature, utility, condition, and other special circumstances of his country."[154] Furthermore, as Althusius relates, proper law "indicates the peculiar way, means, and manner by which this natural equity among men can be upheld, observed, and cultivated in any given commonwealth. Therefore, proper law is nothing other than the practice of this common natural law as adapted to a particular polity."[155] The purpose of proper (also known as positive) law is to specify how individual citizens of any given commonwealth are able to seek and attain natural equity. Given the purpose of proper law, it makes sense that Althusius referred to it as "the servant and handmaiden of common law, and a teacher leading us to the observance of common law."[156]

Having proposed a definition of proper law, Althusius now moves to a discussion of the two principal reasons for the establishment of proper law. "The first reason is that not all men have sufficient natural capacity that they are able to draw from these general principles of common law the particular conclusions and laws suitable to the nature and condition of an activity and its circumstances. The second reason is that natural law is not so completely written on the hearts of men that it is sufficiently efficacious in restraining men from evil and impelling them to good."[157] Particularly in the latter case, as Zanchi stated earlier, natural law merely teaches, inclines, and accuses people of that which is wrong and ought to be avoided. Thus, given natural law's insufficient efficacy in restraining men from evil, Althusius believes it is necessary for there to be "a proper law by which men who are led neither by the love of virtue nor by the hatred of vice may be restrained by the fear of punishment that this law assigns to transgressions of common law."[158]

There are, therefore, two parts to proper law that indicate how it is related to common law but also how the former is distinct from the latter: the first is proper law's agreement with common law, and the second is its difference from it. If proper law taught nothing distinct from common law, then it would not be a different species of law. Whereas, if it proscribed something entirely contrary to common law, it would be evil, because it would make mutable an otherwise immutable common law. "It is truly necessary, therefore, that it not entirely depart from common law, that it not be generally contrary to it, and it not completely combine with it and thus be identical with it."[159]

Proper law is thought to agree with common law in those matters that are common to each law; namely, in terms of starting point, subject, and purpose. Althusius explains each condition in consecutive order: "The starting point is the right and certain reason upon which both laws rely, and by which each decides what is just and declares it. The subject under consideration is the joint business and action to which both laws relate themselves and give directions. The purpose of each is justice and piety, or sanctity, and the same equity and common good in human society."[160] However, proper law and common law differ at times, specifically when proper law must be accommodated to particular and special circumstances and something must be added to or subtracted from common law. In Althusius's judgment, contingency and mutability are necessarily introduced into proper law for the following two reasons:

One reason is that, because of a better understanding by the legislator of order and utility, a law that for a long time was looked upon as just is changed. The other is the nature and condition of an activity so far as persons, things, circumstances, place, or time are concerned. Since the nature and condition of these circumstances may be diverse, inconstant, and changeable, it is not possible for proper law to acknowledge one and the same disposition of common law for everything and in everything, as Junius and Zanchius, together with the jurists, say.[161]

So, as far as Althusius is concerned, proper law may differ from common law with respect to changing circumstances, but it cannot differ in those areas where agreement is maintained with common law. Moreover, according to him, there is no civil or proper law "in which something of natural and divine immutable equity has not been mixed."[162] Thus, civil laws that depart from these strictures relinquish the moral authority that stands behind all duly enacted law. Nonetheless, while common law teaches that evildoers ought to be punished, it proposes nothing concerning the punishment. Proper law determines what the just punishment should be for specific crimes. Common law commands in general. Proper law makes these commands specific, and accommodates them to the experience and utility of the commonwealth and the circumstances of each activity. "For this reason," writes Althusius, "the moral precepts of the Decalogue, having no certain, special, and fixed punishment attached to them, are general. The forensic and political law then makes specific determinations, which it relates to the circumstances of any act."[163] There are, of course, various forms of proper law such as that of the Jews, the Romans, and the Germans of Althusius's day. However, he observes that nearly all European polities in the early seventeenth century used the Roman law as described in the Digest, Code, Novels, and Institutes to provide stability and support for their juridical structures.[164]

The duty of the magistrate, in light of the preceding distinction between common and proper law, is to administer the commonwealth according to the proper law of Moses "so far as moral equity or common law are expressed therein."[165] As Althusius describes it, the magistrate is required to conform to everything in the Mosaic law that is in harmony with common law, but is "by no means required to conform in those things in which the proper law of Moses, in order to be accommodated to the polity of the Jews, differs from common law."[166] Magistrates that establish such laws as absolutely necessary, which are by nature mutable or obsolete, destroy

Christian liberty, impede consciences, and become ensnared in a yoke of slavery. Thus, in opposition to the proponents of theonomy both then and now, Althusius argues against the improper application of Mosaic penology and civil law to contemporary juridical structures.

> Unless proper laws are changed with changing circumstances because of which they broadly exist, they become wicked and attain neither to the equity of the second table of the Decalogue nor to the piety of the first. Thus they cease to contain the common foundation of right reason. Accordingly, the magistrate who makes the proper law of Moses compulsory in his commonwealth sins grievously. For those particular circumstances and considerations because of which the Jewish proper law was promulgated should bear no weight in his commonwealth.[167]

Conclusion

This chapter has argued that Althusius's doctrine of natural law is fully consistent with the theological strictures of Reformed orthodoxy. His doctrine of natural law should be viewed as a further elaboration and application of Jerome Zanchi's doctrine of natural law. Like Zanchi, Althusius held that the precepts of the Decalogue were a renewed and re-enforced subspecies of the logically prior general precepts of morality found in the natural law (the natural knowledge of morality God inscribed in the human mind at creation). By placing Althusius's thought in the context of his contemporaries, it becomes evident that he was both a faithful expositor of Reformed doctrine and an innovative early seventeenth-century political theorist.

As we move from the Reformation (Chapters Three and Four) through early orthodoxy (Chapter Five) into the era of high orthodoxy (Chapter Six), there is a consequent increase in the sophistication with which the doctrines of natural revelation, natural theology, and natural law are developed in Reformed theological systems. Francis Turretin's *Institutio theologiae elencticae*, as we will see in the next chapter, can be viewed as the crowning achievement of nearly a century and a half of Reformed doctrinal development.

6

Francis Turretin and the
Natural Knowledge of God the Creator

Francis Turretin's Contribution to the
Development of Reformed Theological Ethics

There is no hyperbole in applying to the dearth of scholarship concerning Francis Turretin (1623-1687) what Richard Muller has said of the Reformed scholastic theologians generally: "There is a large body of late sixteenth- and seventeenth-century Reformed writing on ethics, philosophy, and natural theology that has been, for the most part, forgotten and/or ignored by modern Reformed theologians and philosophers."[1] This state of affairs is true indeed even for theologians of Francis Turretin's stature. In Reformed circles Turretin's name is virtually synonymous with scholasticism, which, depending upon the perspective of the commentator, kindles either positive or negative connotations. One favorable commentator, in fact, has assigned to him the epitaph of "champion and grandmaster of Reformed polemics."[2] Another has stated that it is customary to regard his system, the *Institutio theologiae elencticae*,[3] as standing "at the apex of the development of scholastic theology in the post-Reformation era, prior to the decline of the Protestant system under the impact of rationalism, pietism, and the Enlightenment of the eighteenth century."[4]

Turretin received his training in philosophy and theology at the Academy of Geneva, the institution where his father, Bénédict Turretin, had served as professor of theology from 1611 to 1631. After completing his studies in 1644, he decided to go abroad to expose himself to "the principal luminaries of Reformed theology in Leiden, Utrecht, Paris, and Saumur."[5] He returned to Geneva at the close of 1647 and was called to become the pastor of the Italian church in 1648, to which he was ordained in December 1649. James T.

Dennison Jr. remarks of Turretin's "postgraduate" sojourn that "he would incorporate his reflections on Saumur in particular into his *Institutio*."[6] As Turretin embarked on his career, the controversy surrounding Amyraldianism — a school of Remonstrant theology that taught hypothetical universalism, toleration, rationalism, and ecumenism — was beginning to gather momentum among the Reformed churches in France. However, as history reveals, the controversy would inevitably spread beyond the boundaries of Paris and Saumur to Geneva, the citadel of Reformed orthodoxy, where the representatives of Amyraldianism in that city (Charles Maurice, Pierre Mussard, Louis Tronchin, Phillippe Mestrezat, and Jean-Robert Chouet) would encounter Francis Turretin's fierce opposition. In 1653, Turretin was appointed to the chair of theology at the Academy, the position he held concurrently with his pastoral duties until his death in 1687.

One of the crowning but short-lived achievements of Turretin's career was the successful campaign he waged in support of the *Helvetic Consensus Formula*. In 1678, he persuaded the Venerable Company to adopt the *Consensus,* which was an orthodox refutation of Salmurian doctrine, but this — as Dennison quips — was "a Pyrrhic victory."[7] For the *Consensus* would soon be repudiated by Jean-Alphonse Turretin, Francis Turretin's only child to survive infancy, who spearheaded the movement for abrogation beginning in 1706.[8] The most enduring legacy of his distinguished career, nonetheless, was the publication of the *Institutio theologiae elencticae* — his mature statement of orthodox Reformed doctrine. Turretin's final years, writes Dennison, "were spent summing up his remarkable career by preparing what he had taught and defended for years — Genevan orthodoxy. The *Institutio* was published *seriatum:* volume one in 1679; volume two in 1682; and volume three in 1685. Turretin was planning a major revision of the whole when he died."[9]

Turretin's theological system is self-consciously scholastic in that he adopts the technical vocabulary and methodological patterns of argumentation characteristic of theologians from the late twelfth century onward, and self-consciously Reformed in that he articulates the doctrinal distinctives of the Reformed wing of the Reformation at a high level of sophistication. Unlike Luther, Calvin, Zwingli, and other early Reformers who had little concern for prolegomena or little interest in elaborating a positive relationship between theology and philosophy, Turretin's system may appear at first reckoning to be an entirely different project from what the Reformers had in mind. Yet, to argue that his system is discontinuous from theirs because it employs refined techniques of scholastic argumentation and is philosophically and methodologically more astute is to draw an invalid conclusion from flawed premises.

In this respect, the differences between Luther's and Melanchthon's theological methods point to divergences that existed even among the first generation of Reformers. If the Reformation brought about a crisis in dogmatics and in effect necessitated a thoroughgoing recalibration of the theological task, "it was not Luther himself who turned to the constructive work of producing a 'reformed' theological structure: he remained, to the end of his life, a thinker whose theology must be elicited from exegetical works, from sermons, and from polemical treatises of a frequently occasional nature. It was left to others to develop explicit dogmatic *loci* out of the text of Scripture and/or commentaries and treatises themselves based on exegesis and to bring about the beginnings of Protestant theology as system."[10] Luther's antagonism toward philosophy and the more speculative elements of traditional theological systems, however, should not be viewed as a repudiation of the use of *recta ratio* or Aristotle's logic, rhetoric, or poetics in theological formulation.[11] Regardless, Melanchthon, in contrast to Luther, "offered a clarity of formulation and a refined method for eliciting doctrinal topics and organizing them into teachable bodies of doctrine. The pedagogical, confessional, systematic, and philosophical impact of Melanchthon's work on the shape of Protestant teaching was enormous."[12]

Among the Reformed, theologians such as first-generation Reformer Martin Bucer and second- and third-generation codifiers such as Peter Martyr Vermigli and Jerome Zanchi utilize the scholastic training of their early formation as they develop and defend Reformed doctrine. What has been said of Bartholomaus Keckermann's continuity with the Reformers and the older scholastics would, by extension, also apply to Turretin: "theological continuity with the early Reformers, Luther and Zwingli, by way of the more philosophically minded men of the second generation, Melanchthon, Vermigli, Zanchi, Ursinus; philosophical and, to a limited extent, methodological continuity with the older scholasticism by way of a modified Thomistic pattern that set faith and theology carefully in accord with but nevertheless above reason and philosophy."[13]

While Turretin's precise doctrinal formulation at the end of the seventeenth century consolidated orthodox Reformed identity for many generations to come (as seen, for example, in Charles Hodge's *Systematic Theology*), it is odd that very few commentators today have expressed sustained, career-length interest in his theological system.[14] Since 1950, only John Walter Beardslee III,[15] Timothy Phillips,[16] and Stephen Robert Spencer[17] have written English-language dissertations on aspects of Turretin's system. A handful of authors have also sporadically addressed topics ranging from Turretin's use of the patristics in doctrinal formulation[18] to his understanding of the covenant of works,[19] special revelation,[20] predestination,[21] the object and nature of theology,[22] the noetic effects of the fall on reason,[23] and finally the metaphysical structure of his concept of God.[24] Beyond these limited studies, however, Francis Turretin's theology has simply been, to a great extent, neglected. Ironically, nearly as much work has been done to document how representatives of Enlightened Orthodoxy — of which Jean-Alphonse Turretin was a preeminent exponent — converted the scholastic orthodoxy they inherited from the Academy to a type of Socinian-Remonstrant rationalism that eschewed metaphysics in favor of apologetics and maintained only those doctrinal aspects of the Christian faith that could be harmonized with reason.[25]

Although nominal attention has been paid to Turretin's prolegomena and doctrine of God, no real interest has been taken yet in his ethics. This is a striking oversight not only because his treatment of natural law is broadly affirmative of the realist natural-law tradition (the Thomist and Scotist trajectories), but also because his formulation of natural-law doctrine is systematic and integrated seamlessly with the adjacent doctrines of natural revelation and natural theology. The purpose of this chapter, like Chapters Three (Calvin) and Four (Vermigli), is to lay out the doctrinal parameters of Turretin's understanding of natural revelation, natural theology, and natural law. By approaching our task in this manner it will become apparent how he arranges the relations between those *loci*, which will also enable us to ascertain what is distinctive about Turretin's formulation of natural law in relation to his predecessors.

Like Vermigli, Zanchi, and Althusius, Turretin affirms unequivocally that natural revelation is essential to supernatural theology; yet he is also clear it has boundaries circumscribing its limited sphere of usefulness. "It is one thing to allow some knowledge of God as Creator and preserver however imperfect, corrupt, and obscure; another to have a full, entire, and clear knowledge of God as Redeemer and of the lawful worship due to him. Natural theology [and likewise natural law] has the former in that which may be known of God. Revelation alone has the latter in the faith that is gained only from the word."[26] After the fall, salvation depends upon the "the revealed Word of the Law and the Gospel."[27] The issue for Turretin, then, is not the mere existence of a true natural knowledge of God, as it is for Barth: "we may admit, indeed, some sort of natural theology arising

from the light of nature, upon which supernatural theology may be built —
for example, that God exists, that God is to be worshipped."[28] Rather, it is
that such knowledge cannot provide adequate or proper foundations for
true religion — even if it does, like philosophy, perform a valuable ancillary
role in supernatural theology.

According to Richard Muller, Turretin's regenerate natural theology
exhibits a "pedagogical or legal use of natural theology as described by
[Stephen] Charnock and [a general parallelism of sorts] with the Reformed
doctrine of the threefold use of the Law."[29] In Turretin's case, as Muller
shows, the parallelism certainly obtains between his use of pagan natural
theology and the preevangelical, pedagogical use of the law (the so-called
usus elenchticus sive paedagogicus), but a "less accurate parallel" may also
exist between his regenerate natural theology and the postevangelical, normative use of the law (the so-called *tertius usus legis*).[30] However, even if
the latter parallel can be sustained, there is no evidence to suggest that "the
Reformed orthodox recognition of the parallel between natural law and the
Decalogue led to a view of pagan natural theology (*theologia falsa*) as a kind
of *praeparatio evangelica:* from Musculus to Polanus and Alsted, to
Du Moulin, Charnock, Turretin, and Heidegger, this form of natural theology carries with it only *the* elenctical or condemnatory function of the Law,
not the full *usus paedagogicus.*"[31] Regenerate natural theology only leaves
men without excuse; it offers no positive or *soteriologically* useful content
for either the regenerate or the unregenerate. Yet, unlike Barth, even after
acknowledging the inherent limitations of natural revelation and natural
theology, Turretin avers, "Although the human understanding is very dark,
yet there still remains in it some rays of natural light and certain first principles, the truth of which is unquestionable. . . . These first principles are
true not only in nature, but also in grace and the mysteries of faith. Faith,
so far from destroying, on the contrary, borrows them from reason and uses
them to strengthen its own doctrines."[32]

Natural Revelation as a True Source for Knowledge of God

For Turretin, as for many of the Reformed scholastics, the doctrine of natural revelation functions as an uncontroversial primer to the doctrine of natural theology and a statement of religious epistemology. The existence of
such a doctrine attests to both the institutionalization and the increasing
sophistication of Protestant theological systems, particularly with respect

to prolegomena, throughout the post-Reformation era. Most of what Turretin writes on natural revelation is interspersed throughout his treatment of natural theology and natural law. Given the purpose of this chapter, therefore, it makes sense to clarify precisely what is meant by natural revelation, the knowledge that such a doctrine yields, and the means by which such knowledge is imparted.

Natural revelation is a species of true knowledge of God that is accessible to all but assimilated in varying degrees. "What is natural, subjectively and constitutively, always exists in the same manner, but not what is such qualitatively and consecutively (for qualities admit of increase and diminution). Natural [revelation] is so called not in the first, but in the second sense. Hence it is not surprising that it should vary as to degree in relation to its subjects, who differ in intellectual acumen."[33] In articulating the doctrine of natural revelation, Turretin presents the broad parameters of a theory of knowledge. In the first place, like Vermigli, he distinguishes between two principal types of knowledge: innate and acquired. In the strict sense of the term, all *actual* knowledge is acquired knowledge. "For," as he relates, "it is certain that no actual knowledge is born with us and that, in this respect, man is like a smooth tablet *(tabula rasa)*."[34] Yet, it is also the case that all human beings — in some only *potentia*, in others *actus* — have been endowed with a natural faculty[35] that "embraces not only the capability of understanding, but also the natural first principles of knowledge from which conclusions both theoretical and practical are deduced."[36] The human mind, according to Turretin, apprehends first principles immediately through intuition, whereas other forms of knowledge are acquired mediately through chains of discursive reasoning. "The mind of man is a *tabula rasa* not absolutely but relatively as to discursion and dianoetical knowledge (which is acquired necessarily by inferring one thing from another); but not as to apprehensive and intuitive knowledge."[37]

Turretin employs the mind's natural capability of apprehending first principles immediately and of appropriating knowledge derived by inference to supply the requisite data upon which to construct the doctrines of natural theology and natural law. Reformed orthodoxy, as Turretin summarizes, "uniformly teach[es] that there is a natural theology, partly innate (derived from the book of conscience by means of common notions [*koinas ennoias*]) and partly acquired (drawn from the book of creatures discursively)."[38] In this noetic structure, the first principles of theoretical knowledge constitute the foundation of natural theology, while the first principles of practical knowledge constitute the foundation of natural law. At this point, therefore, it is sufficient to acknowledge that the doctrines of natural theology and natural law are constructed from knowledge that is partly innate (derived by means of commonly implanted notions) and partly acquired (derived by means of inscription, revelation, observation, or inference).

Like Calvin, Vermigli, and Zanchi, Turretin holds that Scripture (Ps. 19:1; Acts 14:15-17; 17:23; Rom. 1:19-20; 2:14-15) demonstrates that God has provided human beings with both an innate and acquired knowledge of himself. Turretin believes the apostle in Romans 1:18-20 refers to "the true notions of God contained in natural revelation," when in verse 18 he speaks of the wicked as holding down the truth in unrighteousness and when in verse 19 he says that which may be known of God is manifest in them, for God has shown it to them. The true notions of God are revealed "partly in their hearts [innate] and partly in the works of creation [acquired]."[39] Turretin also holds that the literary structure of Romans 1 and 2 indicates the existence of an innate knowledge of God. The apostle, he contends, "wants to demonstrate that neither the Gentiles by nature (chap. 1) nor the Jews by the law (chap. 2) could be justified (because all are sinners), but only by the gospel revealed by Christ. . . . *Poiēmata* [1:20] refers to the works of the creation of the world because the invisible things of God are said to be manifest in them from the creation of the world."[40]

Moreover, Romans 2:14-15 likewise points to knowledge of God that is partly acquired and partly innate. As the apostle states, "The Gentiles, which have not the law, do by nature the things contained in the law, these, having not the law, are a law unto themselves: which show the work of the law written in their hearts, their conscience also bearing witness, and their thoughts the meanwhile accusing or else excusing one another." Such could not be said of the Gentiles, remarks Turretin, "if conscience did not dictate to each one that there is a deity who approves of good actions and disapproves and punishes evil deeds."[41] The immediate awareness of the law written on the heart "necessarily implies the knowledge of God, the legislator, by whose authority it binds men to obedience and proposes rewards or punishments."[42] So moral knowledge can be derived not only from common notions (or first principles of morality) implanted in the mind; it can also be acquired from internal inscription on the conscience or external revelation in the written form of the law of Moses. "Inscription," as Turretin explains, "implies a natural revelation of [the moral] law to the conscience as opposed to the external revelation made to the Jews by the writing upon stony tablets. Hence it is expressed by the conscience, which exerts itself both in observation (*synteresei*) and in consciousness (*syneidesei*) (v. 15)."[43]

Although God provides true knowledge of himself in the works of creation and providence, natural revelation is a nonsalvific but morally culpable source of information about God. Natural revelation is insufficient for salvation not only as it pertains to the subject (namely, human beings), because in this species of revelation the Holy Spirit does not nullify the noetic effects of sin (obfuscation, partiality, blindness) on the mind, but also as it pertains to the object (namely, God), because the mysteries of salvation (Trinity, Incarnation, Atonement) are not ascertainable through the order of natural revelation. In natural revelation, as Turretin explains,

> God (as an object of knowledge) indeed presents himself, but not as an object of faith; God the Creator, but not the Redeemer; the power and the Godhead (i.e., the existence of the deity and his infinite power may be derived from the work of creation), but not his saving grace and mercy. Therefore it was necessary that the defect of the former revelation (made useless and insufficient by sin) should be supplied by another more clear (not only as to degree, but also as to species), not only that God should use mute teachers, but that his sacred voice should also not only declare the excellence of his attributes, but open to us also the mystery of his will in order to [attain] our salvation.[44]

While natural revelation provides essential information concerning God's existence, attributes, will, and works, apart from supernatural verbal revelation it cannot attain a saving knowledge of God. Insofar as natural revelation portrays God's will (as contained in natural law), it is imperfectly or obscurely revealed; however, insofar as the mystery of the gospel is concerned, natural revelation entirely conceals it. Natural revelation, Turretin writes, "displays the works of creation and providence (Ps. 19:1-3; Acts 14:15-17; 17:23-28; Rom. 1:19-20), but does not rise up to the works of redemption and grace which can become known to us by the word alone (Rom. 10:17; 16:25-26)."[45]

Natural Theology as a Reliable but Soteriologically Insufficient Source for Knowledge of God

As stated earlier, Turretin constructs the doctrine of natural theology from natural knowledge that is partly innate and partly acquired. The argument is that universal attestation of the deity and the institution of religions provide content to and justification for natural theology. He enumerates the following five uses for natural theology:

> (1) as a witness of the goodness of God toward sinners unworthy even of these remains of light (Acts 14:16-17; Jn. 1:5); (2) as a bond of external discipline among men to prevent the world from becoming utterly corrupt (Rom. 2:14-15); (3) as a subjective condition in man for the admission of the light of grace because God does not appeal to brutes and stocks, but to rational creatures; (4) as an incitement to the search for this more illustrious revelation (Acts 14:27); (5) to render men inexcusable (Rom. 1:20) both in this life, in the judgment of an accusing conscience (Rom. 2:15) and, in the future life, in the judgment that God shall judge concerning the secrets of men (Rom. 2:16).[46]

In addition to affirming these conventional uses, he also indicates its chief limitation: Natural theology cannot warrant salvation, but it does render all inexcusable for the knowledge each, in fact, possesses.[47] More knowledge is required to obtain salvation than to incur damnation justly and without excuse. For, as Turretin relates, "evil arises from some defect, but the good requires a whole cause. For example, he who offends in one point is guilty of all (Jam. 2:10); but not, therefore, he who does well in one point is just in all. The commission of one sin can render a man inexcusable, but the performance of one good work is not sufficient to save him. Thus the Gentiles were inexcusable because they substituted gods without number in place of that one God whom they could know from the light of nature; but we cannot infer from this that the knowledge of the one God is sufficient absolutely for salvation."[48] He is opposed, therefore, to the Socinian and Remonstrant position that natural theology teaches a common religion by which all may procure salvation.[49]

Before examining Turretin's use of the proofs for God's existence, it is necessary to make some preliminary observations on how the proofs are structured in Reformed orthodoxy. First, as both Platt and Muller point out, the question of the existence of God does not uniformly appear in Reformed scholastic systems, but when it does, it has an apologetical and polemical function rather than a substantive or formative one.[50] Second, as Muller shows, arguments for the existence of God, including the more strictly rhetorical ones drawn from the common consent of mankind (*e consensu gentium*), generally occur in two places in the orthodox systems: "in prolegomena prior to discussion of saving knowledge . . . [or] in the *lo-*

cus de Deo as part of the necessary refutation of atheism."[51] Muller contends the rhetorical form of the proofs indicates, among other things, that their primary force "is not so much to *demonstrate* as to *persuade* the opponent of the existence of God. The Reformed orthodox version of the proofs, therefore, neither operates at a primarily theoretical level nor serves to ground their theological system in a rational foundation. The proofs are directed primarily against those who, for a variety of reasons, ignore the reality of God's power and grace in human life and act as if God were an absent deity."[52] Third, the presence of proofs in Reformed orthodox theology should not, as Muller insists, "be taken as an indication that they held God to be comprehensible or that they believed the proofs to be an easy point of entry into the doctrine of God."[53] Fourth, contrary to the Socinians (and, one might add, latter-day Barthians), the orthodox theologians held there is a minimal *sensus divinitatis* and a genuine natural revelation that can be used to engage in disputation with opponents of the faith.[54]

The indubitable first principle of religion is the existence of deity. And while, in Turretin's mind, it is not only impious but also irrational to deny that proposition, he reluctantly concedes that atheists have made the existence of God a necessary question. The question is not whether all people have a true and saving knowledge of God through natural revelation, but "whether such a knowledge of the deity is implanted in men by nature, that no one can be wholly ignorant of him; or whether the existence of God can be demonstrated by unanswerable arguments, not only from the Scriptures, but also from nature herself."[55] He explains precisely what is meant by an innate knowledge of deity (*sensus divinitatis*) in the following quotation:

> It makes little difference whether we explain this sense by a natural knowledge of God implanted, or a common notion, or a conception of the mind, or (as more recently) by the idea of God as the most perfect being impressed upon our minds. These all come to the same thing, viz., that there is implanted in each one from his birth a sense of deity which does not allow itself to be concealed and which spontaneously exerts itself in all adults of sound mind. Only let us observe that the idea of God can with less propriety be said to be impressed upon us, if by it is meant a certain intelligible species and image of God in our minds representing to us clearly and distinctly the whatness (*quidditatem*) and essence of God (which both his infinite majesty rejects and our finite and weak intelligence cannot take in).[56]

Universal experience thus confirms that knowledge of the deity is naturally present in all persons but to varying degrees. If this is true, it can be inferred that "what is commonly and immutably in all men without exception must be in them naturally because natural things agree in all and are immutable."[57]

In Turretin's model, the proofs divide into rational and rhetorical categories. Turretin speaks of four foundations of demonstration: 1) the "universal voice of nature"; 2) contemplation of the human being; 3) the "testimony of conscience"; and 4) the general "consent of peoples." In Muller's judgment, "The first of these categories contains all of the standard a posteriori arguments with the exception of Aquinas' third way (which is omitted by Turretin). The second could be viewed as a form of causal argument, but the third and fourth are purely rhetorical."[58]

God is known to exist, first of all, on account of the fact that nature is necessarily contingent and dependent. "Nature proves the being of God," reasons Turretin, "since she proclaims that she not only is, but is from another and could not be without another. For if it is certain and indubitable that out of nothing, nothing is made and that nothing can be the cause of itself . . . , it is also certain that we must grant some first and unproduced being from whom all things are, but who is himself from no one."[59] Given the undesirability of ending up in an infinite regress of causes to explain the origin of the universe, Turretin states: "We must necessarily stop in some cause which is so the first as to recognize no superior,"[60] by which he means God.

The beauty and order of the universe also show that God's existence can be discerned from nature. "For God, the wonderful artificer of the universe," as he eloquently states, "has so deeply stamped upon all its parts the impression of his majesty that what was commonly said of the shield of Minerva (into which Phidias had so skillfully introduced his likeness that it could not be taken out without loosening the whole work) has a far juster application here. God cannot be wrested from nature without totally confusing and destroying it."[61] Thus, if order requires wisdom and intelligence, the most perfect forms of order (such as the movement of heavenly bodies) would naturally suppose the most perfectly necessary and infinite wisdom, which is God. Only blindness and wickedness, Turretin remarks, can keep a person from seeing the wonderful beauty and order of the universe. "So not only do the heavens declare the glory of God, but every blade of grass and flower in the field, every pebble on the shore and every shell in the ocean proclaim not only his power and goodness, but also his manifold wisdom, so near each one that even by feeling, God can be found."[62]

The architecture of the human body, in the second place, is a spectac-ular testament to the Creator's wisdom. Conscious reflection upon the de-sign of the body and the capacities of the mind reveal, in Turretin's judg-ment, a clear witness to divinity. "For whence is the body constructed with such wonderful and truly stupendous skill? . . . Whence the mind, a parti-cle of divine breath, possessed of so many faculties, furnished with so many gifts, unless from a supreme intelligence?"[63] Humanity visibly portrays its prototype, and anyone who stays attentive to the microcosm within "will not only hear and see God present in himself, but also in a manner touch and feel him."[64]

The power and stimulus of conscience, in the third place, testifies to a universally implanted sense of deity. "For how comes it," asks Turretin, "that the conscience is tormented after a crime committed (even in secret and with remote judges), where no danger threatened from men (even in those who held supreme power) unless because it is affected by a most inti-mate sense of deity (as appears from the cases of Nero, Caligula, and oth-ers)?"[65] How can the terrors of conscience be explained when they do not arise from fear of temporal punishment? Why do those who appear to have divested their minds of a sense of deity, tremble at an angry God and im-plore his aid with ejaculatory prayers, when unforeseen danger or sudden fear arises? Turretin retorts, "Willing or unwilling, they must believe that there is a God whom right reason itself teaches them to fear and orders them to recognize as the Lord and Judge of all."[66] Or, as he stated earlier in a slightly different formulation, "Although the knowledge of God is natu-ral, it does not follow that no mortal can deny his existence. For if any have denied him, they have done so not so much through ignorance as through perverseness, their own consciences convicting them. . . . Therefore the reason for the denial was not so much an absolute ignorance of God as their corruption and wickedness choking the implanted knowledge and all but destroying it in order that they might sin more freely."[67]

Widespread belief in deity that ought to be worshipped, in the fourth place, attests to a universally implanted sense of divinity. Indeed, Cicero's observation that no nation is so savage as to deny that God exists, has struck its roots so deeply in the human mind, declares Turretin, "that men would rather believe there is a god than that there is none and preferred to have a false god than no god."[68] The mere existence of atheists should no more be taken as counterevidence to the *sensus divinitatis* than "instances of insanity [should] overturn the definition of man as a rational crea-ture."[69] Since humanity's universal consent to a sense of deity is not reducible to wish fulfillment, state policy, or ancestral tradition, Turretin claims it arises from the evidence of the thing itself. That evidence "is so great that no one possessed of a sound mind can be ignorant of it. It is evident from the most intimate sense of deity, impressed by God upon each one, so as to deprive them of the pretext of ignorance. Since men may understand that there is a God and that he is his maker, they are condemned by their own testimony for not worshipping him."[70]

In addition to the aforementioned points, the institution of religions implies a naturally implanted sense of deity in all persons. For what else would adequately explain the propensity of people toward religion, or would prompt a philosopher such as Plato to call man the most religious animal, unless human beings experience a sense of deity whom they feel compelled to worship. "Nor," reasons Turretin, "would people have been disposed to embrace idolatry even in its most shocking forms and to receive so readily false and counterfeit religions that imposters by political contrivance devised to keep men under subjection, unless they had been impelled by some natural instinct to religion and the worship of some deity."[71] While some nations and persons may be so debased as to appear to have no sense of deity, their darkened state does not mean they are devoid of all knowledge of God. For, as Turretin relates, "There can indeed be barren seeds of religion lying dormant in them (on account of their gross blindness and lust) by which they seem to resemble beasts and brutes, but yet they do remain in them."[72] A similar argument can be made with respect to the "cauterization of conscience" in the wicked, as will be seen in the next section. But the origin, foundation, and nature of the natural moral law must be examined first.

Natural Law and the Natural Right of God

Based on the preceding sections, it is now possible to see both how Turretin's formulation of natural-law doctrine is part of a larger doctrinal complex and how his understanding of natural law is broadly affirmative of the realist natural-law tradition. As might be expected, he discusses the origin, foundation, and nature of natural law under topic eleven ("The Law of God") in the first and second questions. His objective in the first question is to affirm the existence of natural law and to clarify how it differs from the law of Moses, while in the second question it is to specify the sense in which moral precepts are of natural and indispensable right. Turretin's doctrine of natural law is not only systematically arranged (and compactly set forth) but also developed as an apologetic for the indispensability of the moral law over against the excesses associated with some late medieval nominalist doctrines of natural law. Relative to the issues of law and right in topic eleven, and particularly on the indispensability of the precepts, Turretin's position seems to reflect a dual *via antiqua* and Scotist accent, while on the more fundamental issues of the liberty of the divine will[73] and the operation of the divine power[74] addressed in the *locus de Deo,* he seems to adopt the philosophical framework of Scotus's "synchronic contingency" model.[75]

The first question of topic eleven starts off by defining the nature of law and by indicating its multiple uses in theology. Turretin begins his treatment of law by enumerating three basic uses of the *lex moralis;* which, as a starting point, is a fairly standard way of addressing the topic in both Lutheran and Reformed scholastic systems. The law has three principal uses in theology. First, it provides direction for life as "a perfect rule of God's right over man and of man's duty toward God." Second, it provides knowledge of sin, because sin's heinousness is ascertained "from no other source than the law" (Rom. 3:20). Third, it provides preparation for grace in that "from the declaration of man's sin and misery, the necessity of saving grace may be unfolded and a desire for it excited in us" (Gal. 3:24).[76] Like Zanchi, Turretin anticipates a discussion of law in general by analyzing the etymology of the word. The Hebrews employ the word *torah* for law, which in the Hiphel means "to teach," because by it all are reminded of their duty. The Greeks call it *nomos* (from *nemein*), which denotes both "to rule" and "to distribute," because by it all ought to be governed and one's due rendered. The Latins derive it either from *legendo,* because, as Cicero observes, it is usually read when enacted so that it may become known to all or is exposed on public tablets to be read; or inasmuch as *legere* is used for *deligere* because it contains a choice of things to be done or avoided; or finally from *ligando* (according to Thomas Aquinas and most of the scholastics after him), because it binds people as it were by a chain. In this latter sense, remarks Turretin, *laws* are frequently referred to as *bonds* in Scripture (Ps. 2:3; Jer. 5:5).[77]

Scripture itself, moreover, refers to law in different ways. At times, the word *law* is used broadly to signify either the "whole word of God" (Ps. 1:2; 19:7-8), the Pentateuch (Luke 24:44; Rom. 3:21), the old covenant as opposed to the new covenant (Heb. 7:12; John 1:17), the covenant of works versus the covenant of grace (Rom. 6:14), or, most important for us, as "the rule of things to be done and avoided, which God has prescribed to rational creatures under the sanction of rewards and punishments."[78]

These different senses of law can be categorized into natural and positive species, which as Turretin contends, parallel the twofold right of God. "As the right of God is twofold (one natural, founded in the perfectly just and holy nature of God; the other positive, depending on the will of God alone in which he also shows his own liberty), so there is a positive law of God built on the free and positive right of God (with respect to which things are then good because God commands them)."[79] Positive law is law God is free to institute, to withhold, or to suspend as he sees fit. Scriptural examples of positive law are Old Testament restrictions relating to food, cult, and ceremony, in which God freely commands something to be done or avoided because it suits his purpose and not because the law pertains to moral goodness or evil per se. Natural law, however, prescribes indispensable duties to human beings that must be performed by all, always, and everywhere. Turretin describes this species of law: "There is another (natural) founded on the natural right of God, with regard to which things are not called just because they are commanded, but are commanded because they were just and good antecedently to the command of God (being founded on the very holiness and wisdom of God)."[80] The Decalogue (the *lex moralis*) and the natural law, in Turretin's system, refer to substantially the same law: "The moral law is the same as to substance with the natural, which is immutable and founded upon the rational nature; both because the sum of the law . . . is impressed upon man by nature and because all its precepts are derived from the light of nature and nothing is found in them which is not taught by sound reason; nothing which does not pertain to all nations in every age; nothing which it is not necessary for human nature to follow in order to attain its end."[81]

It is possible, moreover, to distinguish between two senses of natural law: a broad and a specific sense. The broad sense refers to what Aquinas called *eternal law*, whose jurisdiction extended to governance of the physical world: inanimate objects, plants, animals, and human society. Turretin, like Zanchi, considers the broad sense to be an improper use of the term *natural law* because it "denotes nothing else than the most wise government of the providence of God over creatures and the most efficacious direction to their ends."[82] Yet, like both Aquinas and Zanchi but unlike Scotus, Turretin holds that "the moral law (which is the pattern of God's image in man)" corresponds with "the eternal and archetypal law in God, since it is its copy and shadow *(aposkimation)*, in which he has manifested his justice and holiness."[83] Taken in its strict and proper sense, therefore, natural law refers to "the practical rule of moral duties to which human beings are bound by nature."[84] Concerning the specific sense, Turretin writes, "it is here inquired whether there is such a natural law of God obtaining among all (as the rule of justice and injustice) antecedently to the positive laws of men; or whether justice and virtue depend upon man's will alone and spring from the consent of human society and are to be measured by each one's own utility."[85] According to him, Reformed orthodoxy affirms the former; libertines such as Thomas Hobbes the latter.

The orthodox position is that natural law arises from God having stamped on the conscience the moral obligation to do that which is good and avoid what is evil (i.e., to use Thomistic terminology, the conscience has been stamped with *per se nota* knowledge of the first precept of law). According to Turretin, Reformed orthodoxy affirms "there is a natural law, not arising from a voluntary contract or law of society, but from a divine obligation being impressed by God upon the conscience of man in his very creation, on which the difference between right and wrong is founded and which contains the practical principles of immovable truth (such as 'God should be worshipped,' 'parents honored,' 'we should live virtuously,' 'injure no one,' 'do to others what we would wish them to do to us' and the like)."[86] So much of the innate knowledge of first principles remains after the fall that no person can escape its force. But this does not negate the epistemological reality that natural knowledge of morality has been, to some extent, corrupted and obscured by sin. Before engaging in a discussion of natural law's origin and foundation, Turretin clarifies precisely what orthodoxy understood by the adjective *natural* in natural law: "Now they wish this law to be called natural, not because it has its origin from bare nature (since it depends upon God the supreme lawgiver), but because it becomes known from the aspect of creatures and of the relation of man to God, and the knowledge of it is impressed upon the mind by nature, not acquired by tradition or instruction."[87]

According to Turretin, natural law originates from the right of nature. To avoid misinterpretation of what the phrase *right of nature* means, however, he distinguishes his usage from the more customary one in the *Corpus Iuris Civilis* (1) and in Justinian's *Institutions* (1.2), where it is defined as "that which nature teaches all animals." The semantic range of the phrase is circumscribed in Turretin's usage to that which pertains only to rational creatures. For this reason, then, he rejects the broader interpretation of the right of nature that historically included the law of nations (common law that all nations use) and the civil law (particular laws that each state or community determines for itself). The right of nature is thus "rightly described by common practical notions, or the light and dictation of conscience (which God has engraven by nature upon every individual, to distinguish between virtue and vice, and to know the things to be avoided and the things to be done)."[88]

Now of the "common practical notions," some are primary (which he calls principles) and others are secondary (called conclusions). Principles, in Turretin's schema, are indispensable, apprehended immediately, oriented to the common good, and with the assistance of reason enable valid conclusions to be drawn. Conclusions, on the other hand, always have the end of the common good in view, and may be "either more near, immediate and (as they say) of the first dictation of nature (which are proximately gathered from the principles and readily come into knowledge); or mediate and more remote (which by remoter consequence and with greater difficulty are deduced from the principles)."[89] Primary notions do not vary, but secondary notions display widespread variation in their applications. While mediate and remoter conclusions more easily succumb to the corrupting effects of sin, the fundamental nature of moral knowledge and obligation is still "the same among all, as to first principles and the immediate conclusions thence deduced."[90] "Although various practical notions have been obscured after sin and for a time even obliterated, it does not follow either that they were entirely extinguished or that they never existed at all. For the commonest principle (that good should be done and evil avoided) is unshaken in all, although in the particular conclusions and in the determinations of it good men may often err because vice deceives us under the appearance and shadow of virtue."[91]

Yet it still remains to be seen on what foundation the right of nature rests. According to Turretin, the right of nature rests on two principal foundations: (1) the nature of God, the Creator; and (2) the condition of rational creatures themselves. In the first instance, the right of nature is thought to rest ultimately on the divine being because God, on the basis of his holiness, prescribes duties to his creatures that proceed directly from his nature. In the second instance, the right of nature is thought to rest proximately on rational creatures who, "on account of their necessary dependence upon God in the genus of morals, no less than in the genus of being, are bound to perform or avoid those things that sound reason and the dictates of conscience enjoin upon them to do or avoid."[92]

Before turning attention to the indispensability of the moral law, which is addressed in the second question of topic eleven, it is important to be clear on how Turretin understands the relationship between the *lex naturalis* and the *lex divina*. How does natural law agree with or differ from the moral law as expressed in the Decalogue? "It agrees as to substance and with regard to principles, but differs as to accidents and with regard to conclusions."[93] Substantively, both types of law prescribe the same duties toward God and neighbor and thus share the same moral content. The principal accidental difference between them pertains to the mode of delivery: "In the moral law, these duties are clearly, distinctly, and fully declared; while in the natural law they are obscurely and imperfectly declared both because many intimations have been lost and obliterated by sin and because it has been variously corrupted by the vanity and wickedness of men (Rom. 1:20-22)."[94] The natural law is written on the heart, is universal in scope, and contains only primary or secondary moral propositions, whereas the moral law is written on stone tablets, is limited to those called by the word, and contains both moral and ceremonial propositions. After the fall, God deemed it necessary to promulgate natural law in written form because, as Turretin exclaims, "so great was the blindness of mind, such the perversity of will and disturbance of the affections that only remains of this law [i.e., natural law] survived in the hearts of all (like rubbed pictures of the same, which on that account ought to be retouched by the voice and hand of God as by a new brush)."[95]

Turretin's treatment of topic eleven's second question, "Whether the precepts of the Decalogue are of natural and indispensable right?" repudiates the speculative excesses associated with certain late medieval nominalist doctrines of natural law. In a straightforward sense, his polemic against those formulations is merely an expansion of his earlier remarks on the twofold right of God, which as we saw established the fundamental categories into which the various species of law were placed. Given this state of affairs, it makes sense to take a close look at Turretin's understanding of the divine right. Analysis of the divine right will illuminate Turretin's position that the precepts of the moral law (but not of the ceremonial or civil law) are of natural right, and so are necessary (not only hypothetically from the sanction of the divine will, but absolutely on the part of the thing itself), and thus incapable of being dispensed with, not only by human beings but also by God.[96]

Corresponding with the twofold right of God, Turretin observes in relation to creatures that the divine right pertains either to dominion or government. Dominion is described as "the right of possessing, disposing and using creatures, as a lord or proprietor, who is able to use and enjoy his own property at pleasure."[97] But government "refers to rational creatures whom [God] governs as ruler and legislator; to whom belong legislation, judgment and execution, so as to have the power of enacting laws, of judging in accordance with them and of carrying out the sentence pronounced."[98] As with law in general, the divine right of government is divided into natural and positive species, which is then applied to creatures:

> the former [i.e., natural], according to which [God] must prescribe to rational creatures their duties (the opposites of which imply a contradiction because they are not founded simply on the divine will, but on the perfection, eminence, holiness, and rectitude of the divine nature); the latter [i.e., positive], however, according to which he freely and from his mere good pleasure prescribes such duties as he either was able not to prescribe, or the opposites of which antecedently to the open intimation of the divine will, he might have willed and enjoined without any prejudice to his perfection and holiness, and without embarrassing contradiction.[99]

Therefore, whatever is connected with the nature, perfection, eminence, or holiness of God (such as primary moral precepts) belongs to natural right. However, all those things of which it cannot be said God was not bound by his nature or in which he could or actually has made some change in the moral obligation (such as the ceremonial laws of the Old Testament) belong to positive right.[100]

Moreover, in addition to the "uncreated" or "primary" natural divine right founded on the very nature and holiness of God and described in the previous paragraph, Turretin now introduces what he calls a "created" or "secondary" natural divine right founded on the nature of things — "according to the constitution established by God and the mutual suitableness or fitness of things to each other."[101] This secondary natural divine right does not enjoy the same degree of necessity or obligation as its primary counterpart: its necessity arises from the order instituted by God (according to which he willed such to be the nature of things *de potentia ordinata*). For, as Turretin explains,

> the former [i.e., primary] is immutably absolute; nor is there any case in which God can relax it because thus he would appear to deny his own nature, on which it is based. Hence he never could command or

approve hatred of himself, idolatry, perjury and falsehood. But the latter [i.e., secondary] (although containing the natural rule of rectitude, because it supposes a certain state of things) could in certain cases (the circumstances of things and persons being altered) be changed, but only by his authority who established it. For example, murder and stealing (forbidden in the sixth and eighth commandments) could become lawful, some circumstance being changed — for instance, a divine command or public authority being given. In this respect, it can be referred to positive right; not indeed absolutely and simply such and merely free (which has no foundation except in the will of God alone), but relatively, inasmuch as (although based upon the order of things and created nature) it can still admit of a change in accordance with the wisdom of the legislator, who established that order.[102]

Thus, in contrast to the primary version, the secondary one is a species of positive right, not absolutely (that is, arising from the will of God alone) but only relatively (that is, arising from the created order of things), so that changes in the moral order can occur "in accordance with the wisdom of the legislator, who established that order."

Thus, it seems, Turretin adopts the fundamental philosophical structure of Scotus's "synchronically contingent" doctrine of natural law (in which the first table belongs to natural law in a strict or proper sense: practical principles known from their terms or conclusions necessarily entailed by such, from which there can be no dispensation even by God himself; whereas the second table belongs to natural law in a secondary or extended sense: precepts that "are exceedingly in harmony" with those of the first table, even though they do not follow necessarily from them). Yet, even in his affirmation of the contingency of the moral order, critical qualifications are placed around both the nature (he rejects an operationalized view of the *potentia absoluta*) and the extent (any dispensation is temporary and circumstantially based) of the moral law's mutability. But has God ever relaxed any moral precept? Turretin's response to that question is more in line with the *via antiqua* than with the *via moderna*. In his judgment, the celebrated "hard cases" of late medieval scholastic disputation — to which he provides alternative explanations — do not demonstrate any *actual* dispensations of the moral law: God's command to "hate" himself (third commandment), to blaspheme (first commandment), to lie (ninth commandment),[103] or to forge the images of the cherubim and the serpent (second commandment),[104] changes in Sabbath observance (fourth commandment),[105]

Christ's command to "hate" one's parents (fifth commandment),[106] the "homicide" of Isaac and the "suicide" of Samson (sixth commandment),[107] the abolition of the natural right to self-defense in Christ's command to love one's enemies (sixth commandment),[108] the introduction and sanction of slavery (eighth commandment),[109] the practice of polygamy among the patriarchs (seventh commandment),[110] the permissibility of divorce (seventh commandment),[111] the theft of Egyptian property (eighth commandment),[112] and Hosea's marriage to Gomer (seventh commandment).[113]

Turretin's categorization of the precepts into natural and positive parallels the prior distinction concerning the divine right, which incidentally has a direct bearing upon why some moral precepts are indispensable and others are *potentially* dispensable in his system. Nearly everyone agrees, on the one hand, "those things that have so close a connection with the nature of God that [the rational creature] cannot but be bound to do them (such as that he should subject himself to and reverence God; should have him for his one only God; and the like), without controversy belong to natural right."[114] And, on the other, those duties that "flow from the free good will of God and that he was perfectly free to establish or not establish, ought to be referred to positive right."[115]

What is up for dispute, however, is precisely which precepts belong to natural right and which to positive right. As will be recalled in Althusius's case, God sometimes relaxes the restrictions of the second table (but never any of the first table), presumably because Althusius thought the moral requirements of those precepts were derivatives of the "created" or "secondary" natural divine right founded on the nature of things, which as Turretin specified above, is a species of divine positive right and thus mutable. In any event, Althusius is clear that the power of dispensation vis-à-vis any precept has not been granted to human beings.[116] This chapter does not arbitrate that dispute but shows instead that Turretin's view of the indispensability of the moral law is continuous in certain respects with the *via antiqua* and Duns Scotus's natural-law doctrine but unsympathetic to the nominalist natural-law theories of William of Occam and Pierre d'Ailly.

Indispensability can be understood in two ways: "either absolutely and simply with respect to God as well as to us; or comparatively and relatively with respect to us and not to God."[117] It follows from this distinction, therefore, that some precepts are absolutely indispensable by God as well as by us, while others are relatively dispensable by God but not by us because, as creatures subject to the moral law, we cannot add to or take away from it. "Yet this is not the case with respect to God, who, as supreme Lord and lawgiver, could in certain cases dispense with some law given by himself without sin."[118] The question, then, is: Are the precepts of the moral law of natural right and thus necessary and incapable of being dispensed with, not only by human beings but also by God? In response, Turretin surveys the "celebrated opinions" of three schools of late medieval thought, which provides him with the opportunity to identify the schools with which he is most closely aligned.

The first, and most extreme, opinion is that all precepts of the moral law are potentially dispensable. The moral law, in this viewpoint, is founded on positive right alone (the free will of God), which means it can be changed at God's good pleasure. According to Turretin, William of Occam, Jean Gerson, Pierre d'Ailly, Almayno, and the Socinians all hold to this position. In the case of Occam et al., he believes their argument stems from "a rash desire to expunge the second precept from the Decalogue and by the power which they claim for their pope of dispensing with the precepts of God."[119] The Socinians, on the other hand, insist upon potential dispensability so the Mosaic law can be shown to be imperfect and in need of correction. Intriguingly, Turretin alludes to the existence of some within the Reformed camp who are also attracted to this opinion: "These are joined by those of our party who maintain that the moral goodness and wickedness of things flows from no other source than the free will of God; so that things are good and just only because they are commanded, not commanded because they were just antecedently. Thus there is nothing to hinder [God's] commanding the contrary to them if he wishes."[120]

The second, and middle, opinion holds that the first three precepts are indispensable, the fourth partially dispensable, and the remaining five fully dispensable. Turretin identifies this position with Duns Scotus and Gabriel Biel, who thought second table precepts should not be seen as belonging to natural divine right. As with the first opinion, some within Reformed orthodoxy "maintain that certain moral precepts of the Decalogue that flow absolutely from the nature of God are absolutely indispensable (such as the first, second, third, seventh, and ninth), but the others, depending upon the free will of God (as the fourth partly, and the fifth, sixth, eighth, and tenth), although immovable and indispensable as to us, still are dispensable as to God (who can for certain reasons command the contrary and yet do nothing repugnant to his own nature)."[121]

The third is the opinion of those (such as Thomas Aquinas, Richard of Middleton, Peter Paludanus, and others) who hold that all precepts of the moral law are indispensable because they each contain "the intrinsic reason of justice and duty; not as proceeding from the law, but as founded on the nature of God and arising from the intrinsic constitution of the thing and the proportion between object and act, compared with right reason or the rational nature."[122] According to Turretin, the third is the common opinion among the orthodox — at least on this particular point — and the one to which he also subscribes, but with the following qualification: All moral precepts are not equally based on the primary right of nature. Some descend in an absolute sense from God's nature and "command such things as God wills most freely indeed but yet necessarily (and so necessarily and immutably that he cannot will the contrary without a contradiction)."[123] Others, however, flow from the constitution of the nature of things (the free will of God coming in between) "so they should not be thought to hold an equal degree of necessity and immutability."[124] In the case of the latter, states Turretin, "Although a dispensation properly so called does not have place in them, still a declaration or interpretation is sometimes given concerning them, the circumstances of the things or persons being changed."[125] He provides technical definitions of the terms *dispensation* and *declaration* or *interpretation* at the outset of question two: "Obligation is the right of the law over man on account of which the man who is under law is bound to obey it. Dispensation is when, in any case in which the law really prevails and obliges, the obligation of the law is taken away from some man in particular, the rest remaining under obligation. A declaration or interpretation of law is when it is declared that the law does not bind in a particular case."[126]

Conclusion

For our purposes, there are three critical points with respect to Francis Turretin's theological system. First, analysis of Turretin's prolegomena uncovers not only a high degree of doctrinal sophistication in comparison with such early Reformers as Luther, Calvin, and Zwingli, but also seamless integration of the doctrines of natural revelation, natural theology, and natural law. Second, Turretin's doctrine of God and ethics are symbiotically interconnected, which as such provided Reformed orthodoxy with a further line of defense against the emerging rationalism (à la Amyraldianism) already apparent in Geneva at the end of the seventeenth century. Third, and following from both of the preceding points, Turretin's doctrine of natural law is part of a larger complex of related doctrines, while at the same time his formulation of natural law is broadly affirmative of the realist natural-law tradition (in its Thomist and Scotist trajectories). Turretin's repudiation of nominalist natural-law theories should be understood as stemming primarily from what he said concerning the natural right of God and from his concern to uphold the stability of the moral law in a way that is characteristic of the *via antiqua*.

Conclusion

The preceding chapters have shown that the Reformed wing of the magisterial Reformation inherited the natural-law tradition as a noncontroversial legacy of late medieval scholasticism, even though twentieth-century representatives of the Reformed tradition — Karl Barth, G. C. Berkouwer, Herman Dooyeweerd, and Cornelius Van Til — have typically rejected that tradition because it allegedly glossed over the noetic effects of sin on the natural human faculties and because it was ostensibly based on a dualistic nature-grace dichotomy. Both of these criticisms — which are reiterated many times over in the scholarship of those representatives — are sharpened to a fine point in Barth's angry response to Brunner in the 1934 debate. Apart from the event of God's self-revelation in Jesus Christ, Barth argues humanity possesses no "capacity for revelation" or even "the possibility of being addressed."[1] In Barth's judgment, Brunner's natural theology meant humanity possessed an inherent natural capacity to receive soteriologically weighted revelation, not merely the natural knowledge of God's eternal power and divine nature that nullifies every possible excuse for breaking the moral law. Thus, if humanity could "somehow" and "to some extent"[2] know and do God's will apart from a special divine encounter as Brunner now held, it was clear to Barth his co-conspirator had become essentially indistinguishable from "a Thomist" or "a neo-Protestant modernist."[3]

What changed in the minds of Protestant theologians to shift from viewing the natural knowledge of God as a hallmark of orthodoxy to a harbinger of modernism? While a comprehensive treatment of this question would take many more pages to develop than remain in this book, it is possible to suggest a preliminary answer by sketching a brief history of intellectual developments within Protestant theology and ethics from the seventeenth to the twentieth century. This narrative, which merely touches upon an assortment of seminal figures involved in the emergence and development of the modern natural-law tradition, commences with the widespread desire for peace and religious toleration that settled over Europe in the aftermath of the intraconfessional warfare of the sixteenth and seventeenth centuries. The main Protestant theologians and jurists associated with this movement, unlike their scholastic and orthodox counterparts, demonstrate strong theological affinities with Remonstrant and Socinian thought. With the Socinians, they share the belief that the fall did not fundamentally mar human rational capacities; with the Remonstrants, they rely upon reason to establish the probability of Christian teachings and to furnish the foundation upon which theological doctrines are built and ultimately authenticated.

Although it is a commonplace among legal and moral historians that the Reformation began to unravel the stable medieval synthesis of natural law, reason, and human moral obligation, such a claim is difficult to sustain with respect to the representatives of Reformed orthodoxy in this book. However, when the Protestant tradition is viewed in a broad and undifferentiated way, it is possible to see why certain key legal and moral theorists in the seventeenth century would be regarded as the architects of the modern, secularized natural-law tradition.

It was the Anglican Thomas Hobbes (1588-1679) who first formulated an internally consistent contractual theory of the state free of any trace of higher law. According to him, the first precept of the law of nature (in the sense of the most primitive natural instinct) is self-preservation.[4] Once stripped of all appearances of stability and civilization, the primeval human condition was one in which individuals, isolated and unsupported by any mutually reinforcing association, were the potential prey of every other individual. This meant the natural self-preservation instinct was felt in the form of constant apprehension and the life of the primeval individual was, in Hobbes's famous phrase, "solitary, poor, nasty, brutish, and short."[5] Always at war with one's neighbors, then, the primeval individual could enjoy neither security nor even the elementary comforts of life, and was deprived of a life free from chaos and disorder. The only means of escape from such a dismal existence was, as Hobbes taught, for individuals to surrender their sovereignty and independence to the rule of an absolute sovereign, whose principal role was to guarantee the security of all without prejudice.[6] As legal historian J. M. Kelly observes, "Hobbes's form of social contract is thus one of subjection, and the subjection was to a sovereign, whose name (and the name of Hobbes's book) has become proverbial for the ruler of an absolutist state: *Leviathian*."[7] Hobbes's appeal to the law of nature in the *Leviathian* is not to a transcendent moral standard believed to undergird all forms of law as the medievals held, but rather to a body of prudential maxims based upon empirical observation and materialist psychology and designed to improve the desperate and fragile condition of humanity in the state of nature. In disavowing the transcendent validity of natural law, Hobbes broke with both the realist and nominalist natural-law traditions of the late medieval era.

Likewise in the seventeenth century, the Dutch Remonstrant theologian Hugo de Groot, or Grotius (1583-1645), pioneered a middle way between the Augustinian-Thomistic tradition of a divinely implanted natural law, which had retained its vitality in such figures as Sir John Fortescue (ca. 1394-1476), Richard Hooker (1554-1600), and the later Puritan divines, and the merely prudential system of Hobbes. Grotius's theory of natural law, although influenced significantly by late medieval voluntarism, falls squarely within the stream of philosophical realism or essentialism found in Thomas Aquinas, Duns Scotus, Francisco Suárez, and the Spanish jurist-theologians of Salamanca. In Kelly's judgment, the Grotian mediating position had "been prefigured by several catholic writers of the later Middle Ages, but was first thoroughly elaborated into a system by . . . [Grotius], [who is] regarded as the founder of modern international law."[8]

Grotius's involvement in various political and theological controversies forced him to spend much of his life in exile; in fact, his magnum opus *De iure belli et pacis* (1625) was written while he lived in Paris and worked in the diplomatic service of the king of Sweden. According to J. M. Kelly, Grotius's great work "sought to articulate rules of engagement to lessen the atrocities of war, atrocities he noted that were far worse in the contemporary Thirty Years War in Germany than in the Dutch revolt from Spain. Grotius's reputation as the founder of international law is due to him having put the subject of a law binding nations into a common legal order on a thoroughly organized and scientific basis."[9]

At the heart of Grotius's treatment of international law is the notion that humans possess "not only a strong bent toward social life . . . but also a power of discrimination that enables [them] to decide what things are agreeable or harmful (as to both things present and things to come)."[10] Whatever is at variance with such judgments is understood to be contrary also to the law of nature, that is, to the divinely implanted knowledge of right and wrong insinuated into every human mind at creation. According to Grotius, this understanding of human sociality and natural law would have validity even if God, hypothetically speaking, did not exist or had not been interested in human affairs. "What we have been saying," writes Grotius, "would have a degree of validity even if we should concede that which cannot be conceded without the utmost wickedness, that there is no God, or that the affairs of men are of no concern to him. The very opposite of this view has been implanted in us partly by reason, partly by unbroken tradition, and confirmed by many proofs as well as by miracles attested by all ages."[11] While being openly critical of the bloody intraconfessional warfare that continued to wound and divide Christendom, in Kelly's estimation, Grotius's hypothetical divorce of "natural law from a divine being (though he himself disclaimed belief in any such separation, and actually ascribed natural law to God as its author) was bound to recommend his construction to a Protestant world suspicious of all doctrine carrying a whiff of the medieval Catholic world of St. Thomas."[12]

Grotius's starting point, in converting natural law into a set of legal principles to govern international relations, was the notion — later articulated more fully by Samuel von Pufendorf (1632-1694), professor of law at Heidelberg and afterwards at Lund in Sweden, in *De officio hominis et civis* — that humans are by nature sociable. "But among the traits characteristic of man is an impelling desire for society, that is, for the social life — not of any and every sort, but peaceful, and organized according to the measure of intelligence, with those who are of his own kind; this social trend the Stoics called 'sociableness.' Stated as a universal truth, therefore, the assertion that every animal is impelled by nature to seek only its good cannot be conceded."[13] A paragraph later he specifies more precisely just what social life organized according to intelligence means: "This maintenance of the social order, which we have roughly sketched, and which is consonant with human intelligence, is the source of law properly so called. To this sphere of law belong the abstaining from that which is another's, the restoration to another of anything of his which we may have, together with any gain which we may have received from it; the obligation to fulfill promises, the making good of a loss incurred through our fault, and the inflicting of penalties upon men according to their deserts."[14]

Despite Grotius's repeated affirmations of God as the ultimate source and promulgator of law, his famous hypothetical formula *etsiami daretur non esse Deum* ("even if we should concede that which cannot be conceded without the utmost wickedness, that there is no God"), relates Kelly, "was to be decisive in unhooking the doctrine of natural law — in the ethical sense, not as a prudential derivative of desire to cure a savage state of nature — from theology."[15] When viewed from the perspective of later writers such as Pufendorf and the fatigue experienced by Europeans generally in the wake of the religious wars, it is not surprising that Grotius's hypothesis would spark interest in formulating a science of morals free of any connection with divine revelation, and derivable strictly from rationalistic premises.[16]

In Germany, Pufendorf was part of the post-scholastic Lutheran reaction to Grotius. The German debate principally focused on the relationship between natural law and moral theology, with most orthodox Lutherans insisting the former was based on the latter. According to Knud Haakonssen, in rejecting certain scholastic doctrinal formulations (the relics of the *imago Dei*), orthodox Lutherans "rejected the possibility that men could have any rational knowledge of God's nature on the basis of which they could draw moral lessons for themselves — technically expressed, for example, as a denial that we can know that the natural law 'participates' in God's eternal law."[17] Where Luther had made practical use of natural law in the earthly realms of law, politics, economics, and ethics, Pufendorf now sought to develop a complete science of morals that could be sustained on exclusively earthly or scientific (that is, rational) grounds. Pufendorf's insistence on the scientific character of natural law, inspired by Cartesianism and by Hobbes, was, he thought, "a renewal of Grotius's ambition to use mathematics as the guiding ideal for natural law, an ideal mostly submerged by [Grotius's] humanist learning."[18]

Like Hobbes, Pufendorf thought the fundamental features of human nature were reducible to a constant concern for self-preservation, need for assistance from others, sociability, and the recognition of one's inability to provide for one's own security.[19] Thus groups of people would eventually invent moral rules (or conventions) that enable them to live together and to form institutions for their mutual benefit. Like Grotius, however, Pufendorf acknowledged that the divine will generates the moral obligation implicit in the law of nature.[20] Yet, as Haakonssen observes, "the rest of morals [particularly the rules or conventions] is thus a human creation of which we have 'maker's knowledge,' that is, demonstrative knowledge. In this respect, as in many others, Pufendorf's theory is clearly a precursor of Locke's in the *Essay Concerning Human Understanding*."[21] If the primary accent in Pufendorf's theory of natural law is on self-preservation, then moral obligation reduces to a form of Hobbesian self-interest. But if the primary accent is on human sociability, then, as Haakonssen shows, an interesting dilemma arises. "Sociability can be understood as a given, ultimate feature of human nature. This would dispense with any role for the Deity, except as creator. Morals would be entirely self-contained as a human enterprise, and the discipline dealing with it, natural jurisprudence, would be completely segregated from all theology. This segregation was one of Pufendorf's main concerns, and there is therefore a strong case for interpreting sociability as a natural ability or inclination."[22]

The ambiguities in Pufendorf's moral theory occasioned a fierce debate in German theological circles that lasted well into the eighteenth century. The fundamental questions concerned the role of God in the moral world and, following from that, the relationship between theological ethics and natural law. From one side, Pufendorf was accused of being Hobbesian, or as Haakonssen says, "of excluding God from human morals by making the content of the latter entirely dependent upon post-lapsarian human nature and its exertions."[23] From the other side, he "was charged with ascribing to God, if not too large a role, at least a mistaken one, by making all obligation dependent upon God's will."[24] Valentin Alberti (1635-1697), the orthodox Lutheran theologian, advanced the Hobbesian critique of Pufendorf's theory of natural law. Alberti argued natural law could be derived only from a pre-lapsarian knowledge of human innocence (*status integritatis*) as presented in special revelation. "To base any universal natural law on the de facto sociality of fallen human nature instead of on the original human nature which God created in the purity of his own image was [for Alberti] plainly as impossible as it was impious."[25]

The chief supporter of Pufendorf's thesis concerning the sharp separation of natural law and theological ethics was his influential disciple, the Pietist Lutheran theologian Christian Thomasius (1655-1728). In his monumental *Institutiones jurisprudentiae divinae* (1688), Thomasius maintained the independence of natural law from special revelation by arguing in effect that "we cannot rationally know more about God's authorship of the law than the mere fact and that we can learn the rest from human rationality considered as a social practice."[26] After experiencing a period of intense self-doubt, Thomasius restates his position in *Fundamenta juris naturae et gentium* (1705) to lessen the agnosticism of his earlier formulation, where, in Haakonssen's summary, he "reduces the status of *ius naturae* from one of law proper to that of divine advice or a matter of conscience and stresses the role of positive law and social morality."[27]

Throughout the eighteenth century writers on legal subjects tended to acknowledge a law of nature in terms of reason and rational nature, even as its relationship to the medieval theology that had given it shape was gradually dissociated. This is not to imply that all references to God were either nonexistent or merely ornamental in the great natural jurisprudential systems of the century. However, as Kelly recounts, "Particularly in Germany, natural law was taken — of course in the secular sense which Grotius had given to it — to be a material from which whole systems of municipal law could be fashioned, just as Grotius had extracted from it a structure of international law."[28] German universities soon became the settings within which the architectonic study of natural law, natural jurisprudence, and positive law occurred. "The first chair formally devoted to the law of nature had been Pufendorf's at Heidelberg in the previous century, but such professorships now proliferated, and in the eighteenth century were standard features of the German centers of learning."[29]

The most celebrated proponent of this approach was the Pietist philosopher Christian Wolff (1679-1754), professor at Marburg and at Halle. In his juridical works, Wolff attempted to deduce an entire system of law from a purely theoretical starting point. In the 1740s he produced an eight-volume work in which he presented a jurisprudential system based on his theory of human nature. He later incorporated this material, along with a system of international law, into the *Institutiones* of 1752, which, according to the title, addressed "the law of nature and of nations, in which all rights and all obligations are deduced, by an unbroken chain of connection, from man's own nature."[30] The fundamental axiom of Wolff's system is that human nature tends toward its own perfection. From that starting point he derives the primary legal injunction, namely, to facilitate human beings in advancing to the most perfect condition possible. The corresponding moral injunction, therefore, is to strive toward this condition for oneself, and to shun all acts inhibiting one's progression. Beyond one's duty to oneself, which is primary, one also has secondary obligations to assist in the perfection of one's neighbors. However, the duty to perfect one's neighbor takes second place to the duty to perfect oneself. Still, the obligation not to retard the progression of one's neighbor is absolute. In Wolff's scheme, states Kelly, "These general propositions represented man's goals set by the law of nature; but as the achievement of a goal requires access to appropriate means, the law of nature also authorizes the provision of such means."[31] From the rational premise that all people are by nature equal, Wolff deduced a range of human rights such as liberty, security, and the right of self-defense. "Into this frame of theory Wolff was able to fit, under one head or another, the entire body of contemporary positive law."[32] Wolff's rationalist approach to law, philosophy, biblical studies, and a range of other subjects exerted considerable influence on such contemporaries as Emmerich de Vattel (1714-1767), Immanuel Kant (1724-1804), and Johann Salomo Semler (1725-1791).[33]

In Geneva of the late seventeenth century many of the same tendencies apparent in Germany and France were beginning to show up in the heirs of Reformed orthodoxy. By the late eighteenth century the triumph of reason over revelation succeeded in dismantling the hard-won scholastic theological achievements of Francis Turretin. This eclipse was achieved through the work of key members in the theology department at the Academy of Geneva. At the forefront of the movement known as Enlightened Orthodoxy was Jean-Alphonse Turretin (1671-1737), rector and professor of theology at the Academy and the son of Francis Turretin (1623-1687), the stalwart defender of Reformed orthodoxy against Remonstrant, Socinian, and Salmurian theology in Geneva.

Francis Turretin's successors developed new and expanded uses for reason in theological discourse, principally in the area of natural theology. "Natural theology was important," recounts Martin Klauber, "because it provided common ground for discussion with the unbeliever or the deist. It was the least objectionable form of revelation and helped to make Christianity a reasonable faith."[34] Jean-Alphonse and his successor to the chair of theology at the Academy, Jacob Vernet (1698-1789), felt the only effective way to respond to deism and atheism, the most formidable challenges at the time to the Christian faith, was to abandon the "doctrinaire" and "arcane" Reformed scholastic formulations and to construct a more simplified system of natural theology that would serve as a nearly independent source of religious and moral knowledge.[35] Although they did not completely replace Scripture with natural religion, they "gave rational arguments equality with biblical revelation, stating that both are in complete harmony."[36] They treated natural theology as the necessary prerequisite for special revelation, and considered self-evident principles (such as that the whole is greater than the part, each is to be rendered its due, and the same thing cannot both exist and not exist at the same time) to be foundational to natural theology.[37] Unfortunately, as history would show in the aftermath of David Hume's (1711-1776) devastating critique of theoretical and practical reason, the Enlightened Orthodox strategy of defending the Christian faith through extensive use of natural theology would instead increase the onus against it.

In the wake of Louis XIV's Revocation of the Edict of Nantes (1685),

it is not surprising to find French Huguenot intellectuals turning to a secularized version of natural-law theory to demonstrate what held state and
society together in the absence of religious affiliations. Interestingly, while
the two leading theorists — Pierre Bayle (1647-1706) and Pierre Jurieu
(1637-1713) — both drew from a common fund of natural-law authorities
emphasizing the role of conscience, they developed very different religious
and political strategies for action. As T. J. Hochstrasser puts it, "While both
Bayle and Jurieu started from the claims of conscience, that *pointe de l'âme*,
which neither could nor should be the subject of coercion by government
or by the church of the majority, Bayle supported absolutism in politics and
toleration of religious diversity, while Jurieu supported popular sovereignty
in the political sphere and the maintenance of religious uniformity."[38]

Bayle's support for absolutism derived from his understanding of the
doctrines of election and original sin: apart from the elect, most in society
were so fallen and corrupt that the rule of an absolute monarch was necessary to keep them in tow. Since the only true believers were the elect, it
made very little sense in Bayle's mind to devote much attention to the outward forms and expressions of religion, as no clear link between moral
practice and election could be demonstrated. "For this reason," remarks
Hochstrasser, "even atheists could form functional societies and ancient
history served amply to prove this point. If it were the case that true religion was a matter of the inward relationship between the 'wandering conscience' of the individual and God, then toleration was the morally correct
position for the state to adopt, as persecution could only touch externals
and, by encouraging a mere surface conformity, breed hypocritical subjects."[39] Although Bayle's political views were unpopular among Huguenots of the diaspora, his understanding of toleration and his distaste for
externalist approaches to religion were easily detached from his Augustinian pessimism and justified on rationalistic premises, "notably those used
by Locke in his contemporaneous *Letter on Toleration*."[40] Yet Bayle's account of toleration is not a rights-based account in the Lockean tradition.
Rather, as Hochstrasser urges, Bayle is "a participant in the discourse of
natural jurisprudence, in that he uses natural law arguments to support his
view that sound moral intuitions are accessible to reason."[41] If atheists and
Christians could coexist together by means of natural law, then it seemed to
Bayle that religious refugees posed no real threat to the civil authority.

The opposite pattern emerged in the case of Jurieu, relates Hochstrasser, "whose militant politics were in tune with the first phase of refu-
gee politics (being especially well received by those Protestants still in

France who had access to the pages of the *Pastoral Letters*), but lost popularity later partly through an intolerant refusal to allow for diversity of religious belief and even more because his prophetic dreams of ultimate Protestant triumphalism and imminent papal apocalypse were shown to be mistaken."[42] For Jurieu, tolerance would only lead to religious indifference among the populace and would alienate the secular powers without whose assistance Christianity would have never established itself in the first place. In his mind, "it was axiomatic that to tolerate religious minorities was incompatible with the security of the state, as religious pluralism must lead inexorably to political dissent."[43] Thus the purpose of his dissident *Pastoral Letters* "was not so much to incite the rebellion of French Protestants directly, but to justify to them the invasion of England by William of Orange and so raise their hopes of a similar invasion of France. Nevertheless, this was not how they were read by Bayle, who viewed Jurieu's populism as a disastrous messianic delusion which would only antagonize Louis XIV further, rendering the circumstances of Protestants within France and in the *Refuge* much more difficult."[44]

The Treaty of Rijswijk (1697) at the end of the War of the League of Augsburg (1689-1697) showed the Huguenot refugees there was no hope of a return from exile or a reprieve of Protestant persecution in France. Bayle's advocacy of political absolutism and Jurieu's apocalyptic predictions and arguments for religious uniformity now seemed distant and discredited. The new generation of intellectuals — of whom Jean Barbeyrac (1674-1744) was one — preferred to pursue a strategy of assimilation while retaining a strong commitment to civil toleration, as Bayle had proposed. Barbeyrac, known widely for his French translations of the major works in the early modern natural-law tradition by Grotius, Pufendorf, and Cumberland, exerted great influence in his modest role as translator, mediator, critic, and interpreter of these works. In Hochstrasser's judgment, the distinctiveness of Barbeyrac's work consists in the emphasis placed on the conscience and its regulation of the public expression of religious belief. Barbeyrac equated conscience with the dictates of natural reason and then developed "a version of the sociability thesis that owed rather more to Grotian natural benevolence and to Locke than to Pufendorf's more utilitarian view."[45] Jean-Jacques Burlamaqui (1694-1748), Barbeyrac's younger contemporary and professor of natural and civil law at Geneva, "follows Barbeyrac in mitigating the harsher aspects of Pufendorf's theory with recourse to Grotius and Locke; but he also adds elements of Wolffian natural law theory. . . . He follows Pufendorf and Barbeyrac in still upholding the residual right of the sovereign to define and control the content of natural religion, but believes he can avert any authoritarian dangers implicit in this concession by building provisos around his concept of sovereignty that guarantee the rights of subjects."[46]

In the eighteenth and nineteenth centuries, it was standard practice for Protestant theologians to formulate natural theological arguments as demonstrations of God's existence, the immortality of the soul, and the elementary content of morality. Samuel Clarke (1675-1729), Joseph Butler (1692-1752), William Paley (1743-1805), and Thomas Chalmers (1780-1847) were prominent theologians who thought Christian doctrine not only could but also should be proved through the use of logic and rational argumentation. In this respect, therefore, they sought to articulate distinctively Christian doctrines such as the Trinity and the two natures of Christ in rational terms and then to engage the objections of critics through a vast array of apologetical treatises, many of which exerted influence on Protestant theologians well into the nineteenth century. This influence can be detected in the orthodox Presbyterian Charles Hodge (1797-1878), professor of systematic theology and principal of Princeton Seminary, who made references throughout his *Systematic Theology* to the works of Clarke, Butler, Paley, and Chalmers. In one such instance, in the context of developing a biblical argument in support of natural theology, he wrote, "It cannot, therefore, be reasonably doubted that not only the being of God, but also his eternal power and Godhead, are so revealed in his works, as to lay a stable foundation for natural theology. To the illustration of this subject many important works have been devoted, a few of which are the following: 'Wolf de Theologia Naturali,' 'The Bridgewater Treatises,' Butler's 'Analogy,' Paley's 'Natural Theology.'"[47]

The nineteenth-century Dutch Reformed theologian Herman Bavinck (1854-1921), although a staunch defender of philosophical realism and the natural knowledge of God, was more wary than Hodge of the rationalist tenor in Clarke, Butler, and Paley. He attributed the decline of Protestant theology after 1750 to the predominance of two intellectual streams: Socinian rationalism and Pietistic mysticism.[48] These streams, wrote Bavinck, "represent the mystical and the rational element in religion and theology. Socinianism remains caught up in the Catholic separation of nature and grace and develops it into an antithesis in which nature in the end completely banishes grace. . . . Man, being of the earth, and therefore earthly, has nothing in common with God except dominion, power, and free will, but not knowledge, righteousness, or life. . . . Anabaptism proceeds from the same basic idea: the natural and the supernatural, the human and the divine, stand irreconcilably side by side. But whereas Socinianism abandons grace in favor of nature, Anabaptism sacrifices nature to grace. Adam was 'of the earth earthly' (1 Cor. 15:47); creation and all of nature is of a lower order: material, physical, carnal, impure."[49]

To avert the rationalist and subjectivist shoals of nineteenth-century liberalism, Bavinck sought to develop a philosophical foundation via ordinary experience upon which to erect his orthodox Reformed dogmatics: "The starting point of the theory of knowledge ought to be ordinary daily experience, the universal and natural certainty of human beings concerning the objectivity and truth of their knowledge."[50] By trusting our senses, he reasoned, we are led to believe in an objective world external to us, and our mental representations of that world point back to that reality. Thus he develops a religious epistemology that is universal, intuitive, immediate, and self-evident: akin, it could be said, to the "certainty of faith." Bavinck saw that Christian thinkers from Augustine to Aquinas and through the Reformed scholastics rejected various forms of rationalism and empiricism in favor of a philosophical realism that acknowledges the primacy of the senses and the constraints placed by reality on the human mind.[51] Instead of rejecting natural theology and natural law as species of "Thomism" and "neo-Protestant modernism" as Barth and a host of twentieth-century theologians would do, Bavinck reaffirmed the philosophical and theological categories of catholic Christianity, and on that basis worked to construct a Reformed dogmatics that would address the issues and concerns of his own generation.

One of the primary sources of twentieth-century Protestant suspicion toward the natural-law tradition was, as we saw in the Introduction, its close association with Roman Catholic moral theology. Because natural law not only arose from but also received sophisticated doctrinal definition in the patristic and medieval eras of Christian theology, twentieth-century Protestant theologians and ethicists have been reluctant to authorize its use in contemporary theological ethics. The fundamental problem with this position is that it rests on faulty assumptions regarding the nature and scope of the reform effort in the sixteenth century, as Richard Muller points out.

> The Reformation, in spite of its substantial contribution to the history of doctrine and the shock it delivered to theology and the church in the sixteenth century, was not an attack upon the whole of medieval theology or upon Christian tradition. The Reformation assaulted a limited

spectrum of doctrinal and practical abuses with the intention of reaffirming the values of the historical church catholic. Thus, the mainstream Reformers reconstructed the doctrines of justification and the sacraments and then modified their ideas of the *ordo salutis* and of the church accordingly; but they did not alter the doctrines of God, creation, providence, and Christ, and they maintained the Augustinian tradition concerning predestination, human nature and sin. The reform of individual doctrines, like justification and the sacraments, occurred within the bounds of a traditional, orthodox, and catholic system that, on the grand scale, remained substantively unaltered.[52]

For Barth, Berkouwer, Dooyeweerd, and Van Til, by contrast, the Protestant Reformers intended to make a clean and total break with Rome, which, if applied as an historical and methodological assumption, renders moot any substantive investigation of continuities and discontinuities in Protestant doctrinal formulation with earlier periods of Christian theology. It also undermines any attempt to recover the catholicity of Protestant doctrinal and ethical formulations in relation to the broader and older Christian traditions of the West and the East.

Such an assumption is implicit, for example, in Barth's response to Brunner's appeal to Calvin. To support his case for a Christian natural theology, Brunner cited a broad array of texts from Calvin's corpus (126 citations) to establish the feasibility of his theses. Barth reeled at Brunner's suggestion and informed readers he had asked his brother, Peter Barth, to look into Brunner's claim in a longer and forthcoming historical essay in the periodical *Theologische Existenz heute,*[53] which, as it turns out, precipitated additional responses that would preoccupy Calvin scholars for a significant portion of the twentieth century, as we saw in Chapter One.

Barth rejected Brunner's appeal to Calvin because, above all, he thought it rested on an insufficient appreciation of the Reformer's place in the history of dogma. For better or worse, held Barth, Luther and Calvin failed to strike the root of the problem with Roman Catholicism. Yet to their credit, in Barth's words, they decisively treated "the material problem of the relation between the will and work of man and the reconciliation once and for all effected in Christ"[54] that had sprung up in the Pelagian formulations of the later nominalists. However, what they left undone was to clarify "the problem of the *formal* relation between reason with its interpretation of nature and history, on the one hand, and the absolute claims of revelation, on the other."[55]

In Barth's judgment, the Reformers did not follow through the logic of their material criticism of Roman Catholic works righteousness. Had they taken a supposedly more consistent and straightforward interpretation of *sola gratia-sola fide,* they would have opted for an actualistic theology of revelation like his, instead of maintaining the traditional Augustinian distinction between humanity's destroyed supernatural endowments and corrupted natural endowments, including the natural knowledge of God.[56] That this was indeed Barth's viewpoint can be seen from the following lengthy quotation:

> The Reformers did not perceive the extent to which even *Augustine,* to whom they were so fond of appealing, has to be regarded as a Roman Catholic theologian, and the reserve with which he has therefore to be taken. Hence they were not in a position to foresee all the reservations with which Roman Catholic theology has since, i.e., since the rediscovery of St. Thomas, learnt to surround its (materially unchanged) definitions. For the substance of these definitions has since, in an idealist form, i.e., in that of a secularized Thomism (which has found its mature form in Schleiermacher's *Glaubenslehre*), but without consciousness of its real connections, become part of the armory of modernist Protestantism. If we really wish to maintain the Reformers' position over against that of Roman Catholicism and neo-Protestantism, we are not in a position today to repeat the statements of Luther and Calvin without at the same time making them more pointed than they themselves did.[57]

This paragraph calls attention to Barth's desire to go further than the Reformers in repudiating the Augustinian deposit in prolegomena because of its so-called Roman Catholic roots and its secularized reappearance in nineteenth-century liberalism. In fairness to Barth, it is also worth mentioning here that Brunner shared Barth's disdain for Augustine's legacy in Protestant theology, especially concerning two key doctrines: the relics of the *imago Dei* and original sin.[58]

Given both the magnitude of Barth's influence in twentieth-century theology and the sheer force of his ire against natural theology, it is not difficult to understand why questions pertaining to antecedent intellectual influences (such as Aristotle and the medieval debates) on the Reformers and Reformed orthodoxy would fall on such hard times in contemporary Protestant and Reformed theology. A principal issue raised by the Barth-Brunner debate that requires further attention, though it is beyond the scope of the present investigation, concerns the nature of the relationship between Protestantism and Thomism in the Reformation and post-Reformation eras. As David Steinmetz has observed in relation to Luther, "The story of Thomas Aquinas and Protestantism has yet to be written, and it is not identical with the story of Thomas and Luther."[59] On a related point, but arising from the research of Chapter Two, more historical and systematic analysis is needed to clarify the nature of the relationship between the intellect and will *post-lapsum* in the ethics of Reformed orthodoxy.

A secondary but no less important issue apparent both in the Barth-Brunner debate and the anti-scholastic milieu of twentieth-century theology was, as we have seen, that scholars assumed, tacitly at the very least, a view of Calvin as the chief early codifier of Reformed doctrine. An unfortunate consequence of this assumption in the Barth-Brunner debate was that it set historical and theological parameters that would seldom be questioned or modified as battle lines were drawn by partisans of both sides in the twentieth-century debate over the knowledge of God and the integrally related doctrines of natural theology and natural law.

As argued in Chapter One, the debate had two significant and long-term consequences for the twentieth-century Protestant theological appropriation of the natural-law tradition. First, theologically, it brought into question the legitimate and circumscribed use of natural law in Reformed ethics by identifying it as a "Thomistic" and "neo-Protestant" doctrine and, therefore, too rationalistic in its formulation of the *imago Dei*, sin, and the natural human faculties. Second, historically, and resulting from the preceding theological consequence, subsequent discussion of natural law in most cases did not examine how Protestant orthodoxy had modified the medieval natural-law tradition it received through the Reformers. The focus of most commentators instead was on whether John Calvin had either formulated a doctrine of natural law or could be said to have laid the foundation for a doctrine of natural law. As a result, twentieth-century discussion of the place of natural law in Reformed theological ethics largely overlooked any precedent it may have had in Reformed orthodoxy, which left many contemporary theologians without a sound basis from which to resist adopting the widely publicized Barthian objections to natural theology and natural law. Moreover, as history shows, to the extent that Protestant and Reformed theologians endorsed Barth's theological and philosophical presuppositions, they tended to develop divine command theories with many of the same problems (such as actualism and occasionalism) that were already evident in his own theory.[60]

Since 1990 there has been an identifiable resurgence of interest in the natural-law tradition by Protestant historians, theologians, ethicists, and social commentators. Understandably, in light of the immense number of twentieth-century studies devoted to Calvin's theology, these Protestant authors more frequently appeal to him than to any other Protestant theologian for assistance in formulating a doctrine of natural law. However, to avert a relapse of the Calvin as chief early codifier thesis among those currently interested in natural law, the scope of the discussion should be expanded beyond Calvin to include his contemporaries and Reformed orthodox successors. While this study has centered around Peter Martyr Vermigli, a fellow Reformer and older contemporary of Calvin, and the Reformed scholastics Jerome Zanchi, Johannes Althusius, and Francis Turretin, the scope could even be widened beyond them to include Martin Bucer (1491-1551),[61] Philip Melanchthon (1497-1560),[62] Wolfgang Musculus (1497-1563),[63] Heinrich Bullinger (1504-1575),[64] Theodore Beza (1519-1605),[65] Lambert Daneau (1530-1595),[66] Zacharius Ursinus (1534-1583),[67] Andrew Willet (1562-1621),[68] Bartholomaeus Keckermann (1571-1609),[69] William Ames (1576-1633),[70] Anthony Burgess (d. 1664),[71] Edward Leigh (1602-1671),[72] Adrianus Heereboord (1614-1661),[73] Richard Baxter (1615-1691),[74] Stephen Charnock (1628-1680),[75] Matthew Henry (1662-1714),[76] and many others.

Where Barth, Berkouwer, Dooyeweerd, Van Til, and the generations of those following them either ignored or dismissed the doctrinal contributions of Reformed orthodoxy as "rationalistic" and "discontinuous with the Reformation," research into post-Reformation orthodoxy over the last three decades has shed new light on the continuities — as well as the discontinuities — that the Reformers and their successors maintained with the earlier patristic and medieval eras in Christian theology. This is no less true with respect to this study. As we have seen, orthodox Reformed theologians after Calvin begin to develop the doctrinal foundation for circumscribed uses of natural theology and natural law. Moreover, in addition to affirming the utility of the doctrines, Vermigli, Zanchi, Althusius, and Turretin also provide increasingly sophisticated and comprehensive formulations of natural law, which they situate in the broader context of the grand moral tradition with Aristotle, Cicero, Augustine, Aquinas, Scotus, and many others. An important discovery of this investigation is that greater lines of continuity exist between the realist natural-law tradition (in its Thomist and Scotist trajectories) and the previously mentioned representatives than twentieth-century Protestant commentators have generally acknowledged.

Calvin, Vermigli, and the Reformed scholastics all share the conviction that Scripture is the cognitive foundation *(principium cognoscendi)* of theology and that moral arguments can be based on axioms derived from that *principium.* Consequently, they recognize the existence of a natural knowledge of God that is present in the natural order and discernible either in conjunction with or apart from Scripture. This knowledge, however, has no saving efficacy and merely serves to render all people to be "without excuse" for their moral infractions, as Romans 1:20 attests. This study has endeavored to rediscover the contribution of select representatives of Reformed orthodoxy in three interrelated areas of prolegomena — natural revelation, natural theology, and natural law. We have seen, contrary to current scholarly opinion, that some of the most formative voices in the Reformed tradition thought the diminished natural human faculties still function sufficiently to reveal the general precepts of the natural moral law.

Notes

Notes to the Introduction

1. Virgil, *Eclogues,* trans. H. Rushton Fairclough, rev. G. P. Goold (Cambridge, Mass.: Harvard University Press, 1999: Loeb Classical Library 63: 1916), 3.60. Calvin also refers to this passage in Virgil when commenting on Acts 17:28, "Certain of your own poets"; see his *Commentary on the Acts of the Apostles,* 2 vols., ed. David W. Torrance and Thomas F. Torrance, trans. John W. Fraser (Grand Rapids: Wm. B. Eerdmans Publishing Company, 1966), vol. 2, p. 121.

2. "I count it sufficient to have said that nothing may be found in the world so abject or lowly that it gives no witness to God. The poet said, 'All things are full of Jove.' So long as it endures, whatever is in the world has the power of God hidden under it. If this is discovered through inquiry and knowledge of nature, God will be revealed to us." Peter Martyr Vermigli, *Most learned and fruitful commentaries of D. Peter Martir Vermilius, professor of divinity in the school of Tigure, upon the Epistle of S. Paul to the Romans: wherein are diligently and most profitably entreated all such matters and chief common places of religion touched in the same Epistle,* trans. Sir Henry Billingsley (London: John Daye, 1568), f. 22r. The same passage can also be found in Peter Martyr Vermigli, *Common places,* ed. Robert Masson, trans. Anthonie Marten (London: Henri Denham, Thomas Chard, William Broom, and Andrew Maunsell, 1583), 1.2.4.

3. Russell Hittinger, *The First Grace: Rediscovering the Natural Law in a Post-Christian World* (Wilmington, Del.: ISI Books, 2003), p. 34.

4. Hittinger, *The First Grace,* p. 34.

5. Hittinger, *The First Grace,* p. xxiii.

6. John T. McNeill's classic study, "Natural Law in the Teaching of the Reformers," *Journal of Religion* 26, no. 3 (July 1946): 168-82, has functioned as the *locus classicus* for this position in the secondary literature on the subject. See also Clemens Bauer, "Melanchthons Naturrechtslehre," *Archiv für Reformationsgeschichte* 42 (1951): 64-100; Josef Bohatec, *Calvin und das Recht* (Feudingen: Buchdruck und Verlags-Anstalt, 1934), pp. 2-4, 98-99, 103-29; Lee W. Gibbs, "The Puritan Natural Law Theory of William Ames," *Harvard Theological Review* 64, no. 1 (January 1971): 37-57; W. J. Torrance Kirby,

"Richard Hooker's Theory of Natural Law in the Context of Reformation Theology," *Sixteenth Century Journal* 30, no. 3 (1999): 681-703; Robert Letham, "The *Foedus Operum:* Some Factors Accounting for Its Development," *Sixteenth Century Journal* 14, no. 4 (Winter 1983): 457-67; and Susan E. Schreiner, *The Theater of His Glory: Nature and the Natural Order in the Thought of John Calvin* (Durham, N.C.: Labyrinth Press, 1991; Grand Rapids: Baker Book House, 1995), p. 73.

7. McNeill, "Natural Law in the Teaching of the Reformers," p. 168.

8. McNeill, "Natural Law in the Teaching of the Reformers," p. 168.

9. Richard A. Muller, *Post-Reformation Reformed Dogmatics: The Rise and Development of Reformed Orthodoxy, ca. 1520 to ca. 1725,* 4 vols. (Grand Rapids: Baker Academic, 2003), vol. 1, p. 37.

10. A *strong* divine command theory can be defined as one where God's command is both necessary and sufficient for an action to have moral value. Whereas a *weak* divine command theory, by contrast, can be defined as one where God's command is necessary but not sufficient for an action to have moral value. See Robert Merrihew Adams, "A Modified Divine Command Theory of Ethical Wrongness," in *The Virtue of Faith and Other Essays in Philosophical Theology* (New York: Oxford University Press, 1987), pp. 97-122.

11. Jacques Ellul, *The Theological Foundation of Law,* trans. Marguerite Wieser (London: S.C.M. Press, 1961), pp. 44-71.

12. Stanley Hauerwas, "Natural Law, Tragedy, and Theological Ethics," *American Journal of Jurisprudence* 20 (1975): 1-19; and Hauerwas, *With the Grain of the Universe: The Church's Witness and Natural Theology* (Grand Rapids: Brazos Press, 2001), pp. 36-37, 132-40.

13. Carl F. H. Henry, *Christian Personal Ethics* (Grand Rapids: Wm. B. Eerdmans Publishing Company, 1957), pp. 145-263, 350-418; and Henry, "Natural Law and a Nihilistic Culture," *First Things* 49 (January 1995): 54-60.

14. Paul Lehmann, *Ethics in a Christian Context* (New York: Harper and Row, 1963), pp. 13-73, 148-61, 223-24, 246.

15. Reinhold Niebuhr, *An Interpretation of Christian Ethics* (New York: Harper and Brothers Publishers, 1935), pp. 144-61; Niebuhr, "Christian Faith and Natural Law," in *Love and Justice: Selections from the Shorter Writings of Reinhold Niebuhr,* ed. D. B. Robertson (Louisville: Westminster/John Knox Press, 1957), pp. 46-54; and Niebuhr, *The Nature and Destiny of Man: A Christian Interpretation,* 2 vols. (New York: Charles Scribner's Sons, 1951), vol. 1, pp. 265-300.

16. Helmut Thielicke, *Theological Ethics,* vol. 1, *Foundations,* ed. William H. Lazareth (Grand Rapids: Wm. B. Eerdmans Publishing Company, 1979), pp. 383-451.

17. Herman Dooyeweerd, *A New Critique of Theoretical Thought,* 4 vols., trans. David H. Freeman and William S. Young (Jordan Station, Ontario: Paideia Press, 1984), vol. 1, pp. 510-23; and Dooyeweerd, *Roots of Western Culture: Pagan, Secular, and Christian Options,* ed. Mark Vander Vennen and Bernard Zylstra, trans. John Kraay (Toronto: Wedge Publishing Foundation, 1979), pp. 111-47.

18. Cornelius Van Til, *In Defense of the Faith,* vol. 3, *Christian Theistic Ethics* (Philadelphia: den Dulk Christian Foundation, 1974), pp. 18-40; and Van Til, *Common Grace and the Gospel* (Nutley, N.J.: Presbyterian and Reformed Publishing Company, 1974), pp. 23-95. Cf. Peter J. Leithart, "Stoic Elements in Calvin's Doctrine of the Christian Life.

Part I: Original Corruption, Natural Law, and the Order of the Soul," *Westminster Theological Journal* 55, no. 1 (Spring 1993): 31-54.

19. Gordon Spykman, *Reformational Theology: A New Paradigm for Doing Dogmatics* (Grand Rapids: Wm. B. Eerdmans Publishing Company, 1992), pp. 20-25.

20. G. C. Berkouwer, *General Revelation* (Grand Rapids: Wm. B. Eerdmans Publishing Company, 1955), pp. 187-214; and Berkouwer, *A Half Century of Theology: Movements and Motives,* ed. and trans. Lewis B. Smedes (Grand Rapids: Wm. B. Eerdmans Publishing Company, 1977), pp. 39-74. Cf. Hendrikus Berkhof, *Two Hundred Years of Theology: Report of a Personal Journey,* trans. John Vriend (Grand Rapids: Wm. B. Eerdmans Publishing Company, 1989), pp. 114, 212.

21. Albrecht Ritschl, *Die christliche Lehre von der Rechtfertigung und Versohnung,* 3 vols. (Bonn: A. Marcus, 1895-1903); and Ritschl, *Theologie und Metaphysik: zur Verstandigung und Abwehr* (Bonn: A. Marcus, 1881).

22. Adolf von Harnack, *What Is Christianity?,* 2d ed., rev., trans. Thomas Bailey Saunders (New York: G. P. Putnam's Sons, 1901). For a particularly insightful analysis of the impact of ethical theology upon nineteenth-century Dutch Reformed theology, see James Hutton Mackay's *Religious Thought in Holland during the Nineteenth Century* (New York: Hodder and Stoughton, 1911), pp. 85-130, 179-225.

23. Herman Bavinck, "Common Grace," trans. Raymond C. Van Leeuwen, *Calvin Theological Journal* 24, no. 1 (April 1989): 57. Cf. Herman Bavinck, *Reformed Dogmatics,* vol. 1, *Prolegomena,* ed. John Bolt, trans. John Vriend (Grand Rapids: Baker Academic, 2003), pp. 67-70, 170-74, 541-48; and Bavinck, "De Theologie van Albrecht Ritschl," *Theologische Studien* 6 (1888): 369-403.

24. While it is possible to unearth a plethora of articles addressing various facets of natural-law theory, there are very few book-length monographs to be found on the subject. The following are exceptions: Ernest F. Kevan, *The Evangelical Doctrine of Law* (London: Tyndale Press, 1956); Kevan, *The Grace of Law: A Study in Puritan Theology* (Grand Rapids: Baker Book House, 1965); C. S. Lewis, *The Abolition of Man* (New York: Macmillan, 1947); Ellul, *Theological Foundation of Law;* Otto Friedrich von Gierke, *Natural Law and the Theory of Society, 1500-1800,* trans. Ernest Barker (Cambridge: Cambridge University Press, 1950); Ian T. Ramsey, ed., *Christian Ethics and Contemporary Philosophy* (London: S.C.M. Press, 1966), chap. 20; A. R. Vidler and W. A. Whitehouse, eds., *Natural Law: A Christian Reconsideration* (London: S.C.M. Press, 1946); and Thielicke, *Theological Ethics,* vol. 1, pp. 383-451. The amount of literature available in German-language monographs is somewhat larger. For a review of this literature published during the period 1950-1975, see Heinz-Horst Schrey, "Diskussion um das Naturrecht 1950-1975," *Theologische Rundschau* 41, no. 1 (February 1976): 60-62, 82-88.

25. These dissertations were the only ones that a search of University Microfilms International database yielded on the subject terms *natural law, natural-law theory,* and *natural theology:* Dale Eugene Burrington, "The Place of Natural Law in Protestant Ethics: An Examination of Emil Brunner's Ethical Theory" (Ph.D. diss., The Johns Hopkins University, 1966); Paul B. Henry, "Types of Protestant Theology and the Natural-Law Tradition" (Ph.D. diss., Duke University, 1970); Taina M. Holopainen, "William of Ockham's Theory of the Foundations of Ethics" (Th.D. diss., Helsingin Yliopisto University, 1991); Gerhart von Kap-Herr, "Natural Law and Religion in the Thought of Samuel Pufendorf" (Ph.D. diss., Concordia University, 1991); William James Kirsch, "Contem-

porary Protestant Thought on Natural Law" (Ph.D. diss., University of Illinois at Urbana-Champaign, 1967); John Lewis Marshall, "Natural Law and the Covenant: The Place of Natural Law in the Covenantal Framework of Samuel Rutherford's *Lex, Rex*" (Ph.D. diss., Westminster Theological Seminary, 1995); J. Bruce McCallum, "Modernity and the Dilemma of Natural Theology: The Barth-Brunner Debate, 1934" (Ph.D. diss., Marquette University, 1994); Isabel Wood Rogers, "A Contemporary Protestant Critique of the Natural-Law Tradition" (Ph.D. diss., Duke University, 1961); and David VanDrunen, "Natural Law and Common Law: The Relationship of Law and Custom in the Moral Theology of Thomas Aquinas" (Ph.D. diss., Loyola University-Chicago, 2001).

26. Cf. Henry, "Types of Protestant Theology and the Natural-Law Tradition," chapter 2, "The Reformers and the Natural-Law Tradition," pp. 67-101, and chapter 3, "Protestant Orthodoxy and the Natural-Law Tradition," pp. 102-35.

27. Cf. McCallum, "Modernity and the Dilemma of Natural Theology."

28. Cf. Burrington, "The Place of Natural Law in Protestant Ethics: An Examination of Emil Brunner's Ethical Theory"; Marshall, "Natural Law and the Covenant: The Place of Natural Law in the Covenantal Framework of Samuel Rutherford's *Lex, Rex*"; and von Kap-Herr, "Natural Law and Religion in the Thought of Samuel Pufendorf."

29. Cf. Rogers, "A Contemporary Protestant Critique of the Natural-Law Tradition."

30. Cf. Kirsch, "Contemporary Protestant Thought on Natural Law."

31. Muller, *Post-Reformation Reformed Dogmatics*, vol. 1, p. 37.

32. Jacques-Auguste de Thou (1553-1617), the French Reformed historian and first president of the Parlement of Paris, recorded a statement (most likely from an interview) to this effect made by his former teacher, Joseph Justus Scaliger (1540-1609), the renowned Reformed philologist and historian of the University of Leiden, who said:

> Les plus excellens Théologiens du seizième Siècle, selon Jos. Scaliger, étoient Calvin & Martyr: celui-là a traité les Saintes Lettres comme il les falloit traiter purement & simplement, sans aucunes *argumentations* Scholastiques; & cét homme doué d'un jugement divin a deviné bien des choses, qui ne peuvent être devinées que par ceux qui sont très-savans dans la Langue Hébraïque: & cependant il n'étoit pas de ce nombre. Quant à Martyr, comme il voyoit qu'il avoit affaire à des Sophistes, *Sophisticâ illos devicit*, il les battit & les vainquit avec leurs armes.
>
> Petrus Martyr, dit ailleurs Scaliger, *seliciter initiatus*, bien sondé *in Philosophia, Historia, Linguis, excellens Theologus, & styli puri, ac quàm Theologum deceat melioris.*

Jacques-Auguste de Thou, *Les éloges des hommes savans, tirez de l'Histoire de M. de Thou*, 4th éd. rev., corr., & augm., outré un très-grand nombre de nouvelles remarques, d'un quatrième tome, French trans. Antoine Teissier (Leiden: T. Haaa, 1715), vol. 2, p. 84, cf. pp. 79-89.

B. B. Warfield translated a portion of the previously quoted extract in his address, "John Calvin the Theologian," reprinted in *Calvin and Augustine*, ed. Samuel G. Craig (Philadelphia: Presbyterian and Reformed Publishing Company, 1956), p. 481: "The two most excellent theologians of our times, remarks Joseph Scaliger, are Calvin and Martyr, the former of whom has dealt with the Holy Scriptures as they ought to be dealt with — with sincerity, I mean, and purity and simplicity, without any scholastic subtleties. . . . Peter Martyr, because it seemed to fall to him to engage the Sophists, has overcome them sophistically, and struck them down with their own weapons." For more references to Martyr and Calvin by both Thou and Scaliger, see Jacques-Auguste de Thou, *Monumenta litteraria siue, Obitus et elogia doctorum virorum. Ex historiis illustris viri Iac. Aug. Thuani. Opera C.B.* (London: John Norton Sumptibus & Tho. Warren, 1640), pp. 86-87, 96; Anthony Grafton, *Joseph Scaliger: A Study in the History of Classical Scholarship,* vol. 2, *Historical Chronology* (Oxford: Clarendon Press, 1993), pp. 322-23; and H. J. De Jonge, "The Study of the New Testament," in *Leiden University in the Seventeenth Century: An Exchange of Learning,* ed. Th. H. Lunsingh Scheurleer and G. H. M. Posthumus Meyjes (Leiden: Universitaire Pers Leiden/E. J. Brill, 1975), p. 67, p. 107, n. 260.

33. Muller, *Post-Reformation Reformed Dogmatics,* vol. 1, p. 45.

34. The preeminent exception to this generalization is Emil Brunner, who, in the face of great opposition, developed and defended what he referred to as "a Christian *theologia naturalis.*" A Christian natural theology, according to him, was a form of theological thinking that tried to account for the phenomena of natural life. Thus, he distinguished between "ordinances of creation" such as monogamous marriage, which as an institution can be viewed apart from sin and knowable through the order of creation, and "ordinances of preservation" such as the State, which is always seen in relation to sin. Emil Brunner and Karl Barth, *Natural Theology* ("Nature and Grace" by Brunner and the reply "No!" by Barth), trans. Peter Fraenkel (London: Geoffrey Bles, 1946), p. 30. Brunner published several other works over approximately the next decade that developed and applied the idea of a Christian natural theology. Brunner, *The Divine Imperative: A Study in Christian Ethics,* trans. Olive Wyon (New York: Macmillan, 1937); Brunner, *Justice and the Social Order,* trans. Mary Hottinger (London: Lutterworth Press, 1945); and Brunner, *Christianity and Civilization* (New York: Charles Scribner's Sons, 1948-49). On a lesser scale, see also James Luther Adams, "The Law of Nature: Some General Considerations," *Journal of Religion* 25, no. 2 (April 1945): 88-96; Frederick S. Carney, "Outline of a Natural Law Procedure for Christian Ethics," *Journal of Religion* 47, no. 1 (January 1967): 25-38; Paul Ramsey, "Natural Law and the Nature of Man," *Christendom* 9, no. 3 (Summer 1944): 369-81; and Douglas Sturm, "Naturalism, Historicism, and Christian Ethics: Toward a Christian Doctrine of Natural Law," *Journal of Religion* 44 (January 1964): 40-51.

35. Rufus Black, "Is the New Natural-Law Theory Christian?" in *The Revival of Natural Law: Philosophical, Theological, and Ethical Responses to the Finnis-Grisez School,* ed. Nigel Biggar and Rufus Black (Burlington, Vt.: Ashgate, 2000), p. 148.

36. Nigel Biggar and Rufus Black, eds., *The Revival of Natural Law: Philosophical, Theological, and Ethical Responses to the Finnis-Grisez School* (Burlington, Vt.: Ashgate, 2000).

37. Rufus Black, *Christian Moral Realism: Natural Law, Narrative, Virtue, and the Gospel* (New York: Oxford University Press, 2000).

38. Carl Braaten, "Protestants and Natural Law," in *Being Christian Today: An American Conversation,* ed. Richard John Neuhaus and George Weigel (Washington, D.C.: Ethics and Public Policy Center, 1992), pp. 105-21.

39. J. Budziszewski, *Written on the Heart: The Case for Natural Law* (Downers

Grove, Ill.: InterVarsity Press, 1997); Budziszewski, *The Revenge of Conscience: Politics and the Fall of Man* (Dallas: Spence Publishing Company, 1999); Budziszewski, "The Second Tablet Project," *First Things* (June/July 2002): 23-31; and Budziszewski, *What We Can't Not Know: A Guide* (Dallas: Spence Publishing Company, 2003).

40. Michael Cromartie, ed., *A Preserving Grace: Protestants, Catholics, and Natural Law* (Grand Rapids: Wm. B. Eerdmans Publishing Company/Ethics and Public Policy Center, 1997); and Cromartie, "Religious Conservatives in American Politics 1980-2000: An Assessment," *The Witherspoon Fellowship Lectures*, No. 15, April 16, 2001.

41. Jean Bethke Elshtain, *Augustine and the Limits of Politics* (Notre Dame: University of Notre Dame Press, 1995); and Elshtain, *Just War Theory*, ed. Jean Bethke Elshtain (New York: New York University Press, 1992).

42. Arthur F. Holmes, *Fact, Value, and God* (Grand Rapids: Wm. B. Eerdmans Publishing Company, 1997); see also Holmes's earlier essays, "Concept of Natural Law," *Christian Scholar's Review* 2, no. 3 (1972): 195-208; and "Human Variables and Natural Law," in *God and the Good: Essays in Honor of Henry Stob*, ed. Clifton Orlebeke and Lewis Smedes (Grand Rapids: Wm. B. Eerdmans Publishing Company, 1975), pp. 63-79.

43. Paul Helm, *John Calvin's Ideas* (Oxford: Oxford University Press, 2004), pp. 209-45, 347-88.

44. Alister E. McGrath, *A Scientific Theology*, 3 vols. (Grand Rapids: Wm. B. Eerdmans Publishing Company, 2001-2003), vol. 1, pp. 200-205, 249-306; and vol. 2, pp. 72-96.

45. Susan Schreiner, *The Theater of His Glory*; and Schreiner, "Calvin's Use of Natural Law," in *A Preserving Grace: Protestants, Catholics, and Natural Law*, ed. Michael Cromartie (Grand Rapids: Wm. B. Eerdmans Publishing Company/Ethics and Public Policy Center, 1997), pp. 51-76.

46. David VanDrunen, *Law & Custom: The Thought of Thomas Aquinas and the Future of the Common Law* (New York: Peter Lang, 2003); VanDrunen, "Natural Law, Custom, and Common Law in the Theology of Aquinas and Calvin," *University of British Columbia Law Review* 33 (2000): 699-717; and VanDrunen, "The Context of Natural Law: John Calvin's Doctrine of the Two Kingdoms," *Journal of Church and State* 46, no. 3 (Summer 2004): 503-25.

47. Daniel Westberg, *Right Practical Reason: Aristotle, Action, and Prudence in Aquinas* (Oxford: Clarendon Press, 1994); Westberg, "The Reformed Tradition and Natural Law," in *A Preserving Grace: Protestants, Catholics, and Natural Law*, ed. Michael Cromartie (Grand Rapids: Wm. B. Eerdmans Publishing Company/Ethics and Public Policy Center, 1997), pp. 103-17; Westberg, "The Relation Between Positive and Natural Law in Aquinas," *Journal of Law and Religion* 11 (1994-1995): 1-22; and Westberg, "Thomistic Law and the Moral Theory of Richard Hooker," *American Catholic Philosophical Quarterly: Supplement* 68 (1994): 201-14.

48. See John Bolt's monumental recent book, *A Free Church, A Holy Nation: Abraham Kuyper's American Public Theology* (Grand Rapids: Wm. B. Eerdmans Publishing Company, 2001), pp. 81-122, 407-42; and Vincent E. Bacote, *The Spirit in Public Theology: Appropriating the Legacy of Abraham Kuyper* (Grand Rapids: Baker Academic, 2005).

49. See Richard J. Mouw's recently published Stob Lecture, *He Shines in All That's Fair: Culture and Common Grace* (Grand Rapids: Wm. B. Eerdmans Publishing Company,

2001), pp. 1-8; and Mouw, "Klaas Schilder as Public Theologian," *Calvin Theological Journal* 38, no. 2 (November 2003): 281-98.

50. For an insightful treatment of this juxtaposition in relation to Calvin's views about ethics, and particularly about the ethical capacities of those who are outside of the church, see Helm, *John Calvin's Ideas,* pp. 382-88.

51. The first statement of the group, "Evangelicals and Catholics Together: The Christian Mission in the Third Millennium," first issued in March 1994, can be found in Charles Colson and Richard John Neuhaus, eds., *Evangelicals and Catholics Together: Toward a Common Mission* (Dallas: Word, 1995), pp. xv-xxxiii. The second statement, "Evangelicals and Catholics Together: The Gift of Salvation," issued in December 1997, was published in *Christianity Today,* December 8, 1997, pp. 35-38. The conversations and statements of the group are independent of the official conversations between the Roman Catholic Church and various Protestant churches, and thus speak unofficially and only represent the viewpoint of those who endorsed the documents.

52. Cf. Cromartie, ed., *A Preserving Grace: Protestants, Catholics, and Natural Law.*

53. *The Creeds of Christendom,* vol. 3, *The Evangelical Protestant Creeds,* 6th ed., ed. Philip Schaff, rev. David S. Schaff (Grand Rapids: Baker Book House, 1990), p. 588.

54. Braaten, "Protestants and Natural Law," p. 110.

55. Thielicke, *Theological Ethics,* vol. 1, p. 420.

56. Thielicke, *Theological Ethics,* vol. 1, p. 147.

57. Thielicke, *Theological Ethics,* vol. 1, p. 420.

58. Thielicke, *Theological Ethics,* vol. 1, p. 421.

59. Thielicke, *Theological Ethics,* vol. 1, p. 422.

60. Thielicke, *Theological Ethics,* vol. 1, p. 422.

61. Thielicke, *Theological Ethics,* vol. 1, p. 428.

62. Thielicke, *Theological Ethics,* vol. 1, p. 428.

63. Thielicke, *Theological Ethics,* vol. 1, p. 430. For an informative discussion of Barth's criticism of the "orders of creation and preservation" idea in relationship to the use of "orders" language in Emil Brunner, Reinhold Niebuhr, Paul Tillich, and Dietrich Bonhoeffer, see Louis C. Midgley, "Karl Barth and Moral Natural Law: The Anatomy of a Debate," *Natural Law Forum* 13 (1968): 108-26.

64. Thielicke, *Theological Ethics,* vol. 1, p. 430.

65. Thielicke, *Theological Ethics,* vol. 1, p. 430.

66. Thielicke, *Theological Ethics,* vol. 1, p. 431.

67. Thielicke, *Theological Ethics,* vol. 1, p. 432.

68. Braaten, "Protestants and Natural Law," p. 111.

69. For a survey of the influence of Aristotle's *Ethics* and the natural-law tradition on Reformed orthodoxy, see Wilhelm Geesink's 1897 Rectoral Address "De Geschiedenis der Gereformeerde Ethiek," reprinted in *Gereformeerde Ethiek,* Tweede Deel (Kampen: Kok, 1931), pp. 453-511, especially pp. 453-77; Donald Sinnema, "Aristotle and Early Reformed Orthodoxy: Moments of Accommodation and Antithesis," in *Christianity and the Classics: The Acceptance of a Heritage,* ed. Wendy E. Helleman (Lanham, Md.: University Press of America, 1990), pp. 119-48; and Sinnema, "The Discipline of Ethics in Early Reformed Orthodoxy," *Calvin Theological Journal* 28, no. 1 (April 1993): 10-44. For an acknowledgement of the role and importance of natural theology and the natural-law tradition in Protestant theology two years prior to the Barth-Brunner debate, see

Hans von Steubing, *Naturrecht und natürliche Theologie im Protestantismus* (Göttingen: Vandenhoeck and Ruprecht, 1932), pp. 85-161.

70. Brunner and Barth, *Natural Theology,* p. 102. Cf. Karl Barth, *The Theology of John Calvin,* trans. Geoffrey W. Bromiley (Grand Rapids: Wm. B. Eerdmans Publishing Company, 1995), pp. 162-72.

71. Richard A. Muller, *After Calvin: Studies in the Development of a Theological Tradition* (New York: Oxford University Press, 2003), p. 4.

72. Muller, *After Calvin,* p. 5.

73. For an abbreviated list of seminal contributions to this growing body of knowledge, consult the following sources: Richard A. Muller, *Post-Reformation Reformed Dogmatics;* Muller, *After Calvin;* Muller, "The Problem of Protestant Scholasticism — A Review and Definition," in *Reformation and Scholasticism: An Ecumenical Enterprise,* ed. Willem J. Van Asselt and Eef Dekker (Grand Rapids: Baker Book House, 2001), pp. 45-64; Muller, *The Unaccommodated Calvin: Studies in the Foundation of a Theological Tradition* (New York: Oxford University Press, 2000); John Platt, *Reformed Thought and Scholasticism: The Arguments for the Existence of God in Dutch Theology, 1575-1650* (Leiden: E. J. Brill, 1982); Carl R. Trueman and R. S. Clark, eds., *Protestant Scholasticism: Essays in Reassessment* (Carlisle, U.K.: Paternoster Press, 1999); and Willem J. Van Asselt and Eef Dekker, eds., *Reformation and Scholasticism: An Ecumenical Enterprise* (Grand Rapids: Baker Book House, 2001).

74. Richard A. Muller, *Scholasticism and Orthodoxy in the Reformed Tradition: An Attempt at Definition* (Grand Rapids: Calvin Theological Seminary, 1995), p. 8. A revised and updated version of this monograph can be found in Muller, *After Calvin,* pp. 25-46.

75. Carl R. Trueman and R. S. Clark, "Introduction," in *Protestant Scholasticism: Essays in Reassessment,* ed. Carl R. Trueman and R. S. Clark (Carlisle, U.K.: Paternoster Press, 1999), p. xiv.

76. Brunner and Barth, *Natural Theology,* pp. 94-105. Cf. Barth, *Theology of John Calvin,* pp. 13-68.

77. Trueman and Clark, "Introduction," p. xii. For a scathing condemnation of this type of historiography, see Barr, *Biblical Faith and Natural Theology,* p. 109; and Richard A. Muller, "The Barth Legacy: New Athanasius or Origen Redivivus? A Response to T. F. Torrance," *The Thomist* 54 (1990): 673-704.

78. Muller, *Post-Reformation Reformed Dogmatics,* vol. 1, p. 37.

79. Muller, *Post-Reformation Reformed Dogmatics,* vol. 1, pp. 44-45.

80. Schreiner, *The Theater of His Glory,* p. 77.

81. Muller, *Post-Reformation Reformed Dogmatics,* vol. 1, p. 67.

82. Cf. Muller, *Post-Reformation Reformed Dogmatics,* vol. 1, pp. 51-52, 67-71, 90-96; vol. 4, pp. 391-97.

83. John Patrick Donnelly, S.J., *Calvinism and Scholasticism in Vermigli's Doctrine of Man and Grace* (Leiden: E. J. Brill, 1976), p. 202. Cf. pp. 197-207.

84. Donnelly, *Calvinism and Scholasticism,* p. 205. Cf. Donnelly's article "Calvinist Thomism," *Viator: Medieval and Renaissance Studies* 7 (1976): 443-45.

85. Louis Bouyer, *The Spirit and Forms of Protestantism,* trans. A. V. Littledale (London: Harvill Press, 1956), pp. 162-65; Michael Bertram Crowe, *The Changing Profile of the Natural Law* (The Hague: Martinus Nijhoff, 1977), pp. 192-222; A. P. d'Entrèves, *Natural Law: An Historical Survey* (New York: Harper and Row, 1951), pp.

69-70; Heinrich Denifle, *Luther und Luthertum in der ersten Entwickelung*, 2 vols. in 4 parts (Mainz: F. Kirchheim, 1904-1909), vol. 1, pt. 2, pp. 522, 536, 587; Etienne Gilson, *The Spirit of Medieval Philosophy*, trans. A. H. C. Downes (New York: Charles Scribner's Sons, 1940), pp. 321-23 and 333-37; Joseph Lortz, *The Reformation in Germany*, 2 vols., trans. Ronald Walls (New York: Herder and Herder, 1968), vol. 1, pp. 195-200; Heinrich A. Rommen, *The Natural Law: A Study in Legal and Social History and Philosophy*, trans. Thomas R. Hanley, O.S.B. (Indianapolis: Liberty Fund, Inc., 1998), pp. 51-58; and John Todd, *Martin Luther: A Biographical Study* (Westminster, Md.: Newman Press, 1964), pp. 53-56.

86. Several recent studies have significantly challenged the consensus of the authors in the preceding footnote. John L. Farthing, *Thomas Aquinas and Gabriel Biel: Interpretations of St. Thomas Aquinas in German Nominalism on the Eve of the Reformation* (Durham, N.C.: Duke University Press, 1988); Frank A. James III, *Peter Martyr Vermigli and Predestination: The Augustinian Inheritance of an Italian Reformer* (Oxford: Clarendon Press, 1998); Steven Ozment, "*Homo Viator:* Luther and Late Medieval Theology," in *The Reformation in Medieval Perspective*, ed. Steven Ozment (Chicago: Quadrangle Books, 1971), pp. 142-54; Heiko A. Oberman, *The Harvest of Medieval Theology: Gabriel Biel and Late Medieval Nominalism*, 3rd ed. (Grand Rapids: Baker Book House, 2000); Oberman, *Forerunners of the Reformation* (New York: Holt, Rinehart, and Winston, 1966); Oberman, "Luther and the *Via Moderna:* The Philosophical Backdrop of the Reformation Breakthrough," *Journal of Ecclesiastical History* 54, no. 4 (October 2003): 641-70; Charles Trinkhaus and Heiko A. Oberman, eds., *The Pursuit of Holiness in Late Medieval and Renaissance Religion* (Leiden: E. J. Brill, 1974); David C. Steinmetz, *Misericordia Dei: The Theology of Johannes von Staupitz in Its Late Medieval Setting* (Leiden: E. J. Brill, 1968); and Steinmetz, *Luther and Staupitz: An Essay in the Intellectual Origins of the Protestant Reformation* (Durham, N.C.: Duke University Press, 1980). On Augustine's voluntarism, see Vernon J. Bourke, S.J., "Voluntarism in Augustine's Ethico-Legal Thought," *Augustinian Studies* 1 (1970): 3-17.

87. Stephen J. Grabill, "Introduction to D. Hieronymus Zanchi's 'On the Law in General,'" *Journal of Markets & Morality* 6, no. 1 (Spring 2003): 309-16.

88. For a similar treatment of the nature of "fundamental principles" *(principia)* in general and their role in theology in particular, see Bavinck, *Reformed Dogmatics*, vol. 1, pp. 210-14.

89. For a description of actualism as a motif in Barth's theology, see George Hunsinger, *How to Read Karl Barth: The Shape of His Theology* (New York: Oxford University Press, 1991), pp. 30-32, 67-70, 96-99.

90. Cf. Paul Althaus, *Die Prinzipien der deutschen reformierten Dogmatik im Zeitalter der aristotelischen Scholastik* (Leipzig: Deichert, 1914); Wilhelm Gass, *Geschichte der protestantischen Dogmatik in ihrem Zusammenhange mit der Theologie*, 4 vols. (Berlin: Georg Reimer, 1854-67); Heinrich Heppe, "Der Charakter der deutsch-reformirten Kirche und das Verhältniss derselben zum Luthertum und zum Calvinismus," in *Theologische Studien und Kritiken*, 1850 (Heft 3), pp. 669-706; Heppe, *Die confessionelle Entwicklung der altprotestantischen Kirche Deutschlands, die altprotestantische Union und die gegenwärtige confessionelle Lage und Aufgabe des deutschen Protestantismus* (Marburg: Elwert, 1854); Heppe, *Die Dogmatik des deutschen Protestantismus im sechzehnten Jahrhundert*, 3 vols. (Gotha: Perthes, 1857); Alexander

Schweizer, *Die Glaubenslehre der evangelisch-reformierten Kirche dargestellt und aus den Quellen belegt,* 2 vols. (Zürich: Orell, Füssli, und Comp., 1844-47); Schweizer, *Die protestantischen Centraldogmen in ihrer Entwicklung innerhalb der reformierten Kirche,* 2 vols. (Zürich: Orell, Füssli, und Comp., 1854-56); Thomas F. Torrance, *The Hermeneutics of John Calvin* (Edinburgh: Scottish Academic Press, 1988); Torrance, "Knowledge of God and Speech about Him according to John Calvin," in *Theology in Reconstruction* (Grand Rapids: Wm. B. Eerdmans Publishing Company, 1966), pp. 76-98; Hans Emil Weber, *Der Einfluss der protestantischen Schulphilosophie auf die orthodox-lutherische Dogmatik* (Leipzig: Deichert, 1908); Weber, *Die philosophische Scholastik des deutschen Protestantismus in Zeitalter der Orthodoxie* (Leipzig: Quelle und Meyer, 1907); and Weber, *Reformation, Orthodoxie und Rationalismus,* 2 vols. in 3 parts (1937-51; reprint Darmstadt: Wissenschaftliche Buchgesellschaft, 1966).

91. Muller, *Post-Reformation Reformed Dogmatics,* vol. 1, pp. 29, 44-46.

Notes to Chapter 1

1. Emil Brunner and Karl Barth, *Natural Theology* ("Nature and Grace" by Brunner and the Reply "No!" by Barth), trans. Peter Fraenkel (London: Geoffrey Bles, 1946). In some respects, the Barth-Brunner debate can be seen as the continuation of an earlier discussion dating back to the turn of the century. For a bibliography of key contributions that predate the debate and that examine Calvin's understanding of natural revelation, natural theology, and natural law, see the following chronologically arranged entries: Herman Bavinck, "Calvin and Common Grace," in *Calvin and the Reformation,* ed. William Park Armstrong, trans. Geerhardus Vos (Grand Rapids: Baker Book House, 1980 [orig. pub. 1909]), pp. 99-130; August Lang, "The Reformation and Natural Law," in *Calvin and the Reformation,* ed. William Park Armstrong, trans. J. G. Machen (Grand Rapids: Baker Book House, 1980 [orig. pub. 1909]), pp. 56-98; Benjamin B. Warfield, "Calvin's Doctrine of the Knowledge of God," in *Calvin and the Reformation,* ed. William Park Armstrong (Grand Rapids: Baker Book House, 1980 [orig. pub. 1909]), pp. 131-214; Gisbert Beyerhaus, *Studien zur Staatsanschauung Calvins: Mit besonderer Berücksichtigung seines Souveränitätsbegriffs* (Berlin: Trowitzsch und Sohn, 1910), pp. 65-77; Ernst Troeltsch, "Calvin and Calvinism," *Hibbert Journal* 8, part 1 (1909-10): 102-21; Troeltsch, *The Social Teachings of the Christian Churches,* vol. 2, trans. Olive Wyon (Louisville: Westminster/John Knox Press, 1992 [orig. pub. 1912]), pp. 602-17; Émile Doumergue, *Jean Calvin: Les hommes et les choses de son temps,* vol. 5, *La pensée ecclésiastique et la pensée politique de Calvin* (Lausanne: Georges Bridel, 1917), pp. 454-74; Herman Kuiper, *Calvin on Common Grace* (Grand Rapids: Smitter Book Company, 1928), pp. 5-26, 50-52, 157-58, 182-87; and Josef Bohatec, *Calvin und das Recht* (Feudingen: Buchdruck und Verlags-Anstalt, 1934), pp. 1-93. Yet in other respects, particularly in terms of the historiographical method employed, the debate has functioned as an interpretive grid through which much of the subsequent scholarly discussion has taken place in regard to Calvin's understanding of the natural knowledge of God.

2. Brunner and Barth, *Natural Theology,* p. 59.

3. In "Modernity and the Dilemma of Natural Theology: The Barth-Brunner Debate, 1934" (Ph.D. diss., Marquette University, 1994), pp. 267-73, J. Bruce McCallum

provides an extended and insightful discussion of the rhetorical features of the debate. He identifies the debate as having "the literary characteristics of a conflict narrative in the genre of a German *Auseinandersetzung*" (p. 267). Interestingly, like McCallum, Brunner also considers the genre of the debate to be an *Auseinandersetzung* rather than a *Streitschrift,* which serves to reinforce the dialectical distance and closeness of the disputants and to invite further exchange. According to McCallum, Brunner takes the irenic stance of a friendly advisor who shows that what Barth really desires is what he also desires, but disputes Barth's erroneous conclusions. The literary trope in his presentation is synecdoche and the figure is paradox. Barth, however, assumes the mantle of an angry truth-seeker who stuns his opponent with irony and polemical counter-questions. Barth evidences the trope of irony and uses dialectic as a literary device. McCallum concludes, "The synechdochal rhetorical strategy of Brunner reflects his eristic theology which connects with his opponents in order to say the opposite, while the ironic tone of Barth reflects his interiorization of natural theology by denying the positionality of his negation of natural theology" (p. 268).

4. Brunner and Barth, *Natural Theology,* p. 104.

5. Brunner and Barth, *Natural Theology,* p. 71.

6. For studies that examine Calvin's understanding of *natural law,* see Irena Backus, "Calvin's Concept of Natural and Roman Law," *Calvin Theological Journal* 38, no. 1 (April 2003): 7-26; Andrew Beck, "Natural Law and the Reformation," *The Clergy Review* 21 (April 1941): 73-81; R. S. Clark, "Calvin on the *Lex Naturalis,*" *Stulos Theological Journal* 6, nos. 1-2 (May-November 1998): 1-22; Paul Helm, "Calvin and Natural Law," *Scottish Bulletin of Evangelical Theology* 2 (1984): 5-22; John T. McNeill, "Natural Law in the Teaching of the Reformers," *Journal of Religion* 26, no. 3 (July 1946): 168-82; S. H. Rae, "Calvin, Natural Law, and Contemporary Ethics: A Brief Note," *Reformed Theological Review* 30, no. 1 (January-April 1971): 14-20; Susan E. Schreiner, "Calvin's Use of Natural Law," in *A Preserving Grace: Protestants, Catholics, and Natural Law,* ed. Michael Cromartie (Grand Rapids: Wm. B. Eerdmans Publishing Company/Ethics and Public Policy Center, 1997), pp. 51-76; Schreiner, *The Theater of His Glory: Nature and the Natural Order in the Thought of John Calvin* (Durham, N.C.: Labyrinth Press, 1991; Grand Rapids: Baker Book House, 1995), pp. 73-95; David VanDrunen, "Natural Law, Custom, and Common Law in the Theology of Aquinas and Calvin," *University of British Columbia Law Review* 33 (2000): 699-717; VanDrunen, "The Context of Natural Law: John Calvin's Doctrine of the Two Kingdoms," *Journal of Church and State* 46, no. 3 (Summer 2004): 503-25; and Allen Verhey, "Natural Law in Aquinas and Calvin," in *God and the Good: Essays in Honor of Henry Stob,* ed. Clifton Orlebeke and Lewis Smedes (Grand Rapids: Wm. B. Eerdmans Publishing Company, 1975), pp. 80-92.

For studies that examine Calvin's understanding of *natural theology,* see John Beversluis, "Reforming the 'Reformed' Objection to Natural Theology," *Faith and Philosophy* 12, no. 2 (April 1995): 189-206; L. Harold DeWolf, "The Theological Rejection of Natural Theology: An Evaluation," *Journal of Religious Thought* 15, no. 2 (Spring-Summer 1958): 91-106; Paul Helm, "John Calvin, the *sensus divinitatis,* and the Noetic Effects of Sin," *International Journal for Philosophy of Religion* 43, no. 2 (April 1998): 87-107; Richard A. Muller, "*Duplex Cognitio Dei* in the Theology of Early Reformed Orthodoxy," *Sixteenth Century Journal* 10, no. 2 (Summer 1979): 51-61; Muller, *Post-Reformation Reformed Dogmatics: The Rise and Development of Reformed Orthodoxy, ca.*

1520 to ca. 1725, 4 vols. (Grand Rapids: Baker Academic, 2003), vol. 1, pp. 270-76, 270-310; Gerald J. Postema, "Calvin's Alleged Rejection of Natural Theology," *Scottish Journal of Theology* 24, no. 4 (November 1971): 423-34; David C. Steinmetz, "Calvin and the Natural Knowledge of God," in *Via Augustini: Augustine in the Later Middle Ages, Renaissance, and Reformation: Essays in Honor of Damasus Trapp, O.S.A.*, ed. Heiko A. Oberman and Frank A. James III (Leiden: E. J. Brill, 1991), pp. 142-56; reprinted in *Calvin in Context* (New York: Oxford University Press, 1995), pp. 23-39; Michael Czapkay Sudduth, "Calvin, Plantinga, and the Natural Knowledge of God: A Response to Beversluis," *Faith and Philosophy* 15, no. 1 (January 1998): 92-103; and Sudduth, "The Prospects for a 'Mediate' Natural Theology in John Calvin," *Religious Studies* 31, no. 2 (March 1995): 53-68.

7. Karl Barth, *The Knowledge of God and the Service of God according to the Teaching of the Reformation, Recalling the Scottish Confession of 1560*, trans. J. L. M. Haire and Ian Henderson (London: Hodder and Stoughton, 1938), pp. 3-12; Peter Barth, *Das Problem der natürlichen Theologie bei Calvin* (Munich: Chr. Kaiser, 1935), pp. 3-5; Peter Brunner, "Allgemeine und besondere Offenbarung in Calvins *Institutio*," *Evangelische Theologie* 1, no. 5 (1934): 189-216; Günter Gloede, *Theologia Naturalis bei Calvin* (Stuttgart: W. Kohlhammer, 1935), pp. 2-49; Derek S. Jeffreys, "How Reformed Is Reformed Epistemology? Alvin Plantinga and Calvin's 'Sensus Divinitatis,'" *Religious Studies* 33, no. 4 (December 1997): 419-31; D. Brent Laytham, "The Place of Natural Theology in the Theological Method of John Calvin and Jacob Arminius," in *Church Divinity 1989/90*, ed. John H. Morgan (Bristol, Ind.: Wyndham Hall Press, 1990), pp. 22-44; Wilhelm Niesel, *The Theology of Calvin*, trans. Harold Knight (Philadelphia: Westminster Press, 1956), pp. 39-53; T. A. Noble, "Our Knowledge of God according to John Calvin," *Evangelical Quarterly* 54, no. 1 (January-March 1982): 2-13; T. H. L. Parker, *The Doctrine of the Knowledge of God: A Study in Calvin's Theology*, rev. ed. (Grand Rapids: Wm. B. Eerdmans Publishing Company, 1959), pp. 15-71; John Newton Thomas, "The Place of Natural Theology in the Thought of John Calvin," *Journal of Religious Thought* 15, no. 2 (Spring-Summer 1958): 107-36; James Torrance, "Interpreting the Word by the Light of Christ or the Light of Nature? Calvin, Calvinism, and Barth," in *Calviniana: Ideas and Influence of Jean Calvin*, ed. Robert V. Schnucker (Kirksville, Mo.: Sixteenth Century Journal Publishers, Inc., 1988), pp. 255-67; T. F. Torrance, *Calvin's Doctrine of Man* (Grand Rapids: Wm. B. Eerdmans Publishing Company, 1957), pp. 154-83; Torrance, "Knowledge of God and Speech about Him according to John Calvin," in *Theology in Reconstruction* (Grand Rapids: Wm. B. Eerdmans Publishing Company, 1966), pp. 76-98.

8. Peter Barth, *Das Problem der natürlichen Theologie bei Calvin*, pp. 6-26; Edward A. Dowey Jr., *The Knowledge of God in Calvin's Theology*, rev. ed. (Grand Rapids: Wm. B. Eerdmans Publishing Company, 1994), pp. 41-49; Gloede, *Theologia Naturalis bei Calvin*, pp. 50-71; Dewey J. Hoitenga Jr., "Faith and Reason in Calvin's Doctrine of the Knowledge of God," in *Rationality in the Calvinian Tradition*, ed. Hendrik Hart, Johan Van der Hoeven, and Nicholas Wolterstorff (Lanham, Md.: University Press of America, 1983), pp. 17-42; T. F. Torrance, *Calvin's Doctrine of Man*, pp. 128-53; and Cornelis P. Venema, "The 'Twofold Knowledge of God' and the Structure of Calvin's Theology," *Mid-America Journal of Theology* 4, no. 2 (Fall 1988): 156-82.

9. Peter Barth, *Das Problem der natürlichen Theologie bei Calvin*, pp. 38-60; Marc-Édouard Chenevière, *La pensée politique de Calvin* (Geneva: Éditions Labor et Fides, 1937), pp. 61-90; Arthur C. Cochrane, "Natural Law in Calvin," in *Church-State Rela-*

tions in Ecumenical Perspective, ed. Elwyn A. Smith (Louvain: Duquesne University Press, 1966), pp. 176-217; Dowey, *The Knowledge of God in Calvin's Theology,* pp. 222-38; Jacques Ellul, *The Theological Foundation of Law,* trans. Marguerite Wieser (London: S.C.M. Press, 1961), pp. 61-71; Gloede, *Theologia Naturalis bei Calvin,* pp. 159-281; Harro P. Höpfl, *The Christian Polity of John Calvin* (Cambridge: Cambridge University Press, 1982), pp. 179-87; William Klempa, "Calvin on Natural Law," in *John Calvin and the Church: A Prism of Reform,* ed. Timothy George (Louisville: Westminster/John Knox Press, 1990), pp. 72-95; David Little, "Calvin and the Prospects for a Christian Theory of Natural Law," in *Norm and Context in Christian Ethics,* ed. Gene H. Outka and Paul Ramsey (New York: Scribner's, 1968), pp. 175-97; Charles E. Morton, "What Protestants Think About Natural Law," *Catholic World* 190, no. 1 (February 1960): 294-300; Niesel, *The Theology of Calvin,* pp. 102-3; J. Peter Pelkonen, "The Teaching of John Calvin on the Nature and Function of the Conscience," *The Lutheran Quarterly* 21, no. 1 (February 1969): 74-88; Henry Stob, "Natural-Law Ethics: An Appraisal," *Calvin Theological Journal* 20, no. 1 (April 1985): 58-68; Ronald S. Wallace, *Calvin's Doctrine of the Christian Life* (Edinburgh: Oliver and Boyd, 1959), pp. 141-47; and François Wendel, *Calvin: The Origins and Development of His Religious Thought,* trans. Philip Mairet (New York: Harper and Row, 1963), pp. 161-65.

10. James Barr, *Biblical Faith and Natural Theology* (Oxford: Clarendon Press, 1993), p. 13.

11. Brunner and Barth, *Natural Theology,* pp. 101-10.

12. Brunner and Barth, *Natural Theology,* p. 105.

13. Brunner and Barth, *Natural Theology,* p. 102.

14. Brunner and Barth, *Natural Theology,* p. 101.

15. The primary focus of this book is on the historical consequence; however, it is impossible to separate the historical outcome of the debate from its theological argument. The question of whether Calvin espoused a doctrine of natural law, and, if so, how to understand it in relation to the *duplex cognitio Dei,* will be taken up in Chapter Three.

16. Barth's actualism lies at the root of his criticism of natural theology and natural law. Actualism is present whenever he speaks in the language of occurrence, happening, event, history, decisions, and act. In George Hunsinger's estimation, "At the most general level [actualism] means that he thinks primarily in terms of events and relationships rather than monadic or self-contained substances" (p. 30). An implication of this actualist motif for Barth's ethics is that it is not possible for humans to enter into fellowship with God on the basis of an innate capacity; thus this relationship must be initiated by God and takes place, so to speak, over our heads. "The church, the inspiration of Scripture, faith, and all other creaturely realities in their relationship to God are always understood as events. They are not self-initiating and self-sustaining. They are not grounded in a neutral, ahistorical, or ontological relationship to God independent of the event of grace. Nor are they actualizations of certain ontologically given creaturely capacities. Rather, they have not only their being but also their possibility only as they are continually established anew according to the divine good pleasure" (p. 31). Hunsinger, *How to Read Karl Barth: The Shape of His Theology* (New York: Oxford University Press, 1991).

17. James M. Gustafson defines occasionalism as "a view of moral action that emphasizes the uniqueness of each moment of serious moral choice in contrast to a view

that emphasizes the persistent, perduring order of moral life and the continuities of human experience" (p. 71). Gustafson observes that occasionalism has been deeply influenced by existentialism and is grounded in the conviction that if there is a moral order it is not knowable by human reason. It makes sense, then, that occasionalists usually develop intensely subjective ethical theories. For them, "the moral life is without the props of principles of natural law, which have provided a basis for great objective certitude and for moral absolutes universally valid across time to all who share a common human nature" (pp. 71-72). Gustafson, *Protestant and Roman Catholic Ethics: Prospects for Rapprochement* (Chicago: University of Chicago Press, 1978). Evidence of Barth's occasionalism will be apparent throughout this chapter; however, for an explicit statement of it, see Karl Barth, *Church Dogmatics*, II.2, *The Doctrine of God*, ed. G. W. Bromiley and T. F. Torrance, trans. G. W. Bromiley (Edinburgh: T. & T. Clark, 1957), pp. 663-64.

18. Brunner and Barth, *Natural Theology*, p. 37.

19. Brunner and Barth, *Natural Theology*, p. 41.

20. Heinz Zahrnt, *The Question of God: Protestant Theology in the Twentieth Century*, trans. R. A. Wilson (New York: Harcourt Brace Jovanovich, Inc., 1969), p. 60.

21. E. David Willis, *Calvin's Catholic Christology: The Function of the So-Called Extra Calvinisticum in Calvin's Theology* (Leiden: E. J. Brill, 1966), p. 102; Steinmetz, "Calvin and the Natural Knowledge of God," p. 142; and Zahrnt, *The Question of God*, pp. 54-55.

22. Brunner and Barth, *Natural Theology*, p. 106.

23. Barth, *The Knowledge of God and the Service of God*, p. 8.

24. Barth, *The Knowledge of God and the Service of God*, pp. 8-9.

25. Barth, *The Knowledge of God and the Service of God*, p. 9.

26. Brunner and Barth, *Natural Theology*, p. 107.

27. Brunner and Barth, *Natural Theology*, p. 108.

28. Dowey, *The Knowledge of God in Calvin's Theology.*

29. Parker, *The Doctrine of the Knowledge of God.*

30. Willis, *Calvin's Catholic Christology*, p. 103. Although Dowey is distinctly Brunnerian, Parker's reading of Calvin's exegesis of Psalm 104 is heavily indebted to Barth.

31. Dowey, *The Knowledge of God in Calvin's Theology*, p. 41.

32. Dowey, *The Knowledge of God in Calvin's Theology*, p. 42.

33. Dowey, *The Knowledge of God in Calvin's Theology*, p. 43.

34. Dowey, *The Knowledge of God in Calvin's Theology*, p. 43.

35. Willis, *Calvin's Catholic Christology*, p. 103.

36. Parker, *The Doctrine of the Knowledge of God*, p. 119.

37. Parker, *The Doctrine of the Knowledge of God*, p. 11.

38. Parker, *The Doctrine of the Knowledge of God*, p. 12.

39. Parker, *The Doctrine of the Knowledge of God*, p. 12.

40. Richard Muller was among the first to argue against the central dogma theory; see Richard A. Muller, "Predestination and Christology in Sixteenth-Century Reformed Theology" (Ph.D. diss., Duke University, 1976), pp. 3-6; Muller, *Post-Reformation Reformed Dogmatics*, vol. 1, pp. 42-44; and Charles Partee, "Calvin's Central Dogma Again," *Sixteenth Century Journal* 18, no. 2 (Summer 1987): 191-99.

41. Laytham, "The Place of Natural Theology in the Theological Method of John

Calvin," p. 25. See also Noble, "Our Knowledge of God according to John Calvin," pp. 2-3.

42. Laytham, "The Place of Natural Theology in the Theological Method of John Calvin," p. 25. Noble even goes so far as to say that the knowledge of God "is a theme which if not a basic principle in the sense that it determines all of Calvin's substantive doctrines is nevertheless a perspective or horizon within which Calvin's theology may be seen as a whole." Noble, "Our Knowledge of God according to John Calvin," p. 2.

43. Torrance, "Knowledge of God and Speech about Him according to John Calvin," p. 76.

44. Jean-Daniel Benoît, "The History and Development of the *Institutio:* How Calvin Worked," in *John Calvin,* ed. G. E. Duffield, trans. Ford Lewis Battles (Grand Rapids: Wm. B. Eerdmans Publishing Company, 1966), p. 109.

45. Dowey, *The Knowledge of God in Calvin's Theology,* pp. 46-47.

46. Dowey, *The Knowledge of God in Calvin's Theology,* p. 48.

47. Richard A. Muller, "Establishing the *Ordo docendi:* The Organization of Calvin's *Institutes,* 1536-1559," in *The Unaccommodated Calvin: Studies in the Foundation of a Theological Tradition* (New York: Oxford University Press, 2000), p. 118.

48. Muller, "Establishing the *Ordo docendi,*" p. 137.

49. Muller, "Establishing the *Ordo docendi,*" p. 137.

50. Muller, "Establishing the *Ordo docendi,*" pp. 137-38.

51. Paul B. Henry, "Types of Protestant Theology and the Natural-Law Tradition" (Ph.D. diss., Duke University, 1970), p. 196; and Karl Barth, *The Humanity of God,* trans. J. T. Thomas (Richmond, Va.: John Knox Press, 1960), p. 43.

52. James Barr would challenge this more charitable qualification in method. According to him, the basic lines of Barth's early absolute denial of natural theology were never dismantled, revised, or abandoned either in his later writing or among his proponents. "The new position, one might say, was that only through the death of all sorts of the older natural theology could one come to the resurrection of a new natural theology. Since this is so, we are justified in taking the position of complete denial of natural theology, Barth's position in his Gifford Lectures, in his controversy with Brunner, and in the earlier volumes of the *Church Dogmatics,* as the classic Barthian position." Barr, *Biblical Faith and Natural Theology,* pp. 13-14.

53. Karl Barth, *Church Dogmatics,* IV.1, *The Doctrine of Reconciliation,* ed. G. W. Bromiley and T. F. Torrance, trans. G. W. Bromiley (Edinburgh: T. & T. Clark, 1992), p. 360.

54. Barth, *CD,* IV.1, pp. 360-61.

55. Barth, *CD,* IV.1, p. 361.

56. Barth, *CD,* IV.1, p. 362. This statement is a good example of Barth's actualism.

57. Barth, *CD,* IV.1, p. 362.

58. Barth, *CD,* IV.1, p. 364.

59. Barth, *CD,* IV.1, p. 365.

60. Barth, *CD,* IV.1, p. 368.

61. Barth, *CD,* IV.1, pp. 368-69.

62. Barth, *CD,* IV.1, p. 372.

63. Barth, *CD,* IV.1, p. 373.

64. Barth, *CD,* IV.1, p. 374.

65. For more, see Barth, *CD*, IV.1, pp. 369-72, especially pp. 371-72, and p. 388.

66. Barth, *CD*, IV.1, p. 389.

67. Barth, *CD*, IV.1, p. 389.

68. Muller, *Post-Reformation Reformed Dogmatics,* vol. 1, p. 283.

69. Karl Barth, *Church Dogmatics,* I.1, *The Doctrine of the Word of God,* ed. G. W. Bromiley and T. F. Torrance, trans. G. W. Bromiley (Edinburgh: T. & T. Clark, 1975), p. 130.

70. Barth, *CD*, I.1, p. 131.

71. Barth, *CD*, I.1, p. 131.

72. Barth, *CD*, I.1, p. 131.

73. Barth, *CD*, I.1, p. 131.

74. Barth, *CD*, I.1, pp. 238-39.

75. Barth, *CD*, I.1, p. 241.

76. Barth, *CD*, I.1, p. xiii.

77. Barth, *CD*, II.2, pp. 513, 515.

78. Barth, *CD*, II.2, p. 518.

79. Barth, *CD*, II.2, p. 527.

80. Karl Barth, *Ethics,* ed. Dietrich Braun, trans. Geoffrey W. Bromiley (New York: Seabury Press, 1981), p. 30.

81. Barth, *CD*, II.2, p. 532.

82. Barth, *Ethics,* p. 31.

83. Barth, *Ethics,* p. 32.

84. Barth, *Ethics,* p. 32. Cf. Barth, *CD*, II.2, p. 532. G. C. Berkouwer provides a more nuanced discussion of the remnant idea in relation to the Belgic Confession and the Canons of Dort. However, Barth's influence upon him is apparent, particularly in terms of Berkouwer's disposition to see in the remnant concept a *quantitative* idea that leads to a relativizing of human corruption. See Berkouwer's *Man: The Image of God,* trans. Dirk W. Jellema (Grand Rapids: Wm. B. Eerdmans Publishing Company, 1962), p. 120, and pp. 119-47.

85. Barth, *CD*, II.2, p. 532.

86. Barth, *Ethics,* p. 32.

87. Karl Barth, "The Christian Community and the Civil Community," in *Community, State, and Church: Three Essays,* ed. Will Herberg (Garden City, N.Y.: Anchor Books, 1960), p. 163.

88. Barth, "The Christian Community and the Civil Community," p. 165.

89. Barth, "The Christian Community and the Civil Community," pp. 167-68.

90. Barth, "The Christian Community and the Civil Community," p. 168.

91. Karl Barth, *This Christian Cause: A Letter to Great Britain from Switzerland,* ed. John A. Mackay (New York: Macmillan, 1941), n.p. Unfortunately, there are no numbered pages in this small book.

92. Barth, *This Christian Cause,* n.p.

93. Barth, *This Christian Cause,* n.p.

94. Barth, *This Christian Cause,* n.p.

95. For a thorough survey of the literature and a trenchant criticism of this approach, see Richard A. Muller, "Calvin and the 'Calvinists': Assessing Continuities and Discontinuities Between the Reformation and Orthodoxy. Part I," *Calvin Theological*

Journal 30, no. 2 (November 1995): 345-75; and Muller, "Calvin and the 'Calvinists': Assessing Continuities and Discontinuities Between the Reformation and Orthodoxy. Part II," *Calvin Theological Journal* 31, no. 1 (April 1996): 125-60.

96. Brunner and Barth, *Natural Theology,* p. 105.

97. Muller, *Post-Reformation Reformed Dogmatics,* vol. 1, p. 45.

98. Arthur F. Holmes scrutinizes Ellul's theological and philosophical assumptions in his essay, "A Philosophical Critique of Ellul on Natural Law," in *Jacques Ellul: Interpretative Essays,* ed. Clifford G. Christians and Jay M. Van Hook (Urbana, Ill.: University of Illinois Press, 1981), pp. 229-50.

99. Jacques Ellul, *The Theological Foundation of Law,* trans. Marguerite Wieser (London: S.C.M. Press, 1961), p. 44.

100. Ellul, *The Theological Foundation of Law,* pp. 45-46.

101. Ellul, *The Theological Foundation of Law,* p. 46.

102. Ellul, *The Theological Foundation of Law,* p. 45.

103. Ellul, *The Theological Foundation of Law,* p. 69.

104. Ellul, *The Theological Foundation of Law,* p. 61.

105. Ellul, *The Theological Foundation of Law,* pp. 61-62.

106. Ellul, *The Theological Foundation of Law,* p. 64.

107. Ellul, *The Theological Foundation of Law,* p. 65.

108. Ellul, *The Theological Foundation of Law,* p. 71.

109. Henry Stob, *Summoning Up Remembrance* (Grand Rapids: Wm. B. Eerdmans Publishing Company, 1995), pp. 191, 208, 213-14, 218, 277, 284-85.

110. Cf. John Bolt, "Grand Rapids between Kampen and Amsterdam: Herman Bavinck's Reception and Influence in North America," *Calvin Theological Journal* 38, no. 2 (November 2003): 270-73.

111. Stob, *Summoning Up Remembrance,* p. 139. In his master's thesis, "The Christian Conception of Revelation" (Hartford Theological Seminary, 1936), Stob appropriates the conceptual structure of Barth's doctrine of revelation as his own starting point (cf. pp. 52-56, 94-102). Several decades later, his fundamental assessment of Barth remained congenial: "Karl Barth is an ethicist of the first rank. The ideas he propounds in the field of morals are as important and stimulating as those he develops in Dogmatics." Henry Stob, "Themes in Barth's Ethics," *Reformed Journal* 12, no. 4 (April 1962): 19, 19-23.

112. Stob, "Natural-Law Ethics: An Appraisal," pp. 58-59.

113. Stob, "Natural-Law Ethics: An Appraisal," p. 60. This is where Stob introduces an actualist motif.

114. Stob, "Natural-Law Ethics: An Appraisal," p. 60.

115. Stob, "Natural-Law Ethics: An Appraisal," pp. 60-61.

116. Stob, "Natural-Law Ethics: An Appraisal," p. 61.

117. Stob, "Natural-Law Ethics: An Appraisal," p. 61.

118. Stob, "Natural-Law Ethics: An Appraisal," p. 61.

119. Stob, "Natural-Law Ethics: An Appraisal," p. 62.

120. Herman Dooyeweerd, *Roots of Western Culture: Pagan, Secular, and Christian Options,* ed. Mark Vander Vennen and Bernard Zylstra, trans. John Kraay (Toronto: Wedge Publishing Foundation, 1979), p. 114.

121. Arvin Vos argues that contemporary Protestant theologians such as Bruce

Demarest, Cornelius Van Til, Colin Brown, Francis Schaeffer, Reinhold Niebuhr, and Herman Dooyeweerd fundamentally misunderstand Aquinas on nature and grace. He speculates that the Protestant distortion of Aquinas is attributable to an original Catholic distortion of Aquinas that took place in the sixteenth century by the Spanish scholastic theologians Suárez, Cajetan, and John of St. Thomas. For a full discussion of this view, see Vos's *Aquinas, Calvin, and Contemporary Protestant Thought: A Critique of Protestant Views on the Thought of Thomas Aquinas* (Washington, D.C., and Grand Rapids: Christian University Press and Wm. B. Eerdmans Publishing Company, 1985), chapter 6.

122. Stob, "Natural-Law Ethics: An Appraisal," p. 62. This quotation seems to point toward occasionalism.

123. Stob, "Natural-Law Ethics: An Appraisal," pp. 62-63.

124. Stephen K. Moroney has done significant work in this area of study; see Moroney, "The Noetic Effects of Sin: An Exposition of Calvin's View and a Constructive Theological Proposal" (Ph.D. diss., Duke University, 1995); Moroney, "How Sin Affects Scholarship: A New Model," *Christian Scholar's Review* 28, no. 3 (Spring 1999): 432-51; and Moroney, *The Noetic Effects of Sin: A Historical and Contemporary Exploration of How Sin Affects Our Thinking* (Lanham, Md.: Lexington Books, 2000). For a recent critique of Moroney's book, see Dewey J. Hoitenga, Jr., "The Noetic Effects of Sin: A Review Article," *Calvin Theological Journal* 38, no. 1 (April 2003): 68-102. For a discussion of the topic in Reformed orthodoxy, see Steinmetz, "Calvin and the Natural Knowledge of God," pp. 23-39; and Muller, *Post-Reformation Reformed Dogmatics,* vol. 1, pp. 270-310.

125. Stob, "Natural-Law Ethics: An Appraisal," p. 64.

126. Stob, "Natural-Law Ethics: An Appraisal," p. 65.

127. For more on Stob's understanding of the antithesis, see his "Observations on the Concept of the Antithesis," in *Perspectives on the Christian Reformed Church: Studies in Its History, Theology, and Ecumenicity,* ed. Peter De Klerk and Richard R. De Ridder (Grand Rapids: Baker Book House, 1983), pp. 241-58.

128. Stob, "Natural-Law Ethics: An Appraisal," p. 67.

129. For a definition of the scope and object of ethics, see Henry Stob, "Ethics: An Account of Its Subject Matter," in *Ethical Reflections: Essays on Moral Themes* (Grand Rapids: Wm. B. Eerdmans Publishing Company, 1978), pp. 7-30.

130. Stob, "Natural-Law Ethics: An Appraisal," pp. 67-68. Stob elaborates further on his understanding of the relationship between the revelation in Christ and the immanent Logos in his essay "Calvin and Aquinas," in *Theological Reflections: Essays on Related Themes* (Grand Rapids: Wm. B. Eerdmans Publishing Company, 1981), pp. 126-30.

131. John E. Hare, *God's Call: Moral Realism, God's Commands, and Human Autonomy* (Grand Rapids: Wm. B. Eerdmans Publishing Company, 2001), p. 50.

132. Hare, *God's Call,* p. 50.

133. Richard Cross, *Duns Scotus* (New York: Oxford University Press, 1999), pp. 89-95.

134. Allan B. Wolter, O.F.M., "Native Freedom of the Will as a Key to the Ethics of Scotus," in *The Philosophical Theology of John Duns Scotus,* ed. Marilyn McCord Adams (Ithaca and London: Cornell University Press, 1990), pp. 160-62; and Wolter, *Duns Scotus on the Will and Morality: Selected and Translated with an Introduction by Allan B. Wolter, O.F.M.* (Washington, D.C.: Catholic University of America Press, 1986), pp. 57-63, 263-88.

135. Hannes Möhle, "Scotus's Theory of Natural Law," in *The Cambridge Companion to Duns Scotus*, ed. Thomas Williams (Cambridge: Cambridge University Press, 2003), pp. 312-31, especially p. 312.

136. Cross, *Duns Scotus*, p. 89.

137. Cross, *Duns Scotus*, p. 90.

138. For a critical treatment of John Hare's argument for Calvin as a divine command theorist in the line of Duns Scotus, see Paul Helm, *John Calvin's Ideas* (Oxford: Oxford University Press, 2004), pp. 349-54.

139. Hare, *God's Call*, p. x. To my knowledge, no representative of the Christian natural-law tradition has ever claimed that post-lapsarian natural inclinations provide "an authoritative source of guidance for how we must and must not live."

140. Hare, *God's Call*, p. 49.

141. Hare, *God's Call*, p. 49.

142. Cf. Hare, *God's Call*, pp. 55-59.

143. Hare, *God's Call*, p. 57.

144. John E. Hare, *Why Bother Being Good? The Place of God in the Moral Life* (Downers Grove, Ill.: InterVarsity Press, 2002), p. 7.

145. John E. Hare, *The Moral Gap: Kantian Ethics, Human Limits, and God's Assistance* (Oxford: Clarendon Press, 1996).

146. Hare, *Why Bother Being Good?* p. 29.

147. Hare, *Why Bother Being Good?* p. 102.

148. Hare, *Why Bother Being Good?* pp. 101-3, 136-42.

149. Cf. David Little, *Religion, Order, and Law: A Study in Pre-Revolutionary England* (New York: Harper and Row, 1969), pp. 37-41.

150. Richard J. Mouw, *The God Who Commands: A Study in Divine Command Ethics* (Notre Dame: University of Notre Dame Press, 1990), p. 67, n. 26, which cites Dooyeweerd's *Roots of Western Culture*, chapters 5 and 6.

151. Richard J. Mouw, *He Shines in All That's Fair: Culture and Common Grace* (Grand Rapids: Wm. B. Eerdmans Publishing Company, 2001), p. 90.

152. Mouw, *The God Who Commands*, p. 97.

153. Mouw, *The God Who Commands*, p. 97.

154. Mouw, *The God Who Commands*, p. 97.

155. Mouw, *The God Who Commands*, pp. 97-98.

156. Mouw, *The God Who Commands*, p. 98.

157. Mouw, *He Shines in All That's Fair*, p. 3.

158. For a brief and sporadic treatment of this issue, see Won Ha Shin, "Two Models of Social Transformation: A Critical Analysis of the Theological Ethics of John H. Yoder and Richard J. Mouw" (Ph.D. diss., Boston University, 1997), pp. 92-95, 113-19, 189-92, 195-200.

159. Mouw, *He Shines in All That's Fair*, p. 7.

160. Mouw, *He Shines in All That's Fair*, p. 13.

161. Mouw, *He Shines in All That's Fair*, p. 90.

162. Mouw, *He Shines in All That's Fair*, p. 90.

163. Susan E. Schreiner, *The Theater of His Glory: Nature and the Natural Order in the Thought of John Calvin* (Durham, N.C.: Labyrinth Press, 1991; Grand Rapids: Baker Book House, 1995), pp. 79-95.

Notes to Chapter 2

1. Anthony Quinton, "British Philosophy," in *The Encyclopedia of Philosophy,* vol. 1, ed. Paul Edwards (New York: Macmillan Publishing Company, 1972), p. 373.

2. Arthur F. Holmes, *Fact, Value, and God* (Grand Rapids: Wm. B. Eerdmans Publishing Company, 1997), p. 77, pp. 173-80.

3. See Herman Dooyeweerd, *A New Critique of Theoretical Thought,* 4 vols., trans. David H. Freeman and William S. Young (Jordan Station, Ontario: Paideia Press, 1984), vol. 1, pp. 169-88; Craig M. Gay, *The Way of the (Modern) World: Or, Why It's Tempting to Live As If God Doesn't Exist* (Grand Rapids: Wm. B. Eerdmans Publishing Company, 1998), pp. 119-21; and Tage Lindbom, *The Myth of Democracy* (Grand Rapids: Wm. B. Eerdmans Publishing Company, 1996), p. 20.

4. Hans Blumenberg, *The Legitimacy of the Modern Age,* trans. Robert M. Wallace (Cambridge: MIT Press, 1983 [orig. pub. 1966]). For other mainstream academic critiques of nominalism, see Louis K. Dupré, *Passage to Modernity: An Essay in the Hermeneutics of Nature and Culture* (New Haven: Yale University Press, 1993); and Rudolph Lorenz, *Die unvollendete Befreiung vom Nominalismus: Martin Luther und die Grenzen hermeneutischer Theologie bei Gerhard Ebeling* (Gütersloh: Gütersloher Verlagshaus Mohn, 1973).

5. See Blumenberg, *The Legitimacy of the Modern Age,* pp. 125-226, but especially pp. 152-79. For a multivalent critique of Blumenberg's view of nominalism and his misunderstanding of the dialectic of *potentia absoluta/potentia ordinata,* see Heiko A. Oberman, *Contra vanam curiositatem: ein Kapitel der Theologie zwischen Seelenwickel und Weltall* (Zurich: Theologischer Verlag, 1974); Oberman, "Reformation and Revolution: Copernicus' Discovery in an Era of Change," in *The Dawn of the Reformation: Essays in Late Medieval and Early Reformation Thought* (Grand Rapids: Wm. B. Eerdmans Publishing Company, 1992), pp. 191-98; and Oberman, *The Two Reformations: The Journey from the Last Days to the New World,* ed. Donald Weinstein (New Haven and London: Yale University Press, 2003), p. 24.

6. John Patrick Donnelly, S.J., *Calvinism and Scholasticism in Vermigli's Doctrine of Man and Grace* (Leiden: E. J. Brill, 1976), p. 202. This judgment reverberates throughout Louis Bouyer's *The Spirit and Forms of Protestantism,* trans. A. V. Littledale (London: Harvill Press, 1956), pp. 162-65; Heinrich Denifle's *Luther und Luthertum in der ersten Entwickelung,* 2 vols. in 4 parts (Mainz: F. Kirchheim, 1904-1909), vol. 1, pt. 2, pp. 522, 536, 587; Etienne Gilson's *History of Christian Philosophy in the Middle Ages* (New York: Random House, 1955), pp. 471-72, 489, 498, 499-520; Joseph Lortz's *The Reformation in Germany,* 2 vols., trans. Ronald Walls (New York: Herder and Herder, 1968), vol. 1, pp. 195-200; and John Todd's *Martin Luther: A Biographical Study* (Westminster, Md.: Newman Press, 1964), pp. 53-56.

7. For a concise statement of the differences between the via *antiqua* and the via *moderna,* see William J. Courtenay, "*Antiqui* and *Moderni* in Late Medieval Thought," *Journal of the History of Ideas* 48, no. 1 (January-March 1987): 3-10.

8. Denifle, *Luther und Luthertum,* vol. 1, pt. 2, pp. 523, 547; and Lortz, *The Reformation in Germany,* vol. 1, pp. 170, 396.

9. John L. Farthing, *Thomas Aquinas and Gabriel Biel: Interpretations of St. Thomas Aquinas in German Nominalism on the Eve of the Reformation* (Durham, N.C.: Duke Uni-

versity Press, 1988); Steven Ozment, *"Homo Viator:* Luther and Late Medieval Theology," in *The Reformation in Medieval Perspective,* ed. Steven Ozment (Chicago: Quadrangle Books, 1971), pp. 142-54; Heiko A. Oberman, *The Harvest of Medieval Theology: Gabriel Biel and Late Medieval Nominalism,* 3rd ed. (Grand Rapids: Baker Book House, 2000); Oberman, *Forerunners of the Reformation* (New York: Holt, Rinehart, and Winston, 1966); Oberman, "Luther and the *Via Moderna:* The Philosophical Backdrop of the Reformation Breakthrough," *Journal of Ecclesiastical History* 54, no. 4 (October 2003): 641-70; Charles Trinkhaus and Heiko A. Oberman, eds., *The Pursuit of Holiness in Late Medieval and Renaissance Religion* (Leiden: E. J. Brill, 1974); David C. Steinmetz, *Misericordia Dei: The Theology of Johannes von Staupitz in Its Late Medieval Setting* (Leiden: E. J. Brill, 1968); Steinmetz, *Luther and Staupitz: An Essay in the Intellectual Origins of the Protestant Reformation* (Durham, N.C.: Duke University Press, 1980); and Steinmetz, "Luther Among the Anti-Thomists," in *Luther in Context,* 2d ed. (Grand Rapids: Baker Academic, 2002), pp. 47-58.

10. Heiko A. Oberman, "Some Notes on the Theology of Nominalism: With Attention to Its Relation to the Renaissance," *Harvard Theological Review* 53, no. 1 (January 1960): 54-55; Oberman, *Archbishop Thomas Bradwardine: A Fourteenth-Century Augustinian. A Study of His Theology in Its Historical Context* (Utrecht: Kemink & Zoon, 1957); Oberman, *Masters of the Reformation: Emergence of a New Intellectual Climate in Europe,* trans. Dennis Martin (Cambridge: Cambridge University Press, 1981); Oberman, *The Harvest of Medieval Theology;* Frank A. James III, "A Late Medieval Parallel in Reformation Thought: *Gemina Praedestinatio* in Gregory of Rimini and Peter Martyr Vermigli," in *Via Augustini: Augustine in the Later Middle Ages, Renaissance, and Reformation: Essays in Honor of Damasus Trapp, O.S.A.,* ed. Heiko A. Oberman and Frank A. James III (Leiden: E. J. Brill, 1991), pp. 157-88; James, "Translator's Introduction," in *Predestination and Justification: Two Theological Loci,* vol. 8, *The Peter Martyr Library,* ed. and trans. Frank A. James III (Kirksville, Mo.: Truman State University Press, 2003), pp. xxx-xxxi; and Francis Oakley, *The Western Church in the Later Middle Ages* (Ithaca, N.Y.: Cornell University Press, 1979), pp. 133-38.

11. Michael Bertram Crowe, *The Changing Profile of the Natural Law* (The Hague: Martinus Nijhoff, 1977), p. 212.

12. From the perspective of the early twentieth-century modernist debates, quite aside from the broader historical and theological issues surrounding the Reformation, it makes sense that certain Roman Catholic intellectual communities would go to great lengths to show that nominalism did not arise from an "authentic" Catholic root. As Halsey relates, "After the encyclical *Pascendi Dominici gregis* (1907) Thomism was legislated and literally institutionalized as the only proper mode of Catholic thought. In *Doctoris Angelici* (1914) Pius X warned teachers of Catholic theology and philosophy 'that if they deviated so much as a step from Aquinas, especially in metaphysics, they exposed themselves to grave risk'" (p. 141). In 1914, to assist teachers of Catholic theology and to ensure doctrinal conformity among Catholic theologians, the Congregation of Studies compiled a list of twenty-four theses deemed to be the essential and principal teachings of Aquinas. However, ironically enough, in 1917, Wlodimir Ledochowski, General of the Society of Jesus, pointed out to the newly elected Benedict XV that Francisco Suárez, the revered Spanish Scholastic of the sixteenth century, actually denied twenty-three of the Congregation's twenty-four theses. This striking revelation forced

the pope to concede that there was "at least a modicum of diversity within the Scholastic household" (p. 141). William M. Halsey, *The Survival of American Innocence: Catholicism in an Era of Disillusionment, 1920-1940* (Notre Dame: University of Notre Dame Press, 1980).

13. Allan B. Wolter, O.F.M., "The Realism of Scotus," in *The Philosophical Theology of John Duns Scotus,* ed. Marilyn McCord Adams (Ithaca and London: Cornell University Press, 1990), pp. 42-53.

14. Crowe, *The Changing Profile of the Natural Law,* p. 212.

15. Crowe, *The Changing Profile of the Natural Law,* p. 213.

16. A. P. d'Entrèves, *Natural Law: An Historical Survey* (New York: Harper and Row, 1951), p. 70.

17. Heinrich Rommen, *The Natural Law: A Study in Legal and Social History and Philosophy,* trans. Thomas R. Hanley, O.S.B. (Indianapolis, Ind.: Liberty Fund, Inc., 1998), pp. 54-55.

18. D'Entrèves, *Natural Law: An Historical Survey,* p. 68.

19. John W. Sap, *Paving the Way for Revolution: Calvinism and the Struggle for a Democratic Constitutional State* (Amsterdam: VU Uitgeverij, 2001); and Henk E. S. Woldring, "The Constitutional State in the Political Philosophy of Johannes Althusius," *European Journal of Law and Economics* 5 (1998): 123-32.

20. Johannes Althusius is the preeminent example of a late sixteenth- and seventeenth-century Reformed jurist whose work fits this description. Harold Berman, Daniel Elazar, Thomas Hueglin, and James Skillen concur with this judgment. See Harold J. Berman, *Law and Revolution, II: The Impact of the Protestant Reformations on the Western Legal Tradition* (Cambridge, Mass.: Harvard University Press, 2003), pp. 110-11, 125-26; Daniel J. Elazar, *Covenant Tradition in Politics,* vol. 1, *Covenant and Polity in Biblical Israel: Biblical Foundations and Jewish Expressions* (New Brunswick, N.J.: Transaction Publishers, 1995), p. 26, pp. 19-33; Thomas Hueglin, "Johannes Althusius: Medieval Constitutionalist or Modern Federalist?" *Publius: The Journal of Federalism* 9, no. 4 (Fall 1979): 21-28; James W. Skillen, "The Development of Calvinistic Political Theory in the Netherlands, with Special Reference to the Thought of Herman Dooyeweerd" (Ph.D. diss., Duke University, 1974), pp. 191-217; Skillen, "The Political Theory of Johannes Althusius," *Philosophia Reformata* 39 (1974): 170-90; and Skillen, "From Covenant of Grace to Equitable Public Pluralism: The Dutch Calvinist Contribution," *Calvin Theological Journal* 31, no. 1 (April 1996): 72-77.

21. Frederick S. Carney, "Associational Thought in Early Calvinism," in *Voluntary Associations: A Study of Groups in Free Societies,* ed. D. B. Robertson (Richmond, Va.: John Knox Press, 1966), p. 43, pp. 42-46.

22. One of the better (but historically inaccurate at points) examinations of the evolution of the natural-law tradition is Stephen J. Pope's "Natural Law and Christian Ethics," in *The Cambridge Companion to Christian Ethics,* ed. Robin Gill (Cambridge: Cambridge University Press, 2001), pp. 77-95. Pope's treatment of the relation between voluntarism and Protestantism, though cursory, tends toward the position advocated by Crowe, d'Entrèves, and Rommen precisely because he fails to distinguish between the various strands of the Reformation and because he confines his analysis to representative figures such as Luther and Calvin, ignoring entirely either their forerunners or successors.

23. One prominent medievalist describes the development of the two types of natural-law theories as follows: ". . . in the later Middle Ages and persisting on into the sixteenth and seventeenth centuries there had been two main traditions of natural-law thinking. One of them was grounded in one or other form of ontological essentialism (or 'realism,' to use the medieval term). The other was grounded in the type of theological voluntarism characteristic of William of Ockham (d. 1349) and of his fourteenth- and fifteenth-century nominalist successors" (p. 221). Francis Oakley, "Locke, Natural Law, and God: Again," in *Politics and Eternity: Studies in the History of Medieval and Early-Modern Political Thought* (Leiden: E. J. Brill, 1999), pp. 219-24. See also Kevin McDonnell, "Nominalist Natural-Law Theory Revisited: Gabriel Biel," in *The Medieval Tradition of Natural Law,* ed. Harold J. Johnson (Kalamazoo, Mich.: Medieval Institute Publications and Western Michigan University Press, 1987), pp. 129-36.

24. Liberty Fund's publication of the *Natural Law and Enlightenment Classics* series, a series planning over forty volumes (to be completed in 2008) spanning the seventeenth and eighteenth centuries, has itself contributed to a revival of interest in the modern (i.e., Enlightenment) natural-law tradition. Under the general editorship of Knud Haakonssen, the series includes works by Hugo Grotius, Samuel von Pufendorf, Richard Cumberland, Francis Hutcheson, George Turnbull, Jean-Jacques Burlamaqui, Emmerich de Vattel, Jean Louis De Lolme, and many others.

25. Allan B. Wolter, O.F.M., "Native Freedom of the Will as a Key to the Ethics of Scotus," in *The Philosophical Theology of John Duns Scotus,* ed. Marilyn McCord Adams (Ithaca and London: Cornell University Press, 1990), p. 161; and cf. Robert Prentice, O.F.M., "The Voluntarism of Duns Scotus, As Seen in His Comparison of the Intellect and the Will," *Franciscan Studies* 28 (1968): 63-103.

26. Wolter, "Native Freedom of the Will," p. 161; A. Vos Jaczn., H. Veldhuis, A. H. Looman-Graaskamp, E. Dekker, and N. W. Den Bok, "Introduction, Translation, and Commentary," in John Duns Scotus, *Contingency and Freedom: Lectura I 39* (Dordrecht: Kluwer Academic Publishers, 1994), pp. 23-36; Antonie Vos, "Scholasticism and Reformation," in *Reformation and Scholasticism: An Ecumenical Enterprise,* ed. Willem J. Van Asselt and Eef Dekker (Grand Rapids: Baker Book House, 2001), pp. 110-15, pp. 99-119; Vos, "The Scotian Notion of Natural Law," *Vivarium* 38, no. 2 (2000): 200-202; and Andreas J. Beck, "Gisbertus Voetius (1589-1676): Basic Features of His Doctrine of God," in *Reformation and Scholasticism,* pp. 205-26.

27. In this respect, so-called voluntarist accents can be discerned in Aquinas's otherwise intellectualist anthropology: "Reason has its power of moving from the will, as stated above [*S.T.* I-II, 17, 1], for it is due to the fact that one wills the end that the reason issues its commands as regards things ordained to the end. But in order that the volition of what is commanded may have the nature of law, it needs to be in accord with some rule of reason." In *S.T.* I-II, 17, 1, Aquinas goes further: "Now the first mover, among the powers of the soul, to the doing of an act is the will, as stated above [*S.T.* I-II, 9, 1]. Since therefore the second mover does not move, save in virtue of the first mover, it follows that the very fact that the reason moves by commanding, is due to the power of the will. Consequently, it follows that command is an act of the reason, presupposing an act of the will, in virtue of which the reason, by its command, moves (the power) to the execution of the act." Thomas Aquinas, *Summa Theologica,* 5 vols., trans. Fathers of the English

Dominican Province (New York: Benziger Brothers, Inc., 1948), vol. 2, I-II, 90, 1 (Reply to Obj. 3).

28. Etienne Gilson, *The Christian Philosophy of St. Thomas Aquinas*, trans. L. K. Shook (New York: Random House, 1956), p. 244.

29. For a unique discussion of this concept in the history of ideas, see Louis I. Bredvold, "The Meaning of the Concept of Right Reason in the Natural-Law Tradition," *University of Detroit Law Journal* 36 (December 1959): 120-29.

30. Donald Sinnema's fine article is the clear exception to this statement; "The Discipline of Ethics in Early Reformed Orthodoxy," *Calvin Theological Journal* 28, no. 1 (April 1993): 10-44.

31. Francis Oakley, *Omnipotence, Covenant, and Order: An Excursion in the History of Ideas from Abelard to Leibniz* (Ithaca: Cornell University Press, 1984), p. 82; and Oakley, "'Adamantine Fetters of Destiny': The Absolute Power of God and King in the Sixteenth and Seventeenth Centuries," in *Politics and Eternity: Studies in the History of Medieval and Early-Modern Political Thought* (Leiden: E. J. Brill, 1999), pp. 292-307.

32. The distinction first appeared in Otto von Gierke's *Das deutsche Genossen-schaftsrecht*, vol. 3, *Die Staats- und Korporationslehre des Altertums und des Mittelalters und ihre Aufnahme in Deutschland* (1880), which his son, Julius von Gierke, later published separately under the title *Johannes Althusius und die Entwicklung der naturrechtlichen Staatstheorien: Zugleich ein Beitrag zur Geschichte der Rechtssystematik,* 5th ed. (Aalen: Scientia, 1958), pp. 73-74, n. 44. Gierke reiterated the distinction without modification in his celebrated Cambridge lectures of 1900, which were later published under the title *Political Theories of the Middle Ages*, trans. Frederic W. Maitland (Cambridge: Cambridge University Press, 1951), pp. 172-74, n. 256. Citations will be taken from *Political Theories of the Middle Ages.*

33. Ernst Troeltsch, *The Social Teachings of the Christian Churches*, 2 vols., trans. Olive Wyon (Louisville, Ky.: Westminster/John Knox Press, 1992 [orig. pub. 1912]), vol. 1, pp. 158-61.

34. Paul Vignaux, "Nominalisme," s.v. in *Dictionnaire de théologie catholique* (1931), vol. 11, cols. 717-84; Vignaux, *Justification et predestination au XIVe siècle: Duns Scot, Pierre d'Auriole, Guillaume d'Occam, Grégoire de Rimini* (Paris: E. Leroux, 1934); Vignaux, *Nominalisme au XIVe siècle* (Montreal: Institute D'Études Médiévales, 1948); Vignaux, *Philosophy in the Middle Ages*, trans. E. C. Hall (New York: Meridian Books, 1959); Parthenius Mignes, *Der Gottesbegriff des Duns Scotus auf seinen angeblich exzessiven Indeterminismus* (Vienna: Mayer, 1907); Mignes, *Das Verhältnis zwischen Glauben und Wissen, Theologie und Philosophie nach Duns Scotus* (Paderborn: F. Schöningh, 1908); Mignes, *Der angebliche exzessive Realismus des Duns Scotus* (Münster: Aschendorff, 1908); Mignes, *Ioannis Duns Scoti doctrina philosophica et theologica quoad res praecipuas proposita et exposita,* 2 vols. (Ad Claras Aquas: Collegium S. Bonaventurae, 1930); Francis Oakley, "Medieval Theories of Natural Law: William of Occam and the Significance of the Voluntarist Tradition," *Natural Law Forum* 6 (1961): 65-83; Oakley, "Christian Theology and the Newtonian Science: The Rise of the Concept of the Laws of Nature," *Church History* 30, no. 4 (December 1961): 433-57; Oakley, "Pierre d'Ailly and the Absolute Power of God: Another Note on the Theology of Nominalism," *Harvard Theological Review* 56, no. 1 (January 1963): 59-73; Oakley, *The Political Thought of Pierre d'Ailly: The Voluntarist Tradition* (New Haven: Yale University

Press, 1964); Oakley, "Jacobean Political Theology: The Absolute and Ordinary Powers of the King," *Journal of the History of Ideas* 29, no. 3 (July-September 1968): 323-46; Heiko A. Oberman, "Some Notes on the Theology of Nominalism," pp. 47-76; and Oberman, *The Harvest of Medieval Theology.*

35. Oakley, "Locke, Natural Law, and God: Again," p. 222.

36. "Nominalism," remarks Troeltsch, "resulted not merely in the destruction of dogma, but also, above all, in that of social ethics; while the stressing of the opposition between Reason and Revelation created a yawning gulf between Church and State." Troeltsch, *Social Teachings of the Christian Churches,* vol. 1, p. 278.

37. Gierke, *Political Theories of the Middle Ages,* p. 173.

38. Gierke, *Political Theories of the Middle Ages,* p. 173.

39. Gierke, *Political Theories of the Middle Ages,* p. 173.

40. In questions 91 and 93 of the *Summa Theologica,* Aquinas defines eternal law and describes its relationship to other forms of law. Law, as he defines it, in question 90, article 1, is something pertaining to reason. *Lex* (law) is a derivative of *ligare* (to bind), because it binds one to act. Thus law is "a certain rule or measure of acts whereby man is induced to act or is restrained from acting." But reason is "the rule and measure of human acts . . . which is the first principle of human acts . . . since it belongs to reason to direct to the end, which is the first principle in all matters of action" (*S.T.* I-II, 90, 1). Ultimately, for Aquinas, reason, not will, can be said to move humans to act properly because reason derives its power to move from the will, "for it is due to the fact that one wills the end that the reason issues its commands as regards things ordained to the end. But in order that the volition of what is commanded may have the nature of law, it needs to be in accord with some rule of reason" (*S.T.* I-II, 90, 1, Reply Obj. 3).

Having established the essence of law in question 90, Aquinas then moves on to discuss the various types of law in questions 91 through 95. In question 91, article 1, he explains how law, which is "a dictate of practical reason in the ruler of a perfect community," when combined with the fact that the world is ruled by divine providence, generates the concept of eternal law. "Now it is evident," declares Aquinas, "granted that the world is ruled by divine providence . . . that the whole community of the universe is governed by divine reason. Wherefore, the very idea of the government of things in God the Ruler of the universe has the nature of a law. And since the divine reason's conception of things is not subject to time but is eternal . . . therefore it is that this kind of law must be called eternal" (*S.T.* I-II, 91, 1).

In question 93, article 1, Aquinas shows how God is related to the world of which he is creator and ruler as an artist is related to the products of his art. Just as in the mind of every artist an idea preexists of the art that will be produced, so too in every ruler there preexists the idea of the order to be followed by those subject to his rule. In God's case, however, it is through his wisdom — by which all things were created — that he stands as the artist in relation to the products of his art. Furthermore, just as the type of divine wisdom, which created all things, has the nature of art, exemplar, or idea, so the type of divine wisdom, which moves all things to their due end, has the nature of law. It follows, therefore, from what was said in question 91, article 1, concerning the rule of divine providence, that "the eternal law is nothing else than the type of divine wisdom, as directing all actions and movements" (*S.T.* I-II, 93, 1).

In question 93, articles 2 through 6, Aquinas addresses several significant epistemological matters pertaining to eternal law. Questioning whether eternal law is known by all, he responds that, while only God can know it *in se*, every rational creature is able to know it in its reflection, to a greater or lesser extent. "For every knowledge of truth is a kind of reflection and participation of the eternal law, which is the unchangeable truth. . . . Now, all men know the truth to a certain extent, at least as to the common principles of the natural law, and as to the others, they partake of the knowledge of truth, some more, some less, and in this respect are more or less cognizant of the eternal law" (*S.T.* I-II, 93, 2). However, of the two ways in which things are subject to eternal law, the first involves an immediate intuitive awareness of the law by the rational creature, while the second partakes of eternal law through "an inward motive principle" (as in the case of irrational creatures). Rational creatures are subject to eternal law in both ways, reasons Aquinas, because they have some "imprinted" knowledge of it, and because they have "a natural inclination to that which is in harmony with the eternal law, for 'we are naturally adapted to be the recipients of virtue'" (*S.T.* I-II, 93, 6). But these ways of knowing eternal law are imperfect and susceptible to corruption because the natural inclination to virtue is diminished by vicious habits and the natural knowledge of good is darkened by passions and habits of sin. Nevertheless, despite a possibly imperfect knowledge of eternal law, "in no man does the prudence of the flesh dominate so far as to destroy the whole good of his nature, and consequently, there remains in man the inclination to act in accordance with the eternal law" (*S.T.* I-II, 93, 6).

Now that Aquinas's understanding of eternal law has been introduced, what remains is to show how he relates it to natural law. As a rule and measure, therefore, law can be in a person in two ways. In the first way, law is said to be in the person himself who rules and measures; that is, in the promulgator of the law. In the second way, which is the relevant sense for natural law, law is said to be "in that which is ruled and measured, since a thing is ruled or measured insofar as it partakes of the rule or measure" (*S.T.* I-II, 91, 2). In the following critical citation (*S.T.* I-II, 91, 2) Aquinas explains how it is that natural law is the rational creature's participation in eternal law:

> Wherefore, since all things subject to divine providence are ruled and measured by the eternal law . . . it is evident that all things partake somewhat of the eternal law insofar as, namely, from its being imprinted on them, they derive their respective inclinations to their proper acts and ends. Now among all others, the rational creature is subject to divine providence in a more excellent way, insofar as it partakes of a share of providence, by being provident both for itself and for others. Wherefore it has a share of the eternal reason, whereby it has a natural inclination to its proper act and end, and this participation of the eternal law in the rational creature is called the natural law.

It should be recognized that the principal means by which the rational creature "participates" in eternal law is through the use of *recta ratio* (right reason) to apprehend as good those things to which the creature already has a natural inclination.

41. Thus, Aquinas states, ". . . since God's will is His very Essence, it is subject neither to the Divine government nor to the eternal law but is the same thing as the eternal law" (*S.T.* I-II, 93, 4).

42. Gierke, *Political Theories of the Middle Ages,* p. 172. Cf. Aquinas, *S.T.* I-II, 94, 5 (Reply Obj. 2).

43. For further elaboration of this point, see Anton-Hermann Chroust, "A Summary of the Main Achievements of the Spanish Jurist-Theologians in the History of Jurisprudence," *American Journal of Jurisprudence* 26 (1981): 114-15; and Paul Rooney, "Divine Commands, Natural Law and Aquinas," *Scottish Journal of Religious Studies* 16 (Autumn 1995): 117-40.

44. Oakley, "Medieval Theories of Natural Law," pp. 66, 68; cf. n. 33.

45. Max Shephard, "William of Occam and the Higher Law, I," *American Political Science Review* 26, no. 6 (December 1932): 1009.

46. Shephard, "William of Occam and the Higher Law, I," p. 1009. Cf. Shephard's follow-up article, "William of Occam and the Higher Law, II," *American Political Science Review* 27, no. 1 (February 1933): 24-38.

47. Heiko A. Oberman, "*Via Antiqua* and *Via Moderna*: Late Medieval Prolegomena to Early Reformation Thought," in *The Impact of the Reformation* (Grand Rapids: Wm. B. Eerdmans Publishing Company, 1994), p. 8.

48. See Richard Cross, *Duns Scotus* (New York: Oxford University Press, 1999), pp. 47-60, 83-88; Henri Veldhuis, "Ordained and Absolute Power in Scotus' *Ordinatio I 44*," *Vivarium* 38, no. 2 (2000): 222-30; Allan B. Wolter, O.F.M., "Duns Scotus on the Nature of Man's Knowledge of God," *Review of Metaphysics* 1, no. 2 (December 1947): 3-36; Wolter, *Duns Scotus on the Will and Morality: Selected and Translated with an Introduction by Allan B. Wolter, O.F.M.* (Washington, D.C.: Catholic University of America Press, 1986), pp. 56-57, 255-62; and Wolter, "The Realism of Scotus," pp. 42-53. On the history of the two powers distinction, see William J. Courtenay, *Capacity and Volition: A History of the Distinction of Absolute and Ordained Power* (Bergamo: P. Lubrina, 1990).

49. Aquinas, *S.T.* I-II, 93, 1.

50. Oakley, *Omnipotence, Covenant, and Order*, p. 80.

51. Oakley, "Locke, Natural Law, and God: Again," pp. 230-31.

52. Anton-Hermann Chroust contends that the controversy between the realists and the nominalists had two effects on the development of the natural-law tradition. First, he argues that the controversy "to a large extent determined the subsequent history of philosophy and the development of natural-law theories" (p. 112), thus supporting Oakley's earlier assessment. However, even given his recognition of the controversy's significance, he does not clearly distinguish between the various types of natural-law theories, which in turn undermines his ability to discern the extent to which the Thomistic Salamancan theologians (i.e., Dominico Banez, Francisco Vitoria, Ludovico Molina, Gabriel Vazquez, and Francisco Suárez) draw elements of their natural-law theory from those in the lines of Scotus and Occam. Second, he asserts that the controversy led to an "emphatic revival of essentially Thomistic natural-law theories during the sixteenth and early part of the seventeenth century" (p. 116) among the Spanish jurist-theologians. Yet, such a generalization cannot sufficiently account for the Occamist accents that are unmistakably present in the natural-law theories of Gabriel Vazquez and Francisco Suárez, to mention only two of the Salamancan theologians. Chroust, "A Summary of the Main Achievements of the Spanish Jurist-Theologians," pp. 112-24.

53. Oberman, "*Via Antiqua* and *Via Moderna*," p. 9; and Oberman, *The Harvest of Medieval Theology*, pp. 30-36.

54. Oberman, *The Harvest of Medieval Theology*, p. 35. For insightful analysis of Biel's nominalist theory of natural law, see Oberman, *The Harvest of Medieval Theology*,

pp. 90-119; and McDonnell, "Nominalist Natural-Law Theory Revisited: Gabriel Biel," pp. 129-36.

55. Oberman, *"Via Antiqua* and *Via Moderna,"* p. 9.

56. William J. Courtenay, "Nominalism and Late Medieval Religion," in *The Pursuit of Holiness in Late Medieval and Renaissance Religion: Papers from the University of Michigan Conference,* ed. Charles Trinkaus and Heiko A. Oberman (Leiden: E. J. Brill, 1974), p. 37. Cf. William J. Courtenay, "Late Medieval Nominalism Revisited: 1972-1982," *Journal of the History of Ideas* 44, no. 1 (January-March 1983): 159-64; Courtenay, "The Dialectic of Divine Omnipotence in the High and Late Middle Ages," in *Divine Omniscience and Omnipotence in Medieval Philosophy,* ed. T. Rudavsky (Dordrecht: D. Reidel Publishing Company, 1985), pp. 243-69; and the collection of Courtenay's essays, *Covenant and Causality in Medieval Thought: Studies in Philosophy, Theology, and Economic Practice* (London: Variorum Reprints, 1984). In *Capacity and Volition,* pp. 18-21, Courtenay has made minor modifications to his earlier understanding of the distinction based upon a closer reading of twelfth- and thirteenth-century sources.

57. Courtenay, "Nominalism and Late Medieval Religion," p. 37. See also Heiko A. Oberman, "The 'Extra' Dimension in the Theology of Calvin," in *The Dawn of the Reformation: Essays in Late Medieval and Early Reformation Thought* (Grand Rapids: Wm. B. Eerdmans Publishing Company, 1992), p. 256.

58. Aquinas, *S.T.* I-I, 25, 4, 5.

59. Courtenay, "Nominalism and Late Medieval Religion," p. 39.

60. Heiko A. Oberman, "The Shape of Late Medieval Thought: The Birthpangs of the Modern Era," in *The Dawn of the Reformation: Essays in Late Medieval and Early Reformation Thought* (Grand Rapids: Wm. B. Eerdmans Publishing Company, 1992), p. 27.

61. Courtenay, "Nominalism and Late Medieval Religion," p. 27. Commenting on this quotation, Oberman thinks "Courtenay has convincingly countered the charge of arbitrariness" concerning the *potentia Dei absoluta.* Oberman, *"Via Antiqua* and *Via Moderna,"* p. 9.

62. Oakley, *The Western Church in the Later Middle Ages,* p. 144.

63. Oakley, *The Western Church in the Later Middle Ages,* p. 145.

64. Francis Oakley, *Omnipotence and Promise: The Legacy of the Scholastic Distinction of Powers* (Toronto: Pontifical Institute of Medieval Studies, 2002), p. 10.

65. Katherine H. Tachau, "Logic's God and the Natural Order in Late Medieval Oxford: The Teaching of Robert Holcot," *Annals of Science* 53 (1996): 242, 235-67.

66. Eugenio Randi, "A Scotist Way of Distinguishing Between God's Absolute and Ordained Powers," in *From Ockham to Wyclif,* ed. Anne Hudson and Michael Wilks (Oxford: Basil Blackwell, 1987), pp. 43-50; and Randi, "Ockham, John XXII and the Absolute Power of God," *Franciscan Studies* 46 (1986): 205-16.

67. Oakley, *Omnipotence and Promise,* p. 12.

68. Oakley, *Omnipotence and Promise,* p. 12. For an insightful analysis of the relationship between voluntarism and conciliarism in Oakley's thought, see Constantin Fasolt, "Voluntarism and Conciliarism in the Work of Francis Oakley," *History of Political Thought* 22, no. 1 (Spring 2001): 41-52.

69. Oakley, *The Western Church in the Later Middle Ages,* p. 146.

70. Cf. Courtenay, "Nominalism and Late Medieval Religion," p. 43; Courtenay, "Covenant and Causality in Pierre d'Ailly," *Speculum* 46, no. 1 (January 1971): 116-19;

Oakley, *Omnipotence, Covenant, and Order,* pp. 84-86; Oakley, "Locke, Natural Law, and God: Again," pp. 234-35; and Oberman, "The Shape of Late Medieval Thought," p. 29.

71. Oberman, "*Via Antiqua* and *Via Moderna,*" p. 20.

72. To see how, for example, Suárez and Biel remained consistent nominalists and yet affirmed the immutability of natural-law precepts, see David Williams, "The Immutability of Natural Law According to Suárez," *The Thomist* 62, no. 1 (January 1998): 97-115; and Oberman, *The Harvest of Medieval Theology,* pp. 100-103, 105-8.

73. Courtenay, "Nominalism and Late Medieval Religion," p. 46.

74. Holmes, *Fact, Value, and God,* p. 77.

75. Jerome Hall thinks that the nominalist phase of the natural-law tradition fostered legal positivism because of its stress on law as the command of the sovereign: ". . . an examination of certain natural law writing is illuminating as regards the source of some of the basic legal ideas which are usually assumed to be the invention of the positivists." Hall, *Studies in Jurisprudence and Criminal Theory* (New York: Oceana Publications, 1958), pp. 31-32. Oakley says of Hall's thesis, "there can be little doubt that he is basically correct." Oakley, "Medieval Theories of Natural Law," p. 74. See also Rommen's concurring opinion, *The Natural Law,* pp. 51-53.

76. Courtenay, "Nominalism and Late Medieval Religion," p. 47. Oberman reinforces Courtenay's point in an observation about Gabriel Biel's theology: "Against the Thomistic emphasis on the priority of God's intellect, the priority of God's will is not stressed as much as the simplicity of God's being and the resulting unity of his intellect and essence. As the simplicity of God's being also implies a unity of essence and will, God's very essence guarantees the unbreakable relation and cooperation of intellect and will in God's *opera ad extra*. . . . Biel constantly tries to make clear that, whereas the will of God is the immediate cause of every act, these acts are certainly not arbitrary products of God's will alone. On the contrary, God's will operates according to God's essential wisdom, though this may be hidden from man." Oberman, *The Harvest of Medieval Theology,* p. 99.

77. Anna Case-Winters, *God's Power: Traditional Understandings and Contemporary Challenges* (Louisville: Westminster/John Knox Press, 1990), pp. 39-93; Richard A. Muller, "Scholasticism in Calvin: A Question of Relation and Disjunction," in *The Unaccommodated Calvin: Studies in the Foundation of a Theological Tradition* (New York: Oxford University Press, 2000), pp. 39-61; Francis Oakley, "The Absolute and Ordained Power of God in Sixteenth- and Seventeenth-Century Theology," *Journal of the History of Ideas* 59, no. 3 (1998): 437-61; Susan Schreiner, "Exegesis and Double Justice in Calvin's Sermons on Job," *Church History* 58, no. 3 (September 1989): 322-38; Schreiner, "Through a Mirror Dimly: Calvin's Sermons on Job," *Calvin Theological Journal* 21, no. 2 (November 1986): 175-93; Schreiner, *Where Shall Wisdom Be Found? Calvin's Exegesis of Job from Medieval and Modern Perspectives* (Chicago: University of Chicago Press, 1994); David Steinmetz, "Calvin and the Absolute Power of God," in *Calvin in Context* (New York: Oxford University Press, 1995), pp. 40-52; Heiko A. Oberman, *Initia Calvini: The Matrix of Calvin's Reformation* (Amsterdam: Koninklijke Nederlandse Akademie van Wetenschappen, 1991), pp. 11-17; Oberman, "The 'Extra' Dimension in the Theology of Calvin"; and Oberman, "*Via Antiqua* and *Via Moderna*."

78. Muller, "Scholasticism in Calvin," p. 41.

79. Muller, "Scholasticism in Calvin," p. 41.

80. Francis Turretin thought that Calvin objected to the abuse of the distinction by certain late medieval scholastics and not the distinction itself. See Francis Turretin, *Institutes of Elenctic Theology,* 3 vols., ed. James T. Dennison Jr., trans. George Musgrave Giger (Phillipsburg, N.J.: Presbyterian and Reformed Publishing Company, 1992-1997), 3.21.5.

81. Steinmetz, "Calvin and the Absolute Power of God," p. 48.

82. John Calvin, *Institutes of the Christian Religion,* 2 vols., ed. John T. McNeill, trans. Ford Lewis Battles (Philadelphia: Westminster Press, 1960), 3.23.2.

83. Calvin, *Institutes,* 3.23.2.

84. Steinmetz, "Calvin and the Absolute Power of God," p. 48.

85. Calvin, *Institutes,* 3.23.2.

86. Muller, "Scholasticism in Calvin," p. 47.

87. Oberman, "The 'Extra' Dimension in the Theology of Calvin," p. 255.

88. Oberman, "The 'Extra' Dimension in the Theology of Calvin," p. 256.

89. Oberman, "The 'Extra' Dimension in the Theology of Calvin," p. 256.

Notes to Chapter 3

1. Cf. Emil Brunner and Karl Barth, *Natural Theology* ("Nature and Grace" by Brunner and the Reply "No!" by Barth), trans. Peter Fraenkel (London: Geoffrey Bles, 1946), p. 106.

2. Cf. Aurelius Augustine, "A Treatise on Nature and Grace, Against Pelagius," in *Nicene and Post-Nicene Fathers of the Christian Church* (First Series), vol. 5, ed. Philip Schaff, trans. Peter Holmes and Robert Ernest Wallis (Grand Rapids: Wm. B. Eerdmans Publishing Company, 1956), chaps. 3 (p. 122), 21 (pp. 127-28), 22 (p. 128). Irena Backus makes a similar observation in her excellent article, "Calvin's Concept of Natural and Roman Law," *Calvin Theological Journal* 38, no. 1 (April 2003): 14-15.

3. John Calvin, *Institutes of the Christian Religion,* ed. John T. McNeill, trans. Ford Lewis Battles (Philadelphia: Westminster Press, 1960), 2.2.12-17. For a full treatment of this distinction and Calvin's view of reason, see David Jon Van Houten, "Earthly Wisdom and Heavenly Wisdom: The Concept of Reason in the Theology of John Calvin" (Ph.D. diss., University of Chicago Divinity School, 1993), chap. 3, "Reason Naturally Implanted in Us," pp. 94-165; and chap. 4, "Vitiated Reason," pp. 166-257.

4. Calvin, *Institutes,* 2.2.13.

5. Calvin, *Institutes,* 1.15.8.

6. Calvin, *Institutes,* 2.2.13.

7. John Calvin, *Commentaries on the Twelve Minor Prophets,* 5 vols., trans. John Owen (Grand Rapids: Wm. B. Eerdmans Publishing Company, 1950), vol. 3, pp. 39-43 (viz., Jon. 1:6).

8. John Calvin, *Commentary on the Gospel according to St. John,* 2 vols., ed. David W. Torrance and Thomas F. Torrance, trans. T. H. L. Parker (Grand Rapids: Wm. B. Eerdmans Publishing Company, 1959), vol. 1, pp. 7-15 (viz., John 1:1-9).

9. John Calvin, *Commentary on the Acts of the Apostles,* 2 vols., ed. David W. Torrance and Thomas F. Torrance, trans. John W. Fraser (Grand Rapids: Wm. B. Eerdmans Publishing Company, 1966), vol. 2, pp. 109-23 (viz., Acts 17:22-29).

10. John Calvin, *Commentary on the Epistles of Paul the Apostle to the Romans and the Thessalonians*, ed. David W. Torrance and T. F. Torrance, trans. Ross Mackenzie (Grand Rapids: Wm. B. Eerdmans Publishing Company, 1961), pp. 29-39 (viz., Rom. 1:18-32); and pp. 47-50 (viz., Rom. 2:14-16).

11. Calvin, *Institutes*, 1.3.1.

12. Calvin, *Institutes*, 2.2.22.

13. Calvin, *Institutes*, 2.2.17.

14. Calvin, *Institutes*, 2.2.24; cf. 1.15.8.

15. Calvin, *Institutes*, 2.2.12.

16. Calvin, *Institutes*, 2.2.24.

17. Calvin, *Institutes*, 3.23.2. "For [God's] will is, and rightly ought to be, the cause of all things that are. For if it has any cause, something must precede it, to which it is, as it were, bound; this is unlawful to imagine. For God's will is so much the highest rule of righteousness that whatever he wills, by the very fact that he wills it, must be considered righteous."

18. Calvin, *Institutes*, 2.8.5. "The Lord, in giving the rule of perfect righteousness, has referred all its parts to his will, thereby showing that nothing is more acceptable to him than obedience."

19. Karl Reuter, *Das Grundverständnis der Theologie Calvins* (Neukirchen: Neukirchener Verlag, 1963); Thomas F. Torrance, *The Hermeneutics of John Calvin* (Edinburgh: Scottish Academic Press, 1988); Torrance, "Knowledge of God and Speech about Him According to John Calvin," in *Theology in Reconstruction* (Grand Rapids: Wm. B. Eerdmans Publishing Company, 1966), pp. 76-98; Alister E. McGrath, "John Calvin and Late Medieval Thought: A Study in Late Medieval Influences upon Calvin's Theological Development," *Archiv für Reformationsgeschichte* 77 (1986): 58-78; David C. Steinmetz, "Calvin and the Absolute Power of God," in *Calvin in Context* (New York: Oxford University Press, 1995), pp. 40-52; Heiko A. Oberman, *Initia Calvini: The Matrix of Calvin's Reformation* (Amsterdam: Koninklijke Nederlandse Akademie van Wetenschappen, 1991), pp. 11-17; Oberman, "The 'Extra' Dimension in the Theology of Calvin," in *The Dawn of the Reformation: Essays in Late Medieval and Early Reformation Thought* (Grand Rapids: Wm. B. Eerdmans Publishing Company, 1992), p. 255; and Richard A. Muller, "Scholasticism in Calvin: A Question of Relation and Disjunction," in *The Unaccommodated Calvin: Studies in the Foundation of a Theological Tradition* (New York: Oxford University Press, 2000), pp. 40-41.

20. Cf. Armand Aime LaVallee, "Calvin's Criticism of Scholastic Theology" (Ph.D. diss., Harvard University, 1967), pp. 242-49; Alexandre Ganoczy, *The Young Calvin*, trans. David Foxgrover and Wade Provo (Philadelphia: Westminster Press, 1987), pp. 173-78; the response by Reuter, *Vom Scholaren bis zum jungen Reformator* (Neukirchen: Neukirchener Verlag, 1981); and the surresponses by A. N. S. Lane, "Calvin's Use of Bernard of Clairvaux," in *John Calvin: Student of the Church Fathers* (Grand Rapids: Baker Book House, 1999), pp. 87-114; and Lane, "Calvin's Sources of Bernard of Clairvaux," in *John Calvin: Student of the Church Fathers*, pp. 115-50.

21. Calvin, *Institutes*, 1.15.7.

22. Calvin, *Institutes*, 2.2.26. "Therefore whether or not man is impelled to seek after good by an impulse of nature has no bearing upon freedom of the will. This instead

is required: that he discern good by right reason; that knowing it he choose it; that having chosen it he follow it."

23. Dewey J. Hoitenga Jr., *John Calvin and the Will: A Critique and Corrective* (Grand Rapids: Baker Book House, 1997), pp. 6-8, 45-52.

24. Hoitenga, *John Calvin and the Will*, p. 8. For more on Augustine's legal and ethical voluntarism, see Vernon J. Bourke, S.J., "Voluntarism in Augustine's Ethico-Legal Thought," *Augustinian Studies* 1 (1970): 3-17.

25. A. N. S. Lane, "Calvin and the Fathers in His *Bondage and Liberation of the Will*," in *John Calvin: Student of the Church Fathers*, pp. 151-78; and Lane, "The Influence upon Calvin of His Debate with Pighius," in *John Calvin: Student of the Church Fathers*, pp. 179-90.

26. Cf. Backus, "Calvin's Concept of Natural and Roman Law," p. 8, n. 9; and Richard A. Muller, "*Fides* and *Cognitio* in Relation to the Problem of Intellect and Will in the Theology of John Calvin," in *The Unaccommodated Calvin: Studies in the Foundation of a Theological Tradition* (New York: Oxford University Press, 2000), pp. 161-64.

27. Calvin, *Institutes*, 2.8.1.

28. Cf. Robert Letham, "The *Foedus Operum*: Some Factors Accounting for Its Development," *Sixteenth Century Journal* 14, no. 4 (Winter 1983): 461-63; and Richard A. Muller, "The Covenant of Works and the Stability of Divine Law in Seventeenth-Century Reformed Orthodoxy: A Study in the Theology of Herman Witsius and Wilhelmus à Brakel," in *After Calvin: Studies in the Development of a Theological Tradition* (New York: Oxford University Press, 2003), pp. 182-83.

29. John Calvin, *Commentary on the Book of Psalms*, 5 vols., trans. James Anderson (Grand Rapids: Wm. B. Eerdmans Publishing Company, 1949), vol. 4, p. 38.

30. That is, the faculty that "does not allow man to suppress within himself what he knows" to be true. Calvin, *Institutes*, 4.10.3.

31. That is, the faculty that distinguishes good from evil, right from wrong, and what should be followed from what should be avoided. Calvin, *Institutes*, 1.15.8.

32. John Calvin, *The Bondage and Liberation of the Will: A Defense of the Orthodox Doctrine of Human Choice Against Pighius*, ed. A. N. S. Lane, trans. G. I. Davies (Grand Rapids: Baker Books, 1996), 1.248; 2.259, 266-67; 3.313; 4.327-30, 339-46; 6.387.

33. Muller, "*Fides* and *Cognitio*," pp. 164-67, 170-73; and Muller, "Foreword," in *John Calvin and the Will*, pp. 6-10.

34. Richard A. Muller, *Post-Reformation Reformed Dogmatics: The Rise and Development of Reformed Orthodoxy, ca. 1520 to ca. 1725*, 4 vols. (Grand Rapids: Baker Academic, 2003), vol. 1, pp. 288-89.

35. Torrance, "Knowledge of God and Speech about Him According to John Calvin," p. 76.

36. Richard A. Muller, "*Duplex Cognitio Dei* in the Theology of Early Reformed Orthodoxy," *Sixteenth Century Journal* 10, no. 2 (Summer 1979): 54. Cf. Muller, "Predestination and Christology in Sixteenth-Century Reformed Theology" (Ph.D. diss., Duke University, 1976), pp. 53-67.

37. Pierre Viret, *A Very Familiar and Fruitful Exposition of the Twelve Articles of the Christian Faith Contained in the Common Creed, Called the Apostle's Creed* (London: John Day, 1548), f. Avii.

38. Viret, *Apostle's Creed*, f. Avii.

39. Viret, *Apostle's Creed,* f. Aviii.
40. Viret, *Apostle's Creed,* f. Avii.
41. Viret, *Apostle's Creed,* f. Aviii.
42. Viret, *Apostle's Creed,* f. Bi.
43. Viret, *Apostle's Creed,* f. Bi.
44. Viret, *Apostle's Creed,* f. Bi.
45. Viret, *Apostle's Creed,* ff. Bi-ii.
46. Muller, *Post-Reformation Reformed Dogmatics,* vol. 1, pp. 289-90.
47. Viret, *Apostle's Creed,* ff. Bi-Bv.
48. Viret, *Apostle's Creed,* f. Biii.
49. Muller, *Post-Reformation Reformed Dogmatics,* vol. 1, p. 290.
50. Muller, *Post-Reformation Reformed Dogmatics,* vol. 1, p. 290.
51. Calvin, *Institutes,* 1.2.1.
52. Calvin, *Institutes,* 1.2.1.
53. Muller, *Post-Reformation Reformed Dogmatics,* vol. 3, p. 173.
54. Muller, *Post-Reformation Reformed Dogmatics,* vol. 3, p. 174.
55. Calvin, *Institutes,* 1.3.1. For rich and learned analyses of the Stoic seed metaphor in moral and theological treatises of the Renaissance and Reformation periods, see Robert A. Greene, "Synderesis, the Spark of Conscience, in the English Renaissance," *Journal of the History of Ideas* 52, no. 2 (April-June 1991): 195-219; Maryanne Cline Horowitz, "The Stoic Synthesis of the Idea of Natural Law in Man: Four Themes," *Journal of the History of Ideas* 35, no. 1 (January-March 1974): 3-16; and Horowitz, *Seeds of Virtue and Knowledge* (Princeton, N.J.: Princeton University Press, 1998).
56. Calvin, *Institutes,* 1.3.1.
57. Calvin, *Institutes,* 1.4.1.
58. Calvin, *Institutes,* 1.3.1.
59. Calvin, *Institutes,* 1.3.2.
60. Calvin, *Institutes,* 1.3.2.
61. Calvin, *Institutes,* 1.4.1.
62. Calvin, *Institutes,* 1.4.1.
63. Calvin, *Institutes,* 1.4.1.
64. Calvin, *Institutes,* 1.5.8.
65. Egil Grislis, "Calvin's Use of Cicero in the *Institutes* I:1-5 — A Case Study in Theological Method," *Archiv für Reformationsgeschichte* 62 (1971): 21.
66. Calvin, *Institutes,* 1.3.2.
67. Calvin, *Institutes,* 1.3.2.
68. Calvin, *Institutes,* 1.3.2.
69. Calvin, *Institutes,* 1.5.11.
70. Calvin, *Institutes,* 1.5.11.
71. Grislis, "Calvin's Use of Cicero in the *Institutes* I:1-5," p. 25.
72. Calvin, *Institutes,* 1.5.2.
73. Calvin, *Commentary on the Acts of the Apostles,* vol. 2, p. 119.
74. Calvin, *Institutes,* 1.5.2.
75. Calvin, *Institutes,* 1.5.3. Cf. *Institutes,* vol. 1, p. 54, n. 9, where John T. McNeill remarks, "This notion recurs in many later writers. It was frequently utilized in the Re-

naissance and became a literary commonplace"; and Grislis, "Calvin's Use of Cicero in the *Institutes* I:1-5," pp. 9-11.

76. Calvin, *Institutes*, 1.2.1. Calvin's language here is similar to Viret's.

77. Calvin, *Institutes*, 1.6.2.

78. Calvin, *Institutes*, 1.6.2.

79. Calvin, *Institutes*, 1.5.12. Cf. Calvin, *Commentary on the Acts of the Apostles*, vol. 2, pp. 112-14, 118-19.

80. Calvin, *Institutes*, 1.1.1.

81. For a full treatment of Calvin's ordering and reordering of topics in the various editions of the *Institutes*, see Richard A. Muller, "Establishing the *Ordo docendi:* The Organization of Calvin's *Institutes*, 1536-1559," in The *Unaccommodated Calvin: Studies in the Foundation of a Theological Tradition* (New York: Oxford University Press, 2000), pp. 118-39.

82. Calvin, *Institutes*, 1.2.1.

83. Calvin, *Institutes*, 1.6.1.

84. Calvin, *Institutes*, 1.10.1.

85. Calvin, *Institutes*, 1.13.9, 11.

86. Edward A. Dowey Jr., *The Knowledge of God in Calvin's Theology*, rev. ed. (Grand Rapids: Wm. B. Eerdmans Publishing Company, 1994), pp. 45-46.

87. Calvin, *Institutes*, 2.6.1.

88. Calvin, *Commentary on Romans*, p. 31.

89. Muller, *Post-Reformation Reformed Dogmatics*, vol. 1, p. 290.

90. Brunner and Barth, *Natural Theology*, p. 108.

91. Muller, *Post-Reformation Reformed Dogmatics*, vol. 1, p. 274.

92. Calvin, *Institutes*, 1.6.1.

93. Ernest F. Kevan, *The Grace of Law: A Study in Puritan Theology* (Grand Rapids: Baker Book House, 1965), pp. 69-77, 109-34.

94. E. David Willis, *Calvin's Catholic Christology: The Function of the So-Called Extra Calvinisticum in Calvin's Theology* (Leiden: E. J. Brill, 1966), p. 104.

95. Willis, *Calvin's Catholic Christology*, pp. 104-5.

96. Willis, *Calvin's Catholic Christology*, p. 109.

97. John Calvin, *Commentaries on the Epistles of Paul the Apostle to the Philippians, Colossians, and Thessalonians*, ed. and trans. John Pringle (Grand Rapids: Wm. B. Eerdmans Publishing Company, 1948), p. 183.

98. Willis, *Calvin's Catholic Christology*, p. 121.

99. Backus, "Calvin's Concept of Natural and Roman Law," pp. 11-13; R. S. Clark, "Calvin on the *Lex Naturalis*," *Stulos Theological Journal* 6, nos. 1-2 (May-November 1998): 4, 7-9, 18, 22; Paul Helm, "Calvin and Natural Law," *Scottish Bulletin of Evangelical Theology* 2 (1984): 10-12; Harro P. Höpfl, *The Christian Polity of John Calvin* (Cambridge: Cambridge University Press, 1982), pp. 179-81; William Klempa, "Calvin on Natural Law," in *John Calvin and the Church: A Prism of Reform*, ed. Timothy George (Louisville: Westminster/John Knox Press, 1990), pp. 80-81; Peter J. Leithart, "Stoic Elements in Calvin's Doctrine of the Christian Life. Part I: Original Corruption, Natural Law, and the Order of the Soul," *Westminster Theological Journal* 55, no. 1 (Spring 1993): 35-45; and Allen Verhey, "Natural Law in Aquinas and Calvin," in *God and the Good: Es-*

says in Honor of Henry Stob, ed. Clifton Orlebeke and Lewis Smedes (Grand Rapids: Wm. B. Eerdmans Publishing Company, 1975), pp. 82-83, 91-92.

100. This is a difficult thesis to establish on historical grounds for two primary reasons. First, because Calvin adopted the natural-law tradition from medieval antecedents with relatively minor alterations and scarce citations, it is difficult to determine what historical ties Calvin sought to maintain or to sever with them. This problem is exacerbated in relation to natural law since Calvin's treatment of the subject is brief and no sources are cited in the formation of his view. In the absence of precise historical relationships, the commentator must remain content to establish the feasibility of an argument on the basis of resemblances between Calvin's thought and a range of possible antecedents. Second, given the polemical context of the sixteenth century and the greater emphasis by the Reformers on the doctrines of justification, the sacraments, and the church, it makes sense that Calvin would be much less concerned to quibble over issues pertaining to natural law, an area in which a significant degree of consensus already existed between the magisterial Reformation and Roman Catholicism. But, as Muller observes, the historiographical problem still remains: "given the varieties of late medieval theology and exegesis, the vagaries of polemical arguments, and the absence of citation, precise sources and antecedents of the Reformers' thought — Calvin's in particular — frequently cannot be determined." Muller, "Scholasticism in Calvin," p. 42.

101. Calvin, *Institutes,* 2.2.22.

102. Cf. Horowitz, *Seeds of Virtue and Knowledge,* pp. 21-34.

103. Calvin, *Institutes,* 2.2.22.

104. Calvin, *Institutes,* 2.8.1.

105. Clark, "Calvin on the *Lex Naturalis,*" pp. 6-7.

106. David C. Steinmetz, "The Reformation and the Ten Commandments," *Interpretation: A Journal of Bible and Theology* 43, no. 3 (July 1989): 260-61; reprinted as "Calvin and the First Commandment," in *Calvin in Context* (New York: Oxford University Press, 1995), pp. 53-63.

107. Aquinas, *S.T.* I-II, 94, 5, 6; 100, 1, 11.

108. Klempa, "Calvin on Natural Law," p. 80.

109. Henry Stob, "Natural-Law Ethics: An Appraisal," *Calvin Theological Journal* 20, no. 1 (April 1985): 58-59.

110. Clark, "Calvin on the *Lex Naturalis,*" pp. 7-8. Cf. Aquinas's discussion of the moral precepts of the Old Law in *S.T.* I-II, 100, 1-12.

111. Clark, "Calvin on the *Lex Naturalis,*" p. 18. Stephen Casselli would take issue with Clark's assessment. For more, see Stephen J. Casselli, "The Threefold Division of the Law in the Thought of Aquinas," *Westminster Theological Journal* 61 (1999): 183-88.

112. Clark, "Calvin on the *Lex Naturalis,*" pp. 13-14.

113. Cf. McGrath, "John Calvin and Late Medieval Thought," pp. 77-78; Alister E. McGrath, *A Life of John Calvin: A Study in the Shaping of Western Culture* (Cambridge, Mass.: Basil Blackwell, 1990), pp. 40-47; and Torrance, *The Hermeneutics of John Calvin,* pp. 35-49, 72-95.

114. Cf. Ganoczy, *The Young Calvin,* p. 177, pp. 173-78.

115. In a recent work Guenther Haas has shown that Calvin uses three out of four different senses of the term *equity* found in Greek and Roman thought. Haas points out

that, for Calvin, equity can mean either natural law, justice as a principle of law, or law that is mitigated by mercy. His thesis is that Calvin sees equity as fundamental not only in civil law but also in Scripture, with God's love for the elect functioning as the template for human instances of equity. Cf. Haas, *The Concept of Equity in Calvin's Ethics* (Waterloo, Ontario: Wilfrid Laurier University Press, 1997). It should also be noted that in Calvin's earliest writing such themes are already seminally present; see *Calvin's Commentary on Seneca's De Clementia*, trans., intro., and notes Ford Lewis Battles and André Malan Hugo (Leiden: E. J. Brill, 1969), pp. 66-67, 76-77, 82-85, 267-71, 300-303, 378-79.

116. Calvin, *Institutes*, 4.20.16.

117. For more on how Calvin's successors handled the subject, see Heinrich Heppe, *Reformed Dogmatics Set Out and Illustrated from the Sources,* rev. and ed. Ernst Bizer, trans. G. T. Thomson (London: Allen and Unwin, 1950), pp. 285-300.

118. John T. McNeill, "Natural Law in the Thought of Luther," *Church History* 10, no. 3 (September 1941): 219-25. In Melanchthon's case, however, the situation is quite different from Calvin's and Luther's. As early as the 1521 *Loci communes theologici* Melanchthon is interested in providing a modified realist natural-law doctrine, which he further refines and expands in subsequent editions and then integrates into his 1540 *Commentary on Romans.* See Philip Melanchthon, *Loci communes (1543),* trans. J. A. O. Preus (St. Louis: Concordia Publishing House, 1992), pp. 57-80; and Melanchthon, *Commentary on Romans,* trans. Fred Kramer (St. Louis: Concordia Publishing House, 1992), pp. 73-91. For helpful treatments of Melanchthon on natural law and the third use of the law, see Clemens Bauer, "Melanchthons Naturrechtslehre," *Archiv für Reformationsgeschichte* 42 (1951): 64-100; Harold J. Berman, *Law and Revolution, II: The Impact of the Protestant Reformations on the Western Legal Tradition* (Cambridge, Mass.: Harvard University Press, 2003), pp. 77-87, 111-13; John Witte Jr., *Law and Protestantism: The Legal Teachings of the Lutheran Reformation* (Cambridge: Cambridge University Press, 2002), pp. 121-40; and Timothy J. Wengert, *Law and Gospel: Philip Melanchthon's Debate with John of Agricola of Eisleben over Poenitentia* (Grand Rapids: Baker Books, 1997), pp. 191-210.

119. Helm, "Calvin and Natural Law," p. 10.

120. Marc-Édouard Chenevière, *La pensée politique de Calvin* (Geneva: Éditions Labor et Fides, 1937), p. 46.

121. Backus, "Calvin's Concept of Natural and Roman Law," p. 10.

122. Backus, "Calvin's Concept of Natural and Roman Law," pp. 11-12. Cf. Terry L. Miethe, "Natural Law, the Synderesis Rule, and St. Augustine," *Augustinian Studies* 11 (1980): 91-97. For a general discussion of the development of these terms throughout the scholastic era, see Michael Bertram Crowe, "Aquinas and Natural Law: Terminology and Definitions in the Late 12th and Early 13th Centuries," in *Sprache und Erkenntnis im Mittelalter: Akten des VI. Internationalen Kongresses für Mittelalterliche Philosophie der Société internationale pour l'étude de la philosophie Médiévale, 29. August–3. September 1977,* 2 vols., ed. Jan P. Beckman and Wolfgang Kluxen (Berlin: Walter de Gruyter, 1981), vol. 2, pp. 614-21. For specialized definitions of the terms as they appear in Protestant orthodoxy, see Richard A. Muller, *Dictionary of Latin and Greek Theological Terms: Drawn Principally from Protestant Scholastic Theology* (Grand Rapids: Baker Book House, 1985), s.v. "conscientia" and "synderesis."

123. Calvin, *Institutes*, 2.2.22.

124. Chenevière, *La pensée politique de Calvin,* pp. 49-50.

125. Calvin, *Institutes,* 4.10.3.

126. Calvin, *Commentary on Romans,* p. 49.

127. Calvin, *Commentary on Romans,* p. 49.

128. "Now as *being* is the first thing that falls under the apprehension simply, so *good* is the first thing that falls under the apprehension of the practical reason, which is directed to action: since every agent acts for an end under the aspect of good. Consequently the first principle in the practical reason is one founded on the notion of good, viz., that *good is that which all things seek after.* Hence this is the first precept of law, that *good is to be done and pursued, and evil is to be avoided.* All other precepts of the natural law are based upon this: so that whatever the practical reason naturally apprehends as man's good (or evil) belongs to the precepts of the natural law as something to be done or avoided." Aquinas, *S.T.* I-II, 94, 2.

129. Calvin, *Commentary on Romans,* p. 48.

130. Calvin, *Commentary on Romans,* p. 48.

131. Calvin, *The Bondage and Liberation of the Will,* 1.248; 2.288-89; 3.304, 308, 311, 313, 316, 320-22, 325; 4.329; 5.352, 354, 362-67, 370; 6.382-94.

132. Timothy C. Potts, "Conscience," in *The Cambridge History of Later Medieval Philosophy: From the Rediscovery of Aristotle to the Disintegration of Scholasticism, 1100-1600,* ed. Norman Kretzmann, Anthony Kenny, and Jan Pinborg (New York: Cambridge University Press, 1982), p. 700.

133. Calvin, *Commentary on Romans,* p. 48.

134. Calvin, *Commentary on Romans,* p. 48.

135. Potts, "Conscience," p. 700.

136. Backus, "Calvin's Concept of Natural and Roman Law," p. 10.

137. Calvin, *Commentary on Romans,* p. 49.

138. Calvin, *Institutes,* 2.8.1.

139. Calvin, *Institutes,* 2.2.23.

Notes to Chapter 4

1. Jacques-Auguste de Thou, *Les éloges des hommes savans, tirez de l'Histoire de M. de Thou,* 4th éd. rev., corr., & augm., outré un très-grand nombre de nouvelles remarques, d'un quatrième tome, French trans. Antoine Teissier (Leiden: T. Haaa, 1715), vol. 2, p. 84, cf. pp. 79-89. Also quoted by B. B. Warfield, "John Calvin the Theologian," in *Calvin and Augustine,* ed. Samuel G. Craig (Philadelphia: Presbyterian and Reformed Publishing Company, 1956), p. 481.

2. John Patrick Donnelly, S.J., *Calvinism and Scholasticism in Vermigli's Doctrine of Man and Grace* (Leiden: E. J. Brill, 1976), pp. 3, 171. For a complete listing of each title, including reprint editions, and a comprehensive register of Vermigli's correspondence, see John Patrick Donnelly, S.J., Robert M. Kingdon, and Marvin W. Anderson, *A Bibliography of the Works of Peter Martyr Vermigli* (Kirksville, Mo.: Sixteenth Century Journal Publishers, 1990).

3. For a fuller treatment, see Donnelly, *Calvinism and Scholasticism,* chap. 7, "The Influence of Martyr's Thought," pp. 170-96.

4. Donnelly, *Calvinism and Scholasticism*, p. 3.

5. Josiah Simler, "Oratio de vita et obitu viri optimi, praestantissimi Theologi D. Petri Martyris Vermilii, Sacrarum literarum in Schola Tigurina Professoris," in *Loci communes* (London: Thomas Vautrollerius, 1583). Simler's oration was first published at Zurich in 1563 and subsequently attached as a preface to many of Martyr's commentaries. A sixteenth-century English translation, "An Oration of the Life and Death of that Worthy Man and Excellent Divine D. Peter Martyr Vermillius, Professor of Divinity in the School of Zurich," was reprinted at the end of the *Common places*, trans. Anthonie Marten (London: Henri Denham, Thomas Chard, William Broom, and Andrew Maunsell, 1583). An annotated, modern English translation of the oration from the 1583 edition of the *Loci communes* is available in *Life, Letters, and Sermons*, vol. 5, *The Peter Martyr Library*, ed. and trans. John Patrick Donnelly, S.J. (Kirksville, Mo.: Truman State University Press, 1999), pp. 9-62.

6. Théodore de Bèze, *Icones, id est verae imagines virorum doctrina simul et pietate illustrium*, . . . (Geneva: I. Laonium, 1580). For an English translation of this text, see *Beza's "Icones": Contemporary Portraits of Reformers of Religion and Letters*, trans. C. G. McCrie (London: Religious Tract Society, 1906), pp. 123-26.

7. John Sleidan, *The General History of the Reformation of the Church from the Errors and Conceptions of the Church of Rome: Begun in Germany by Martin Luther with the Progress thereof in all Parts of Christendom from the Year 1517 to the Year 1556*, trans. Edmund Bohun (London: Edward Jones, Abel Swall, and Henry Bonwicke, 1562), pp. 443, 483-84, 590, 637.

8. John Strype, *Annals of the Reformation and Establishment of Religion and Other Various Occurrences in the Church of England during Queen Elizabeth's Happy Reign Together with an Appendix of Original Papers of State, Records, and Letters*, 4 vols. in 7 parts (London: John Wyat, 1709; New York: Burt Franklin, 1966), vol. 1, part 1, pp. 428-32.

9. Nöel Taillepied, *Histoire de vies, meurs, actes, doctrine et morts des quatre principaux Hérétiques de nostra temps* (Douay: 1580).

10. Anthony à Wood, *Athenae Oxonienses . . . to which are added, the Fasti, or, Annals, of the said university, for the same time*, 2 vols. (London: Tho. Bennet, 1691-1692), vol. 1, pp. 106-8 (no. 144).

11. Friedrich Christoph Schlosser, *Leben des Theodor de Beza und des Peter Martyr Vermili. Ein Beytrag zur Geschichte der Zeiten der Kirchen-Reformation. Mit einem Anhang bisher ungedruckter Briefe Calvins und Beza's und andrer Urkunden ihrer Zeit; aus den Schätzen der herzogl. Bibliothek zu Gotha* (Heidelberg: Mohr und Zimmer, 1809).

12. Charles Schmidt, *Vie de Pierre Martyr Vermigli: Thèse présentée à la Faculté de Théologie de Strasbourg* (Strasbourg: 1834).

13. Charles Schmidt, *Peter Martyr Vermigli. Leben und ausgewahlte Schriften. Nach handschriftlichen und gleichzeitigen Quellen von dr. C. Schmidt* (Elberfeld: R. L. Friderichs, 1858).

14. André Bouvier, *Henri Bullinger, réformateur et conseiller oecuménique: le successeur de Zwingli: d'après sa correspondance avec les réformés et les humanistes de langue française* (Neuchatel: Delachaux and Niestlé, 1940), Part 3, chap. 1, "Bullinger, Pierre Martyr et le Colloque de Poissy," pp. 279-89; W. Hugelshofer, "Zum Porträt des Petrus Martyr Vermilius," *Zwingliana* 5, no. 1 (1930): 127-29; Augusto Jahier, *Riformatori e Riformati Italiani dei Secoli XV° e XVI°: Trenta succinte Biografie con*

illustrazioni e Appendice (Firenze: Società editrice Claudiana, 1924), Parte Seconda, Riformatori e Riformati, "Pietro Martire Vermigli," pp. 52-58; Charles Hugh Egerton Smyth, Cranmer and the Reformation under Edward VI (Cambridge: Cambridge University Press, 1926), chap. 4, "Oxford and Peter Martyr," pp. 108-38; and M. Young, The Life and Times of Aonio Paleario: or, A History of the Italian Reformers in the Sixteenth Century Illustrated by Original Letters and Unedited Documents, 2 vols. (London: Bell and Daldy, 1860), vol. 1, chap. 10, "Peter Martyr Vermiglio," pp. 397-493.

15. Entries by Charles Schmidt in Real-Encyklopädie für protestantische Theologie und Kirche, 1st ed., vol. 16 (Leipzig: J. C. Hinrichs, 1885), s.v. "Vermigli"; Karl Benrath in Realencyclopaedie für protestantische Theologie und Kirche, 2d ed., vol. 20 (Leipzig: J. C. Hinrichs, 1908), s.v. "Vermigli, Pietro Martire"; Karl Benrath in The New Schaff-Herzog Encyclopedia of Religious Knowledge, vol. 12 (New York and London: Funk and Wagnalls Company, 1912), s.v. "Vermigli, Pietro Martire"; and Alexander Gordon in Dictionary of National Biography, ed. Sir Leslie Stephen and Sir Sidney Lee (Oxford: Oxford University Press, 1917; reprinted 1960), s.v. "Vermigli, Pietro Martire."

16. Frédéric Gardy, "Les Livres de Pierre Martyr Vermigli Conservés à la Bibliothèque de Genève," Anzeiger für Schweizerische Geschichte 17 (1919): 1-6. See also Alexandre Ganoczy, La Bibliothèque de l'Académie de Calvin: Le Catalogue de 1572 et ses Enseignements (Geneva: Librairie Droz, 1969), pp. 19-27, 79-80, 337; and Donnelly, Calvinism and Scholasticism, pp. 208-17.

17. Benjamin F. Paist Jr., "Peter Martyr and the Colloquy of Poissy," Princeton Theological Review 20 (April 1922): 212-31; (July 1922): 418-47; and (October 1922): 616-46.

18. Gordon Huelin, "Peter Martyr and the English Reformation" (Ph.D. diss., University of London, 1954).

19. Joseph C. McLelland, The Visible Words of God: An Exposition of the Sacramental Theology of Peter Martyr Vermigli, A.D. 1500-1562 (Edinburgh: Oliver and Boyd, 1957).

20. Philip Murray Jourdan McNair, Peter Martyr in Italy: An Anatomy of Apostasy (Oxford: Clarendon Press, 1967).

21. Klaus Sturm, Die Theologie Peter Martyr Vermiglis während seines ersten Aufenthalts in Straßburg 1542-1547: Ein Reformkatholik unter den Vätern der reformierten Kirche (Neukirchen-Vluyn: Neukirchener Verlag, 1971).

22. Salvatore Corda, Veritas Sacramenti: A Study in Vermigli's Doctrine of the Lord's Supper (Zürich: Theologischer Verlag, 1975).

23. Marvin W. Anderson, Peter Martyr, A Reformer in Exile (1542-1562): A Chronology of Biblical Writings in England and Europe (Nieuwkoop: B. De Graaf, 1975).

24. Donnelly, Calvinism and Scholasticism.

25. Robert M. Kingdon, The Political Thought of Peter Martyr Vermigli: Selected Texts and Commentary (Geneva: Librairie Droz, 1980).

26. Joseph C. McLelland, ed., Peter Martyr Vermigli and Italian Reform (Waterloo, Ontario: Wilfrid Laurier University Press, 1980).

27. Truman State University Press in conjunction with Thomas Jefferson University Press and Sixteenth Century Journal Publishers has assumed the responsibility for publishing The Peter Martyr Library. To date eight volumes have appeared with several more volumes planned: Volume 1, Early Writings: Creed, Scripture, Church, ed. Joseph C.

McLelland, trans. Mario Di Gangi and Joseph C. McLelland (1994); Volume 2, *Dialogue on the Two Natures in Christ*, ed. and trans. John Patrick Donnelly, S.J. (1995); Volume 3, *Sacred Prayers Drawn from the Psalms of David*, ed. and trans. John Patrick Donnelly, S.J. (1996); Volume 4, *Philosophical Works: On the Relation of Philosophy to Theology*, ed. and trans. Joseph C. McLelland (1996); Volume 5, *Life, Letters, and Sermons*, ed. and trans. John Patrick Donnelly, S.J. (1999); Volume 6, *The Commentary on the Lamentations of the Prophet Jeremiah*, ed. and trans. Dan Shute (2002); Volume 7, *The Oxford Treatise and Disputation on the Eucharist*, ed. and trans. Joseph C. McLelland (2000); and Volume 8, *Predestination and Justification: Two Theological Loci*, ed. and trans. Frank A. James III (2003). Joseph C. McLelland and G. E. Duffield also edited a volume on *The Life, Early Letters, and Eucharistic Writings of Peter Martyr* (Appleford, U.K.: Sutton Courtenay Press, 1989). A paperback anthology, which assembles seminal chapters from the Martyr corpus according to topic, has been published recently. Cf. *The Peter Martyr Reader*, ed. John Patrick Donnelly, S.J., Frank A. James III, and Joseph C. McLelland (Kirksville, Mo.: Truman State University Press, 1999).

28. Marvin W. Anderson, "Rhetoric and Reality: Peter Martyr and the English Reformation," *Sixteenth Century Journal* 19, no. 3 (Fall 1988): 451-69; Alan Beesley, "An Unpublished Source of the Book of Common Prayer: Peter Martyr Vermigli's *Adhortatio ad Coenam Domini Mysticam*," *Journal of Ecclesiastical History* 19, no. 1 (April 1968): 83-88; Patrick Collinson, "England and International Calvinism, 1558-1640," in *International Calvinism, 1541-1715*, ed. Menna Prestwich (Oxford: Clarendon Press, 1985), pp. 197-223; Philip Murray Jourdan McNair, "Peter Martyr in England," in *Peter Martyr Vermigli and Italian Reform*, ed. Joseph C. McLelland (Waterloo, Ontario: Wilfrid Laurier University Press, 1980), pp. 85-106; and M. A. Overell, "Peter Martyr in England, 1547-1553: An Alternate View," *Sixteenth Century Journal* 15, no. 1 (Spring 1984): 87-104.

29. See the references in notes 14 and 17.

30. Marvin W. Anderson, "Peter Martyr, Reformed Theologian (1542-1562): His Letters to Heinrich Bullinger and John Calvin," *Sixteenth Century Journal* 4, no. 1 (April 1973): 41-64.

31. Paul F. Grendler, "The Circulation of Protestant Books in Italy," in McLelland, ed., *Peter Martyr Vermigli and Italian Reform*, pp. 5-16; Philip Murray Jourdan McNair, "The Reformation of the Sixteenth Century in Renaissance Italy," in *Studies in Church History*, vol. 17, *Religion and Humanism: Papers Read at the Eighteenth Summer Meeting and the Nineteenth Winter Meeting of the Ecclesiastical History Society*, ed. Keith Robbins (Oxford: Basil Blackwell, 1981), pp. 149-66; Paul V. Murphy, "Between *Spirituali* and *Intransigenti*: Cardinal Ercole Gonzaga and Patrician Reform in Sixteenth-Century Italy," *Catholic Historical Review* 88, no. 3 (July 2002): 446-69; and John Tedeschi, "Italian Reformers and the Diffusion of Renaissance Culture," *Sixteenth Century Journal* 5, no. 2 (October 1974): 79-94.

32. Marvin W. Anderson, "*Vista Tigurina*: Peter Martyr and European Reform (1556-1562)," *Harvard Theological Review* 83, no. 2 (April 1990): 181-206; and David C. Steinmetz, *Reformers in the Wings: From Geiler von Kaysersberg to Theodore Beza*, 2d ed. (Oxford: Oxford University Press, 2001), pp. 106-13.

33. Cf. Marvin W. Anderson, "Peter Martyr Vermigli: Protestant Humanist," in McLelland, ed., *Peter Martyr Vermigli and Italian Reform*, pp. 65-84; Mariano Di Gangi, *Peter Martyr Vermigli, 1499-1562: Renaissance Man, Reformation Master* (Lanham, Md.:

University Press of America, 1993); Joseph C. McLelland, "Peter Martyr Vermigli: Scholastic or Humanist?" in McLelland, ed., *Peter Martyr Vermigli and Italian Reform*, pp. 141-52; Luigi Santini, *Tra spiritualismo e riforma: Saggi di storia religiosa Toscana* (Firenze: Presso lo Stabilimento Poligrafico Fiorentino, 1979), pp. 143-69; and Cesare Vasoli, "*Loci Communes* and the Rhetorical and Dialectical Traditions," in McLelland, ed., *Peter Martyr Vermigli and Italian Reform*, pp. 17-28.

34. Donnelly, *Calvinism and Scholasticism*, pp. 9-12, 19-41, 197-207; Donnelly, "Calvinist Thomism," *Viator: Medieval and Renaissance Studies* 7 (1976): 441-55; Donnelly, "Italian Influences on the Development of Calvinist Scholasticism," *Sixteenth Century Journal* 7, no. 1 (April 1976): 81-101; Donnelly, "Peter Martyr on Fallen Man: A Protestant Scholastic View" (Ph.D. diss., University of Wisconsin–Madison, 1971); Frank A. James III, "Peter Martyr Vermigli: At the Crossroads of Late Medieval Scholasticism, Christian Humanism, and Resurgent Augustinianism," in *Protestant Scholasticism: Essays in Reassessment*, ed. Carl R. Trueman and R. S. Clark (Carlisle, U.K.: Paternoster Press, 1999), pp. 62-78; and Joseph C. McLelland, "Calvinism Perfecting Thomism: Peter Martyr Vermigli's Question," *Scottish Journal of Theology* 31, no. 6 (December 1978): 571-78. For an assessment of Donnelly's thesis, see Willem J. Van Asselt and Eef Dekker, "Introduction," in *Reformation and Scholasticism: An Ecumenical Enterprise*, ed. Willem J. Van Asselt and Eef Dekker (Grand Rapids: Baker Book House, 2001), pp. 22-24.

35. Cf. Robert M. Kingdon, "Peter Martyr Vermigli and the Marks of the True Church," in *Continuity and Discontinuity in Church History: Essays Presented to George Huntston Williams*, ed. F. Forrester Church and Timothy George (Leiden: E. J. Brill, 1979), pp. 198-214; Luigi Santini, "Appunti sulla ecclesiologia di P. M. Vermigli e la edificazione della Chiesa," *Bolletino della Società di Studi Valdesi* 104 (1958): 69-75; and Santini, "'Scisma' e 'eresia' nel pensiero di P. M. Vermigli," *Bolletino della Società di Studi Valdesi* 125 (1969): 27-43.

36. Joseph C. McLelland, "The Reformed Doctrine of Predestination according to Peter Martyr," *Scottish Journal of Theology* 8, no. 3 (September 1955): 255-71.

37. Frank A. James III, "A Late Medieval Parallel in Reformation Thought: *Gemina Praedestinatio* in Gregory of Rimini and Peter Martyr Vermigli," in *Via Augustini: Augustine in the Later Middle Ages, Renaissance, and Reformation: Essays in Honor of Damasus Trapp, O.S.A.*, ed. Heiko A. Oberman and Frank A. James III (Leiden: E. J. Brill, 1991), pp. 157-88; James, "*De Justificatione*: The Evolution of Peter Martyr Vermigli's Doctrine of Justification" (Ph.D. diss., Westminster Theological Seminary, 2000); James, "Juan de Valdés Before and After Peter Martyr Vermigli: The Reception of *Gemina Praedestinatio* in Valdés' Later Thought," *Archiv für Reformationsgeschichte* 83 (1992): 180-208; James, "*Praedestinatio Dei*: The Intellectual Origins of Peter Martyr Vermigli's Doctrine of Double Predestination" (D.Phil. thesis, Oxford University, 1993); James, *Peter Martyr Vermigli and Predestination: The Augustinian Inheritance of an Italian Reformer* (Oxford: Clarendon Press, 1998); and James, "Translator's Introduction," in *Predestination and Justification: Two Theological Loci*, vol. 8, *The Peter Martyr Library*, ed. and trans. Frank A. James III (Kirksville, Mo.: Truman State University Press, 2003), pp. xv-xliv.

38. Marvin W. Anderson, "Biblical Humanism and Roman Catholic Reform 1444-1563: A Study of Renaissance Philology and New Testament Criticism from Laurentius Valla to Pietro Martyre Vermigli" (Ph.D. diss., University of Aberdeen, 1964); and Frank A. James III, "The Biblical Scholarship of Peter Martyr Vermigli (1499-1562)," in

Historical Handbook of Major Biblical Interpreters, ed. Donald K. McKim (Downers Grove, Ill.: InterVarsity Press, 1998), pp. 239-45.

39. Marvin W. Anderson, *Peter Martyr, A Reformer in Exile (1542-1562): A Chronology of Biblical Writings in England and Europe* (Nieuwkoop: B. De Graaf, 1975); and Anderson, "Pietro Martire Vermigli on the Scope and Clarity of Scripture," *Theologische Zeitschrift* 3, no. 2 (March/April 1974): 86-94.

40. Marvin W. Anderson, "Word and Spirit in Exile (1542-1561): The Biblical Writings of Peter Martyr Vermigli," *Journal of Ecclesiastical History* 21, no. 3 (July 1970): 193-201.

41. Marvin W. Anderson, "Peter Martyr on Romans," *Scottish Journal of Theology* 26, no. 4 (November 1973): 401-20.

42. Daniel John Shute, "Peter Martyr and the Rabbinic Bible in the Interpretation of Lamentations" (Ph.D. diss., McGill University, 1994).

43. John L. Thompson, "The Survival of Allegorical Argumentation in Peter Martyr Vermigli's Old Testament Exegesis," in *Biblical Interpretation in the Era of the Reformation: Essays Presented to David C. Steinmetz in Honor of His Sixtieth Birthday,* ed. Richard A. Muller and John L. Thompson (Grand Rapids: Wm. B. Eerdmans Publishing Company, 1996), pp. 255-71.

44. John Patrick Donnelly, S.J., "The Social and Ethical Thought of Peter Martyr Vermigli," in McLelland, ed., *Peter Martyr Vermigli and Italian Reform,* pp. 107-19.

45. The dearth of scholarship here may be explained by two interrelated facts. First, Vermigli never devoted *scholia* in any commentary to a systematic treatment of issues pertaining to natural law. Second, in compiling excerpts from his Romans commentary for Book 1 of the *Loci communes,* Robert Masson only selected passages from Vermigli's exegesis of 1:18-20, excluding entirely his exegesis of 2:14-16 — the preeminent natural-law passage in Scripture.

46. Robert M. Kingdon, "Althusius' Use of Calvinist Sources in His *Politica,*" *Rechtstheorie* 16 (1997): 23-27; Kingdon, "Introduction," in *The Political Thought of Peter Martyr Vermigli: Selected Texts and Commentary,* ed. Robert M. Kingdon (Geneva: Librairie Droz, 1980), pp. i-xxvi; Kingdon, "The Function of Law in the Political Thought of Peter Martyr Vermigli," in *Reformatio Perennis: Essays on Calvin and the Reformation in Honor of Ford Lewis Battles,* ed. B. A. Gerrish and Robert Benedetto (Pittsburgh: Pickwick Press, 1981), pp. 159-72; and Kingdon, "The Political Thought of Peter Martyr Vermigli," in McLelland, ed., *Peter Martyr Vermigli and Italian Reform,* pp. 121-40.

47. Marvin W. Anderson, "Royal Idolatry: Peter Martyr and the Reformed Tradition," *Archiv für Reformationsgeschichte* 69 (1978): 157-200.

48. Richard A. Muller, *Post-Reformation Reformed Dogmatics: The Rise and Development of Reformed Orthodoxy, ca. 1520 to ca. 1725,* 4 vols. (Grand Rapids: Baker Academic, 2003), vol. 4, p. 394.

49. Muller, *Post-Reformation Reformed Dogmatics,* vol. 1, p. 272.

50. Thematic *loci* or *scholia,* digressions in the form of systematic tracts on seminal theological topics, are peppered throughout Martyr's voluminous biblical commentaries. In compiling these tracts into the 1576 edition of the *Loci communes,* Masson frequently excised significant exegetical aspects of the text so the reader would not be encumbered by references to the pericope from which it was drawn. To avert any textual

corruption related to Masson's process of selection, citations will be taken directly from Vermigli's commentaries and will be cross-referenced with the 1583 edition of the *Common places*. Wherever applicable, contemporary English translations of these passages will be drawn from the volumes in *The Peter Martyr Library*.

51. John T. McNeill, "Introduction," in John Calvin, *Institutes of the Christian Religion*, 2 vols., ed. John T. McNeill, trans. Ford Lewis Battles (Philadelphia: Westminster Press, 1960), vol. 1, p. xlviii, n. 28.

52. Donnelly, "The Social and Ethical Thought of Peter Martyr Vermigli," p. 118.

53. Anderson, "Peter Martyr Vermigli: Protestant Humanist," p. 68.

54. For more on the Stoic origins of this idea, see Maryanne Cline Horowitz, "The Stoic Synthesis of the Idea of Natural Law in Man: Four Themes," *Journal of the History of Ideas* 35, no. 1 (January-March 1974): 3-16; and Horowitz, *Seeds of Virtue and Knowledge* (Princeton: Princeton University Press, 1998), pp. 3-34.

55. Peter Martyr Vermigli, *Most learned and fruitful commentaries of D. Peter Martir Vermilius, professor of divinity in the school of Tigure, upon the Epistle of S. Paul to the Romans: wherein are diligently and most profitably entreated all such matters and chief common places of religion touched in the same Epistle* (hereafter *Romans*), trans. Sir Henry Billingsley (London: John Daye, 1568), f. 36v, f. 41r.

56. An English translation is forthcoming of Vermigli's *Commentary on Aristotle's Nicomachean Ethics*, vol. 9, *The Peter Martyr Library*, ed. Emidio Campi and Joseph C. McLelland (Kirksville, Mo.: Truman State University Press, 2006).

57. Peter Martyr Vermigli, "Vermigli's Introduction to the Commentary on the *Nicomachean Ethics*," in *Philosophical Works: On the Relation of Philosophy to Theology*, vol. 4, *The Peter Martyr Library*, ed. Emidio Campi and Joseph C. McLelland (Kirksville, Mo.: Truman State University Press, 2006), p. 6.

58. Vermigli, "Introduction to *Nicomachean Ethics*," p. 7.

59. Vermigli, "Introduction to *Nicomachean Ethics*," p. 7.

60. Vermigli, "Introduction to *Nicomachean Ethics*," p. 7.

61. Vermigli, "Introduction to *Nicomachean Ethics*," pp. 7-8.

62. Vermigli, "Introduction to *Nicomachean Ethics*," p. 8.

63. Vermigli, "Introduction to *Nicomachean Ethics*," p. 8.

64. Vermigli, "Introduction to *Nicomachean Ethics*," p. 8.

65. Vermigli, "Introduction to *Nicomachean Ethics*," p. 8.

66. Vermigli, "Introduction to *Nicomachean Ethics*," p. 8.

67. Donnelly, *Calvinism and Scholasticism*, p. 88.

68. Vermigli, "Introduction to *Nicomachean Ethics*," p. 9.

69. Vermigli, "Introduction to *Nicomachean Ethics*," p. 14.

70. Vermigli, "Introduction to *Nicomachean Ethics*," pp. 14-15.

71. Vermigli, "Introduction to *Nicomachean Ethics*," p. 15.

72. Vermigli, "Introduction to *Nicomachean Ethics*," p. 15.

73. Vermigli, "Introduction to *Nicomachean Ethics*," p. 15.

74. Donnelly, *Calvinism and Scholasticism*, p. 88.

75. Donnelly, *Calvinism and Scholasticism*, p. 88.

76. Vermigli, *Romans*, f. 21v; and *Common places* (hereafter CP), 1.2.1.

77. Vermigli, *Romans*, f. 21v; CP, 1.2.1.

78. Vermigli, *Romans*, f. 21v; CP, 1.2.1.

79. Vermigli, Romans, f. 21r; CP, 1.2.2.

80. Vermigli, Romans, f. 21r; CP, 1.2.2.

81. Vermigli, Romans, f. 21r; CP, 1.2.2.

82. Vermigli, Romans, f. 21r; CP, 1.2.3. Herman Bavinck utilizes the concepts of *prolepseis,* "common notions," and divine ideas as the scientific foundation *(principium)* for his dogmatics. See Herman Bavinck, *Reformed Dogmatics,* 4 vols., ed. John Bolt, trans. John Vriend (Grand Rapids: Baker Academic, 2003-2006), vol. 1, pp. 223-33, 207-33; and vol. 2, pp. 53-91. Cf. Horowitz, "The Stoic Synthesis of the Idea of Natural Law in Man," pp. 5-10; and Horowitz, *Seeds of Virtue and Knowledge,* pp. 23-26, 44-56.

83. John Calvin, *Commentary on the Epistles of Paul the Apostle to the Romans and to the Thessalonians,* ed. David W. Torrance and T. F. Torrance, trans. Ross Mackenzie (Grand Rapids: Wm. B. Eerdmans Publishing Company, 1961), p. 48.

84. Vermigli, Romans, f. 22v; CP, 1.2.3.

85. Vermigli, Romans, f. 20r; CP, 1.2.10.

86. Vermigli, Romans, f. 20r; CP, 1.2.10.

87. Vermigli clearly has Cicero's discussion of Epicurus' notion of *prolepseis* in the background here. Cf. Cicero's *Nature of the Gods,* trans. P. G. Walsh (New York: Oxford University Press, 1998), 1.16-18.

88. Vermigli, Romans, f. 22v; CP, 1.2.3.

89. Vermigli, Romans, f. 22v; CP, 1.2.3.

90. Vermigli, Romans, f. 22v; CP, 1.2.3.

91. Vermigli, Romans, f. 22v; CP, 1.2.4.

92. Vermigli, Romans, f. 22v; CP, 1.2.4.

93. Vermigli, Romans, f. 22v; CP, 1.2.4.

94. Vermigli, Romans, f. 20r; CP, 1.2.9.

95. Vermigli, Romans, f. 22r; CP, 1.2.4. Cf. Romans, f. 38r.

96. Vermigli, Romans, f. 22r; CP, 1.2.4.

97. David C. Steinmetz, "Calvin and the Natural Knowledge of God," in *Calvin in Context* (New York: Oxford University Press, 1995), pp. 23-39; originally published in *Via Augustini: Augustine in the Later Middle Ages, Renaissance, and Reformation: Essays in Honor of Damasus Trapp, O.S.A.,* ed. Heiko A. Oberman and Frank A. James III (Leiden: E. J. Brill, 1991), pp. 142-56.

98. Steinmetz, "Calvin and the Natural Knowledge of God," p. 28.

99. Steinmetz, "Calvin and the Natural Knowledge of God," p. 29. Cf. Calvin, *Commentary on Romans,* pp. 30, 31, 32, 33, 29-39.

100. Steinmetz, "Calvin and the Natural Knowledge of God," p. 29.

101. Calvin, *Commentary on Romans,* p. 31.

102. Calvin, *Commentary on Romans,* pp. 32-39.

103. Steinmetz, "Calvin and the Natural Knowledge of God," p. 29.

104. Steinmetz, "Calvin and the Natural Knowledge of God," p. 31.

105. Steinmetz, "Calvin and the Natural Knowledge of God," p. 31.

106. Vermigli, Romans, f. 22r; CP, 1.2.5.

107. For a detailed grammatical, theological, and philosophical examination of Aquinas's commentary on Romans 1:17-25, see Eugene F. Rogers Jr., *Thomas Aquinas and Karl Barth: Sacred Doctrine and the Natural Knowledge of God* (Notre Dame: University of Notre Dame Press, 1995), chap. 5, "Thomas's Commentary on Romans 1:17-25," pp.

112-56; and chap. 6, "Conclusions about the Natural Cognition of God," pp. 157-80; and Eugene F. Rogers Jr., "The Narrative of Natural Law in Aquinas's Commentary on Romans 1," *Theological Studies* 59, no. 2 (June 1998): 254-76. For further corroboration of Rogers' point about Aquinas and the ineffectiveness of natural law in leading people to the good, see E. A. Goerner, "On Thomistic Natural Law: The Bad Man's View of Thomistic Natural Right," *Political Theory* 7, no. 1 (February 1979): 101-22. Of related interest, Steven C. Boguslawski, Rector of Sacred Heart Major Seminary in Detroit, Michigan, is in the final stages of preparing the first English translation of Aquinas's hefty *Commentary on Romans*.

108. Vermigli, Romans, ff. 20r-21v; CP, 1.2.11. Cf. Romans, f. 70v-r.

109. Rogers, "The Narrative of Natural Law in Aquinas's Commentary on Romans 1," p. 261.

110. Rogers, "The Narrative of Natural Law in Aquinas's Commentary on Romans 1," p. 267.

111. Vermigli, Romans, f. 20r; CP, 1.2.10.

112. Vermigli, Romans, f. 20r; CP, 1.2.9.

113. Vermigli, Romans, f. 22r; CP, 1.2.5.

114. Emil Brunner and Karl Barth, *Natural Theology* ("Nature and Grace" by Brunner and the Reply "No!" by Barth), trans. Peter Fraenkel (London: Geoffrey Bles, 1946), p. 107.

115. Vermigli, Romans, f. 23v; CP, 1.2.8. For a discussion of why good works cannot be the cause of our salvation, see Vermigli, Romans, ff. 39v-40r.

116. The same argument is reiterated again at 2:1-3. Vermigli, Romans, f. 36v-r.

117. Vermigli, Romans, f. 23v; CP, 1.2.8.

118. Cited from Vermigli's essay "Free Will," appendix in *Common places*, f. 102, par. 3. A contemporary English translation of this text is available in *Philosophical Works*, vol. 4, *The Peter Martyr Library*, pp. 271-319. Rudolph Gualther found this tract and two others (a summary statement on free will and an essay on providence and predestination) among Martyr's papers and added them to his 1580 edition of the *Loci communes*, but their authorship has been a matter of considerable dispute. They were commonly attributed to Bullinger, since they were written in an unknown hand but with Bullinger's marginalia. In 1957 Peter Walser ("Die fraglichen drei Traktate," in *Die Prädestination bei Heinrich Bullinger im Zusammenhang mit seiner Gotteslehre* (Zurich: Zwingli Verlag, 1957), pp. 200-210) ascribed them to Vermigli, which was challenged by Joachim Staedtke ("Drei umstrittene Traktate Peter Martyr Vermiglis," *Zwingliana* 11 [1962]: 553-54) who left the question unresolved. Marvin Anderson (*Peter Martyr, A Reformer in Exile*, pp. 89-95) noted some doctrinal anomalies in them in relation to other aspects of Martyr's teaching. Donnelly reviewed the arguments, and concluded that Vermigli was their author (*Calvinism and Scholasticism*, pp. 117-18; and Donnelly, "Three Disputed Tracts," in *Essays Presented to Myron P. Gilmore*, ed. Sergio Bertelli and Gloria Ramakus (Florence: La Nuova Italia, 1978), pp. 37-46), but this was challenged in turn by Frank A. James III ("A Late Medieval Parallel in Reformation Thought," pp. 157-88). This author sides with Donnelly and McLelland, who attribute their authorship to Vermigli. For a detailed survey of positions taken in the debate, see Joseph McLelland's synopsis in *Philosophical Works*, pp. 268-70.

119. Vermigli, Romans, f. 23v; CP, 1.2.8.

120. Vermigli, "Free Will," f. 102, par. 4.
121. Vermigli, Romans, f. 23v; CP, 1.2.8.
122. Vermigli, Romans, f. 36v.
123. Vermigli, Romans, f. 36v.
124. Vermigli, Romans, f. 43r. Cf. Romans, f. 33v.
125. Vermigli, Romans, f. 43r.
126. Vermigli, "Free Will," f. 102, par. 4. Cf. Calvin's nearly identical statement in
Institutes, 1.3.1; 2.2.22; 2.8.1-2; and 4.20.16.
127. Vermigli, Romans, f. 44v.
128. Vermigli, Romans, f. 44v.
129. Vermigli, Romans, f. 44v.
130. Vermigli, Romans, f. 44v.
131. Vermigli, Romans, f. 44v.
132. Vermigli, Romans, f. 44v.
133. Vermigli, Romans, f. 44v.
134. Vermigli, Romans, f. 44v.
135. Vermigli, Romans, f. 44v.
136. Vermigli, Romans, f. 44v.
137. Vermigli, Romans, f. 44r.
138. Vermigli, Romans, f. 44r.
139. Vermigli, Romans, f. 44r.
140. Vermigli, Romans, f. 44r.
141. Vermigli, Romans, f. 44r.

Notes to Chapter 5

1. Johannes Althusius, *Politics,* trans. Frederick S. Carney (Boston: Beacon Press, 1964). A recent unabridged translation of the *Politica* into German has been completed by Heinrich Janssen, edited by Dieter Wyduckel (Berlin: Duncker and Humblot, 2003).
2. Otto von Gierke, *The Development of Political Theory,* trans. Bernard Freyd (New York: W. W. Norton and Company, Inc., 1939; New York: Howard Fertig, 1966), pp. 17-18.
3. Johannes Althusius, "Preface to the 1614 edition," in *Politica: An Abridged Translation of Politics Methodically Set Forth and Illustrated with Sacred and Profane Examples,* ed. and trans. Frederick S. Carney (Indianapolis: Liberty Fund, 1995), p. 14.
4. For an intriguing discussion of how Althusius's "entire system of law" in the *Dicaeologica* contributed to the formation of the new European *jus commune* in the sixteenth to the eighteenth centuries, see Harold J. Berman, *Law and Revolution, Vol. II: The Impact of the Protestant Reformations on the Western Legal Tradition* (Cambridge, Mass.: Harvard University Press, 2003), pp. 110, 124-30.
5. Frederick S. Carney, "Translator's Introduction," in *Politica,* p. xii.
6. Otto Friedrich von Gierke taught law at the universities of Berlin, Breslau, and Heidelberg throughout his long and distinguished career. His chief works were *Das deutsche Genossenschaftsrecht,* 4 vols. (Berlin: Weidmann, 1868-1913) of which *Natural Law and the Theory of Society, 1500-1800,* trans. Ernest Barker (Cambridge: Cambridge Uni-

versity Press, 1950) is a translation of five subsections of the fourth volume; *Johannes Althusius und die Entwicklung der naturrechtlichen Staatstheorien: zugleich ein Beitrag zur Geschichte der Rechtssystematik*, 5th ed. (Aalen: Scientia, 1958), which was translated into English as *The Development of Political Theory*, but first appeared as the third volume in the series above; and *Deutsches privatrecht*, 3 vols. (Leipzig: Duncker and Humblot, 1895-1917).

7. Carney, "Translator's Introduction," in *Politica*, p. ix.

8. Gierke, *Natural Law and the Theory of Society*, p. 70.

9. According to Gierke, "Althusius . . . deduces his system in a rational way from a purely secular concept of society; for him biblical texts are merely examples, and the events of sacred as well as profane history serve as illustrations of the results which have first been reached by rational inference." Gierke, *The Development of Political Theory*, p. 70, cf. p. 75. Unfortunately, Brian Tierney continues to read Althusius in the same vein as Gierke; see Tierney's *Religion, Law, and the Growth of Constitutional Thought, 1150-1650* (Cambridge: Cambridge University Press, 1982), pp. 71-79.

10. Friedrich was a professor of government at Harvard for many years during which he devoted a considerable portion of his scholarly attention to the work of Johannes Althusius. His chief works were Friedrich, "Althusius, Johannes," in *Encyclopaedia of the Social Sciences*, vol. 2 (New York: The Macmillan Company, 1937), pp. 13-14; Friedrich, "Introduction," in *Politica Methodice Digesta of Johannes Althusius* (Cambridge, Mass.: Harvard University Press, 1932), pp. xv-cxviii; Friedrich, *Johannes Althusius und sein Werk im Rahmen der Entwicklung der Theorie von der Politik* (Berlin: Duncker and Humblot, 1975); and Friedrich, "Preface," in *The Politics of Johannes Althusius*, trans. Frederick S. Carney (London: Eyre and Spottiswoode, 1965), pp. vii-xii.

11. Carney, "Translator's Introduction," in *Politica*, p. ix.

12. Thus, writes Friedrich, "I believe that in order to comprehend adequately the place of Althusius in the history of thought, one must realize that he, like Hobbes, is attempting to develop the implications for a science of politics of the rigid determinism that the dogma of predestination meant in the natural order. How near he came to the elimination of a personal God is shown by the strange and oft repeated sentence: 'Quod Deus est in mundo, lex est in societate.' God is here already an impersonal, normative force." Friedrich, "Introduction," p. lxviii.

13. Friedrich, "Introduction," p. lxxiii.

14. Friedrich, "Introduction," p. lxxxviii, pp. lxxxiv-xciv.

15. Friedrich, "Introduction," pp. lxxviii-lxxix.

16. Friedrich, "Introduction," p. xv.

17. A. J. Carlyle, *Political Liberty: A History of the Conception in the Middle Ages and Modern Times* (Oxford: Oxford University Press, 1941; London: Frank Cass and Company, Ltd., 1963), pp. 51-57.

18. A. J. and R. W. Carlyle, *A History of Mediaeval Political Theory in the West*, 6 vols. (Edinburgh and London: William Blackwood and Sons, Ltd., 1936), vol. 6, pp. 357-63, 371-72, 394-95, 405-13, 498-501.

19. William Archibald Dunning, *A History of Political Theories from Luther to Montesquieu* (New York: The Macmillan Company, 1916), pp. 61-67.

20. John Neville Figgis, *Studies of Political Thought: From Gerson to Grotius, 1414-1625* (Cambridge: Cambridge University Press, 1907), pp. 175-85. Cf. John Neville

Figgis, *The Divine Right of Kings*, 2d ed. (Cambridge: Cambridge University Press, 1922), pp. 106-36, 219-55.

21. Contemporary political historian Quentin Skinner also reiterates Gierke's estimate of Althusius as "the pivotal figure in the evolution of modern constitutionalism" and "as the first political philosopher who shook off 'the whole theocratic conception of the State'" (p. 341, n. 1). However, like Gierke in his failure to account for Althusius's use of Ramist logic in organizing the subject matter of the *Politica*, Skinner mistakenly concludes, "Althusius [had] the ambition to emancipate the study of 'politics' from the confines of theology and jurisprudence . . ." (p. 342) and, thus, ". . . outlined the principles of a new, secularized political science in his treatise entitled *Politics Methodically Set Forth*" (p. 350). Quentin Skinner, *The Foundations of Modern Political Thought*, 2 vols. (Cambridge: Cambridge University Press, 1978), vol. 2, pp. 341-50.

22. Alessandro Passerin d'Entrèves, "Giovanni Althusio e il problema metodologico nella storia della filosofia politica e giuridica," *Rivista internazionale di filosofia del dritto* 14 (1934): 109-23.

23. D'Entrèves, "Giovanni Althusio," pp. 115-16.

24. Pierre Mesnard, *L'essor de la philosophie politique de XVIe siècle* (Paris: J. Vrin, 1951).

25. Frederick S. Carney, "Associational Thought in Early Calvinism," in *Voluntary Associations: A Study of Groups in Free Societies*, ed. D. B. Robertson (Richmond, Va.: John Knox Press, 1966), pp. 39-53; and Carney, "The Associational Theory of Johannes Althusius: A Study in Calvinist Constitutionalism" (Ph.D. diss., University of Chicago, 1960).

26. Stanley Parry, "The Political Science of Johannes Althusius" (Ph.D. diss., Yale University, 1953), pp. 60-80, 189-201.

27. Ernst Reibstein, *Johannes Althusius als Fortsetzer der Schule von Salamanca: Untersuchungen zur Ideengeschichte des Recht-Staates und zur altprotestantischen Naturrechtslehr* (Karlsruhe: C. F. Müller, 1955).

28. Peter Joachen Winters, *Die "Politica" des Johannes Althusius und ihre zeitgenössischen Quellen: Zur Grundlegung der politischen Wissenschaft im 16. und im beginnenden 17. Jahrhundert* (Freiburg: Rombach, 1963).

29. Erik Wolf, *Das Problem der Naturrechtslehre: Versuch einer Orientierung* (Karlsruhe: C. F. Müller, 1964); and Wolf, *Grosse Rechtsdenker der deutschen Geistesgeschichte*, 4th ed. (Tübingen: J. C. B. Mohr, 1963).

30. Eckhard Feuerherdt, *Gesellschaftsvertrag und Naturrecht in der Staatslehre des Johannes Althusius* (Köln: R. Pulm, 1962).

31. Reibstein, *Johannes Althusius als Fortsetzer der Schule von Salamanca*, p. 13. For more on this altercation, see Friedrich, "Introduction," pp. xxvii-xxix.

32. Winters, *Die "Politica" des Johannes Althusius und ihre zeitgenössischen Quellen*, pp. 150-51.

33. As a recent addendum to the Reibstein-Winters exchange, Heinrich Janssen has investigated the way in which the Bible functioned as the foundation of Althusius's political theory, particularly with respect to his understanding of law and the relationship between church and state. Beyond stating that Althusius did not develop "a detailed and elaborate natural theology," Janssen argues parallel to Reibstein that Althusius's doctrine of natural law follows in the scholastic line of Aquinas, Covarruvias, and Vásquez,

and not in the early Enlightenment line of Grotius and Pufendorf (pp. 95, 97). Heinrich Janssen, *Die Bibel als Grundlage der politischen Theorie des Johannes Althusius* (Frankfurt am Main: Peter Lang, 1992), pp. 95-99.

34. P. S. Gerbrandy, *National and International Stability: Althusius, Grotius, Van Vollenhoven* (Cambridge, Mass.: Harvard University Press, 1944).

35. James W. Skillen, "The Development of Calvinistic Political Theory in the Netherlands, with Special Reference to the Thought of Herman Dooyeweerd" (Ph.D. diss., Duke University, 1974), pp. 191-217; Skillen, "The Political Theory of Johannes Althusius," *Philosophia Reformata* 39 (1974): 170-90; and more recently, Skillen, "From Covenant of Grace to Equitable Public Pluralism: The Dutch Calvinist Contribution," *Calvin Theological Journal* 31, no. 1 (April 1996): 72-77.

36. Skillen, "From Covenant of Grace to Equitable Public Pluralism," p. 72.

37. Herman Dooyeweerd, *A New Critique of Theoretical Thought*, 4 vols., trans. David H. Freeman and H. de Jongste (Jordan Station, Ontario: Paideia Press, 1984), vol. 3, p. 662, pp. 662-63; also see Dooyeweerd, *De Strijd om het Souvereiniteitsbegrip in de Moderne Rechts- en Staatsleer* (Amsterdam: H. J. Paris, 1950), pp. 7-8.

38. Friedrich, "Introduction," pp. lii-liii.

39. Skillen, "The Development of Calvinistic Political Theory in the Netherlands," p. 201, pp. 198-201; and Skillen, "The Political Theory of Johannes Althusius," p. 178, pp. 177-79.

40. Skillen, "The Political Theory of Johannes Althusius," p. 172. For criticism of Dooyeweerd's understanding of the nature-grace motif in Thomas Aquinas, which undergirds his antipathy toward scholasticism in general, see Arvin Vos, *Aquinas, Calvin, and Contemporary Protestant Thought: A Critique of Protestant Views on the Thought of Thomas Aquinas* (Washington and Grand Rapids: Christian University Press and Wm. B. Eerdmans Publishing Company, 1985), pp. 128-33, 148-52.

41. Neo-Calvinist Gordon Spykman, likewise following Dooyeweerd, falls prey to exactly the same appraisal of Althusius as Skillen does. Like Skillen, Spykman credits Althusius with providing "the systematic climax of Calvinist social thought coming up out of the sixteenth-century Reformation, and with formulating the first clear statement of that complementary principle which in later Calvinist tradition came to be known as sphere sovereignty and sphere universality" (p. 107). However, he contends that it is possible to criticize Althusian social philosophy on a number of dubious points. First, "It betrays remnants of an earlier scholastic notion of a certain hierarchy among social institutions" (p. 107). Second, "It seems that legal norms are derived in part from natural-law theories" (p. 107). Third, "A notion of popular sovereignty is present which leans toward a social contract theory of political authority" (p. 107). Yet, despite these so-called defects, Spykman thinks that Althusius's contribution to a pluralist social philosophy is considerable. Gordon Spykman, "Pluralism: Our Last Best Hope?" *Christian Scholar's Review* 10, no. 2 (1981): 99-115. See also Spykman's *Reformational Theology: A New Paradigm for Doing Dogmatics* (Grand Rapids: Wm. B. Eerdmans Publishing Company, 1992), pp. 20-25.

In contrast to Skillen and Spykman, neo-Calvinist social philosopher Henk Woldring presents a more accurate appraisal of the broad parameters of Althusius's social philosophy, specifically with respect to his doctrine of natural law. Unlike Skillen and Spykman, Woldring does not filter Althusius's understanding of natural law through

Dooyeweerd's anti-scholastic interpretive lens. While Woldring fails to place Althusius's doctrine of natural law in the context of his Reformed contemporaries, he does exhibit a rudimentary understanding of the way in which Althusius conceived "natural law as universal principles of law, such as justice, humanity, reasonableness, and fairness, created by God in human nature, which can be clarified by the moral law of the Ten Commandments and by brotherly love." Henk E. S. Woldring, "Multiform Responsibility and the Revitalization of Civil Society," in *Religion, Pluralism, and Public Life: Abraham Kuyper's Legacy for the Twenty-First Century,* ed. Luis E. Lugo (Grand Rapids: Wm. B. Eerdmans Publishing Company, 2000), p. 178; and Woldring, "The Constitutional State in the Political Philosophy of Johannes Althusius," *European Journal of Law and Economics* 5 (1998): 127-28.

42. Daniel J. Elazar, *Covenant Tradition in Politics,* vol. 1, *Covenant and Polity in Biblical Israel: Biblical Foundations and Jewish Expressions* (New Brunswick, N.J.: Transaction Publishers, 1995), p. 26.

43. Incidentally, Eric Voegelin stands alone among twentieth-century political philosophers and intellectual historians in his unilaterally negative assessment of Althusius for his use of the Ramist method: "The use of the Ramist method will aid us in fixing the rank of Althusius's work — which is still overrated as a consequence of Otto von Gierke's monograph. The *Politica* is by far the most solid work of the Calvinist monarchomachic group; . . . it is the work of an experienced practical lawyer who could digest his rich knowledge, with the aid of his 'method,' into a well-ordered book; but it is definitely not the work of a great political thinker" (p. 56). One suspects, however, that Voegelin's criticism relates more to his displeasure with Althusius's successful integration of Reformed ecclesiology with juridical structure than it does to Althusius's clear repudiation of Jean Bodin's integration of Roman Catholic ecclesiology (*plenitudo potestatis*) to the issue of sovereignty in the commonwealth. Eric Voegelin, *The Collected Works of Eric Voegelin,* vol. 23, *History of Political Ideas,* vol. 5, *Religion and the Rise of Modernity,* ed. James L. Wiser (Columbia: University of Missouri Press, 1998), pp. 55-59.

44. J. Wayne Baker and Charles S. McCoy, *Fountainhead of Federalism: Heinrich Bullinger and the Covenantal Tradition* (Louisville: Westminster/John Knox Press, 1991), chap. 2, "The Development of the Federal Theological Tradition," pp. 29-44; chap. 3, "Federal Political Philosophy: Mornay and Althusius," pp. 45-62.

45. Fabrizio Lomonaco, "Huguenot Critical Theory and 'Ius Maiestatis' in Huber and Althusius," in *New Essays on the Political Thought of the Huguenots of the Refuge,* ed. John Christian Laursen (Leiden: E. J. Brill, 1995), pp. 171-92.

46. Charles McCoy, "The Centrality of Covenant in the Political Philosophy of Johannes Althusius," in *Politische Theorie des Johannes Althusius,* ed. Karl-Wilhelm Dahm, Werner Krawietz, and Dieter Wyduckel (Berlin: Duncker and Humblot, 1988), pp. 187-99; and McCoy, "Der Bund als Grundmetapher in der Politica des Johannes Althusius," in *Gottes Zukunft — Zukunft der Welt* (München: Chr. Kaiser Verlag, 1986), pp. 332-44.

47. Baker and McCoy, *Fountainhead of Federalism,* p. 50.

48. According to McCoy, "In the hands of Althusius, immersed as he is in the federalism of Herborn, the covenant as fundamental political principle encompasses the contractualism of Roman law and the centrality of politics for human living found in the

Aristotelian and natural-law traditions." McCoy, "The Centrality of Covenant in the Political Philosophy of Johannes Althusius," p. 190.

49. In this respect, Daniel Elazar's four-volume *Covenant Tradition in Politics* series is his crowning achievement. Elazar, *Covenant and Polity in Biblical Israel: Biblical Foundations and Jewish Expressions,* vol. 1 (New Brunswick, N.J.: Transaction Publishers, 1995); Elazar, *Covenant and Commonwealth: From Christian Separation Through the Protestant Reformation,* vol. 2 (New Brunswick, N.J.: Transaction Publishers, 1996); Elazar, *Covenant and Constitutionalism: The Great Frontier and the Matrix of Federal Democracy,* vol. 3 (New Brunswick, N.J.: Transaction Publishers, 1998); and Elazar, *Covenant and Civil Society: The Constitutional Matrix of Modern Democracy,* vol. 4 (New Brunswick, N.J.: Transaction Publishers, 1998).

50. Daniel J. Elazar, "Althusius's Grand Design for a Federal Commonwealth," in *Politica: An Abridged Translation of Politics Methodically Set Forth and Illustrated with Sacred and Profane Examples,* ed. and trans. Frederick S. Carney (Indianapolis: Liberty Fund, 1995), p. xxxv. A little further down the page Elazar summarizes Althusius's principal contribution as follows: "Althusius's *Politica* was the first book to present a comprehensive theory of federal republicanism rooted in a covenantal view of human society derived from, but not dependent on, a theological system. It presented a theory of polity-building based on the polity as a compound political association established by its citizens through their primary associations on the basis of consent rather than a reified state imposed by a ruler or an elite" (p. xxxv). Cf. Elazar, *Covenant and Polity in Biblical Israel,* vol. 1, p. 26; and Elazar, *Covenant and Civil Society,* vol. 4, pp. 1-2, 20-21, 27-28.

51. Thomas Hueglin, in contrast to Elazar, argues that while the American Federalists drew from the older European tradition of federalism, for example, in Montesquieu's *The Spirit of Laws* — and, through Montesquieu's use of historical examples there, Althusius's theory of consociational federalism — "an argument can be made that the Federalists' interpretation constituted a deliberate and radical break with [the older European] tradition" of federalism. Hueglin, "Federalism at the Crossroads: Old Meanings, New Significance," *Canadian Journal of Political Science* 36, no. 2 (June 2003): 276, 275-94.

52. Michael Behnen, "Herrscherbild und Herrschaftstechnik in der 'Politica' des Johannes Althusius," *Zeitschrift für historische Forschung* 11 (1984): 417-72.

53. Alain de Benoist, "The First Federalist: Johannes Althusius," *Krisis* 22 (March 1999): 2-34.

54. Ken Endo, "The Principle of Subsidiarity: From Johannes Althusius to Jacques Delors," *Hokkaido Law Review* 44, no. 6 (1994): 629-32, 553-652.

55. Thomas Hueglin, "Covenant and Federalism in the Politics of Althusius," in *The Covenant Connection: From Federal Theology to Modern Federalism,* ed. Daniel J. Elazar and John Kincaid (Lanham, Md.: Lexington Books, 2000), pp. 31-54; Hueglin, *Early Modern Concepts for a Late Modern World: Althusius on Community and Federalism* (Waterloo, Ontario: Wilfrid Laurier University Press, 1999); Hueglin, "Have We Studied the Wrong Authors? On the Relevance of Johannes Althusius," *Studies in Political Thought* 1, no. 1 (1992): 75-93; Hueglin, "Johannes Althusius: Medieval Constitutionalist or Modern Federalist?" *Publius: The Journal of Federalism* 9, no. 4 (Fall 1979): 9-41; and Hueglin, *Sozietaler Föderalismus: Die politische Theorie des Johannes Althusius* (Berlin: Walter de Gruyter, 1991).

56. Patrick Riley, "Three Seventeenth Century German Theorists of Federalism: Althusius, Hugo, and Leibniz," *Publius: The Journal of Federalism* 6, no. 3 (Summer 1976): 7-41.

57. Hueglin, "Have We Studied the Wrong Authors?" p. 89.

58. The massive two-volume *Althusius-Bibliographie* appeared in 1973 as the first publication of the recently founded Johannes Althusius Gesellschaft, now associated with the Faculty of Law at the Technical University of Dresden and renamed as the Society for Research on Early Modern Legal Theory and Constitutional History (http://www.althusius.de), and organizes all that was written by Althusius or about his life and work up to the date of its publication. The major publications of the Society from latest to earliest are as follows: Frederick S. Carney, Heinz Schilling, and Dieter Wyduckel, eds., *Jurisprudenz, politische Theorie und politische Theologie: Beiträge des Herborner Symposions zum 400. Jahrestag der Politica des Johannes Althusius 1603-2003* (Berlin: Duncker & Humblot, 2004); Emilio Bonfatti, Giuseppe Duso, and Merio Scattola, eds., *Politisches Begriffe und historisches Umfeld in der Politica methodice digesta des Johannes Althusius* (Wiesbaden, 2002); Peter Blickle, Thomas Hüglin, and Dieter Wyduckel, eds., *Subsidiarität als rechtliches und politisches Ordnungsprinzip in Kirche, Staat und Gesellschaft: Genese, Geltungsgrundlagen und Perspektiven an der Schwelle des dritten Jahrtausends* (Berlin: Duncker & Humblot, 2002); Giuseppe Duso, Werner Krawietz, and Dieter Wyduckel, eds., *Konsens und Konsoziation in der Politischen Theorie des frühen Föderalismus* (Berlin: Duncker & Humblot, 1997); Karl-Wilhelm Dahm, Werner Krawietz, and Dieter Wyduckel, eds., *Politische Theorie des Johannes Althusius* (Berlin: Duncker & Humblot, 1988); and Dieter Wyduckel, *Althusius-Bibliographie: Bibliographie zur politischen Ideengeschichte und Staatslehre, zum Staatsrecht und zur Verfassungsgeschichte des 16. bis 18. Jahrhunderts*, 2 vols., ed. Hans Ulrich Scupin and Ulrich Scheuner (Berlin: Duncker and Humblot, 1973). For a review of this work, see Theo Veen, "Een *Fundgrube* voor de historische wetenschap: de *Althusius-Bibliografie,*" *Bijdragen en Mededelingen Betreffende de Geschiedenis der Nederlanden* 94, no. 1 (1979): 89-96.

59. The notable exceptions to this generalization are Thomas Eugene Ridenhour Jr., "The Uses of Cicero by Johannes Althusius in the *Politica Methodice Digesta* (M.A. thesis, University of Virginia, 2001); Corrado Malandrino, "Il *Syndikat* di Johannes Althusius a Emden: La ricerca," *Pensiero Politico* 28, no. 3 (1995): 359-83, which endeavors to correct some of the weaknesses in Heinz Werner Antholz's *Die politische Wirksamkeit des Johannes Althusius in Emden* (Aurich: Abhandlungen und Vorträge zur Geschichte Ostfrieslands, 1955), the only major work on the subject; Robert V. Friedeburg, "From Collective Representation to the Right to Individual Defence: James Steuart's *Ius Populi Vindicatum* and the Use of Johannes Althusius's *Politica* in Restoration Scotland," *History of European Ideas* 24, no. 1 (1998): 19-42; Sanford Lakoff, "Althusius, Johannes," in *Political Philosophy: Theories, Thinkers, Concepts,* ed. Seymour Martin Lipset (Washington: Congressional Quarterly Press, 2001), pp. 221-23; Robert M. Kingdon, "Althusius' Use of Calvinist Sources in His *Politica,*" *Rechtstheorie* 16 (1997): 19-28 (Kingdon's article can also be found in Duso et al., eds., *Konsens und Konsoziation*); John Lewis Marshall, "Natural Law and the Covenant: The Place of Natural Law in the Covenantal Framework of Samuel Rutherford's *Lex, Rex*" (Ph.D. diss., Westminster Theological Seminary, 1995); Merio Scattola, "Johannes Althusius und das

Naturrecht des 16. Jahrhunderts," in *Jurisprudenz, Politische Theorie und Politische Theologie*, pp. 371-96; and Christoph Strohm, "Althusius's Rechtslehre im Kontext des reformierten Protestantismus," in *Jurisprudenz, Politische Theorie und Politische Theologie*, pp. 71-102.

60. Cf. Berman, *Law and Revolution, II*; Russell Hittinger, *The First Grace: Rediscovering the Natural Law in a Post-Christian World* (Wilmington: ISI Books, 2003); Joan Lockwood O'Donovan, *Theology of Law and Authority in the English Reformation* (Atlanta: Scholars Press, 1991); Charles J. Reid Jr., *Power over the Body, Equality in the Family: Rights and Domestic Relations in Medieval Canon Law* (Grand Rapids: Wm. B. Eerdmans Publishing Company, 2004); David VanDrunen, "The Context of Natural Law: John Calvin's Doctrine of the Two Kingdoms," *Journal of Church and State* 46, no. 3 (Summer 2004): 503-25; and John Witte Jr., *Law and Protestantism: The Legal Teachings of the Lutheran Reformation* (Cambridge: Cambridge University Press, 2002).

61. Althusius, "Preface to the 1603 edition," in *Politica*, p. 3.

62. Althusius, "Preface to the 1603 edition," in *Politica*, p. 5.

63. Althusius, "Preface to the 1603 edition," in *Politica*, p. 5.

64. Carney, "Translator's Introduction," in *Politica*, pp. xii-xv. For more on Ramism, see Walter Ong, *Ramus, Method, and the Decay of Dialogue* (Cambridge, Mass.: Harvard University Press, 1958); Neal W. Gilbert, *Renaissance Concepts of Method* (New York: Columbia University Press, 1960); and Richard A. Muller, *Post-Reformation Reformed Dogmatics: The Rise and Development of Reformed Orthodoxy, ca. 1520 to ca. 1725*, 4 vols. (Grand Rapids: Baker Academic, 2003), vol. 1, pp. 181-84.

65. Althusius, "Preface to the 1610 edition of Johannes Althusius's *Politica Methodice Digesta*," in *New Essays on the Political Thought of the Huguenots of the Refuge*, ed. John Christian Laursen, trans. Cary J. Nederman (Leiden: E. J. Brill, 1995), p. 198.

66. Althusius, "Preface to the 1610 edition of Johannes Althusius's *Politica*," p. 198. Cf. Althusius, *Politica*, 21.41 (pp. 146-48).

67. Carney, "The Associational Theory of Johannes Althusius," pp. 155-66. Antony Black's understanding of this relationship differs in important respects from Carney's, Gierke's, and Friedrich's. According to Black, "Althusius's conception of social relationships clearly owed a great deal to the Christian idea of love; indeed, in the last resort, mutual love may be said to be the pattern that emerges as he weaves together the various strands of solidarity and exchange. It has been argued that Althusius's use of Scripture was merely ornamental (Bartels, cit. Friedrich 1932, xviii; Mesnard 1936, 614-15). It is certainly true that he insisted that the study of politics was a discipline *sui generis*, and that he often used Scripture, as did the scholastics, to corroborate conclusions arrived at by other means. He rejected the view that one could deduce the normative pattern of social and political life from Scripture alone. The data of politics are provided by observation of human life as we experience it or read about it; the discipline closest to politics is jurisprudence (4). But the picture that finally emerges is inspired, as he explicitly asserts, by those parts of the *Decalogue* which relate to social conduct, interpreted, in the New Testament manner, in terms of the overriding precept of love. In other words, Christianity provides the 'form' and goal of politics, not its material nor its method" (pp. 140-41). Antony Black, *Guild & State: European Political Thought from the Twelfth Century to the Present* (New Brunswick, N.J.: Transaction Publishers, 2003), pp. 136-42.

68. Gierke, *The Development of Political Theory,* p. 70.

69. Carney, "The Associational Theory of Johannes Althusius," p. 153.

70. Friedrich, "Introduction," p. lxiv; and Carney, "The Associational Theory of Johannes Althusius," p. 164.

71. Carney, "The Associational Theory of Johannes Althusius," p. 164.

72. Carney, "The Associational Theory of Johannes Althusius," p. 165.

73. Carney, "The Associational Theory of Johannes Althusius," p. 166.

74. For studies that disagree with Carney's understanding of the relationship between natural law and divine law, see Richard A. Muller, "The Covenant of Works and the Stability of Divine Law in Seventeenth-Century Reformed Orthodoxy: A Study in the Theology of Herman Witsius and Wilhelmus à Brakel," in *After Calvin: Studies in the Development of a Theological Tradition* (New York: Oxford University Press, 2003), pp. 182-83; Robert Letham, "The *Foedus Operum:* Some Factors Accounting for Its Development," *Sixteenth Century Journal* 14, no. 4 (Winter 1983): 461-63; and Lyle D. Bierma, *German Calvinism in the Confessional Age: The Covenant Theology of Caspar Olevianus* (Grand Rapids: Baker Book House, 1996), pp. 112-20.

75. Peter Martyr Vermigli's biblical commentaries and *scholia* pertaining to political topics (namely, Judges 3 on inferior magistrates, that is, *ephors,* and Romans 13 on the right to resist tyrants) were read and frequently cited by Althusius. For more, see Kingdon, "Althusius's Use of Calvinist Sources in His *Politica,*" pp. 23-24.

76. Althusius also appeals to other writers in the Reformed scholastic tradition such as Francis Junius, John Piscator, Benedict Aretius, and Zacharias Ursinus. Cf. Carney, "Translator's Introduction," in *Politica,* pp. xxvi-xxvii.

77. Otto Gründler typifies the older dogmatic assessment of Zanchi: "The key to Zanchi's theology and its unifying principle is the concept of causality. It dominates his doctrine of God; it determines the relation between Creator and creature; it underlies the analogy by which knowledge of God is possible; and it characterizes his doctrines of providence and predestination. . . . In the theology of Zanchi, at the very point of transition from Reformation to Orthodoxy, the spirit of medieval Scholasticism has thus begun to replace that of the Reformers at a point where it counted most. To the extent to which — under the influence of the Thomistic-Aristotelian tradition — the christocentric orientation of Calvin's thinking shifted toward a metaphysics of causality in the thought of his successors, Reformed theology ceased to be a theology of revelation." Gründler, "The Influence of Thomas Aquinas upon the Theology of Girolamo Zanchi (1516-1590)," in *Studies in Medieval Culture,* Series VII, no. 2, ed. John R. Sommerfeldt (Kalamazoo: Western Michigan University, 1964), p. 117. Cf. Gründler, "Thomism and Calvinism in the Theology of Girolamo Zanchi" (1516-1590) (Ph.D. diss., Princeton Theological Seminary, 1961); and Gründler, *Die Gotteslehre Girolami Zanchis und ihre Bedeutung für seine Lehre von der Pradestination* (Neukirchen-Vluyn: Neukirchener Verlag, 1965).

Fortunately, John L. Farthing has shown, in a variety of recent publications, that the older dogmatic assessment of Zanchi's theology is not only false but also a caricature of considerable inflation. Cf. Farthing, "*De coniugio spirituali:* Jerome Zanchi on Ephesians 5:22-33," *Sixteenth Century Journal* 24, no. 3 (1993): 621-52; Farthing, "*Foedus Evangelicum:* Jerome Zanchi on the Covenant," *Calvin Theological Journal* 29, no. 1 (April 1994): 149-67; Farthing, "Christ and the Eschaton: The Reformed Eschatology of Jerome Zanchi," in *Later Calvinism: International Perspectives,* ed. W. Fred Graham

(Kirksville, Mo.: Sixteenth Century Journal Publishers, 1994), pp. 333-54; Farthing, "Holy Harlotry: Jerome Zanchi and the Exegetical History of Gomer (Hosea 1–3)," in *Biblical Interpretation in the Era of the Reformation: Essays Presented to David C. Steinmetz in Honor of His Sixtieth Birthday*, ed. Richard A. Muller and John L. Thompson (Grand Rapids: Wm. B. Eerdmans Publishing Company, 1996), pp. 292-312; and Farthing, "Zanchi, Jerome (1516-1590)," in *Historical Handbook of Major Biblical Interpreters*, ed. Donald K. McKim (Downers Grove, Ill.: InterVarsity Press, 1998), pp. 245-49.

78. Carney, "Translator's Introduction," in *Politica*, p. xxvii.

79. Carney, "Translator's Introduction," in *Politica*, p. xxii.

80. Althusius, *Politica*, 21.29 (p. 144), emphasis added. See also Jerome Zanchi's elaboration of this idea in his *Confession of Christian Religion* (Cambridge: John Legat, 1599), 10.3 (p. 48). Cf. Kingdon, "Althusius's Use of Calvinist Sources in His *Politica*," pp. 19-28.

81. Zacharias Ursinus, *The Commentary of Dr. Zacharias Ursinus on the Heidelberg Catechism*, trans. G. W. Willard (Columbus, Ohio, 1852; Phillipsburg, N.J.: Presbyterian and Reformed Publishing Company, 1985), p. 492.

82. For studies related to Zanchi's biography, see Christopher J. Burchill, "Girolamo Zanchi: Portrait of a Reformed Theologian and His Work," *Sixteenth Century Journal* 15, no. 2 (1984): 185-207; Burchill, "Girolamo Zanchi in Strasbourg 1553-1563" (Ph.D. diss., Cambridge University, 1980); Charles Schmidt, "Girolamo Zanchi," *Studium und Kritiken* 32 (1859): 625-708; and Joseph N. Tylenda, "Girolamo Zanchi and John Calvin: A Study in Discipleship as Seen through Their Correspondence," *Calvin Theological Journal* 10, no. 2 (November 1975): 101-41.

83. This chapter has been translated by Jeffrey J. Veenstra and published in the scholia section of the *Journal of Markets & Morality* 6, no. 1 (Spring 2003): 317-98. All subsequent page references will be to the scholia folios and not to those of the *Journal of Markets & Morality* folios. The original citation is *Operum theologicorum*, tome 4, *De primi hominis lapsu, de peccato, & de legi Dei* (Geneva: Sumptibus Samuelis Crispini, 1617), fols. 185-221.

84. The treatise on law is a shorthand reference for *S.T.* I-II, questions 90-114.

85. These chapters were originally published under separate cover as the *Tractatus de redemptione* while Zanchi was still in residence at Heidelberg.

86. John Patrick Donnelly, S.J., "Calvinist Thomism," *Viator: Medieval and Renaissance Studies* 7 (1976): 444.

87. Donnelly, "Calvinist Thomism," p. 444.

88. Zanchi, "On the Law in General," p. 2.

89. Zanchi, "On the Law in General," p. 2.

90. Zanchi, "On the Law in General," p. 2.

91. Zanchi, "On the Law in General," pp. 2-3.

92. Zanchi, "On the Law in General," p. 3.

93. Zanchi, "On the Law in General," p. 4.

94. Zanchi, "On the Law in General," p. 5.

95. Zanchi, "On the Law in General," pp. 4-5.

96. Zanchi, "On the Law in General," p. 12.

97. Zanchi, "On the Law in General," p. 5.

98. Zanchi, "On the Law in General," p. 5.

99. Zanchi, "On the Law in General," p. 6.

100. Zanchi, "On the Law in General," p. 6.

101. Zanchi, "On the Law in General," p. 8; cf. Gratian, *Decretum,* 1.7.

102. Zanchi, "On the Law in General," p. 8. Althusius typically employs the Roman law terminology of *common law (jus commune)* when speaking of natural law, whereas Zanchi prefers the more conventional Thomistic terminology of *lex naturalis* or *lex naturae.*

103. Cf. Aquinas's treatment of natural law in relation to moral precepts of the Old Law in *S.T.* I-II, 100, 1, 3, 11.

104. Zanchi, "On the Law in General," p. 9.

105. Zanchi, "On the Law in General," p. 9.

106. Zanchi, "On the Law in General," p. 9.

107. Zanchi, "On the Law in General," p. 9. Cf. Zanchi, *Confession,* 5.6-8 (pp. 24-25); 10.3 (p. 48).

108. Zanchi, "On the Law in General," pp. 9-10.

109. Zanchi, *Confession,* 7.1-9 (pp. 31-37).

110. Zanchi, "On the Law in General," p. 10.

111. Zanchi, "On the Law in General," pp. 12-13.

112. Zanchi, "On the Law in General," p. 14. For a parallel anthropological discussion of the remnants of human free will after the fall, see Zanchi, *Confession,* 8.1-9 (pp. 38-42).

113. Zanchi, "On the Law in General," p. 11.

114. Zanchi, "On the Law in General," p. 13.

115. Zanchi, "On the Law in General," p. 13.

116. Zanchi, "On the Law in General," p. 14. Both Calvin and Vermigli employ a similar notion — namely, the concept of *prolepseis* — to refer to the knowledge of justice and rectitude that has been implanted by God in the human mind. For an informative treatment of the origin of the spark metaphor in Stoicism and its reappearance in the early modern era, see Maryanne Cline Horowitz, "The Stoic Synthesis of the Idea of Natural Law in Man: Four Themes," *Journal of the History of Ideas* 35, no. 1 (January-March 1974): 14-16; and Horowitz, *Seeds of Virtue and Knowledge* (Princeton, N.J.: Princeton University Press, 1998), pp. 3-20, 32-34.

117. Zanchi, "On the Law in General," p. 16.

118. Zanchi, "On the Law in General," p. 16.

119. Zanchi, "On the Law in General," p. 16.

120. Althusius, "Preface to the 1610 edition of Johannes Althusius's *Politica,*" p. 198.

121. Zanchi, "On the Law in General," p. 16.

122. Zanchi, "On the Law in General," p. 17.

123. Zanchi, "On the Law in General," p. 17.

124. Zanchi, "On the Law in General," p. 17.

125. A few pages later, Zanchi clarifies how the Decalogue relates to the natural law: "[B]ecause the Decalogue defines and describes the same things that are called natural law, the Ten Commandments themselves are often called 'natural law'. . . . In closing, it must be mentioned that just as Christ is the fulfillment of the entire Mosaic law, so, too, is he the fulfillment of natural law because, as human beings are convicted of sin

through the law, they flee to Christ for forgiveness." Zanchi, "On the Law in General," p. 21.

126. Zanchi, "On the Law in General," p. 17.

127. Zanchi, "On the Law in General," p. 19.

128. Zanchi, "On the Law in General," p. 19. For an extended treatment of two interrelated and important topics, namely, the regenerate person's free choice and power to do good and good works respectively, see Zanchi, *Confession*, 20.1-9 (pp. 156-62); and 21.1-9 (pp. 163-69). Cf. Aquinas's discussion of the ineffectiveness of natural law in leading people to the good in his commentary on Romans 1. Eugene F. Rogers Jr., "The Narrative of Natural Law in Aquinas's Commentary on Romans 1," *Theological Studies* 59, no. 2 (June 1998): 256-62.

129. Zanchi, "On the Law in General," pp. 58-59, 58-61.

130. Johannes Althusius, *Dicaelogicae Libri Tres, Totum & universum Jus, quo utimur methodicè complectentes: . . .* , 2d ed. (Frankfurt: Christopher Corvini, 1649; Aalen: Scientia, 1967). I want to acknowledge my debt to Jeff Veenstra for his assistance with the translations from the *Dicaeologica*. The elided sections of the texts contain only abbreviated references to classical, contemporary, and biblical authorities that support Althusius's argument.

131. Althusius, *Politica*, 21.15 (p. 138).

132. Althusius, *Politica*, 21.16-17 (p. 139).

133. Althusius, *Politica*, 21.18 (p. 139). Cf. Zanchi, "On the Law in General," pp. 5, 11.

134. Althusius, "Preface to the 1610 edition of Johannes Althusius's *Politica*," p. 198.

135. There is an earlier, less detailed treatment of this distinction in the *Politica* at 1.11-22 (pp. 19-22). There is another treatment of this distinction in the *Dicaeologica* at 1.13.6: "There is a two part classification of law: natural/common law and civil/proper law . . . just as the utility and necessity of human life that produce the law has two aspects, that is, a common one and one proper to each individual area." ("Coustitutio juris est duplex: naturalis, communis: vel civilis, propria . . . prout utilitas et necessitas vitae humanae, quae jus peperit, duplex est, communis, vel loci alicujus certi propria.")

136. Althusius, *Politica*, 21.19 (p. 139).

137. Althusius, *Dicaeologica*, 1.13.7: "Naturalis et communis est, quam recta ratio communis, propter communem humanae vitae socialis necessitatem et utilitatem parit. Unde jus naturale vocatur."

138. Althusius, *Dicaeologica*, 1.13.18: "Hoc commune jus alii distinguunt in jus naturale, vel gentium. . . . Paulo aliter. . . . Alii vero utrumque hoc rectius naturale vocant . . . jus naturale solis hominibus tribuit et quod jus gentium dicitur, hoc saepe naturale a J Cris vocatur. . . . Jus naturale quod vocant, dicitur, quod recta simplex noetica, αναποδεικτως, hominem, quatenus homo et animal rationale, docet . . . ad sancta et pie vivendum. . . . Unde a quibusdam jus rationalis vocatur . . . quamnis idipsum non innaseatur proprie, sed tantium, εννοιαι, notions ejusdem, seu potius facultas juris hujus cognoscendi a natura ingeneretur. Vocatur quoque lex naturae . . . naturalis aequitas . . . quod jus bruta animalia nonunquam imitantur, et cujus simulachra quaedam habere dicuntur. . . ."

139. Althusius, *Politica*, 21.20 (p. 140).

140. Althusius, *Dicaeologica*, 1.13.11: "Commune igitur jus est, quod a natura, vel Deo immediate hominum mentibus est inscriptum, et ad quod faciendum, vel omittendum, illi ab eodem moventur, quantum satis est ad publicum bonum societatis humanae conservandum, et ad peccati nocentes convincendum, vel innocents excusandum. . . . Unde in homine juris hujus est, tum notitia, tum inclinatio naturalis. Illa homo cognoseit id quod justum est, hac vero impellitur arcano naturae instinctu ad faciendum, vel omittendum id quod justum, vel injustum esse cognovit." Cf. Zanchi, "On the Law in General," p. 11, pp. 11-14. At this point Zanchi enumerates possible definitions of natural and common law before providing his own definition in the next thesis (Thesis 8).

141. Althusius, *Politica*, 21.20 (p. 140).

142. Althusius, *Dicaeologica*, 1.13.14: "Docet autem et inscribit mentibus hominum Deus generalia principia boni et aequi, mali et iniqui, ad quae sacienda, vel omittenda, omnes obligat, impellit et incitat, atque negligentes in hisce per conscientiam intus accusat et sacientes excusat. Itaque ad bonum impellit, et a malo avocat. Si ductum illius ad bonum secutus suerit, excusat: sin minus, accusat eundem." Cf. Zanchi, "On the Law in General," p. 12.

143. Althusius, *Politica*, 21.21 (p. 140). Cf. Zanchi, "On the Law in General," pp. 18-19.

144. Althusius, *Politica*, 21.21 (p. 140).

145. Althusius, *Politica*, 21.22-23 (p. 140). Cf. Zanchi, "On the Law in General," pp. 17, 21.

146. Althusius, *Politica*, 21.26 (p. 141). Althusius's reference here to the first table as a superior law, in my judgment, points toward a Scotistic understanding of natural law and the relations between the tables. For ample documentation to support this claim, see Allan Wolter's commentary (pp. 60-64) and the translated portions of Scotus' *Ordinatio* III, distinction 37, in *Duns Scotus on the Will and Morality: Selected and Translated with an Introduction by Allan B. Wolter, O.F.M.* (Washington: Catholic University of America Press, 1986), pp. 269-89.

147. Althusius, *Politica*, 21.26 (p. 142).

148. Althusius, *Politica*, 21.28 (pp. 143-44). On the question of the dispensability of the precepts, which will be addressed more fully in Chapter Six, it is clear that Althusius's position is in line with Duns Scotus's.

149. Althusius, *Politica*, 21.29 (p. 144), emphasis added. Cf. Zanchi, *Confession*, 10.3 (p. 48).

150. Althusius, *Dicaeologica*, 1.13.18: ". . . jus naturale solis hominibus tribuit et quod jus gentium dicitur, hoc saepe naturale à J Cris vocatur. . . ." Cf. Zanchi, "On the Law in General," pp. 8, 17.

151. Zanchi, "On the Law in General," p. 63. Zanchi's affirmative view of philosophy is seen especially in his praise of Aristotle during the course of his lectures in Strasbourg on the philosopher's *Physics*: "The method of Moses is not so very different from the one that Aristotle followed. It is therefore useful to observe, when you are reading Moses, who recounts the works of God in separate days, that, when you are looking for a longer explanation of these matters, you know where to turn to: namely to Aristotle's works, in which these matters are discussed more widely." As translated and

quoted by J. A. Van Ruler, *The Crisis of Causality: Voetius and Descartes on God, Nature, and Change* (Leiden: E. J. Brill, 1995), pp. 80-81.

152. Zanchi, "On the Law in General," p. 63.

153. Zanchi, "On the Law in General," pp. 63-64.

154. Althusius, *Politica*, 21.30 (p. 144). Cf. Althusius, *Politica*, 1.19-21 (pp. 21-22).

155. Althusius, *Politica*, 21.30 (p. 144).

156. Althusius, *Politica*, 21.30 (p. 144).

157. Althusius, *Politica*, 21.31 (p. 144). He borrows these reasons directly from Zanchi. Cf. Zanchi, *Operum theologicorum*, tome 4, *De primi hominis lapsu, de peccato, & de legi Dei* (Geneva: Sumptibus Samuelis Crispini, 1617), Cap. XI, "De Decalogo," fols. 222-26 (Thesis 1).

158. Althusius, *Politica*, 21.31 (p. 144).

159. Althusius, *Politica*, 21.32 (p. 145).

160. Althusius, *Politica*, 21.32 (p. 145).

161. Althusius, *Politica*, 21.32 (p. 145).

162. Althusius, *Politica*, 9.21 (p. 72).

163. Althusius, *Politica*, 21.33 (p. 146). Althusius's "entire system of law" as presented in the *Dicaeologica* is an attempt to make such "specific determinations" on the basis of common and customary law for the polity of Emden.

164. Althusius, *Politica*, 21.34 (p. 146).

165. Althusius, *Politica*, 22.3 (p. 148). Zanchi states a similar position in his *Confession*: "Lastly, in as much as Christ in his gospel did not take away the political laws of the nations, which were not contrary to the law of nature: Therefore we think it lawful and free for any governors to bring among their subjects such political laws as were delivered to the people of Israel, and by the same, (than which none are more just) to rule and govern the people. Therefore, they do exceeding great injury to the Gospel of Christ, that say it troubles or overthrows commonwealths." Zanchi, *Confession*, 13.8 (p. 98).

166. Althusius, *Politica*, 22.3 (p. 148).

167. Althusius, *Politica*, 22.4 (p. 148).

Notes to Chapter 6

1. Richard A. Muller, "Foreword," in Dewey J. Hoitenga Jr., *John Calvin and the Will: A Critique and Corrective* (Grand Rapids: Baker Book House, 1997), p. 11.

2. Anri Morimoto, "The Seventeenth-Century Ecumenical Interchanges," in *Christian Ethics in Ecumenical Context: Theology, Culture, and Politics in Dialogue*, ed. Shin Chiba, George R. Hunsberger, and Lester Edwin J. Ruiz (Grand Rapids: Wm. B. Eerdmans Publishing Company, 1995), p. 86.

3. This work was first published in three volumes between the years 1679-1685. George Musgrave Giger, professor of classics at Princeton University (1847-1865), produced an 8,000-page handwritten translation of the *Institutio*, which was edited and annotated by James T. Dennison Jr. much later and published recently (1992-1997) in three volumes by the Presbyterian and Reformed Publishing Company. Subsequent cita-

tions to this work will be referenced according to the following documentation system: topic, question, and paragraph numbers.

4. Richard A. Muller, "Scholasticism Protestant and Catholic: Francis Turretin on the Object and Principles of Theology," *Church History* 55, no. 2 (June 1986): 195.

5. James T. Dennison Jr., "The Life and Career of Francis Turretin," in *Institutes of Elenctic Theology*, 3 vols., trans. George Musgrave Giger, ed. James T. Dennison Jr. (Phillipsburg, N.J.: Presbyterian and Reformed Publishing Company, 1997), vol. 3, p. 642.

6. Dennison, "The Life and Career of Francis Turretin," in *Institutes*, vol. 3, p. 642. For more on this history, see also James T. Dennison Jr., "The Twilight of Scholasticism: Francis Turretin at the Dawn of the Enlightenment," in *Protestant Scholasticism: Essays in Reassessment*, ed. Carl R. Trueman and R. S. Clark (Carlisle, U.K.: Paternoster Press, 1999), pp. 244-55.

7. Dennison, "The Life and Career of Francis Turretin," in *Institutes*, vol. 3, p. 646.

8. On the transitions of this era, see Martin I. Klauber, *Between Reformed Scholasticism and Pan-Protestantism: Jean-Alphonse Turretin (1671-1737) and Enlightened Orthodoxy at the Academy of Geneva* (Selinsgrove, Pa.: Susquehanna University Press, 1994); Klauber, "Jean-Alphonse Turrettini and the Abrogation of the Formula Consensus in Geneva," *Westminster Theological Journal* 53 (1991): 325-38; Klauber, "Jean-Alphonse Turrettini (1671-1737) on Natural Theology: The Triumph of Reason over Revelation at the Academy of Geneva," *Scottish Journal of Theology* 47, no. 3 (1994): 301-25; Klauber, "Reason, Revelation, and Cartesianism: Louis Tronchin and Enlightened Orthodoxy in Late Seventeenth-Century Geneva," *Church History* 59 (1990): 326-39; Klauber, "Reformed Orthodoxy in Transition: Bénédict Pictet (1655-1724) and Enlightened Orthodoxy in Post-Reformation Geneva," in *Later Calvinism: International Perspectives*, ed. W. Fred Graham (Kirksville, Mo.: Sixteenth Century Journal Publishers, 1994), pp. 93-113; Klauber, "The Context and Development of the Views of Jean-Alphonse Turrettini (1671-1737) on Religious Authority" (Ph.D. diss., University of Wisconsin–Madison, 1987); Klauber, "The Eclipse of Reformed Scholasticism in Eighteenth-Century Geneva: Natural Theology from Jean-Alphonse Turretin to Jacob Vernet," in *The Identity of Geneva: The Christian Commonwealth, 1564-1864*, ed. John B. Roney and Martin I. Klauber (Westport, Conn.: Greenwood Press, 1998), pp. 129-42; Klauber, "The Helvetic Consensus Formula (1675): An Introduction and Translation," *Trinity Journal* 11 (Spring 1990): 103-23; Klauber, "Theological Transition in Geneva: From Jean-Alphonse Turretin to Jacob Vernet," in *Protestant Scholasticism: Essays in Reassessment*, ed. Carl R. Trueman and R. S. Clark (Carlisle, U.K.: Paternoster Press, 1999), pp. 256-70; and Martin I. Klauber and Glenn S. Sunshine, "Jean-Alphonse Turrettini on Biblical Accommodation: Calvinist or Socinian?" *Calvin Theological Journal* 25, no. 1 (April 1990): 7-27.

9. Dennison, "The Life and Career of Francis Turretin," in *Institutes*, vol. 3, p. 646.

10. Richard A. Muller, *Post-Reformation Reformed Dogmatics: The Rise and Development of Reformed Orthodoxy, ca. 1520 to ca. 1725*, 4 vols. (Grand Rapids: Baker Academic, 2003), vol. 1, p. 53.

11. Muller, *Post-Reformation Reformed Dogmatics*, vol. 1, pp. 96-99. Cf. David C. Steinmetz, *Luther in Context*, 2d ed. (Grand Rapids: Baker Academic, 2002), pp. 24-27, 38-41, 63-67.

12. Muller, *Post-Reformation Reformed Dogmatics*, vol. 1, p. 53.

13. Richard A. Muller, "*Vera Philosophia cum sacra Theologia nusquam pugnat*: Keckermann on Philosophy, Theology, and the Problem of Double Truth," *Sixteenth Century Journal* 15, no. 3 (1984): 362. For an extended treatment of the eclectic manner in which the Reformed appropriated medieval scholastic models, see Muller, *Post-Reformation Reformed Dogmatics*, vol. 1, pp. 88-122; vol. 4, pp. 391-97.

14. The notable exception is John Walter Beardslee III, who sought to revive interest in Turretin's theology by providing English translations of key sections of the *Institutio* several decades before the Giger-Dennison translation appeared in print. Cf. *Reformed Dogmatics: J. Wollebius, G. Voetius, F. Turretin*, ed. and trans. John W. Beardslee III (New York: Oxford University Press, 1965); and *The Doctrine of Scripture: Locus 2 of Institutio theologiae elencticae*, ed. and trans. John W. Beardslee III (Grand Rapids: Baker Book House, 1981).

15. John Walter Beardslee III, "Theological Development at Geneva under Francis and Jean-Alphonse Turretin (1648-1737)" (Ph.D. diss., Yale University, 1956).

16. Timothy Phillips, "Francis Turretin's Idea of Theology and Its Bearing upon His Doctrine of Scripture" (Ph.D. diss., Vanderbilt University, 1986).

17. Stephen Robert Spencer, "Reformed Scholasticism in Medieval Perspective: Thomas Aquinas and François Turrettini on the Incarnation" (Ph.D. diss., Michigan State University, 1988).

18. E. P. Meijering, *Reformierte Scholastik und patristische Theologie: die Bedeutung des Vaterbeweises in der Institutio theologiae elencticae F. Turrettins: unter besonderer Berucksichtigung der Gotteslehre und Christologie* (Nieuwkoop: De Graaf, 1991); and Meijering, "The Fathers and Calvinist Orthodoxy: Systematic Theology (A. Polanus, J. Wolleb, and F. Turrettini)," in *The Reception of the Church Fathers in the West: From the Carolingians to the Maurists*, 2 vols., ed. Irena Backus (Leiden: E. J. Brill, 1997), vol. 2, pp. 867-87.

19. Stephen R. Spencer, "Francis Turretin's Concept of the Covenant of Nature," in Graham, ed., *Later Calvinism: International Perspectives*, pp. 71-91.

20. Martin I. Klauber, "Francis Turretin on Biblical Accommodation: Loyal Calvinist or Reformed Scholastic?" *Westminster Theological Journal* 55, no. 1 (Spring 1993): 73-86.

21. Joel R. Beeke, "The Order of the Divine Decrees at the Genevan Academy: From Bezan Supralapsarianism to Turretinian Infralapsarianism," in Roney and Klauber, eds., *The Identity of Geneva: The Christian Commonwealth, 1564-1864*, pp. 57-76.

22. Muller, "Scholasticism Protestant and Catholic," pp. 193-205; and Timothy R. Phillips, "The Dissolution of Francis Turretin's Vision of *Theologia*: Geneva at the End of the Seventeenth Century," in Roney and Klauber, eds., *The Identity of Geneva: The Christian Commonwealth, 1564-1864*, pp. 77-92.

23. Sebastian Rehnman, "Alleged Rationalism: Francis Turretin on Reason," *Calvin Theological Journal* 37, no. 2 (November 2002): 255-69. Cf. Paul K. Helseth, "Right Reason and the Princeton Mind: The Moral Context," *Journal of Presbyterian History* 77, no. 1 (Spring 1999): 13-28.

24. Sebastian Rehnman, "Theistic Metaphysics and Biblical Exegesis: Francis Turretin on the Concept of God," *Religious Studies* 38, no. 2 (June 2002): 167-86.

25. Cf. Martin Klauber's publications in note 8.

26. Turretin, *Institutes*, 1.4.6 .

27. Turretin, *Institutes*, 1.4.2.

28. Turretin, *Institutes*, 1.4.3.

29. Muller, *Post-Reformation Reformed Dogmatics*, vol. 1, p. 300. Cf. Stephen Charnock, "Discourse of the Knowledge of Christ," in *The Works of the Late Learned Divine Stephen Charnock, B.D.: Being Several Discourses upon Various Divine Subjects*, 2 vols. (London: Printed by A. Maxwell and R. Roberts for Tho. Cockeril, 1684), vol. 2, pp. 486-88, 474-552.

30. Muller, *Post-Reformation Reformed Dogmatics*, vol. 1, p. 308. Cf. Richard A. Muller, *Dictionary of Latin and Greek Theological Terms: Drawn Principally from Protestant Scholastic Theology* (Grand Rapids: Baker Book House, 1985), s.v. "usus legis."

31. Muller, *Post-Reformation Reformed Dogmatics*, vol. 1, p. 308.

32. Turretin, *Institutes*, 1.9.5.

33. Turretin, *Institutes*, 1.3.12.

34. Turretin, *Institutes*, 1.3.2.

35. Turretin contends that the faculty is "spontaneously endowed" in all adults of sound mind.

36. Turretin, *Institutes*, 1.3.2.

37. Turretin, *Institutes*, 1.3.11.

38. Turretin, *Institutes*, 1.3.4. Althusius makes reference to the idea of "common notions" in *Dicaeologica*, 1.13.18; as does Charnock in "Discourse of the Knowledge of Christ," pp. 474-88. Calvin and Vermigli also refer to "common notions."

39. Turretin, *Institutes*, 1.3.6.

40. Turretin, *Institutes*, 1.3.6.

41. Turretin, *Institutes*, 1.3.5.

42. Turretin, *Institutes*, 1.3.5.

43. Turretin, *Institutes*, 1.3.5.

44. Turretin, *Institutes*, 2.1.5. Turretin's reference here to the "uselessness" and "insufficiency" of natural revelation concerns its *ultimate* soteriological value and not its *proximate* utility in law, politics, or ethics.

45. Turretin, *Institutes*, 2.1.6.

46. Turretin, *Institutes*, 1.3.4.

47. Turretin, *Institutes*, 1.4.8-10.

48. Turretin, *Institutes*, 1.4.9.

49. Turretin, *Institutes*, 1.4.5-23.

50. John Platt, *Reformed Thought and Scholasticism: The Arguments for the Existence of God in Dutch Theology, 1575-1650* (Leiden: E. J. Brill, 1982); and Muller, *Post-Reformation Reformed Dogmatics*, vol. 1, pp. 293-304; vol. 3, pp. 170-95.

51. Muller, *Post-Reformation Reformed Dogmatics*, vol. 3, p. 178.

52. Muller, *Post-Reformation Reformed Dogmatics*, vol. 3, p. 179.

53. Muller, *Post-Reformation Reformed Dogmatics*, vol. 3, p. 181.

54. Muller, *Post-Reformation Reformed Dogmatics*, vol. 3, p. 182, pp. 181-93.

55. Turretin, *Institutes*, 3.1.4.

56. Turretin, *Institutes*, 3.1.18.

57. Turretin, *Institutes*, 1.3.7. Jerome Zanchi, interestingly enough, employs precisely the same idea to support his argument that natural law originates ultimately in

God and not in nature: "if [natural law] came from nature, then it would exist equally in all people; for those things that are shared by all people naturally exist equally in all people. However, we see among different peoples that some are wiser, more devoted to justice and honesty, and more zealous for God; but one would never find people who deny that God exists and who could not differentiate between right and wrong." Zanchi, "On the Law in General," trans. Jeffrey J. Veenstra, *Journal of Markets & Morality* 6, no. 1 (Spring 2003): 13 (p. 329).

58. Muller, *Post-Reformation Reformed Dogmatics,* vol. 3, p. 184, pp. 185-93.

59. Turretin, *Institutes,* 3.1.6.

60. Turretin, *Institutes,* 3.1.6.

61. Turretin, *Institutes,* 3.1.5.

62. Turretin, *Institutes,* 3.1.10.

63. Turretin, *Institutes,* 3.1.13.

64. Turretin, *Institutes,* 3.1.13.

65. Turretin, *Institutes,* 3.1.14.

66. Turretin, *Institutes,* 3.1.14.

67. Turretin, *Institutes,* 1.3.14.

68. Turretin, *Institutes,* 3.1.16.

69. Turretin, *Institutes,* 3.1.16.

70. Turretin, *Institutes,* 3.1.17.

71. Turretin, *Institutes,* 1.3.8.

72. Turretin, *Institutes,* 1.3.9.

73. Cf. Turretin, *Institutes,* 3.14, 15, 17, 18.

74. Cf. Turretin, *Institutes,* 3.21.

75. Cf. A. Vos Jaczn., H. Veldhuis, A. H. Looman-Graaskamp, E. Dekker, and N. W. Den Bok, "Introduction, Translation, and Commentary," in John Duns Scotus, *Contingency and Freedom: Lectura I 39* (Dordrecht: Kluwer Academic Publishers, 1994), pp. 23-36; Antonie Vos Jaczn., "De Kern van de klassieke gereformeerde theologie: Een traditiehistorisch gesprek," *Kerk en theologie* 47 (1996): 114-22; Vos, "Scholasticism and Reformation," in *Reformation and Scholasticism: An Ecumenical Enterprise,* ed. Willem J. Van Asselt and Eef Dekker (Grand Rapids: Baker Book House, 2001), pp. 110-15; Andreas J. Beck, "Gisbertus Voetius (1589-1676): Basic Features of His Doctrine of God," in *Reformation and Scholasticism,* pp. 205-26; and Muller, *Post-Reformation Reformed Dogmatics,* vol. 3, pp. 443-52.

76. Turretin, *Institutes,* 11.1.1.

77. Turretin, *Institutes,* 11.1.2.

78. Turretin, *Institutes,* 11.1.3.

79. Turretin, *Institutes,* 11.1.4.

80. Turretin, *Institutes,* 11.1.4.

81. Turretin, *Institutes,* 11.2.17.

82. Turretin, *Institutes,* 11.1.5.

83. Turretin, *Institutes,* 11.2.16.

84. Turretin, *Institutes,* 11.1.5.

85. Turretin, *Institutes,* 11.1.5.

86. Turretin, *Institutes,* 11.1.7. Cf. Aquinas, *S.T.* I-II, 94, 2; 100, 3. It should be acknowledged that Turretin is making a strong metaphysical claim here with respect to

natural law: Natural law has ontic validity, was divinely promulgated, and is true regardless of the clarity with which it is known.

87. Turretin, *Institutes*, 11.1.7. Zanchi makes exactly the same point as Turretin does here. Cf. Zanchi, "On the Law in General," pp. 12-14.

88. Turretin, *Institutes*, 11.1.10.

89. Turretin, *Institutes*, 11.1.11.

90. Turretin, *Institutes*, 11.1.11.

91. Turretin, *Institutes*, 11.1.20.

92. Turretin, *Institutes*, 11.1.9.

93. Turretin, *Institutes*, 11.1.22; cf. 11.2.17.

94. Turretin, *Institutes*, 11.1.22.

95. Turretin, *Institutes*, 11.1.23.

96. Turretin, *Institutes*, 11.2.9, 34. For further discussion of this issue, particularly in its relationship to late medieval views of divine omnipotence, see Chapter Two, "Development of the Natural-Law Tradition through the High Middle Ages." Cf. Turretin, *Institutes*, 3.21.

97. Turretin, *Institutes*, 11.2.4.

98. Turretin, *Institutes*, 11.2.4.

99. Turretin, *Institutes*, 11.2.4.

100. Turretin, *Institutes*, 11.2.5.

101. Turretin, *Institutes*, 11.2.6.

102. Turretin, *Institutes*, 11.2.6.

103. Turretin, *Institutes*, 11.2.5.

104. Turretin, *Institutes*, 11.2.10.

105. Turretin, *Institutes*, 11.2.21.

106. Turretin, *Institutes*, 11.2.22.

107. Turretin, *Institutes*, 11.2.23.

108. Turretin, *Institutes*, 11.2.24.

109. Turretin, *Institutes*, 11.2.19.

110. Turretin, *Institutes*, 11.2.26-28.

111. Turretin, *Institutes*, 11.2.29-30.

112. Turretin, *Institutes*, 11.2.32-33.

113. Turretin, *Institutes*, 11.2.25.

114. Turretin, *Institutes*, 11.2.7.

115. Turretin, *Institutes*, 11.2.7.

116. Johannes Althusius, *Politica: An Abridged Translation of Politics Methodically Set Forth and Illustrated with Sacred and Profane Examples*, ed. and trans. Frederick S. Carney (Indianapolis: Liberty Fund, 1995), 21.26 (p. 141).

117. Turretin, *Institutes*, 11.2.8.

118. Turretin, *Institutes*, 11.2.8.

119. Turretin, *Institutes*, 11.2.10. For historical support for Turretin's allegation, see Francis Oakley, "'Adamantine Fetters of Destiny': The Absolute and Ordained Powers of God and King in the Sixteenth and Seventeenth Centuries," in *Politics and Eternity: Studies in the History of Medieval and Early-Modern Political Thought* (Leiden: E. J. Brill, 1999), pp. 279-91; Oakley, "Pierre d'Ailly and the Absolute Power of God: Another Note on the Theology of Nominalism," *Harvard Theological Review* 56, no. 1 (Janu-

ary 1963): 59-73; Oakley, *The Political Thought of Pierre d'Ailly: The Voluntarist Tradition* (New Haven: Yale University Press, 1964); Eugenio Randi, "Ockham, John XXII, and the Absolute Power of God," *Franciscan Studies* 46 (1986): 205-16; and Taina M. Holopainen, "William of Ockham's Theory of the Foundations of Ethics" (Th.D. diss., Helsingin Yliopisto University, 1991).

120. Turretin, *Institutes,* 11.2.10.

121. Turretin, *Institutes,* 11.2.10. For more on Scotus's view, see Mary Elizabeth Ingham, *Ethics and Freedom: An Historical-Critical Investigation of Scotist Ethical Thought* (Lanham, Md.: University Press of America, 1989); Robert Prentice, O.F.M., "The Contingent Element Governing the Natural Law on the Last Seven Precepts of the Decalogue according to Duns Scotus," *Antonianum* 42 (1967): 259-92; Thomas Williams, "The Libertarian Foundations of Scotus's Moral Philosophy," *The Thomist* 62, no. 2 (April 1998): 193-215; Allan B. Wolter, O.F.M., "Native Freedom of the Will as a Key to the Ethics of Scotus," in *The Philosophical Theology of John Duns Scotus,* ed. Marilyn McCord Adams (Ithaca and London: Cornell University Press, 1990), pp. 160-62; and Wolter, *Duns Scotus on the Will and Morality: Selected and Translated with an Introduction by Allan B. Wolter, O.F.M.* (Washington, D.C.: Catholic University of America Press, 1986), pp. 57-63, 263-88.

122. Turretin, *Institutes,* 11.2.10.

123. Turretin, *Institutes,* 11.2.11.

124. Turretin, *Institutes,* 11.2.11. Althusius's remarks concerning the dispensability of the fifth, sixth, and eighth precepts (cf. *Politica,* 21.28 [pp. 143-44]) should probably be taken in the sense that Turretin specifies here.

125. Turretin, *Institutes,* 11.2.11.

126. Turretin, *Institutes,* 11.2.2.

Notes to Conclusion

1. Emil Brunner and Karl Barth, *Natural Theology* ("Nature and Grace" by Brunner and the Reply "No!" by Barth), trans. Peter Fraenkel (London: Geoffrey Bles, 1946), pp. 78-81, 91, 96.

2. Brunner and Barth, *Natural Theology,* p. 87.

3. Brunner and Barth, *Natural Theology,* p. 90.

4. Thomas Hobbes, *Leviathan: or the Matter, Forme and Power of a Commonwealth Ecclesiastical and Civil,* ed. Michael Oakeshott (New York: Collier Books, 1961), pp. 103-4.

5. Hobbes, *Leviathan,* p. 100.

6. Hobbes, *Leviathan,* pp. 129-33.

7. J. M. Kelly, *A Short History of Western Legal Theory* (Oxford: Clarendon Press, 1992), p. 212, pp. 212-14.

8. Kelly, *A Short History of Western Legal Theory,* p. 224.

9. Kelly, *A Short History of Western Legal Theory,* p. 225.

10. Hugo Grotius, *Prolegomena to the Law of War and Peace,* trans. Francis W. Kelsey (Indianapolis: Bobbs-Merrill Company, 1957), p. 9.

11. Grotius, *Prolegomena to the Law of War and Peace,* p. 10.

12. Kelly, *A Short History of Western Legal Theory*, p. 225.

13. Grotius, *Prolegomena to the Law of War and Peace*, p. 6.

14. Grotius, *Prolegomena to the Law of War and Peace*, pp. 8-9.

15. Kelly, *A Short History of Western Legal Theory*, p. 226.

16. Anton-Hermann Chroust provides an important historical corrective to this observation, which, if accurate, is foundational to a contemporary reassessment of Grotius's contribution to the natural-law tradition, even if Grotius's contemporaries had an altogether different interpretation:

> To Gregory of Valencia the lex naturalis is always a "lex indicans," that is, a "declaratory law," declaratory of the absolute good and just, of the absolute moral order. But such a "declaratory law" presupposes the perseitas boni, as well as the total exclusion of any purely voluntaristic or nominalistic interpretation of the essence of Natural Law. Arriaga and others went from these presuppositions so far as to reach the conclusion that Natural Law, as a "lex indicans," would be existing and valid even if there were no God. This often quoted and applied "Etsiamsi daretur non esse Deum" later was taken over by Hugo Grotius, who probably found it mentioned in Francisco Suarez's "De Legibus ac Deo Legislatore." Only by showing to what extent Grotius relied upon Thomistic sources we may be able to understand more completely his own attitude towards the ultimate grounds and problems of Natural Law. Should this thesis prove correct, then the often disputed continuity of Natural Law thinking clearly would stretch from St. Thomas and the Thomistic-Scotistic controversy through the Spanish "Jurist-Theologians" directly down to Hugo Grotius. Should we fully grasp and evaluate the ultimate meaning of the Grotian "etsiamsi daretur non esse Deum," we cannot fail to realize that Grotius adheres to the Thomistic Natural Law tradition. It is, therefore, a great misconception of the true state of affairs to link Grotius to Thomas Hobbes and the nominalistic tradition, as, for instance, Pufendorf tried to do.

Anton-Hermann Chroust, "Hugo Grotius and the Scholastic Natural Law Tradition," *The New Scholasticism* 17, no. 2 (April 1943): 114-16.

17. Knud Haakonssen, *Natural Law and Moral Philosophy: From Grotius to the Scottish Enlightenment* (Cambridge: Cambridge University Press, 1996), p. 36.

18. Haakonssen, *Natural Law and Moral Philosophy*, p. 37.

19. Samuel Pufendorf, *The Whole Duty of Man, According to the Law of Nature*, ed. and intro. Ian Hunter and David Saunders, trans. Andrew Tooke (Indianapolis: Liberty Fund, 2003), 1.3.7.

20. Pufendorf, *The Whole Duty of Man*, 1.3.10; Grotius, *Prolegomena to the Law of War and Peace*, p. 11.

21. Haakonssen, *Natural Law and Moral Philosophy*, p. 38.

22. Haakonssen, *Natural Law and Moral Philosophy*, pp. 42-43.

23. Haakonssen, *Natural Law and Moral Philosophy*, p. 44.

24. Haakonssen, *Natural Law and Moral Philosophy*, p. 44.

25. Haakonssen, *Natural Law and Moral Philosophy*, p. 45, n. 52.

26. Haakonssen, *Natural Law and Moral Philosophy*, p. 45.

27. Haakonssen, *Natural Law and Moral Philosophy*, p. 45.

258   NOTES TO PAGES 181-88

28. Kelly, *A Short History of Western Legal Theory,* p. 260.

28. Kelly, *A Short History of Western Legal Theory,* p. 260.

29. Kelly, *A Short History of Western Legal Theory,* p. 260.

30. Kelly, *A Short History of Western Legal Theory,* p. 260.

31. Kelly, *A Short History of Western Legal Theory,* p. 261.

32. Kelly, *A Short History of Western Legal Theory,* p. 261.

33. Kelly, *A Short History of Western Legal Theory,* pp. 261-62; and John Fletcher Hurst, *History of Rationalism Embracing a Survey of the Present State of Protestant Theology,* rev. ed. (New York: Eaton & Mains, 1901), pp. 104-11.

34. Martin I. Klauber, "The Eclipse of Reformed Scholasticism in Eighteenth-Century Geneva: Natural Theology from Jean-Alphonse Turretin to Jacob Vernet," in *The Identity of Geneva: The Christian Commonwealth, 1564-1864,* ed. John B. Roney and Martin I. Klauber (Westport, Conn.: Greenwood Press, 1998), p. 129.

35. Martin I. Klauber, *Between Reformed Scholasticism and Pan-Protestantism: Jean-Alphonse Turretin (1671-1737) and Enlightened Orthodoxy at the Academy of Geneva* (Selingsgrove, Pa.: Susquehanna University Press, 1994), pp. 77-103.

36. Klauber, *Between Reformed Scholasticism and Pan-Protestantism,* p. 63.

37. Klauber, *Between Reformed Scholasticism and Pan-Protestantism,* p. 74.

38. T. J. Hochstrasser, "The Claims of Conscience: Natural Law Theory, Obligation, and Resistance in the Huguenot Diaspora," in *New Essays on the Political Thought of the Huguenots of the Refuge,* ed. John Christian Laursen (Leiden: E. J. Brill, 1995), pp. 22-23.

39. Hochstrasser, "The Claims of Conscience," pp. 23-24.

40. Hochstrasser, "The Claims of Conscience," p. 24.

41. Hochstrasser, "The Claims of Conscience," p. 31.

42. Hochstrasser, "The Claims of Conscience," pp. 24-25.

43. Hochstrasser, "The Claims of Conscience," p. 26.

44. Hochstrasser, "The Claims of Conscience," pp. 26-27.

45. Hochstrasser, "The Claims of Conscience," p. 39.

46. Hochstrasser, "The Claims of Conscience," p. 47.

47. Charles Hodge, *Systematic Theology,* 3 vols. (Grand Rapids: Wm. B. Eerdmans Publishing Company, 1970), vol. 1, p. 25.

48. Herman Bavinck, *Reformed Dogmatics,* 4 vols., ed. John Bolt, trans. John Vriend (Grand Rapids: Baker Academic, 2003-2007), vol. 1, pp. 183-204.

49. Bavinck, *Reformed Dogmatics,* vol. 1, p. 184.

50. Bavinck, *Reformed Dogmatics,* vol. 1, p. 223.

51. Bavinck, *Reformed Dogmatics,* vol. 1, p. 208, pp. 226-33.

52. Richard A. Muller, *Post-Reformation Reformed Dogmatics: The Rise and Development of Reformed Orthodoxy, ca. 1520 to ca. 1725,* 4 vols. (Grand Rapids: Baker Academic, 2003), vol. 1, p. 97.

53. Brunner and Barth, *Natural Theology,* p. 100; and Peter Barth, *Das Problem der natürlichen Theologie bei Calvin* (Munich: Chr. Kaiser, 1935).

54. Brunner and Barth, *Natural Theology,* pp. 101-2.

55. Brunner and Barth, *Natural Theology,* p. 101.

56. Cf. Aurelius Augustine, "A Treatise on Nature and Grace, Against Pelagius," in *Nicene and Post-Nicene Fathers of the Christian Church* (First Series), vol. 5, ed. Philip

Schaff, trans. Peter Holmes and Robert Ernest Wallis (Grand Rapids: Wm. B. Eerdmans Publishing Company, 1956), chaps. 3 (p. 122), 21 (pp. 127-28), 22 (p. 128).

57. Brunner and Barth, *Natural Theology*, p. 101. Dooyeweerd's assessment of Augustine's theology of revelation bears a striking resemblance to Barth's: "Augustine did accept the ground motive of revelation in its purity. But he could not develop it radically because the Greek ground motive, transmitted by Greek philosophy, placed a firm hold upon his entire worldview. . . . The example of Augustine clearly demonstrates how even in a great father of the church the spiritual power of the Greek ground motive worked as a dangerous counterforce to the ground motive of revelation." Dooyeweerd, *Roots of Western Culture: Pagan, Secular, and Christian Options*, ed. Mark Vander Vennen and Bernard Zylstra, trans. John Kraay (Toronto: Wedge Publishing Foundation, 1979), pp. 114-15.

58. Emil Brunner, *Dogmatics*, vol. 2, *The Christian Doctrine of Creation and Redemption*, trans. Olive Wyon (Philadelphia: Westminster Press, 1952), pp. 49-52, 103-4; and Brunner, *Man in Revolt: A Christian Anthropology*, trans. Olive Wyon (Philadelphia: Westminster Press, 1939), pp. 83-112, 120-22, 143-52. Brunner's view of Augustine's theology of the fall is expressed well in the following extract from *Man in Revolt* (p. 120):

> After the early Christian theologians had developed very contradictory and different views of the fall, and the extent of its effects upon the human race, it was Augustine who gave to the ecclesiastical doctrine its standard form, in which it determined not only the history of Roman Catholic theology but the development of Protestant theology as well.
>
> For our generation, the fact that this narrative is no longer historically credible means that the convincing power of this imposing doctrine, which dominated the thought of Europe for fifteen hundred years and — although modified in different ways — has formed the solid substance of the doctrine of sin of all Christian churches, has completely disappeared. For most of our contemporaries Adam is a kind of legendary figure; it can no longer play any part in the thinking of the succeeding generations as a historical force.
>
> But what we said in connexion with the question of man's origin is still more true here: the re-formulation to which we are forced by scientific knowledge is not a retraction which cannot, "unfortunately," be avoided, but it is an inner necessity, inherent in the very truth apprehended by faith. It is not for scientific reasons, in the main, that the historical form of the doctrine of the fall is questionable, but for religious reasons; it has led to serious distortions of the faith, of the understanding of sin, and of man's responsibility in the sight of God.

59. David C. Steinmetz, "Luther among the Anti-Thomists," in *Luther in Context*, 2d ed. (Grand Rapids: Baker Academic, 2002), p. 58.

60. James M. Gustafson, *Protestant and Roman Catholic Ethics: Prospects for Rapproachment* (Chicago: University of Chicago Press, 1978), pp. 33-46, and especially pp. 62-74.

61. Martin Bucer, *Common places*, ed. and trans. D. F. Wright (Abingdon, U.K.: Sutton Courtenay Press, 1972), pp. 119-42 (on original sin), 143-57 (on free will).

62. Philip Melanchthon, *Loci communes (1543)*, trans. J. A. O. Preus (St. Louis:

Concordia Publishing House, 1992), pp. 57-80; and Melanchthon, *Commentary on Romans*, trans. Fred Kramer (St. Louis: Concordia Publishing House, 1992), pp. 73-85 (viz., Rom. 1:18-32), 89-90 (viz., Rom. 2:14-16).

63. Wolfgang Musculus, *Common places* (London: Reginalde Wolfe, 1563), ff. 28-120.

64. Heinrich Bullinger, *Common places of the Christian Religion,* trans. John Stockwood (London: Printed by Tho. East and H. Middleton for George Byshop, 1572), ff. 62-101; and Bullinger, *The Decades of Henry Bullinger,* 5 vols. in 4, ed. Thomas Harding, trans. H. I. (Cambridge: Cambridge University Press, 1849-52; New York: Johnson Reprint Corporation, 1968), vol. 2, *Second Decade,* the first sermon, pp. 193-209; the second through tenth sermons treat precepts one to seven of the Ten Commandments (pp. 209-435); and vol. 3, *Third Decade,* the first through fourth sermons treat precepts eight to ten of the Ten Commandments (pp. 17-124).

65. Theodore Beza, *A Brief and Pithie Summary of the Christian Faith, made in the form of a Confession, with a confutation of all such Superstitious Errors, as are contrary thereunto,* trans. R. F. (London: William How, 1571), ff. 5-6, 24-43; and Beza, *A booke of Christian Questions and answers, wherein are set forth the chief points of the Christian religion in manner of an abridgement,* trans. Arthur Goldring (London: Printed by William How for Abraham Veale, 1572), ff. 24-32, 47-51.

66. Lambert Daneau, *Ethices Christianae, libri tres: in quibus de veris humanarum actionum principiis agitur : atque etiam legis Diuinae, siue Decalogi, explicatio, illúsque cum scriptis scholasticorum, iure naturali siue philosophico, ciuili Romanorum, & canonico collatio continetur praeterea virtutum & vitiorum, quae passim vel in Sacra Scriptura vel alibi occurru[n]t, quae*que ad singula legis Diuinae praecepta reuocantur, variae definitions* (Geneva: Eustathium Vignon, 1588); and Daneau, *The Wonderful Workmanship of the World: Wherein is Contained an Excellent Discourse of Christian Natural Philosophy, concerning the Form, Knowledge, and Use of All Things Created: Specially Gathered out of the Fountains of Holy Scripture* (London: Andrew Maunsell, 1578).

67. Zacharias Ursinus, *The Commentary of Dr. Zacharias Ursinus on the Heidelberg Catechism,* trans. G. W. Willard (Columbus, Ohio, 1852; Phillipsburg, N.J.: Presbyterian and Reformed Publishing Company, 1985), pp. 476-618.

68. Andrew Willet, *Hexapla: that is, a six-fold commentarie upon the most diuine Epistle of the holy Apostle S. Paul to the Romanes,* 2 vols. (Cambridge: Cantrell Legge, 1620), vol. 1, pp. 57-98 (viz., Rom. 1:18-32), 115-24, 131-40 (viz., Rom. 2:14-16).

69. Bartholomaeus Keckermann, *Systema Ethicae, tribus libris adornatum & publicis praelectionibus traditum in Gymnasio Dantiscano* (London: Nortoniana, 1607).

70. William Ames, *Conscience with the Power and Cases thereof* (Amsterdam: Theatrum Orbis Terrarum; Norwood, N.J.: W. J. Johnson, 1975 [orig. pub. 1639]), pp. 1-55, 99-114, 169-293 (on the precepts of the second table).

71. Anthony Burgess, *Vindiciae Legis: or, A Vindication of the Moral Law and the Covenants, from the Errors of Papists, Arminians, Socinians, and most especially, Antinomians* (London: James Young, 1646), pp. 1-110, 146-219.

72. Edward Leigh, *A System or Body of Divinity: Consisting of Ten Books, wherein the Fundamentals and Main Grounds of Religion are Opened: The Contrary Errors Refuted: Most of the Controversies between Us, the Papists, Arminians, and Socinians Discussed and Handled* (London: Printed by A. M. for William Lee, 1662), pp. 144-57, 1020-1153.

73. Adrianus Heereboord, *Collegium Ethicum, sev Philosophia Moralis* (London: Rogeri Danielis, 1658).

74. Richard Baxter, *The Catechizing of Families: A Teacher of Housholders How to Teach their Housholds: Useful also to School-masters and Tutors of Youth* (London: Printed for T. Parkhurst and B. Simmons, 1683), pp. 19-26; and Baxter, *More Reasons for the Christian Religion and No Reason Against It. Or a Second Appendix to the Reasons of the Christian Religion* (London: Printed for Nevil Simmons, 1672), pp. 118-31.

75. Stephen Charnock, "Discourse of the Knowledge of Christ," in *The Works of the Late Learned Divine Stephen Charnock, B.D.: Being Several Discourses upon Various Divine Subjects*, 2 vols. (London: Printed by A. Maxwell and R. Roberts for Tho. Cockeril, 1684), vol. 2, pp. 474-552.

76. Matthew Henry, *Matthew Henry's Commentary on the Whole Bible*, New Modern Edition Complete and Unabridged in 6 vols. (Peabody, Mass.: Hendrickson Publishers, Inc., 1991 [orig. pub. 1706]), vol. 6, pp. 297-300 (viz., Rom. 1:19-32), 301-4 (viz., Rom. 2:1-16).

Bibliography

Primary Sources

Althusius, Johannes. *Dicaeologicae Libri Tres, Totum & universum Jus, quo utimur methodicè complectentes: . . .* 2d ed. Frankfurt: Christopher Corvini, 1649; Aalen: Scientia, 1967.

————. *Politica.* German translation by Heinrich Janssen. Edited by Dieter Wyduckel. Berlin: Duncker and Humblot, 2003.

————. *Politica: An Abridged Translation of Politics Methodically Set Forth and Illustrated with Sacred and Profane Examples.* Edited and translated by Frederick S. Carney. Indianapolis: Liberty Fund, 1995.

————. *Politics.* Translated by Frederick S. Carney. Boston: Beacon Press, 1964.

————. "Preface to the 1610 edition of Johannes Althusius's *Politica Methodice Digesta.*" In *New Essays on the Political Thought of the Huguenots of the Refuge,* translated by Cary J. Nederman, edited by John Christian Laursen, pp. 197-201. Leiden: E. J. Brill, 1995.

Ames, William. *Conscience with the Power and Cases thereof.* Amsterdam: Theatrum Orbis Terrarum; Norwood, N.J.: W. J. Johnson, 1975.

Augustine, Aurelius. "A Treatise on Nature and Grace, Against Pelagius." In *Nicene and Post-Nicene Fathers of the Christian Church* (First Series), vol. 5, pp. 116-51. Edited by Philip Schaff. Translated by Peter Holmes and Robert Ernest Wallis. Grand Rapids: Wm. B. Eerdmans Publishing Company, 1956.

Baxter, Richard. *More Reasons for the Christian Religion and No Reason Against It. Or a Second Appendix to the Reasons of the Christian Religion.* London: Printed for Nevil Simmons, 1672.

————. *The Catechizing of Families: A Teacher of Housholders How to Teach their Housholds: Useful also to School-masters and Tutors of Youth.* London: Printed for T. Parkhurst and B. Simmons, 1683.

Bèze, Théodore de. *A booke of Christian Questions and answers, wherein are set forth the chief points of the Christian religion in manner of an abridgement.* Translated by Arthur Goldring. London: Printed by William How for Abraham Veale, 1572.

————. *A Brief and Pithie Summary of the Christian Faith, made in the form of a Confession, with a confutation of all such Superstitious Errors, as are contrary thereunto.* Translated by R. F. London: William How, 1571.

————. *Beza's "Icones": Contemporary Portraits of Reformers of Religion and Letters.* Translated by C. G. McCrie. London: Religious Tract Society, 1906.

————. *Icones, id est verae imagines virorum doctrina simul et pietate illustrium, quorum praecipue ministerio partim bonarum literarum studia sunt restituta, partim vera religio in variis orbis Christiani regionibus, nostra patrumque memoria fuit instaurata: additis eorundem vitae & operae descriptionibus, quibus adiectae sunt nonnullae picturae quas emblemata vocant.* Geneva: I. Laonium, 1580.

Bucer, Martin. *Common places.* Edited and translated by D. F. Wright. Abingdon, U.K.: Sutton Courtenay Press, 1972.

Bullinger, Heinrich. *Common places of the Christian Religion.* Translated by John Stockwood. London: Printed by Tho. East and H. Middleton for George Byshop, 1572.

————. *The Decades of Henry Bullinger.* 5 vols. in 4. Edited by Thomas Harding. Translated by H. I. Cambridge: Cambridge University Press, 1849-52; New York: Johnson Reprint Corporation, 1968.

Burgess, Anthony. *Vindiciae Legis: or, A Vindication of the Moral Law and the Covenants, from the Errors of Papists, Arminians, Socinians, and most especially, Antinomians.* London: James Young, 1646.

Calvin, John. *Commentary on Seneca's De Clementia.* Translation, Introduction, and Notes by Ford Lewis Battles and André Malan Hugo. Leiden: E. J. Brill, 1969.

————. *Commentary on the Book of Psalms.* 5 vols. Translated by James Anderson. Grand Rapids: Wm. B. Eerdmans Publishing Company, 1949.

————. *Commentary on the Acts of the Apostles.* 2 vols. Edited by David W. Torrance and Thomas F. Torrance. Translated by John W. Fraser. Grand Rapids: Wm. B. Eerdmans Publishing Company, 1966.

————. *Commentary on the Epistles of Paul the Apostle to the Romans and to the Thessalonians.* Edited by David W. Torrance and T. F. Torrance. Translated by Ross Mackenzie. Grand Rapids: Wm. B. Eerdmans Publishing Company, 1961.

————. *Commentaries on the Epistles of Paul the Apostle to the Philippians, Colossians, and Thessalonians.* Edited and translated by John Pringle. Grand Rapids: Wm. B. Eerdmans Publishing Company, 1948.

————. *Commentary on the Gospel according to St. John.* 2 vols. Edited by David W. Torrance and Thomas F. Torrance. Translated by T. H. L. Parker. Grand Rapids: Wm. B. Eerdmans Publishing Company, 1959.

————. *Commentaries on the Twelve Minor Prophets.* 5 vols. Translated by John Owen. Grand Rapids: Wm. B. Eerdmans Publishing Company, 1950.

————. *Institutes of the Christian Religion.* 1559 ed. Edited by John T. McNeill. Translated by Ford Lewis Battles. Philadelphia: Westminster Press, 1960.

————. *The Bondage and Liberation of the Will: A Defense of the Orthodox Doctrine of Human Choice Against Pighius.* Edited by A. N. S. Lane. Translated by G. I. Davies. Grand Rapids: Baker Books, 1996.

Charnock, Stephen. *The Works of the Late Learned Divine Stephen Charnock, B.D.: Be-*

ing *Several Discourses upon Various Subjects.* 2 vols. London: Printed by
    A. Maxwell and R. Roberts for Tho. Cockeril, 1684.
Cicero, Marcus Tullius. *The Nature of the Gods.* Translation, Introduction, and Notes
    by P. G. Walsh. New York: Oxford University Press, 1998.
Daneau, Lambert. *Ethices Christianae, libri tres : in quibus de veris humanarum
    actionum principiis agitur : atque etiam legis Diuinae, siue Decalogi, explicatio,
    illúsque cum scriptis scholasticorum, iure naturali siue philosophico, ciuili
    Romanorum, & canonico collatio continetur praeterea virtutum & vitiorum, quae
    passim vel in Sacra Scriptura vel alibi occurru[n]t, quae*que ad singula legis
    Diuinae praecepta reuocantur, variae definitions.* Geneva: Eustathium Vignon,
    1588.
————. *The Wonderful Workmanship of the World: Wherein is Contained an Excellent
    Discourse of Christian Natural Philosophy, concerning the Form, Knowledge, and
    Use of All Things Created: Specially Gathered out of the Fountains of Holy Scrip-
    ture.* London: Andrew Maunsell, 1578.
Grotius, Hugo. *Prolegomena to the Law of War and Peace.* Translated by Francis W.
    Kelsey. Indianapolis: Bobbs-Merrill Company, 1957.
Heereboord, Adrianus. *Collegium Ethicum, sev Philosophia Moralis.* London: Rogeri
    Danielis, 1658.
Henry, Matthew. *Matthew Henry's Commentary on the Whole Bible.* New Modern Edi-
    tion Complete and Unabridged in 6 vols. Peabody, Mass.: Hendrickson Pub-
    lishers, Inc., 1991.
Hobbes, Thomas. *Leviathan: or the Matter, Forme and Power of a Commonwealth Eccle-
    siastical and Civil.* Edited by Michael Oakeshott. New York: Collier Books,
    1961.
Keckermann, Bartholomaeus. *Systema Ethicae, tribus libris adornatum & publicis
    praelectionibus traditum in Gymnasio Dantiscano.* London: Nortoniana, 1607.
Leigh, Edward. *A System or Body of Divinity: Consisting of Ten Books, wherein the Fun-
    damentals and Main Grounds of Religion are Opened: The Contrary Errors Refuted:
    Most of the Controversies between Us, the Papists, Arminians, and Socinians Dis-
    cussed and Handled.* London: Printed by A. M. for William Lee, 1662.
Melanchthon, Philip. *Commentary on Romans.* Translated by Fred Kramer. St. Louis:
    Corcordia Publishing House, 1992.
————. *Loci communes (1543).* Translated by J. A. O. Preus. St. Louis, Mo.: Concordia
    Publishing House, 1992.
Musculus, Wolfgang. *Common places.* London: Reginalde Wolfe, 1563.
Pufendorf, Samuel. *The Whole Duty of Man, According to the Law of Nature.* Edited and
    Introduced by Ian Hunter and David Saunders. Translated by Andrew Tooke.
    Indianapolis: Liberty Fund, 2003.
Sleidan, John. *The General History of the Reformation of the Church from the Errors and
    Conceptions of the Church of Rome: Begun in Germany by Martin Luther with the
    Progress thereof in all Parts of Christendom from the Year 1517 to the Year 1556.*
    Translated by Edmund Bohun. London: Edward Jones, Abel Swall, and Henry
    Bonwicke, 1562.
Strype, John. *Annals of the Reformation and Establishment of Religion and Other Various*

Occurrences in the Church of England during Queen Elizabeth's Happy Reign To-gether with an Appendix of Original Papers of State, Records, and Letters. 4 vols. in 7 parts. London: John Wyat, 1709; New York: Burt Franklin, 1966.

Taillepied, Nöel. *Histoire de vies, meurs, actes, doctrine et morts des quatre principaux Hérétiques de nostra temps.* Douay: 1580.

Thomas Aquinas. *Summa Theologica.* 5 vols. Translated by the Fathers of the English Dominican Province. New York: Benziger Brothers, Inc., 1948.

Thou, Jacques August de. *Les éloges des hommes savans, tirez de l'Histoire de M. de Thou.* 4 vols. 4th éd. rev., corr., & augm. French translation by Antoine Teissier. Leiden: T. Haaa, 1715.

———. *Monumenta litteraria siue, Obitus et elogia doctorum virorum. Ex historiis illustris viri Iac. Aug. Thuani. Opera C.B.* London: John Norton Sumptibus & Tho. Warren, 1640.

Turretin, Francis. *Institutes of Elenctic Theology.* 3 vols. Translated by George Musgrave Giger. Edited by James T. Dennison Jr. Phillipsburg, N.J.: Presbyterian and Reformed Publishing Company, 1992-1997.

Ursinus, Zacharias. *The Commentary of Dr. Zacharias Ursinus on the Heidelberg Catechism.* Translated by G. W. Willard. Columbus, Ohio: 1852; Phillipsburg, N.J.: Presbyterian and Reformed Publishing Company, 1985.

Vermigli, Pietro Martire. *Commentary on Aristotle's Nicomachean Ethics.* Vol. 9. *The Peter Martyr Library.* Edited by Emidio Campi and Joseph C. McLelland. Kirksville, Mo.: Truman State University Press, 2005.

———. *Common places.* Edited by Robert Masson. Translated by Anthonie Marten. London: Henri Denham, Thomas Chard, William Broom, and Andrew Maunsell, 1583.

———. *Dialogue on the Two Natures in Christ.* Vol. 2. *The Peter Martyr Library.* Edited and translated by John Patrick Donnelly, S.J. Kirksville, Mo.: Truman State University Press, 1995.

———. *Early Writings: Creed, Scripture, Church.* Vol. 1. *The Peter Martyr Library.* Edited by Joseph C. McLelland. Translated by Mario Di Gangi and Joseph C. McLelland. Kirksville, Mo.: Truman State University Press, 1994.

———. *Life, Letters, and Sermons.* Vol. 5. *The Peter Martyr Library.* Edited and translated by John Patrick Donnelly, S.J. Kirksville, Mo.: Truman State University Press, 1999.

———. *Loci communes.* London: Thomas Vautrollerius, 1583.

———. *Most learned and fruitful commentaries of D. Peter Martir Vermilius, professor of divinity in the school of Tigure, upon the Epistle of S. Paul to the Romans: wherein are diligently and most profitably entreated all such matters and chief common places of religion touched in the same Epistle.* Translated by Sir Henry Billingsley. London: John Daye, 1568.

———. *Philosophical Works: On the Relation of Philosophy to Theology.* Vol. 4. *The Peter Martyr Library.* Edited and translated by Joseph C. McLelland. Kirksville, Mo.: Truman State University Press, 1996.

———. *Predestination and Justification: Two Theological Loci.* Vol. 8. *The Peter Martyr*

Library. Edited and translated by Frank A. James III. Kirksville, Mo.: Truman State University Press, 2003.

————. *Sacred Prayers Drawn from the Psalms of David.* Vol. 3. *The Peter Martyr Library.* Edited and translated by John Patrick Donnelly, S.J. Kirksville, Mo.: Truman State University Press, 1996.

————. *The Commentary on the Lamentations of the Prophet Jeremiah.* Vol. 6. *The Peter Martyr Library.* Kirksville, Mo.: Truman State University Press, 2002.

————. *The Life, Early Letters, and Eucharistic Writings of Peter Martyr.* Edited by Joseph C. McLelland and G. E. Duffield. Appleford, U.K.: Sutton Courtenay Press, 1989.

————. *The Oxford Treatise and Disputation on the Eucharist.* Vol. 7. *The Peter Martyr Library.* Edited and translated by Joseph C. McLelland. Kirksville, Mo.: Truman State University Press, 2000.

————. *The Peter Martyr Reader.* Edited by John Patrick Donnelly, S.J., Frank A. James III, and Joseph C. McLelland. Kirksville, Mo.: Truman State University Press, 1999.

————. *The Political Thought of Peter Martyr Vermigli: Selected Texts and Commentary.* Edited by Robert M. Kingdon. Geneva: Librairie Droz, 1980.

Viret, Pierre. *A Very Familiar and Fruitful Exposition of the Twelve Articles of the Christian Faith Contained in the Common Creed, Called the Apostle's Creed.* London: John Day, 1548.

Virgil. *Eclogues.* Translated by H. Rushton Fairclough. Revised by G. P. Goold. Cambridge, Mass.: Harvard University Press, 1999.

Willet, Andrew. *Hexapla: that is, a six-fold commentarie upon the most diuine Epistle of the holy Apostle S. Paul to the Romanes.* 2 vols. Cambridge: Cantrell Legge, 1620.

Wood, Anthony à. *Athenae Oxonienses . . . to which are added, the Fausti, or, Annals, of said university, for the same time.* 2 vols. London: Tho. Bennet, 1691-1692.

Zanchi, Jerome. *Confession of Christian Religion.* Cambridge: John Legat, 1599.

————. *Operum theologicorum.* Tome 4. *De primi hominis lapsu, de peccato, & de legi Dei.* Geneva: Sumptibus Samuelis Crispini, 1617.

————. "On the Law in General." Translated by Jeffrey J. Veenstra. *Journal of Markets & Morality* 6, no. 1 (Spring 2003): 317-98.

Secondary Sources

Adams, James Luther. "The Law of Nature: Some General Considerations." *Journal of Religion* 25, no. 2 (April 1945): 88-96.

Adams, Robert Merrihew. "A Modified Divine Command Theory of Ethical Wrongness." In *The Virtue of Faith and Other Essays in Philosophical Theology,* pp. 97-122. New York: Oxford University Press, 1987.

Althaus, Paul. *Die Prinzipien der deutschen reformierten Dogmatik im Zeitalter der aristotelischen Scholastik.* Leipzig: Deichert, 1914.

Anderson, Marvin W. "Biblical Humanism and Roman Catholic Reform 1444-1563: A Study of Renaissance Philology and New Testament Criticism from Laurentius

Valla to Pietro Martyre Vermigli." Ph.D. dissertation, University of Aberdeen, 1964.

————. *Peter Martyr, A Reformer in Exile (1542-1562): A Chronology of Biblical Writings in England and Europe.* Nieuwkoop: B. De Graaf, 1975.

————. "Peter Martyr, Reformed Theologian (1542-1562): His Letters to Heinrich Bullinger and John Calvin." *Sixteenth Century Journal* 4, no. 1 (April 1973): 41-64.

————. "Peter Martyr on Romans." *Scottish Journal of Theology* 26, no. 4 (November 1973): 401-20.

————. "Peter Martyr Vermigli: Protestant Humanist." In *Peter Martyr Vermigli and Italian Reform,* edited by Joseph C. McLelland, pp. 65-84. Waterloo, Ontario: Wilfrid Laurier University Press, 1980.

————. "Pietro Martire Vermigli on the Scope and Clarity of Scripture." *Theologische Zeitschrift* 3, no. 2 (March/April 1974): 86-94.

————. "Rhetoric and Reality: Peter Martyr and the English Reformation." *Sixteenth Century Journal* 19, no. 3 (Fall 1988): 451-69.

————. "Royal Idolatry: Peter Martyr and the Reformed Tradition." *Archiv für Reformationsgeschichte* 69 (1978): 157-200.

————. "*Vista Tigurina:* Peter Martyr and European Reform (1556-1562)." *Harvard Theological Review* 83, no. 2 (April 1990): 181-206.

————. "Word and Spirit in Exile (1542-1561): The Biblical Writings of Peter Martyr Vermigli." *Journal of Ecclesiastical History* 21, no. 3 (July 1970): 193-201.

Antholz, Heinz Werner. *Die politische Wirksamkeit des Johannes Althusius in Emden.* Aurich: Abhandlungen und Vorträge zur Geschichte Ostfrieslands, 1955.

Asselt, Willem J. van, and Eef Dekker, eds. *Reformation and Scholasticism: An Ecumenical Enterprise.* Grand Rapids: Baker Book House, 2001.

Backus, Irena. "Calvin's Concept of Natural and Roman Law." *Calvin Theological Journal* 38, no. 1 (April 2003): 7-26.

Bacote, Vincent E. *The Spirit in Public Theology: Appropriating the Legacy of Abraham Kuyper.* Grand Rapids: Baker Academic, 2005.

Baker, J. Wayne, and Charles S. McCoy. *Fountainhead of Federalism: Heinrich Bullinger and the Covenantal Tradition.* Louisville: Westminster/John Knox Press, 1991.

Barr, James. *Biblical Faith and Natural Theology.* Oxford: Clarendon Press, 1993.

Barth, Karl. *Church Dogmatics.* Vol. I.1. *The Doctrine of the Word of God.* Edited by G. W. Bromiley and T. F. Torrance. Translated by G. W. Bromiley. Edinburgh: T. & T. Clark, 1975.

————. *Church Dogmatics.* Vol. II.2. *The Doctrine of God.* Edited by G. W. Bromiley and T. F. Torrance. Translated by G. W. Bromiley. Edinburgh: T. & T. Clark, 1957.

————. *Church Dogmatics.* Vol. IV.1. *The Doctrine of Reconciliation.* Edited by G. W. Bromiley and T. F. Torrance. Translated by G. W. Bromiley. Edinburgh: T. & T. Clark, 1992.

————. *Ethics.* Edited by Dietrich Braun. Translated by Geoffrey W. Bromiley. New York: Seabury Press, 1981.

————. "The Christian Community and the Civil Community." In *Community, State and Church: Three Essays,* edited by Will Herberg, pp. 149-90. Garden City, N.Y.: Anchor Books, 1960.

———. *The Humanity of God.* Translated by J. T. Thomas. Richmond, Va.: John Knox Press, 1960.

———. *The Knowledge of God and the Service of God according to the Teaching of the Reformation, Recalling the Scottish Confession of 1560.* Translated by J. L. M. Haire and Ian Henderson. London: Hodder and Stoughton, 1938.

———. *The Theology of John Calvin.* Translated by Geoffrey W. Bromiley. Grand Rapids: Wm. B. Eerdmans Publishing Company, 1995.

———. *This Christian Cause: A Letter to Great Britain from Switzerland.* Edited by John A. Mackay. New York: Macmillan, 1941.

Barth, Peter. *Das Problem der natürlichen Theologie bei Calvin.* Munich: Chr. Kaiser, 1935.

Bauer, Clemens. "Melanchthons Naturrechtslehre." *Archiv für Reformationsgeschichte* 42 (1951): 64-100.

Bavinck, Herman. "Calvin and Common Grace." In *Calvin and the Reformation,* edited by William Park Armstrong, translated by Geerhardus Vos, pp. 99-130. Grand Rapids: Baker Book House, 1980.

———. "Common Grace." Translated by Raymond C. Van Leeuwen. *Calvin Theological Journal* 24, no. 1 (April 1989): 35-65.

———. "De Theologie van Albrecht Ritschl." *Theologische Studien* 6 (1888): 369-403.

———. *Reformed Dogmatics.* 4 vols. Edited by John Bolt. Translated by John Vriend. Grand Rapids: Baker Academic, 2003-2007.

Beardslee, John W. III. *Reformed Dogmatics: J. Wollebius, G. Voetius, F. Turretin.* Edited and translated by John W. Beardslee III. New York: Oxford University Press, 1965.

———. *The Doctrine of Scripture: Locus 2 of Institutio theologiae elencticae.* Edited and translated by John W. Beardslee III. Grand Rapids: Baker Book House, 1981.

———. "Theological Development at Geneva under Francis and Jean-Alphonse Turretin (1648-1737)." Ph.D. dissertation, Yale University, 1956.

Beck, Andreas J. "Gisbertus Voetius (1589-1676): Basic Features of His Doctrine of God." In *Reformation and Scholasticism: An Ecumenical Enterprise,* edited by Willem J. Van Asselt and Eef Dekker, pp. 205-26. Grand Rapids: Baker Book House, 2001.

Beck, Andrew. "Natural Law and the Reformation." *The Clergy Review* 21 (April 1941): 73-81.

Beeke, Joel R. "The Order of the Divine Decrees at the Genevan Academy: From Bezan Supralapsarianism to Turretinian Infralapsarianism." In *The Identity of Geneva: The Christian Commonwealth, 1564-1864,* edited by John B. Roney and Martin I. Klauber, pp. 57-76. Westport, Conn.: Greenwood Press, 1998.

Beesley, Alan. "An Unpublished Source of the Book of Common Prayer: Peter Martyr Vermigli's *Adhortatio ad Coenam Domini Mysticam.*" *Journal of Ecclesiastical History* 19, no. 1 (April 1968): 83-88.

Behnen, Michael. "Herrscherbild und Herrschaftstechnik in der 'Politica' des Johannes Althusius." *Zeitschrift für historische Forschung* 11 (1984): 417-72.

Benoist, Alain de. "The First Federalist: Johannes Althusius." *Krisis* 22 (March 1999): 2-34.

Benoît, Jean-Daniel. "The History and Development of the *Institutio:* How Calvin Worked." In *John Calvin,* edited by G. E. Duffield, translated by Ford Lewis Battles, pp. 102-17. Grand Rapids: Wm. B. Eerdmans Publishing Company, 1966.

Benrath, Karl. "Vermigli, Pietro Martire." In *Realencyclopaedie für protestantische Theologie und Kirche,* vol. 20, pp. 550-52. 2d ed. Leipzig: J. C. Hinrichs, 1908.

————. "Vermigli, Pietro Martire." In *The New Schaff-Herzog Encyclopedia of Religious Knowledge,* vol. 12, pp. 165-66. New York and London: Funk and Wagnalls Company, 1912.

Bentum, A. van. "Does 'Natural' Law Exist? Protestant Theology and Natural Law." *The Eastern Churches Quarterly* 15 (Winter 1963): 152-63.

Berkhof, Hendrikus. *Two Hundred Years of Theology: Report of a Personal Journey.* Translated by John Vriend. Grand Rapids: Wm. B. Eerdmans Publishing Company, 1989.

Berkouwer, G. C. *A Half Century of Theology: Movements and Motives.* Edited and translated by Lewis B. Smedes. Grand Rapids: Wm. B. Eerdmans Publishing Company, 1977.

————. *General Revelation.* Grand Rapids: Wm. B. Eerdmans Publishing Company, 1955.

————. *Man: The Image of God.* Translated by Dirk W. Jellema. Grand Rapids: Wm. B. Eerdmans Publishing Company, 1962.

Berman, Harold J. *Law and Revolution, II: The Impact of the Protestant Reformations on the Western Legal Tradition.* Cambridge, Mass.: Harvard University Press, 2003.

Beversluis, John. "Reforming the 'Reformed' Objection to Natural Theology." *Faith and Philosophy* 12, no. 2 (April 1995): 189-206.

Beyerhaus, Gisbert. *Studien zur Staatsanschauung Calvins: Mit besonderer Berücksichtigung seines Souveränitätsbegriffs.* Berlin: Trowitzsch und Sohn, 1910.

Bierma, Lyle D. *German Calvinism in the Confessional Age: The Covenant Theology of Caspar Olevianus.* Grand Rapids: Baker Book House, 1996.

Biggar, Nigel. "Karl Barth and Germain Grisez on the Human Good: An Ecumenical Rapprochement." In *The Revival of Natural Law: Philosophical, Theological, and Ethical Responses to the Finnis-Grisez School,* edited by Nigel Biggar and Rufus Black, pp. 164-83. Burlington, Vt.: Ashgate, 2000.

————. *The Hastening That Waits: Karl Barth's Ethics.* Oxford: Clarendon Press, 1993.

Biggar, Nigel, and Rufus Black, eds. *The Revival of Natural Law: Philosophical, Theological, and Ethical Responses to the Finnis-Grisez School.* Burlington, Vt.: Ashgate, 2000.

Black, Antony. *Guild & State: European Political Thought from the Twelfth Century to the Present.* New Brunswick, N.J.: Transaction Publishers, 2003.

Black, Rufus. *Christian Moral Realism: Natural Law, Narrative, Virtue, and the Gospel.* New York: Oxford University Press, 2000.

————. "Is the New Natural Law Theory Christian?" In *The Revival of Natural Law: Philosophical, Theological, and Ethical Responses to the Finnis-Grisez School,* edited by Nigel Biggar and Rufus Black, pp. 148-63. Burlington, Vt.: Ashgate, 2000.

———. "The New Natural Law Theory." In *The Revival of Natural Law: Philosophical, Theological, and Ethical Responses to the Finnis-Grisez School,* edited by Nigel Biggar and Rufus Black, pp. 1-28. Burlington, Vt.: Ashgate, 2000.

Blickle, Peter, Thomas O. Hüglin, and Dieter Wyduckel, eds. *Subsidiarität als rechtliches und politischen Ordnungsprinzip in Kirche, Staat und Gesellschaft: Genese, Geltungsgrundlagen und Perspektiven an der Schwelle des dritten Jahrtausends.* Berlin: Duncker and Humblot, 2002.

Blumenberg, Hans. *The Legitimacy of the Modern Age.* Translated by Robert M. Wallace. Cambridge, Mass.: MIT Press, 1983.

Bohatec, Josef. *Calvin und das Recht.* Feudingen: Buchdruck und Verlags-Anstalt, 1934.

Bolt, John. *A Free Church, A Holy Nation: Abraham Kuyper's American Public Theology.* Grand Rapids: Wm. B. Eerdmans Publishing Company, 2001.

———. "Grand Rapids Between Kampen and Amsterdam: Herman Bavinck's Reception and Influence in North America." *Calvin Theological Journal* 38, no. 2 (November 2003): 263-80.

Bonfatti, Emilio, Giuseppe Duso, and Merio Scattola, eds. *Politisches Begriffe und historisches Umfeld in der Politica methodice digesta des Johannes Althusius.* Wiesbaden, 2002.

Bourke, Vernon J., S.J. "Voluntarism in Augustine's Ethico-Legal Thought." *Augustinian Studies* 1 (1970): 3-17.

Bouvier, André. *Henri Bullinger, réformateur et conseiller oecuménique: le successeur de Zwingli: d'après sa correspondance avec les réformés et les humanistes de langue française.* Neuchatel: Delachaux and Niestlé, 1940.

Bouyer, Louis. *The Spirit and Forms of Protestantism.* Translated by A. V. Littledale. London: Harvill Press, 1956.

Braaten, Carl E. "Protestants and Natural Law." In *Being Christian Today: An American Conversation,* edited by Richard John Neuhaus and George Weigel, pp. 105-21. Washington, D.C.: Ethics and Public Policy Center, 1992.

Bredvold, Louis I. "The Meaning of the Concept of Right Reason in the Natural-Law Tradition." *University of Detroit Law Journal* 36 (December 1959): 120-29.

Brunner, Emil. *Christianity and Civilization.* New York: Charles Scribner's Sons, 1948-1949.

———. *Dogmatics.* Vol. 2. *The Christian Doctrine of Creation and Redemption.* Translated by Olive Wyon. Philadelphia: Westminster Press, 1952.

———. *Justice and the Social Order.* Translated by Mary Hottinger. London: Lutterworth Press, 1945.

———. *Man in Revolt: A Christian Anthropology.* Translated by Olive Wyon. Philadelphia: Westminster Press, 1939.

———. *Revelation and Reason: The Christian Doctrine of Faith and Knowledge.* Translated by Olive Wyon. Philadelphia: Westminster Press, 1946.

———. *The Divine Imperative: A Study in Christian Ethics.* Translated by Olive Wyon. New York: Macmillan, 1937.

Brunner, Emil, and Karl Barth. *Natural Theology* ("Nature and Grace" by Brunner and the Reply "No!" by Barth). Translated by Peter Fraenkel. London: Geoffrey Bles, 1946.

Brunner, Peter. "Allegemeine und besondere Offenbarung in Calvins *Institutio*." *Evangelische Theologie* 1, no. 5 (1934): 189-216.

Budziszewski, J. *The Revenge of Conscience: Politics and the Fall of Man.* Dallas: Spence Publishing Company, 1999.

———. "The Second Tablet Project." *First Things* (June/July 2002): 23-31.

———. *What We Can't Not Know: A Guide.* Dallas: Spence Publishing Company, 2003.

———. *Written on the Heart: The Case for Natural Law.* Downers Grove, Ill.: InterVarsity Press, 1997.

Burchill, Christopher J. "Girolamo Zanchi: Portrait of a Reformed Theologian and His Work." *Sixteenth Century Journal* 15, no. 2 (1984): 185-207.

———. "Girolamo Zanchi in Strasbourg 1553-1563." Ph.D. dissertation, Cambridge University, 1980.

Burrington, Dale Eugene. "The Place of Natural Law in Protestant Ethics: An Examination of Emil Brunner's Ethical Theory." Ph.D. dissertation, The Johns Hopkins University, 1966.

Carlyle, A. J. *Political Liberty: A History of the Conception in the Middle Ages and Modern Times.* Oxford: Oxford University Press, 1941; London: Frank Cass and Company, Ltd., 1963.

Carlyle, R. W., and A. J. Carlyle. *A History of Mediaeval Political Theory in the West.* 6 vols. Edinburgh and London: William Blackwood and Sons, Ltd., 1936.

Carney, Frederick S. "Associational Thought in Early Calvinism." In *Voluntary Associations: A Study of Groups in Free Societies,* edited by D. B. Robertson, pp. 39-53. Richmond, Va.: John Knox Press, 1966.

———. "Outline of a Natural Law Procedure for Christian Ethics." *Journal of Religion* 47, no. 1 (January 1967): 25-38.

———. "The Associational Theory of Johannes Althusius: A Study in Calvinist Constitutionalism." Ph.D. dissertation, University of Chicago, 1960.

———. "Translator's Introduction." In *Politica: An Abridged Translation of Politics Methodically Set Forth and Illustrated with Sacred and Profane Examples,* pp. ix-xxxiv. Indianapolis: Liberty Fund, 1995.

Carney, Frederick S., Heinz Schilling, and Dieter Wyduckel, eds. *Jurisprudenz, politische Theorie und politische Theologie: Beiträge des Herborner Symposions zum 400. Jahrestag der Politica des Johannes Althusius 1603-2003.* Berlin: Duncker & Humblot, 2004.

Case-Winters, Anna. *God's Power: Traditional Understandings and Contemporary Challenges.* Louisville: Westminster/John Knox Press, 1990.

Casselli, Stephen J. "The Threefold Division of the Law in the Thought of Aquinas." *Westminster Theological Journal* 61 (1999): 175-207.

Chenevière, Marc-Édouard. *La pensée politique de Calvin.* Geneva: Éditions Labor et Fides, 1937.

Chroust, Anton-Hermann. "A Summary of the Main Achievements of the Spanish

Jurist-Theologians in the History of Jurisprudence." *American Journal of Juris-prudence* 26 (1981): 112-24.

――――. "Hugo Grotius and the Scholastic Natural Law Tradition." *The New Scholasticism* 17, no. 2 (April 1943): 101-33.

Clark, R. S. "Calvin on the *Lex Naturalis.*" *Stulos Theological Journal* 6, nos. 1-2 (May-November 1998): 1-22.

Cochrane, Arthur C. "Natural Law in Calvin." In *Church-State Relations in Ecumenical Perspective,* edited by Elwyn A. Smith, pp. 176-217. Louvain: Duquesne University Press, 1966.

Collinson, Patrick. "England and International Calvinism, 1558-1640." In *International Calvinism, 1541-1715,* edited by Menna Prestwich, pp. 197-223. Oxford: Clarendon Press, 1985.

Colson, Charles, and Richard John Neuhaus, eds. *Evangelicals and Catholics Together: Toward a Common Mission.* Dallas: Word, 1995.

Corda, Salvatore. *Veritas Sacramenti: A Study in Vermigli's Doctrine of the Lord's Supper.* Zürich: Theologischer Verlag, 1971.

Courtenay, William J. "*Antiqui* and *Moderni* in Late Medieval Thought." *Journal of the History of Ideas* 48, no. 1 (January-March 1987): 3-10.

――――. *Capacity and Volition: A History of the Distinction of Absolute and Ordained Power.* Bergamo: P. Lubrina, 1990.

――――. *Covenant and Causality in Medieval Thought: Studies in Philosophy, Theology, and Economic Practice.* London: Variorum Reprints, 1984.

――――. "Covenant and Causality in Pierre d'Ailly." *Speculum* 46, no. 1 (January 1971): 94-119.

――――. "Late Medieval Nominalism Revisted: 1972-1982." *Journal of the History of Ideas* 44, no. 1 (January-March 1983): 159-64.

――――. "Nominalism and Late Medieval Religion." In *The Pursuit of Holiness in Late Medieval and Renaissance Religion: Papers from the University of Michigan Conference,* edited by Charles Trinkhaus and Heiko A. Oberman, pp. 26-59. Leiden: E. J. Brill, 1974.

――――. "The Dialectic of Divine Omnipotence in the High and Late Middle Ages." In *Divine Omniscience and Omnipotence in Medieval Philosophy,* edited by T. Rudavsky, pp. 243-69. Dordrecht: D. Reidel Publishing Company, 1985.

Cromartie, Michael, ed. *A Preserving Grace: Protestants, Catholics, and Natural Law.* Grand Rapids: Wm. B. Eerdmans Publishing Company/Ethics and Public Policy Center, 1997.

――――. "Religious Conservatives in American Politics 1980-2000: An Assessment." *The Witherspoon Fellowship Lectures* 15 (April 16, 2001).

Cross, Richard. *Duns Scotus.* New York: Oxford University Press, 1999.

Crowe, Michael Bertram. "Aquinas and Natural Law: Terminology and Definitions in the Late 12th and Early 13th Centuries." In *Sprache und Erkenntnis im Mittelalter: Akten des VI. Internationalen Kongresses für Mittelalterliche Philosophie der Société internationale pour l'étude de la philosophie Médiévale, 29. August–3. September 1977,* 2 vols., edited by Jan P. Beckmann and Wolfgang Kluxen, vol. 2, pp. 614-21. Berlin: Walter de Gruyter, 1981.

————. *The Changing Profile of the Natural Law.* The Hague: Martinus Nijhoff, 1977.

————. *Natural Law: An Historical Survey.* New York: Harper and Row, 1951.

Dahm, Karl-Wilhelm, Werner Krawietz, and Dieter Wyduckel, eds. *Politische Theorie des Johannes Althusius.* Berlin: Duncker & Humblot, 1988.

Denifle, Heinrich. *Luther und Luthertum in der ersten Entwickelung.* 2 vols. in 4 parts. Mainz: F. Kirchheim, 1904-1909.

Dennison, James T. Jr. "The Life and Career of Francis Turretin." In *Institutes of Elenctic Theology,* 3 vols., edited by James T. Dennison Jr., translated by George Musgrave Giger, vol. 3, pp. 639-58. Phillipsburg, N.J.: Presbyterian and Reformed Publishing Company, 1997.

————. "The Twilight of Scholasticism: Francis Turretin at the Dawn of the Enlightenment." In *Protestant Scholasticism: Essays in Reassessment,* edited by Carl R. Trueman and R. S. Clark, pp. 244-55. Carlisle, U.K.: Paternoster Press, 1999.

D'Entrèves, A. P. "Giovanni Althusio e il problema metodologico nella storia della filosofia politica e giuridica." *Rivista internazionale di filosofia del diritto* 14 (1934): 109-23.

DeWolf, L. Harold. "The Theological Rejection of Natural Theology: An Evaluation." *Journal of Religious Thought* 15, no. 2 (Spring-Summer 1958): 91-106.

Di Gangi, Mariano. *Peter Martyr Vermigli, 1499-1562: Renaissance Man, Reformation Master.* Lanham, Md.: University Press of America, 1993.

Donnelly, John Patrick, S.J. *Calvinism and Scholasticism in Vermigli's Doctrine of Man and Grace.* Leiden: E. J. Brill, 1976.

————. "Calvinist Thomism." *Viator: Medieval and Renaissance Studies* 7 (1976): 441-55.

————. "Italian Influences on the Development of Calvinist Scholasticism." *Sixteenth Century Journal* 7, no. 1 (April 1976): 81-101.

————. "Peter Martyr on Fallen Man: A Protestant Scholastic View." Ph.D. dissertation, University of Wisconsin-Madison, 1971.

————. "The Social and Ethical Thought of Peter Martyr Vermigli." In *Peter Martyr Vermigli and Italian Reform,* edited by Joseph C. McLelland, pp. 107-19. Waterloo, Ontario: Wilfrid Laurier University Press, 1980.

————. "Three Disputed Tracts." In *Essays Presented to Myron P. Gilmore,* edited by Sergio Bertelli and Gloria Ramakus, pp. 37-46. Florence: La Nuova Italia, 1978.

Donnelly, John Patrick, S.J., Robert M. Kingdon, and Marvin W. Anderson, eds. *A Bibliography of the Works of Peter Martyr Vermigli.* Kirksville, Mo.: Sixteenth Century Journal Publishers, 1990.

Dooyeweerd, Herman. *A New Critique of Theoretical Thought.* 4 vols. Translated by David H. Freeman and William S. Young. Jordan Station, Ontario: Paideia Press, 1984.

————. *De Strijd om het Souvereiniteitsbegrip in de Moderne Rechts- en Staatsleer.* Amsterdam: H. J. Paris, 1950.

————. *Roots of Western Culture: Pagan, Secular, and Christian Options.* Edited by Mark Vander Vennen and Bernard Zylstra. Translated by John Kraay. Toronto: Wedge Publishing Foundation, 1979.

Doumergue, Émile. *Jean Calvin: Les hommes et les choses de son temps.* Vol. 5. *La pensée ecclésiastique et la pensée politique de Calvin.* Lausanne: Georges Bridel, 1917.

Dowey, Edward A. Jr. *The Knowledge of God in Calvin's Theology.* Rev. ed. Grand Rapids: Wm. B. Eerdmans Publishing Company, 1994.

Dunning, William Archibald. *A History of Political Theories from Luther to Montesquieu.* New York: The Macmillan Company, 1916.

Dupré, Louis K. *Passage to Modernity: An Essay in the Hermeneutics of Nature and Culture.* New Haven: Yale University Press, 1993.

Duso, Giuseppe, Werner Krawietz, and Dieter Wyduckel, eds. *Konsens und Konsoziation in der politischen Theorie des frühen Föderalismus.* Berlin: Duncker and Humblot, 1997.

Elazar, Daniel J. "Althusius' Grand Design for a Federal Commonwealth." In *Politica: An Abridged Translation of Politics Methodically Set Forth and Illustrated with Sacred and Profane Examples,* edited and translated by Frederick S. Carney, pp. xxxv-xlvi. Indianapolis: Liberty Fund, 1995.

———. *Covenant Tradition in Politics.* Vol. 1. *Covenant and Polity in Biblical Israel: Biblical Foundations and Jewish Expressions.* New Brunswick, N.J.: Transaction Publishers, 1995.

———. *Covenant Tradition in Politics.* Vol. 2. *Covenant and Commonwealth: From Christian Separation Through the Protestant Reformation.* New Brunswick, N.J.: Transaction Publishers, 1996.

———. *Covenant Tradition in Politics.* Vol. 3. *Covenant and Constitutionalism: The Great Frontier and the Matrix of Federal Democracy.* New Brunswick, N.J.: Transaction Publishers, 1998.

———. *Covenant Tradition in Politics.* Vol. 4. *Covenant and Civil Society: The Constitutional Matrix of Modern Democracy.* New Brunswick, N.J.: Transaction Publishers, 1998.

Ellul, Jacques. *The Theological Foundation of Law.* Translated by Marguerite Wieser. London: S.C.M. Press, 1961.

Elshtain, Jean Bethke. *Augustine and the Limits of Politics.* Notre Dame: University of Notre Dame Press, 1995.

Elshtain, Jean Bethke, ed. *Just War Theory.* New York: New York University Press, 1992.

Endo, Ken. "The Principle of Subsidiarity: From Johannes Althusius to Jacques Delors." *Hokkaido Law Review* 44, no. 6 (1994): 553-652.

"Evangelicals and Catholics Together: The Christian Mission in the Third Millennium." In *Evangelicals and Catholics Together: Toward a Common Mission,* edited by Charles Colson and Richard John Neuhaus, pp. xv-xxxiii. Dallas: Word, 1995.

"Evangelicals and Catholics Together: The Gift of Salvation." *Christianity Today* 41, no. 14 (December 8, 1997): 35-38.

Farthing, John L. "Christ and the Eschaton: The Reformed Eschatology of Jerome Zanchi." In *Later Calvinism: International Perspectives,* edited by W. Fred Graham, pp. 333-54. Kirksville, Mo.: Sixteenth Century Journal Publishers, 1994.

————. "*De coniugio spirituali:* Jerome Zanchi on Ephesians 5:22-23." *Sixteenth Century Journal* 24, no. 3 (1993): 621-52.

————. "*Foedus Evangelicum:* Jerome Zanchi on the Covenant." *Calvin Theological Journal* 29, no. 1 (April 1994): 149-67.

————. "Holy Harlotry: Jerome Zanchi and the Exegetical History of Gomer (Hosea 1–3)." In *Biblical Interpretation in the Era of the Reformation: Essays Presented to David C. Steinmetz in Honor of His Sixtieth Birthday,* edited by Richard A. Muller and John L. Thompson, pp. 292-312. Grand Rapids: Wm. B. Eerdmans Publishing Company, 1996.

————. *Thomas Aquinas and Gabriel Biel: Interpretations of St. Thomas Aquinas in German Nominalism on the Eve of the Reformation.* Durham: Duke University Press, 1988.

————. "Zanchi, Jerome (1516-1590)." In *Historical Handbook of Major Biblical Interpreters,* edited by Donald K. McKim, pp. 245-49. Downers Grove, Ill.: InterVarsity Press, 1998.

Fasolt, Constantin. "Voluntarism and Conciliarism in the Work of Francis Oakley." *History of Political Thought* 22, no. 1 (Spring 2001): 41-52.

Feuerherdt, Eckhard. *Gesellschaftsvertrag und Naturrecht in der Staatslehre des Johannes Althusius.* Köln: R. Pulm, 1962.

Figgis, John Neville. *Studies of Political Thought: From Gerson to Grotius, 1414-1625.* Cambridge: Cambridge University Press, 1907.

————. *The Divine Right of Kings.* 2d ed. Cambridge: Cambridge University Press, 1922.

Friedeburg, Robert V. "From Collective Representation to the Right to Individual Defence: James Steuart's *Ius Populi Vindicatum* and the Use of Johannes Althusius' *Politica* in Restoration Scotland." *History of European Ideas* 24, no. 1 (1998): 19-42.

Friedrich, Carl Joachim. "Althusius, Johannes." In *Encyclopaedia of the Social Sciences,* vol. 2, pp. 13-14. New York: The Macmillan Company, 1937.

————. "Introduction." In *Politica Methodice Digesta of Johannes Althusius,* pp. xv-cxviii. Cambridge, Mass.: Harvard University Press, 1932.

————. *Johannes Althusius und sein Werk im Rahmen der Entwicklung der Theorie von der Politik.* Berlin: Duncker and Humblot, 1975.

————. "Preface." In *The Politics of Johannes Althusius,* translated by Frederick S. Carney, pp. vii-xii. London: Eyre and Spottiswoode, 1965.

Ganoczy, Alexandre. *La Bibliothèque de l'Académie de Calvin: Le Catalogue de 1572 et ses Enseignements.* Geneva: Librairie Droz, 1969.

————. *The Young Calvin.* Translated by David Foxgrover and Wade Provo. Philadelphia: Westminster Press, 1987.

Gardy, Frédéric. "Les Livres de Pierre Martyr Vermigli Conservés à la Bibliothèque de Genève." *Anzeiger für Schweizerische Geschichte* 17 (1919): 1-6.

Gass, Wilhelm. *Geschichte der protestantischen Dogmatik in ihrem Zusammenhange mit der Theologie.* 4 vols. Berlin: Georg Reimer, 1854-1867.

Gay, Craig M. *The Way of the (Modern) World: Or, Why It's Tempting to Live As If God Doesn't Exist.* Grand Rapids: Wm. B. Eerdmans Publishing Company, 1998.

Geesink, Wilhelm. *Gereformeerde Ethiek*. Tweede Deel. Kampen: Kok, 1931.

Gerbrandy, P. S. *National and International Stability: Althusius, Grotius, Van Vollenhoven*. Cambridge, Mass.: Harvard University Press, 1944.

Gibbs, Lee W. "The Puritan Natural Law Theory of William Ames." *Harvard Theological Review* 64, no. 1 (January 1971): 37-57.

Gierke, Otto Friedrich von. *Das deutsche Genossenschaftsrecht*. 4 vols. Berlin: Weidmann, 1868-1913.

———. *Deutsches privatrecht*. 3 vols. Leipzig: Duncker and Humblot, 1895-1917.

———. *Johannes Althusius und die Entwicklung der naturrechtlichen Staatstheorien: zugleich ein Beitrag zur Geschichte der Rechtssystematik*. 5th ed. Aalen: Scientia, 1958.

———. *Natural Law and the Theory of Society, 1500-1800*. Translated by Ernest Barker. Cambridge: Cambridge University Press, 1950.

———. *Political Theories of the Middle Ages*. Translated by Frederic W. Maitland. Cambridge: Cambridge University Press, 1951.

———. *The Development of Political Theory*. Translated by Bernard Freyd. New York: W. W. Norton and Company, Inc.; New York: Howard Fertig, 1966.

Gilbert, Neal W. *Renaissance Concepts of Method*. New York: Columbia University Press, 1960.

Gilson, Etienne. *History of Christian Philosophy in the Middle Ages*. New York: Random House, 1955.

———. *The Christian Philosophy of St. Thomas Aquinas*. Translated by L. K. Shook. New York: Random House, 1956.

———. *The Spirit of Medieval Philosophy*. Translated by A. H. C. Downes. New York: Charles Scribner's Sons, 1940.

Gloede, Günter. *Theologia Naturalis bei Calvin*. Stuttgart: W. Kohlhammer, 1935.

Goerner, E. A. "On Thomistic Natural Law: The Bad Man's View of Thomistic Natural Right." *Political Theory* 7, no. 1 (February 1979): 101-22.

Gordon, Alexander. "Vermigli, Pietro Martire." In *Dictionary of National Biography*, edited by Sir Leslie Stephen and Sir Sidney Lee, pp. 253-56. Oxford: Oxford University Press, 1917. Reprinted 1960.

Grabill, Stephen J. "Introduction to D. Hieronymus Zanchi's 'On the Law in General.'" *Journal of Markets & Morality* 6, no. 1 (Spring 2003): 309-16.

Grafton, Anthony. *Joseph Scaliger: A Study in the History of Classical Scholarship*. 2 vols. Oxford: Clarendon Press, 1993.

Greene, Robert A. "Synderesis, the Spark of Conscience, in the English Renaissance." *Journal of the History of Ideas* 52, no. 2 (April-June 1991): 195-219.

Grendler, Paul F. "The Circulation of Protestant Books in Italy." In *Peter Martyr Vermigli and Italian Reform*, edited by Joseph C. McLelland, pp. 5-16. Waterloo, Ontario: Wilfrid Laurier University Press, 1980.

Grislis, Egil. "Calvin's Use of Cicero in the *Institutes* I:1-5 — A Case Study in Theological Method." *Archiv für Reformationsgeschichte* 62 (1971): 5-37.

Gründler, Otto. *Die Gotteslehre Girolamo Zanchis und ihre Bedeutung für seine Lehre von der Pradestination*. Neukirchen-Vluyn: Neukirchener Verlag, 1965.

———. "The Influence of Thomas Aquinas upon the Theology of Girolamo Zanchi

(1516-1590)." In *Studies in Medieval Culture,* Series VII, no. 2, edited by John R. Sommerfeldt, pp. 102-17. Kalamazoo: Western Michigan University, 1964.

———. "Thomism and Calvinism in the Theology of Girolamo Zanchi (1516-1590)." Ph.D. dissertation, Princeton Theological Seminary, 1961.

Gustafson, James M. *Protestant and Roman Catholic Ethics: Prospects for Rapprochement.* Chicago: University of Chicago Press, 1978.

Haakonssen, Knud. *Natural Law and Moral Philosophy: From Grotius to the Scottish Enlightenment.* Cambridge: Cambridge University Press, 1996.

Haas, Guenther. *The Concept of Equity in Calvin's Ethics.* Waterloo, Ontario: Wilfrid Laurier University Press, 1997.

Hall, Jerome. *Studies in Jurisprudence and Criminal Theory.* New York: Oceana Publications, 1958.

Halsey, William M. *The Survival of American Innocence: Catholicism in an Era of Disillusionment, 1920-1940.* Notre Dame: University of Notre Dame Press, 1980.

Hare, John E. *God's Call: Moral Realism, God's Commands, and Human Autonomy.* Grand Rapids: Wm. B. Eerdmans Publishing Company, 2001.

———. *The Moral Gap: Kantian Ethics, Human Limits, and God's Assistance.* Oxford: Clarendon Press, 1996.

———. *Why Bother Being Good? The Place of God in the Moral Life.* Downers Grove, Ill.: InterVarsity Press, 2002.

Harnack, Adolf von. *What Is Christianity?* 2d ed., rev. Translated by Thomas Bailey Saunders. New York: G. P. Putnam's Sons, 1901.

Hauerwas, Stanley. "Natural Law, Tragedy, and Theological Ethics." *American Journal of Jurisprudence* 20 (1975): 1-19.

———. *With the Grain of the Universe: The Church's Witness and Natural Theology.* Grand Rapids: Brazos Press, 2001.

Helm, Paul. "Calvin and Natural Law." *Scottish Bulletin of Evangelical Theology* 2 (1984): 5-22.

———. *John Calvin's Ideas.* Oxford: Oxford University Press, 2004.

———. "John Calvin, the *sensus divinitatis,* and the Noetic Effects of Sin." *International Journal for Philosophy of Religion* 43, no. 2 (April 1998): 87-107.

Helseth, Paul K. "Right Reason and the Princeton Mind: The Moral Context." *Journal of Presbyterian History* 77, no. 1 (Spring 1999): 13-28.

Henry, Carl F. H. *Christian Personal Ethics.* Grand Rapids: Wm. B. Eerdmans Publishing Company, 1957.

———. "Natural Law and a Nihilistic Culture." *First Things* 49 (January 1995): 54-60.

Henry, Paul B. "Types of Protestant Theology and the Natural-Law Tradition." Ph.D. dissertation, Duke University, 1970.

Heppe, Heinrich. "Der Charakter der deutsch-reformirten Kirche und das Verhältniss derselben zum Luthertum und zum Calvinismus." In *Theologische Studien und Kritiken,* 1850 (Heft 3), pp. 669-706.

———. *Die confessionelle Entwicklung der altprotestantischen Kirche Deutschlands, die altprotestantische Union und die gegenwärtige confessionelle Lage und Aufgabe des deutschen Protestantismus.* Marburg: Elwert, 1854.

————. *Die Dogmatik des deutschen Protestantismus im sechzehnten Jahrhundert.* 3 vols. Gotha: Perthes, 1857.

————. *Reformed Dogmatics Set Out and Illustrated from the Sources.* Revised and edited by Ernst Bizer. Translated by G. T. Thomson. London: Allen and Unwin, 1950.

Hittinger, Russell. *The First Grace: Rediscovering the Natural Law in a Post-Christian World.* Wilmington, Del.: ISI Books, 2003.

Hochstrasser, T. J. "The Claims of Conscience: Natural Law Theory, Obligation, and Resistance in the Huguenot Diaspora." In *New Essays on the Political Thought of the Huguenots of the Refuge,* edited by John Christian Laursen, pp. 15-51. Leiden: E. J. Brill, 1995.

Hodge, Charles. *Systematic Theology.* 3 vols. Grand Rapids: Wm. B. Eerdmans Publishing Company, 1970.

Hoitenga, Dewey J. Jr. "Faith and Reason in Calvin's Doctrine of the Knowledge of God." In *Rationality in the Calvinian Tradition,* edited by Hendrik Hart, Johan Van der Hoeven, and Nicholas Wolterstorff, pp. 17-42. Lanham, Md.: University Press of America, 1983.

————. *John Calvin and the Will: A Critique and Corrective.* Grand Rapids: Baker Book House, 1997.

————. "The Noetic Effects of Sin: A Review Article." *Calvin Theological Journal* 38, no. 1 (April 2003): 68-102.

Holmes, Arthur F. "A Philosophical Critique of Ellul on Natural Law." In *Jacques Ellul: Interpretive Essays,* edited by Clifford G. Christians and Jay M. Van Hook, pp. 229-50. Urbana: University of Illinois Press, 1981.

————. "Concept of Natural Law." *Christian Scholar's Review* 2, no. 3 (1972): 195-208.

————. *Fact, Value, and God.* Grand Rapids: Wm. B. Eerdmans Publishing Company, 1997.

————. "Human Variables and Natural Law." In *God and the Good: Essays in Honor of Henry Stob,* edited by Clifton Orlebeke and Lewis Smedes, pp. 63-79. Grand Rapids: Wm. B. Eerdmans Publishing Company, 1975.

Holopainen, Taina M. "William of Ockham's Theory of the Foundations of Ethics." Th.D. dissertation, Helsingin Yliopisto University, 1991.

Höpfl, Harro P. *The Christian Polity of John Calvin.* Cambridge: Cambridge University Press, 1982.

Horowitz, Maryanne Cline. *Seeds of Virtue and Knowledge.* Princeton, N.J.: Princeton University Press, 1998.

————. "The Stoic Synthesis of the Idea of Natural Law in Man: Four Themes." *Journal of the History of Ideas* 35, no. 1 (January-March 1974): 3-16.

Hueglin, Thomas O. "Covenant and Federalism in the Politics of Althusius." In *The Covenant Connection: From Federal Theology to Modern Federalism,* edited by Daniel J. Elazar and John Kincaid, pp. 31-54. Lanham, Md.: Lexington Books, 2000.

————. *Early Modern Concepts for a Late Modern World: Althusius on Community and Federalism.* Waterloo, Ontario: Wilfrid Laurier University Press, 1999.

————. "Federalism at the Crossroads: Old Meanings, New Significance." *Canadian Journal of Political Science* 36, no. 2 (June 2003): 275-94.

————. "Have We Studied the Wrong Authors? On the Relevance of Johannes Althusius." *Studies in Political Thought* 1, no. 1 (1992): 75-93.

————. "Johannes Althusius: Medieval Constitutionalist or Modern Federalist?" *Publius: The Journal of Federalism* 9, no. 4 (Fall 1979): 9-41.

————. *Sozietaler Föderalismus: Die politische Theorie des Johannes Althusius.* Berlin: Walter de Gruyter, 1991.

Huelin, Gordon. "Peter Martyr and the English Reformation." Ph.D. dissertation, University of London, 1954.

Hugelshofer, W. "Zum Porträt des Petrus Martyr Vermilius." *Zwingliana* 5, no. 1 (1930): 127-29.

Hunsinger, George. *How to Read Karl Barth: The Shape of His Theology.* New York: Oxford University Press, 1991.

Hurst, John Fletcher. *History of Rationalism Embracing a Survey of the Present State of Protestant Theology.* Rev. ed. New York: Eaton & Mains, 1901.

Ingham, Mary Elizabeth. *Ethics and Freedom: An Historical-Critical Investigation of Scotist Ethical Thought.* Lanham, Md.: University Press of America, 1989.

Jahier, Augusto. *Riformatori e Riformati Italiani dei Secoli XV° e XVI°: Trenta succinte Biografie con illustrazioni e Appendice.* Firenze: Società editrice Claudiana, 1924.

James, Frank A. III. "A Late Medieval Parallel in Reformation Thought: *Gemina Praedestinatio* in Gregory of Rimini and Peter Martyr Vermigli." In *Via Augustini: Augustine in the Later Middle Ages, Renaissance, and Reformation: Essays in Honor of Damasus Trapp, O.S.A.,* edited by Heiko A. Oberman and Frank A. James III, pp. 157-88. Leiden: E. J. Brill, 1991.

————. *De Justificatione: The Evolution of Peter Martyr Vermigli's Doctrine of Justification.* Ph.D. dissertation, Westminster Theological Seminary, 2000.

————. "Juan de Valdés Before and After Peter Martyr Vermigli: The Reception of *Gemina Praedestinatio* in Valdés' Later Thought." *Archiv für Reformationsgeschichte* 83 (1992): 180-208.

————. *Peter Martyr Vermigli and Predestination: The Augustinian Inheritance of an Italian Reformer.* Oxford: Clarendon Press, 1998.

————. "Peter Martyr Vermigli: At the Crossroads of Late Medieval Scholasticism, Christian Humanism, and Resurgent Augustinianism." In *Protestant Scholasticism: Essays in Reassessment,* edited by Carl R. Trueman and R. S. Clark, pp. 62-78. Carlisle, U.K.: Paternoster Press, 1999.

————. "*Praedestinatio Dei:* The Intellectual Origins of Peter Martyr Vermigli's Doctrine of Double Predestination." D.Phil. thesis, Oxford University, 1993.

————. "The Biblical Scholarship of Peter Martyr Vermigli (1499-1562)." In *Historical Handbook of Major Biblical Interpreters,* edited by Donald K. McKim, pp. 239-45. Downers Grove, Ill.: InterVarsity Press, 1998.

————. "Translator's Introduction." In *Predestination and Justification: Two Theological Loci,* Vol. 8, *The Peter Martyr Library,* edited and translated by Frank A. James III, pp. xv-xliv. Kirksville, Mo.: Truman State University Press, 2003.

Janssen, Heinrich. *Die Bibel als Grundlage der politischen Theorie des Johannes Althusius.* Frankfurt am Main: Peter Lang, 1992.

Jeffreys, Derek S. "How Reformed Is Reformed Epistemology? Alvin Plantinga and Calvin's 'Sensus Divinitatis.'" *Religious Studies* 33, no. 4 (December 1997): 419-31.

Jonge, H. J. de. "The Study of the New Testament." In *Leiden University in the Seventeenth Century: An Exchange of Learning,* edited by Th. H. Lunsingh Scheurleer and G. H. M. Posthumus Meyjes, pp. 65-110. Leiden: Universitaire Pers Leiden/ E. J. Brill, 1975.

Kap-Herr, Gerhart von. "Natural Law and Religion in the Thought of Samuel Pufendorf." Ph.D. dissertation, Concordia University, 1991.

Kelly, J. M. *A Short History of Western Legal Theory.* Oxford: Clarendon Press, 1992.

Kevan, Ernest F. *The Evangelical Doctrine of Law.* London: Tyndale Press, 1956.

———. *The Grace of Law: A Study in Puritan Theology.* Grand Rapids: Baker Book House, 1965.

Kilner, J. F. "Hurdles for Natural-Law Ethics: Lessons from Grotius." *American Journal of Jurisprudence* 28 (1983): 149-68.

Kingdon, Robert M. "Althusius' Use of Calvinist Sources in His *Politica.*" *Rechtstheorie* 16 (1997): 19-28.

———. "Introduction." In *The Political Thought of Peter Martyr Vermigli: Selected Texts and Commentary,* edited by Robert M. Kingdon, pp. i-xxvi. Geneva: Librairie Droz, 1980.

———. "Peter Martyr Vermigli and the Marks of the True Church." In *Continuity and Discontinuity in Church History: Essays Presented to George Huntston Williams,* edited by F. Forrester Church and Timothy George, pp. 198-214. Leiden: E. J. Brill, 1979.

———. "The Function of Law in the Political Thought of Peter Martyr Vermigli." In *Reformatio Perennis: Essays on Calvin and the Reformation in Honor of Ford Lewis Battles,* edited by B. A. Gerrish and Robert Benedetto, pp. 159-72. Pittsburgh, Pa.: Pickwick Press, 1981.

———. "The Political Thought of Peter Martyr Vermigli." In *Peter Martyr Vermigli and Italian Reform,* edited by Joseph C. McLelland, pp. 121-40. Waterloo, Ontario: Wilfrid Laurier University Press, 1980.

Kirby, W. J. Torrance. "Richard Hooker's Theory of Natural Law in the Context of Reformation Theology." *Sixteenth Century Journal* 30, no. 3 (1999): 681-703.

Kirsch, William James. "Contemporary Protestant Thought on Natural Law." Ph.D. dissertation, University of Illinois at Urbana-Champaign, 1967.

Klauber, Martin I. *Between Reformed Scholasticism and Pan-Protestantism: Jean-Alphonse Turretin (1671-1737) and Enlightened Orthodoxy at the Academy of Geneva.* Selingsgrove, Pa.: Susquehanna University Press, 1994.

———. "Francis Turretin on Biblical Accommodation: Loyal Calvinist or Reformed Scholastic?" *Westminster Theological Journal* 55, no. 1 (Spring 1993): 73-86.

———. "Jean-Alphonse Turrettini (1671-1737) on Natural Theology: The Triumph of Reason over Revelation at the Academy of Geneva." *Scottish Journal of Theology* 47, no. 3 (1994): 301-25.

————. "Jean-Alphonse Turrettini and the Abrogation of the Formula Consensus in Geneva." *Westminster Theological Journal* 53 (1991): 325-38.

————. "Reason, Revelation, and Cartesianism: Louis Tronchin and Enlightened Orthodoxy in Late Seventeenth-Century Geneva." *Church History* 59 (1990): 326-39.

————. "Reformed Orthodoxy in Transition: Bénédict Pictet (1655-1724) and Enlightened Orthodoxy in Post-Reformation Geneva." In *Later Calvinism: International Perspectives,* edited by W. Fred Graham, pp. 93-113. Kirksville, Mo.: Sixteenth Century Journal Publishers, 1994.

————. "The Context and Development of the Views of Jean-Alphonse Turrettini (1671-1737) on Religious Authority." Ph.D. dissertation, University of Wisconsin–Madison, 1987.

————. "The Eclipse of Reformed Scholasticism in Eighteenth-Century Geneva: Natural Theology from Jean-Alphonse Turretin to Jacob Vernet." In *The Identity of Geneva: The Christian Commonwealth, 1564-1864,* edited by John B. Roney and Martin I. Klauber, pp. 129-42. Westport, Conn.: Greenwood Press, 1998.

————. "The Helvetic Consensus Formula (1675): An Introduction and Translation." *Trinity Journal* 11 (Spring 1990): 103-23.

————. "Theological Transition in Geneva: From Jean-Alphonse Turretin to Jacob Vernet." In *Protestant Scholasticism: Essays in Reassessment,* edited by Carl R. Trueman and R. S. Clark, pp. 256-70. Carlisle, U.K.: Paternoster Press, 1999.

Klauber, Martin I., and Glenn S. Sunshine. "Jean-Alphonse Turrettini on Biblical Accommodation: Calvinist or Socinian?" *Calvin Theological Journal* 25, no. 1 (April 1990): 7-27.

Klempa, William. "Calvin on Natural Law." In *John Calvin and the Church: A Prism of Reform,* edited by Timothy George, pp. 72-95. Louisville: Westminster/John Knox Press, 1990.

Kuiper, Herman. *Calvin on Common Grace.* Grand Rapids: Smitter Book Company, 1928.

Lakoff, Sanford. "Althusius, Johannes." In *Political Philosophy: Theories, Thinkers, Concepts,* edited by Seymour Martin Lipset, pp. 221-23. Washington, D.C.: Congressional Quarterly Press, 2001.

Lane, Anthony N. S. "Calvin and the Fathers in His *Bondage and Liberation of the Will.*" In *John Calvin: Student of the Church Fathers,* pp. 151-78. Grand Rapids: Baker Book House, 1999.

————. "Calvin's Sources of Bernard of Clairvaux." In *John Calvin: Student of the Church Fathers,* pp. 115-50. Grand Rapids: Baker Book House, 1999.

————. "Calvin's Use of Bernard of Clairvaux." In *John Calvin: Student of the Church Fathers,* pp. 87-114. Grand Rapids: Baker Book House, 1999.

————. "The Influence upon Calvin of His Debate with Pighius." In *John Calvin: Student of the Church Fathers,* pp. 179-90. Grand Rapids: Baker Book House, 1999.

Lang, August. "The Reformation and Natural Law." In *Calvin and the Reformation,* edited by William Park Armstrong, translated by J. G. Machen, pp. 56-98. Grand Rapids: Baker Book House, 1980.

LaVallee, Armand Aime. "Calvin's Criticism of Scholastic Theology." Ph.D. dissertation, Harvard University, 1967.

Laytham, D. Brent. "The Place of Natural Theology in the Theological Method of John Calvin and Jacob Arminius." In *Church Divinity 1989/90*, edited by John H. Morgan, pp. 22-44. Bristol, Ind.: Wyndham Hall Press, 1990.

Lehmann, Paul. *Ethics in a Christian Context*. New York: Harper and Row, 1963.

Leithart, Peter J. "Stoic Elements in Calvin's Doctrine of the Christian Life. Part I: Original Corruption, Natural Law, and the Order of the Soul." *Westminster Theological Journal* 55, no. 1 (Spring 1993): 31-54.

Letham, Robert. "The *Foedus Operum*: Some Factors Accounting for Its Development." *Sixteenth Century Journal* 14, no. 4 (Winter 1983): 457-67.

Lewis, C. S. *The Abolition of Man*. New York: Macmillan, 1947.

Lindbom, Tage. *The Myth of Democracy*. Grand Rapids: Wm. B. Eerdmans Publishing Company, 1996.

Little, David. "Calvin and the Prospects for a Christian Theory of Natural Law." In *Norm and Context in Christian Ethics*, edited by Gene H. Outka and Paul Ramsey, pp. 175-97. New York: Scribner's, 1968.

———. *Religion, Order, and Law: A Study in Pre-Revolutionary England*. New York: Harper and Row, 1969.

Lomonaco, Fabrizio. "Huguenot Critical Theory and 'Ius Maiestatis' in Huber and Althusius." In *New Essays on the Political Thought of the Huguenots of the Refuge*, edited by John Christian Laursen, pp. 171-92. Leiden: E. J. Brill, 1995.

Lorenz, Rudolph. *Die unvollendete Befreiung vom Nominalismus: Martin Luther und die Grenzen hermeneutischer Theologie bei Gerhard Ebeling*. Gütersloh: Gütersloher Verlagshaus Mohn, 1973.

Lortz, Joseph. *The Reformation in Germany*. 2 vols. Translated by Ronald Walls. New York: Herder and Herder, 1968.

Luscombe, D. E. "Natural Morality and Natural Law." In *The Cambridge History of Later Medieval Philosophy: From the Rediscovery of Aristotle to the Disintegration of Scholasticism, 1100-1600*, edited by Norman Kretzmann, Anthony Kenny, and Jan Pinborg, pp. 705-19. New York: Cambridge University Press, 1982.

Malandrino, Corrado. "Il *Syndikat* di Johannes Althusius a Emden: La ricerca." *Pensiero Politico* 28, no. 3 (1995): 359-83.

Marshall, John Lewis. "Natural Law and the Covenant: The Place of Natural Law in the Covenantal Framework of Samuel Rutherford's *Lex, Rex*." Ph.D. dissertation, Westminster Theological Seminary, 1995.

Mackay, James Hutton. *Religious Thought in Holland during the Nineteenth Century*. New York: Hodder and Stoughton, 1911.

McCallum, J. Bruce. "Modernity and the Dilemma of Natural Theology: The Barth-Brunner Debate, 1934." Ph.D. dissertation, Marquette University, 1994.

McCoy, Charles S. "Der Bund als Grundmetapher in der Politica des Johannes Althusius." In *Gottes Zukunft — Zukunft der Welt*, pp. 332-44. München: Chr. Kaiser Verlag, 1986.

———. "The Centrality of Covenant in the Political Philosophy of Johannes Althusius." In *Politische Theorie des Johannes Althusius*, edited by Karl-Wilhelm

Dahm, Werner Krawietz, and Dieter Wyduckel, pp. 187-99. Berlin: Duncker and Humblot, 1988.

McDonnell, Kevin. "Nominalist Natural Law Theory Revisited: Gabriel Biel." In *The Medieval Tradition of Natural Law,* edited by Harold J. Johnson, pp. 129-36. Kalamazoo: Medieval Institute Publications and Western Michigan University Press, 1987.

McGrath, Alister E. *A Life of John Calvin: A Study in the Shaping of Western Culture.* Cambridge, Mass.: Basil Blackwell, 1990.

————. *A Scientific Theology.* 3 vols. Grand Rapids: Wm. B. Eerdmans Publishing Company, 2001-2003.

————. "John Calvin and Late Medieval Thought: A Study in Late Medieval Influences upon Calvin's Theological Development." *Archiv für Reformationsgeschichte* 77 (1986): 58-78.

McLelland, Joseph C. "Calvinism Perfecting Thomism: Peter Martyr Vermigli's Question." *Scottish Journal of Theology* 31, no. 6 (December 1978): 571-78.

————. "Peter Martyr Vermigli: Scholastic or Humanist?" In *Peter Martyr Vermigli and Italian Reform,* edited by Joseph C. McLelland, pp. 141-52. Waterloo, Ontario: Wilfrid Laurier University Press, 1980.

————. "The Reformed Doctrine of Predestination according to Peter Martyr." *Scottish Journal of Theology* 8, no. 3 (September 1955): 255-71.

————. *The Visible Words of God: An Exposition of the Sacramental Theology of Peter Martyr Vermigli, A.D. 1500-1562.* Edinburgh: Oliver and Boyd, 1957.

McLelland, Joseph C., ed. *Peter Martyr Vermigli and Italian Reform.* Waterloo, Ontario: Wilfrid Laurier University Press, 1980.

McNair, Philip Murray Jourdan. "Peter Martyr in England." In *Peter Martyr Vermigli and Italian Reform,* edited by Joseph C. McLelland, pp. 85-106. Waterloo, Ontario: Wilfrid Laurier University Press, 1980.

————. *Peter Martyr in Italy: An Anatomy of Apostasy.* Oxford: Clarendon Press, 1967.

————. "The Reformation of the Sixteenth Century in Renaissance Italy." In *Studies in Church History,* Vol. 17, *Religion and Humanism: Papers Read at the Eighteenth Summer Meeting and the Nineteenth Winter Meeting of the Ecclesiastical History Society,* edited by Keith Robbins, pp. 149-66. Oxford: Basil Blackwell, 1981.

McNeill, John T. "Natural Law in the Teaching of the Reformers." *Journal of Religion* 26, no. 3 (July 1946): 168-82.

————. "Natural Law in the Thought of Luther." *Church History* 10, no. 3 (September 1941): 211-27.

Meijering, E. P. *Reformierte Scholastik und patristische Theologie: die Bedeutung des Vaterbeweises in der Institutio theologiae elencticae F. Turrettins: unter besonderer Berucksichtigung der Gottslehre und Christologie.* Nieuwkoop: De Graaf, 1991.

————. "The Fathers and Calvinist Orthodoxy: Systematic Theology (A. Polanus, J. Wolleb, and F. Turrettini)." In *The Reception of the Church Fathers in the West: From the Carolingians to the Maurists,* 2 vols., edited by Irena Backus, vol. 2, pp. 867-87. Leiden: E. J. Brill, 1997.

Mesnard, Pierre. *L'essor de la philosophie politique de XVIe siècle.* Paris: J. Vrin, 1951.

Midgley, Louis C. "Karl Barth and Moral Natural Law: The Anatomy of a Debate." *Natural Law Forum* 13 (1968): 108-26.

Miethe, Terry L. "Natural Law, the Synderesis Rule, and St. Augustine." *Augustinian Studies* 11 (1980): 91-97.

Minges, Parthenius. *Das Verhältnis zwischen Glauben und Wissen, Theologie und Philosophie nach Duns Scotus.* Paderborn: F. Schöningh, 1908.

————. *Der angebliche exzessive Realismus des Duns Scotus.* Münster: Aschendorff, 1908.

————. *Der Gottesbegriff des Duns Scotus auf seinen angeblich exzessiven Indeterminismus.* Vienna: Mayer, 1907.

————. *Ioannis Duns Scoti doctrina philosophica et theologica quoad res praecipuas proposita et exposita.* 2 vols. Ad Claras Aquas: Collegium S. Bonaventurae, 1930.

Möhle, Hannes. "Scotus's Theory of Natural Law." In *The Cambridge Companion to Duns Scotus,* edited by Thomas Williams, pp. 312-31. Cambridge: Cambridge University Press, 2003.

Morimoto, Anri. "The Seventeenth-Century Ecumenical Interchanges." In *Christian Ethics in Ecumenical Context: Theology, Culture, and Politics in Dialogue,* edited by Shin Chiba, George R. Hunsberger, and Lester Edwin J. Ruiz, pp. 86-102. Grand Rapids: Wm. B. Eerdmans Publishing Company, 1995.

Moroney, Stephen K. "How Sin Affects Scholarship: A New Model." *Christian Scholar's Review* 28, no. 3 (Spring 1999): 432-51.

————. "The Noetic Effects of Sin: An Exposition of Calvin's View and a Constructive Theological Proposal." Ph.D. dissertation, Duke University, 1995.

————. *The Noetic Effects of Sin: A Historical and Contemporary Exploration of How Sin Affects Our Thinking.* Lanham, Md.: Lexington Books, 2000.

Morton, Charles E. "What Protestants Think About Natural Law." *Catholic World* 190, no. 1 (February 1960): 294-300.

Mouw, Richard J. *He Shines in All That's Fair: Culture and Common Grace.* Grand Rapids: Wm. B. Eerdmans Publishing Company, 2001.

————. "Klaas Schilder as Public Theologian." *Calvin Theological Journal* 38, no. 2 (November 2003): 281-98.

————. *The God Who Commands: A Study in Divine Command Ethics.* Notre Dame: University of Notre Dame Press, 1990.

Muller, Richard A. *After Calvin: Studies in the Development of a Theological Tradition.* New York: Oxford University Press, 2003.

————. "Calvin and the 'Calvinists': Assessing Continuities and Discontinuities Between the Reformation and Orthodoxy. Part I." *Calvin Theological Journal* 30, no. 2 (November 1995): 345-75.

————. "Calvin and the 'Calvinists': Assessing Continuities and Discontinuities Between the Reformation and Orthodoxy. Part II." *Calvin Theological Journal* 31, no. 1 (April 1996): 125-60.

————. *Dictionary of Latin and Greek Theological Terms: Drawn Principally from Protestant Scholastic Theology.* Grand Rapids: Baker Book House, 1985.

———. "*Duplex Cognitio Dei* in the Theology of Early Reformed Orthodoxy." *Sixteenth Century Journal* 10, no. 2 (Summer 1979): 51-61.

———. "Establishing the *Ordo docendi:* The Organization of Calvin's *Institutes,* 1536-1559." In *The Unaccommodated Calvin: Studies in the Foundation of a Theological Tradition,* pp. 118-39. New York: Oxford University Press, 2000.

———. "*Fides* and *Cognitio* in Relation to the Problem of Intellect and Will in the Theology of John Calvin." In *The Unaccommodated Calvin: Studies in the Foundation of a Theological Tradition,* pp. 159-73. New York: Oxford University Press, 2000.

———. *Post-Reformation Reformed Dogmatics: The Rise and Development of Reformed Orthodoxy, ca. 1520 to ca. 1725.* 4 vols. Grand Rapids: Baker Academic, 2003.

———. "Predestination and Christology in Sixteenth-Century Reformed Theology." Ph.D. dissertation, Duke University, 1976.

———. *Scholasticism and Orthodoxy in the Reformed Tradition: An Attempt at Definition.* Grand Rapids: Calvin Theological Seminary, 1995.

———. "Scholasticism in Calvin: A Question of Relation and Disjunction." In *The Unaccommodated Calvin: Studies in the Foundation of a Theological Tradition,* pp. 39-61. New York: Oxford University Press, 2000.

———. "Scholasticism Protestant and Catholic: Francis Turretin on the Object and Principles of Theology." *Church History* 55, no. 2 (June 1986): 193-205.

———. "The Barth Legacy: New Athanasius or Origen Redivivus? A Response to T. F. Torrance." *The Thomist* 54 (1990): 673-704.

———. "The Covenant of Works and the Stability of Divine Law in Seventeenth-Century Reformed Orthodoxy: A Study in the Theology of Herman Witsius and Wilhelmus à Brakel." In *After Calvin: Studies in the Development of a Theological Tradition,* pp. 175-90. New York: Oxford University Press, 2003.

———. "The Problem of Protestant Scholasticism — A Review and Definition." In *Reformation and Scholasticism: An Ecumenical Enterprise,* edited by Willem J. van Asselt and Eef Dekker, pp. 45-64. Grand Rapids: Baker Book House, 2001.

———. *The Unaccommodated Calvin: Studies in the Foundation of a Theological Tradition.* New York: Oxford University Press, 2000.

———. "*Vera Philosophia cum sacra Theologia nusquam pugnat:* Keckermann on Philosophy, Theology, and the Problem of Double Truth." *Sixteenth Century Journal* 15, no. 3 (1984): 341-65.

Murphy, Paul V. "Between *Spirituali* and *Intransigenti:* Cardinal Ercole Gonzaga and Patrician Reform in Sixteenth-Century Italy." *Catholic Historical Review* 88, no. 3 (July 2002): 446-69.

Niebuhr, Reinhold. *An Interpretation of Christian Ethics.* New York: Harper and Brothers Publishers, 1935.

———. "Christian Faith and Natural Law." In *Love and Justice: Selections from the Shorter Writings of Reinhold Niebuhr,* edited by D. B. Robertson, pp. 46-54. Louisville: Westminster/John Knox Press, 1957.

———. *The Nature and Destiny of Man: A Christian Interpretation.* 2 vols. New York: Charles Scribner's Sons, 1951.

Niesel, Wilhelm. *The Theology of Calvin*. Translated by Harold Knight. Philadelphia: Westminster Press, 1956.

Noble, T. A. "Our Knowledge of God according to John Calvin." *Evangelical Quarterly* 54, no. 1 (January-March 1982): 2-13.

O'Donovan, Joan Lockwood. *Theology of Law and Authority in the English Reformation*. Atlanta: Scholars Press, 1991.

Oakley, Francis. "'Adamantine Fetters of Destiny': The Absolute Power of God and King in the Sixteenth and Seventeenth Centuries." In *Politics and Eternity: Studies in the History of Medieval and Early-Modern Political Thought*, pp. 276-332. Leiden: E. J. Brill, 1999.

———. "Christian Theology and the Newtonian Science: The Rise of the Concept of the Laws of Nature." *Church History* 30, no. 4 (December 1961): 433-57.

———. "Jacobean Political Theology: The Absolute and Ordinary Powers of the King." *Journal of the History of Ideas* 29, no. 3 (July-September 1968): 323-46.

———. "Legitimation by Consent: The Question of the Medieval Roots." In *Politics and Eternity: Studies in the History of Medieval and Early-Modern Political Thought*, pp. 96-137. Leiden: E. J. Brill, 1999.

———. "Locke, Natural Law, and God: Again." In *Politics and Eternity: Studies in the History of Medieval and Early-Modern Political Thought*, pp. 217-48. Leiden: E. J. Brill, 1999.

———. "Medieval Theories of Natural Law: William of Occam and the Significance of the Voluntarist Tradition." *Natural Law Forum* 6 (1961): 65-83.

———. *Omnipotence and Promise: The Legacy of the Scholastic Distinction of Powers*. Toronto: Pontifical Institute of Medieval Studies, 2002.

———. *Omnipotence, Covenant, and Order: An Excursion in the History of Ideas from Abelard to Leibniz*. Ithaca, N.Y.: Cornell University Press, 1984.

———. "Pierre d'Ailly and the Absolute Power of God: Another Note on the Theology of Nominalism." *Harvard Theological Review* 56, no. 1 (January 1963): 59-73.

———. *Politics and Eternity: Studies in the History of Medieval and Early-Modern Political Thought*. Leiden: E. J. Brill, 1999.

———. "The Absolute and Ordained Power of God in Sixteenth- and Seventeenth-Century Theology." *Journal of the History of Ideas* 59, no. 3 (1998): 437-61.

———. *The Political Thought of Pierre d'Ailly: The Voluntarist Tradition*. New Haven: Yale University Press, 1964.

———. *The Western Church in the Later Middle Ages*. Ithaca, N.Y.: Cornell University Press, 1979.

Oberman, Heiko A. *Archbishop Thomas Bradwardine: A Fourteenth-Century Augustinian. A Study of His Theology in Its Historical Context*. Utrecht: Kemink & Zoon, 1957.

———. *Contra vanam curiositatem: ein Kapitel der Theologie zwischen Seelenwickel und Weltall*. Zurich: Theologischer Verlag, 1974.

———. *Forerunners of the Reformation*. New York: Holt, Rinehart, and Winston, 1966.

———. "Fourteenth-Century Religious Thought: A Premature Profile." In *The Dawn of the Reformation: Essays in Late Medieval and Early Reformation Thought*, pp. 1-17. Grand Rapids: Wm. B. Eerdmans Publishing Company, 1992.

———. *Initia Calvini: The Matrix of Calvin's Reformation.* Amsterdam: Koninklijke Nederlandse Akademie van Wetenschappen, 1991.

———. "Luther and the *Via Moderna:* The Philosophical Backdrop of the Reformation Breakthrough." *Journal of Ecclesiastical History* 54, no. 4 (October 2003): 641-70.

———. *Masters of the Reformation: Emergence of a New Intellectual Climate in Europe.* Translated by Dennis Martin. Cambridge: Cambridge University Press, 1981.

———. "Reformation and Revolution: Copernicus' Discovery in an Era of Change." In *The Dawn of the Reformation: Essays in Late Medieval and Early Reformation Thought,* pp. 179-203. Grand Rapids: Wm. B. Eerdmans Publishing Company, 1992.

———. "Some Notes on the Theology of Nominalism: With Attention to Its Relation to the Renaissance." *Harvard Theological Review* 53, no. 1 (January 1960): 47-76.

———. "The 'Extra' Dimension in the Theology of Calvin." In *The Dawn of the Reformation: Essays in Late Medieval and Early Reformation Thought,* pp. 234-58. Grand Rapids: Wm. B. Eerdmans Publishing Company, 1992.

———. *The Harvest of Medieval Theology: Gabriel Biel and Late Medieval Nominalism.* 3d ed. Grand Rapids: Baker Book House, 2000.

———. "The Shape of Late Medieval Thought: The Birthpangs of the Modern Era." In *The Dawn of the Reformation: Essays in Late Medieval and Early Reformation Thought,* pp. 18-38. Grand Rapids: Wm. B. Eerdmans Publishing Company, 1992.

———. *The Two Reformations: The Journey from the Last Days to the New World.* Edited by Donald Weinstein. New Haven and London: Yale University Press, 2003.

———. "*Via Antiqua* and *Via Moderna:* Late Medieval Prolegomena to Early Reformation Thought." In *The Impact of the Reformation,* pp. 3-22. Grand Rapids: Wm. B. Eerdmans Publishing Company, 1994.

Ong, Walter. *Ramus, Method, and the Decay of Dialogue.* Cambridge, Mass.: Harvard University Press, 1958.

Overell, M. A. "Peter Martyr in England 1547-1553: An Alternate View." *Sixteenth Century Journal* 15, no. 1 (Spring 1984): 87-104.

Ozment, Steven. "*Homo Viator:* Luther and Late Medieval Theology." In *The Reformation in Medieval Perspective,* edited by Steven Ozment, pp. 142-54. Chicago: Quadrangle Books, 1971.

Paist, Benjamin F. Jr. "Peter Martyr and the Colloquy of Poissy." *Princeton Theological Review* 20 (April 1922): 212-31; (July 1922): 418-47; (October 1922): 616-46.

Parker, T. H. L. *The Doctrine of the Knowledge of God: A Study in Calvin's Theology.* Rev. ed. Grand Rapids: Wm. B. Eerdmans Publishing Company, 1959.

Parry, Stanley Joseph. "The Political Science of Johannes Althusius." Ph.D. dissertation, Yale University, 1953.

Partee, Charles. "Calvin's Central Dogma Again." *Sixteenth Century Journal* 18, no. 2 (Summer 1987): 191-99.

Pelkonen, J. Peter. "The Teaching of John Calvin on the Nature and Function of the Conscience." *The Lutheran Quarterly* 21, no. 1 (February 1969): 74-88.

Phillips, Timothy R. "Francis Turretin's Idea of Theology and Its Bearing upon His Doctrine of Scripture." Ph.D. dissertation, Vanderbilt University, 1986.

———. "The Dissolution of Francis Turretin's Vision of *Theologia:* Geneva at the End of the Seventeenth Century." In *The Identity of Geneva: The Christian Commonwealth, 1564-1864,* edited by John B. Roney and Martin I. Klauber, pp. 77-92. Westport, Conn.: Greenwood Press, 1998.

Platt, John. *Reformed Thought and Scholasticism: The Arguments for the Existence of God in Dutch Theology, 1575-1650.* Leiden: E. J. Brill, 1982.

Pope, Stephen J. "Natural Law and Christian Ethics." In *The Cambridge Companion to Christian Ethics,* edited by Robin Gill, pp. 77-95. Cambridge: Cambridge University Press, 2001.

Postema, Gerald J. "Calvin's Alleged Rejection of Natural Theology." *Scottish Journal of Theology* 24, no. 4 (November 1971): 423-34.

Potts, Timothy C. "Conscience." In *The Cambridge History of Later Medieval Philosophy: From the Rediscovery of Aristotle to the Disintegration of Scholasticism, 1100-1600,* edited by Norman Kretzmann, Anthony Kenny, and Jan Pinborg, pp. 687-704. New York: Cambridge University Press, 1982.

Prentice, Robert, O.F.M. "The Contingent Element Governing the Natural Law on the Last Seven Precepts of the Decalogue According to Duns Scotus." *Antonianum* 42 (1967): 259-92.

———. "The Voluntarism of Duns Scotus, As Seen in His Comparison of the Intellect and the Will." *Franciscan Studies* 28 (1968): 63-103.

Quinton, Anthony. "British Philosophy." In *The Encyclopedia of Philosophy,* edited by Paul Edwards, vol. 1, pp. 369-96. New York: Macmillan Publishing Company, 1972.

Rae, S. H. "Calvin, Natural Law, and Contemporary Ethics: A Brief Note." *Reformed Theological Review* 30, no. 1 (January-April 1971): 14-20.

Ramsey, Ian T., ed. *Christian Ethics and Contemporary Philosophy.* London: S.C.M. Press, 1966.

———. "Towards a Rehabilitation of Natural Law." In *Christian Ethics and Contemporary Philosophy,* edited by Ian T. Ramsey, pp. 382-96. London: S.C.M. Press, 1966.

Ramsey, Paul. "Natural Law and the Nature of Man." *Christendom* 9, no. 3 (Summer 1944): 369-81.

Randi, Eugenio. "A Scotist Way of Distinguishing Between God's Absolute and Ordained Powers." In *From Ockham to Wyclif,* edited by Anne Hudson and Michael Wilks, pp. 43-50. Oxford: Basil Blackwell, 1987.

———. "Ockham, John XXII and the Absolute Power of God." *Franciscan Studies* 46 (1986): 205-16.

Rehnman, Sebastian. "Alleged Rationalism: Francis Turretin on Reason." *Calvin Theological Journal* 37, no. 2 (November 2002): 255-69.

———. "Theistic Metaphysics and Biblical Exegesis: Francis Turretin on the Concept of God." *Religious Studies* 38, no. 2 (June 2002): 167-86.

Reibstein, Ernst. *Johannes Althusius als Fortsetzer der Schule von Salamanca: Unter-*

suchungen zur Ideengeschichte des Recht-Staates und zur altprotestantischen Naturrechtslehr. Karlsruhe: C. F. Müller, 1955.

Reid, Charles J., Jr. *Power over the Body, Equality in the Family: Rights and Domestic Relations in Medieval Canon Law.* Grand Rapids: Wm. B. Eerdmans Publishing Company, 2004.

Reuter, Karl. *Das Grundverständnis der Theologie Calvins.* Neukirchen: Neukirchener Verlag, 1963.

————. *Vom Scholaren bis zum jungen Reformator.* Neukirchen: Neukirchener Verlag, 1981.

Ridenhour, Thomas Eugene Jr. "The Uses of Cicero by Johannes Althusius in the *Politica Methodice Digesta.*" M.A. thesis, University of Virginia, 2001.

Riley, Patrick. "Three Seventeenth Century German Theorists of Federalism: Althusius, Hugo, and Leibniz." *Publius: The Journal of Federalism* 6, no. 3 (Summer 1976): 7-41.

Ritschl, Albrecht. *Die christliche Lehre von der Rechtfertigung und Versohnung.* 3 vols. Bonn: A. Marcus, 1895-1903.

————. *Theologie und Metaphysik: zur Verstandigung und Abwehr.* Bonn: A. Marcus, 1881.

Rogers, Eugene F. Jr. "The Narrative of Natural Law in Aquinas's Commentary on Romans 1." *Theological Studies* 59, no. 2 (June 1998): 254-76.

————. *Thomas Aquinas and Karl Barth: Sacred Doctrine and the Natural Knowledge of God.* Notre Dame: University of Notre Dame Press, 1995.

Rogers, Isabel Wood. "A Contemporary Protestant Critique of the Natural Law Tradition." Ph.D. dissertation, Duke University, 1961.

Rommen, Heinrich A. *The Natural Law: A Study in Legal and Social History and Philosophy.* Translated by Thomas R. Hanley, O.S.B. Indianapolis: Liberty Fund, 1998.

Rooney, Paul. "Divine Commands, Natural Law and Aquinas." *Scottish Journal of Religious Studies* 16 (Autumn 1995): 117-40.

Ruler, J. A. van. *The Crisis of Causality: Voetius and Descartes on God, Nature, and Change.* Leiden: E. J. Brill, 1995.

Santini, Luigi. "Appunti sulla ecclesiologia di P. M. Vermigli e la edificazione della Chiesa." *Bolletino della Società di Studi Valdesi* 104 (1958): 69-75.

————. "'Scisma' e 'eresia' nel pensiero di P. M. Vermigli." *Bolletino della Società di Studi Valdesi* 125 (1969): 27-43.

————. *Tra spiritualismo e riforma: Saggi di storia religiosa Toscana.* Firenze: Presso lo Stabilimento Poligrafico Fiorentino, 1979.

Sap, John W. *Paving the Way for Revolution: Calvinism and the Struggle for a Democratic Constitutional State.* Amsterdam: VU Uitgeverij, 2001.

Scattola, Merio. "Johannes Althusius und das Naturrecht des 16. Jahrhunderts." In *Jurisprudenz, Politische Theorie und Politische Theologie: Beiträge des Herborner Symposions zum 400. Jahrestag der Politica des Johannes Althusius 1603-2003,* edited by Frederick S. Carney, Heinz Schilling, and Dieter Wyduckel, pp. 371-96. Berlin: Duncker & Humblot, 2004.

Schaff, Philip, ed. *The Creeds of Christendom.* Vol. 3. *The Evangelical Protestant Creeds.* 6th ed. Revised by David S. Schaff. Grand Rapids: Baker Book House, 1990.

Schlosser, Friedrich Christoph. *Leben des Theodor de Beza und des Peter Martyr Vermili. Ein Beytrag zur Geschichte der Zeiten der Kirchen-Reformation. Mit einem Anhang bisher ungedruckter Briefe Calvins und Beza's und andrer Urkunden ihrer Zeit; aus den Schätzen der herzogl. Bibliothek zu Gotha.* Heidelberg: Mohr und Zimmer, 1809.

Schmidt, Charles. "Girolamo Zanchi." *Studium und Kritiken* 32 (1859): 625-708.

———. *Peter Martyr Vermigli. Leben und ausgewahlte Schriften. Nach handschriftlichen und gleichzeitigen Quellen von dr. C. Schmidt.* Elberfeld: R. L. Friderichs, 1858.

———. "Vermigli." In *Real-Encyklopädie für protestantische Theologie und Kirche,* vol. 16, pp. 357-61. 1st ed. Leipzig: J. C. Hinrichs, 1885.

———. *Vie de Pierre Martyr Vermigli: Thèse présentée à la Faculté de Théologie de Strasbourg.* Strasbourg: 1834.

Schreiner, Susan E. "Calvin's Use of Natural Law." In *A Preserving Grace: Protestants, Catholics, and Natural Law,* edited by Michael Cromartie, pp. 51-76. Grand Rapids: Wm. B. Eerdmans Publishing Company/Ethics and Public Policy Center, 1997.

———. "Exegesis and Double Justice in Calvin's Sermons on Job." *Church History* 58, no. 3 (September 1989): 322-38.

———. *The Theater of His Glory: Nature and the Natural Order in the Thought of John Calvin.* Durham, N.C.: Labyrinth Press, 1991; Grand Rapids: Baker Book House, 1995.

———. "Through a Mirror Dimly: Calvin's Sermons on Job." *Calvin Theological Journal* 21, no. 2 (November 1986): 175-93.

———. *Where Shall Wisdom Be Found? Calvin's Exegesis of Job from Medieval and Modern Perspectives.* Chicago: University of Chicago Press, 1994.

Schrey, Heinz-Horst. "Diskussion um das Naturrecht 1950-1975." *Theologische Rundschau* 41, no. 1 (February 1976): 59-93.

Schweizer, Alexander. *Die Glaubenslehre der evangelisch-reformierten Kirche dargestellt und aus den Quellen belegt.* 2 vols. Zürich: Orell, Füssli, und Comp., 1844-1847.

———. *Die protestantischen Centraldogmen in ihrer Entwicklung innerhalb der reformierten Kirche.* 2 vols. Zürich: Orell, Füssli, und Comp., 1854-1856.

Sinnema, Donald. "Aristotle and Early Reformed Orthodoxy: Moments of Accommodation and Antithesis." In *Christianity and the Classics: The Acceptance of a Heritage,* edited by Wendy E. Helleman, pp. 119-48. Lanham, Md.: University Press of America, 1990.

———. "The Discipline of Ethics in Early Reformed Orthodoxy." *Calvin Theological Journal* 28, no. 1 (April 1993): 10-44.

Shephard, Max A. "William of Occam and the Higher Law, I." *American Political Science Review* 26, no. 6 (December 1932): 1005-23.

———. "William of Occam and the Higher Law, II." *American Political Science Review* 27, no. 1 (February 1933): 24-38.

Shin, Won Ha. "Two Models of Social Transformation: A Critical Analysis of the Theological Ethics of John H. Yoder and Richard J. Mouw." Ph.D. dissertation, Boston University, 1997.

Shute, Daniel John. "Peter Martyr and the Rabbinic Bible in the Interpretation of Lamentations." Ph.D. dissertation, McGill University, 1994.

Skillen, James W. "From Covenant of Grace to Equitable Public Pluralism: The Dutch Calvinist Contribution." *Calvin Theological Journal* 31, no.1 (April 1996): 67-96.

———. "The Development of Calvinistic Political Theory in the Netherlands, with Special Reference to the Thought of Herman Dooyeweerd." Ph.D. dissertation, Duke University, 1974.

———. "The Political Theory of Johannes Althusius." *Philosophia Reformata* 39 (1974): 170-90.

Skinner, Quentin. *The Foundations of Modern Political Thought.* 2 vols. Cambridge: Cambridge University Press, 1978.

Smyth, Charles Hugh Egerton. *Cranmer and the Reformation under Edward VI.* Cambridge: Cambridge University Press, 1926.

Spencer, Stephen R. "Francis Turretin's Concept of the Covenant of Nature." In *Later Calvinism: International Perspectives,* edited by W. Fred Graham, pp. 71-91. Kirksville, Mo.: Sixteenth Century Journal Publishers, 1994.

———. "Reformed Scholasticism in Medieval Perspective: Thomas Aquinas and François Turrettini on the Incarnation." Ph.D. dissertation, Michigan State University, 1988.

Spykman, Gordon. "Pluralism: Our Last Best Hope?" *Christian Scholar's Review* 10, no. 2 (1981): 99-115.

———. *Reformational Theology: A New Paradigm for Doing Dogmatics.* Grand Rapids: Wm. B. Eerdmans Publishing Company, 1992.

Staedtke, Joachim. "Drei umstrittene Traktate Peter Martyr Vermiglis." *Zwingliana* 11 (1962): 553-54.

Steinmetz, David C. "Calvin and the Absolute Power of God." In *Calvin in Context,* pp. 40-52. New York: Oxford University Press, 1995.

———. "Calvin and the First Commandment." In *Calvin in Context,* pp. 53-63. New York: Oxford University Press, 1995.

———. "Calvin and the Natural Knowledge of God." In *Via Augustini: Augustine in the Later Middle Ages, Renaissance, and Reformation: Essays in Honor of Damasus Trapp, O.S.A.,* edited by Heiko A. Oberman and Frank A. James III, pp. 142-56. Leiden: E. J. Brill, 1991.

———. *Calvin in Context.* New York: Oxford University Press, 1995.

———. "Luther Among the Anti-Thomists." In *Luther in Context,* 2d ed., pp. 47-58. Grand Rapids: Baker Academic, 2002.

———. *Luther and Staupitz: An Essay in the Intellectual Origins of the Protestant Reformation.* Durham, N.C.: Duke University Press, 1980.

———. *Luther in Context.* 2d ed. Grand Rapids: Baker Academic, 2002.

———. *Misericordia Dei: The Theology of Johannes von Staupitz in Its Late Medieval Setting.* Leiden: E. J. Brill, 1968.

———. *Reformers in the Wings: From Geiler von Kaysersberg to Theodore Beza.* 2d ed. Oxford: Oxford University Press, 2001.

————. "The Reformation and the Ten Commandments." *Interpretation: A Journal of Bible and Theology* 43, no. 3 (July 1989): 256-66.

————. "The Scholastic Calvin." In *Protestant Scholasticism: Essays in Reassessment,* edited by Carl R. Trueman and R. S. Clark, pp. 16-30. Carlisle, U.K.: Paternoster Press, 1999.

Steubing, Hans von. *Naturrecht und natürliche Theologie im Protestantismus.* Göttingen: Vandenhoeck and Ruprecht, 1932.

Stob, Henry. "Ethics: An Account of Its Subject Matter." In *Ethical Reflections: Essays on Moral Themes,* pp. 7-30. Grand Rapids: Wm. B. Eerdmans Publishing Company, 1978.

————. "Calvin and Aquinas." In *Theological Reflections: Essays on Related Themes,* pp. 126-30. Grand Rapids: Wm. B. Eerdmans Publishing Company, 1981.

————. "Natural-Law Ethics: An Appraisal." *Calvin Theological Journal* 20, no. 1 (April 1985): 58-68.

————. "Observations on the Concept of the Antithesis." In *Perspectives on the Christian Reformed Church: Studies in Its History, Theology, and Ecumenicity,* edited by Peter De Klerk and Richard R. De Ridder, pp. 241-58. Grand Rapids: Baker Book House, 1983.

————. "Principle and Practice." In *Ethical Reflections: Essays on Moral Themes,* pp. 31-49. Grand Rapids: Wm. B. Eerdmans Publishing Company, 1978.

————. *Summoning Up Remembrance.* Grand Rapids: Wm. B. Eerdmans Publishing Company, 1995.

————. "The Christian Conception of Revelation." M.T.S. thesis, Hartford Theological Seminary, 1936.

————. "Themes in Barth's Ethics." *Reformed Journal* 12, no. 4 (April 1962): 19-23.

Strohm, Christoph. "Althusius' Rechtslehre im Kontext des reformierten Protestantismus." In *Jurisprudenz, Politische Theorie und Politische Theologie: Beiträge des Herborner Symposions zum 400. Jahrestag der Politica des Johannes Althusius 1603-2003,* edited by Frederick S. Carney, Heinz Schilling, and Dieter Wyduckel, pp. 71-102. Berlin: Duncker & Humblot, 2004.

Sturm, Douglas. "Naturalism, Historicism, and Christian Ethics: Toward a Christian Doctrine of Natural Law." *Journal of Religion* 44 (January 1964): 40-51.

Sturm, Klaus. *Die Theologie Peter Martyr Vermiglis während seines ersten Aufenthalts in Straßburg 1542-1547: Ein Reformkatholik unter den Vätern der reformierten Kirche.* Neukirchen-Vluyn: Neukirchener Verlag, 1971.

Sudduth, Michael Czapkay. "Calvin, Plantinga, and the Natural Knowledge of God: A Response to Beversluis." *Faith and Philosophy* 15, no. 1 (January 1998): 92-103.

————. "The Prospects for 'Mediate' Natural Theology in John Calvin." *Religious Studies* 31, no. 2 (March 1995): 53-68.

Tachau, Katherine H. "Logic's God and the Natural Order in Late Medieval Oxford: The Teaching of Robert Holcot." *Annals of Science* 53 (1996): 235-67.

Tedeschi, John. "Italian Reformers and the Diffusion of Renaissance Culture." *Sixteenth Century Journal* 5, no. 2 (October 1974): 79-94.

Thielicke, Helmut. *Theological Ethics.* Vol. 1. *Foundations.* Edited by William H. Lazareth. Grand Rapids: Wm. B. Eerdmans Publishing Company, 1979.

Thomas, John Newton. "The Place of Natural Theology in the Thought of John Calvin." *Journal of Religious Thought* 15, no. 2 (Spring-Summer 1958): 107-36.

Thompson, John L. "The Survival of Allegorical Argumentation in Peter Martyr Vermigli's Old Testament Exegesis." In *Biblical Interpretation in the Era of the Reformation: Essays Presented to David C. Steinmetz in Honor of His Sixtieth Birthday*, edited by Richard A. Muller and John L. Thompson, pp. 255-71. Grand Rapids: Wm. B. Eerdmans Publishing Company, 1996.

Tierney, Brian. *Religion, Law, and the Growth of Constitutional Thought, 1150-1650.* Cambridge: Cambridge University Press, 1982.

———. *The Idea of Natural Rights: Studies on Natural Rights, Natural Law, and Church Law, 1150-1625.* Atlanta: Scholars Press, 1997.

Todd, John. *Martin Luther: A Biographical Study.* Westminster, Md.: Newman Press, 1964.

Torrance, James. "Interpreting the Word by the Light of Christ or the Light of Nature? Calvin, Calvinism, and Barth." In *Calviniana: Ideas and Influence of Jean Calvin*, edited by Robert V. Schnucker, pp. 255-67. Kirksville, Mo.: Sixteenth Century Journal Publishers, Inc., 1988.

Torrance, Thomas F. *Calvin's Doctrine of Man.* Grand Rapids: Wm. B. Eerdmans Publishing Company, 1957.

———. "Knowledge of God and Speech about Him According to John Calvin." In *Theology in Reconstruction*, pp. 76-98. Grand Rapids: Wm. B. Eerdmans Publishing Company, 1966.

———. *The Hermeneutics of John Calvin.* Edinburgh: Scottish Academic Press, 1988.

Trinkhaus, Charles, and Heiko A. Oberman, eds. *The Pursuit of Holiness in Late Medieval and Renaissance Religion.* Leiden: E. J. Brill, 1974.

Troeltsch, Ernst. "Calvin and Calvinism." *Hibbert Journal* 8, Part 1 (1909-1910): 102-21.

———. *The Social Teachings of the Christian Churches.* 2 vols. Translated by Olive Wyon. Louisville: Westminster/John Knox Press, 1992.

Trueman, Carl R., and R. S. Clark, eds. *Protestant Scholasticism: Essays in Reassessment.* Carlisle, U.K.: Paternoster Press, 1999.

Trueman, Carl R., and R. S. Clark. "Introduction." In *Protestant Scholasticism: Essays in Reassessment,* edited by Carl R. Trueman and R. S. Clark, pp. xi-xix. Carlisle, U.K.: Paternoster Press, 1999.

Tylenda, Joseph N. "Girolamo Zanchi and John Calvin: A Study in Discipleship as Seen through Their Correspondence." *Calvin Theological Journal* 10, no. 2 (November 1975): 101-41.

VanDrunen, David. *Law & Custom: The Thought of Thomas Aquinas and the Future of the Common Law.* New York: Peter Lang, 2003.

———. "Natural Law, Custom, and Common Law in the Theology of Aquinas and Calvin." *University of British Columbia Law Review* 33 (2000): 699-717.

———. "Natural Law and Common Law: The Relationship of Law and Custom in the Moral Theology of Thomas Aquinas." Ph.D. dissertation, Loyola University-Chicago, 2001.

————. "The Context of Natural Law: John Calvin's Doctrine of the Two Kingdoms." *Journal of Church and State* 46, no. 3 (Summer 2004): 503-25.

Van Houten, David Jon. "Earthly Wisdom and Heavenly Wisdom: The Concept of Reason in the Theology of John Calvin." Ph.D. dissertation, University of Chicago Divinity School, 1993.

Van Til, Cornelius. *Common Grace and the Gospel.* Nutley, N.J.: Presbyterian and Reformed Publishing Company, 1974.

————. *In Defense of the Faith.* Vol. 3. *Christian Theistic Ethics.* Philadelphia: den Dulk Christian Foundation, 1974.

Vasoli, Cesare. "*Loci Communes* and the Rhetorical and Dialectical Traditions." In *Peter Martyr Vermigli and Italian Reform,* edited by Joseph C. McLelland, pp. 17-28. Waterloo, Ontario: Wilfrid Laurier University Press, 1980.

Veen, Theo. "Een *Fundgrube* voor de historische wetenschap: de *Althusius-Bibliografie.*" *Bijdragen en Mededelingen Betreffende de Geschiedenis der Nederlanden* 94, no. 1 (1979): 89-96.

Veldhuis, Henri. "Ordained and Absolute Power in Scotus' *Ordinatio I 44.*" *Vivarium* 38, no. 2 (2000): 222-30.

Verhey, Allen. "Natural Law in Aquinas and Calvin." In *God and the Good: Essays in Honor of Henry Stob,* edited by Clifton Orlebeke and Lewis Smedes, pp. 80-92. Grand Rapids: Wm. B. Eerdmans Publishing Company, 1975.

Venema, Cornelis P. "The 'Twofold Knowledge of God' and the Structure of Calvin's Theology." *Mid-America Journal of Theology* 4, no. 2 (Fall 1988): 156-82.

Vidler, A. R., and W. A. Whitehouse, eds. *Natural Law: A Christian Reconsideration.* London: S.C.M. Press, 1946.

Vignaux, Paul. *Justification et predestination au XIVe siècle: Duns Scot, Pierre d'Auriole, Guillaume d'Occam, Grégoire de Rimini.* Paris: E. Leroux, 1934.

————. "Nominalisme." In *Dictionnaire de théologie catholique* (1931), vol. 11, cols. 717-84.

————. *Nominalisme au XIVe siècle.* Montreal: Institute D'Ètudes Médiévales, 1948.

————. *Philosophy in the Middle Ages.* Translated by E. C. Hall. New York: Meridian Books, 1959.

Voegelin, Eric. *The Collected Works of Eric Voegelin.* Vol. 23. *History of Political Ideas.* Vol. 5. *Religion and the Rise of Modernity.* Edited by James L. Wiser. Columbia, Mo.: University of Missouri Press, 1998.

Vos, Antonie Jaczn. "De Kern van de klassieke gereformeerde theologie: Een traditiehistorisch gesprek." *Kerk en theologie* 47 (1996): 106-25.

————. "Scholasticism and Reformation." In *Reformation and Scholasticism: An Ecumenical Enterprise,* edited by Willem J. Van Asselt and Eef Dekker, pp. 99-119. Grand Rapids: Baker Book House, 2001.

————. "The Scotian Notion of Natural Law." *Vivarium* 38, no. 2 (2000): 197-221.

Vos, Antonie Jaczn., H. Veldhuis, A. H. Looman-Graaskamp, E. Dekker, and N. W. Den Bok. "Introduction, Translation, and Commentary." In John Duns Scotus, *Contingency and Freedom: Lectura I 39,* pp. 23-36. Dordrecht: Kluwer Academic Publishers, 1994.

Vos, Arvin. *Aquinas, Calvin, and Contemporary Protestant Thought: A Critique of*

Protestant Views on the Thought of Thomas Aquinas. Washington, D.C., and Grand Rapids: Christian University Press and Wm. B. Eerdmans Publishing Company, 1985.

Wallace, Ronald S. *Calvin's Doctrine of the Christian Life.* Edinburgh: Oliver and Boyd, 1959.

Walser, Peter. "Die fraglichen drei Traktate." In *Die Pradestination bei Heinrich Bullinger im Zusammenhang mit seiner Gotteslehre,* pp. 200-10. Zurich: Zwingli Verlag, 1957.

Warfield, Benjamin B. "Calvin's Doctrine of the Knowledge of God." In *Calvin and the Reformation,* edited by William Park Armstrong, pp. 131-214. Grand Rapids: Baker Book House, 1980.

————. "John Calvin the Theologian." In *Calvin and Augustine,* edited by Samuel G. Craig, pp. 481-87. Philadelphia: Presbyterian and Reformed Publishing Company, 1956.

Weber, Hans Emil. *Der Einfluss der protestantischen Schulphilosophie auf die orthodoxlutherische Dogmatik.* Leipzig: Deichert, 1908.

————. *Die philosophische Scholastik des deutschen Protestantismus in Zeitalter der Orthodoxie.* Leipzig: Quelle und Meyer, 1907.

————. *Reformation, Orthodoxie und Rationalismus.* 2 vols. in 3 parts. Darmstadt: Wissenschaftliche Buchgesellschaft, 1966.

Wendel, François. *Calvin: The Origins and Development of His Religious Thought.* Translated by Philip Mairet. New York: Harper and Row, 1963.

Wengert, Timothy J. *Law and Gospel: Philip Melanchthon's Debate with John of Agricola of Eisleben over* Poenitentia. Grand Rapids: Baker Books, 1997.

Westberg, Daniel. *Right Practical Reason: Aristotle, Action, and Prudence in Aquinas.* Oxford: Clarendon Press, 1994.

————. "The Reformed Tradition and Natural Law." In *A Preserving Grace: Protestants, Catholics, and Natural Law,* edited by Michael Cromartie, pp. 103-17. Grand Rapids: Wm. B. Eerdmans Publishing Company/Ethics and Public Policy Center, 1997.

————. "The Relation Between Positive and Natural Law in Aquinas." *Journal of Law and Religion* 11 (1994-1995): 1-22.

————. "Thomistic Law and the Moral Theory of Richard Hooker." *American Catholic Philosophical Quarterly: Supplement* 68 (1994): 201-14.

Williams, David. "The Immutability of Natural Law according to Suarez." *The Thomist* 62, no. 1 (January 1998): 97-115.

Williams, Thomas. "The Libertarian Foundations of Scotus's Moral Philosophy." *The Thomist* 62, no. 2 (April 1998): 193-215.

Willis, E. David. *Calvin's Catholic Christology: The Function of the So-Called Extra Calvinisticum in Calvin's Theology.* Leiden: E. J. Brill, 1966.

Winters, Peter Jochen. *Die "Politica" des Johannes Althusius und ihre zeitgenössischen Quellen: Zur Grundlegung der politischen Wissenschaft im 16. und im beginnenden 17. Jahrhundert.* Freiburg: Rombach, 1963.

Witte, John Jr. *Law and Protestantism: The Legal Teachings of the Lutheran Reformation.* Cambridge: Cambridge University Press, 2002.

Woldring, Henk E. S. "Multiform Responsibility and the Revitalization of Civil Society." In *Religion, Pluralism, and Public Life: Abraham Kuyper's Legacy for the Twenty-First Century,* edited by Luis E. Lugo, pp. 175-88. Grand Rapids: Wm. B. Eerdmans Publishing Company, 2000.

————. "The Constitutional State in the Political Philosophy of Johannes Althusius." *European Journal of Law and Economics* 5 (1998): 123-32.

Wolf, Erik. *Das Problem der Naturrechtslehre: Versuch einer Orientierierung.* Karlsruhe: C. F. Müller, 1964.

————. *Grosse Rechtsdenker der deutschen Geistesgeschichte.* 4th ed. Tübingen: J. C. B. Mohr, 1963.

Wolter, Allan B., O.F.M. "Duns Scotus on the Nature of Man's Knowledge of God." *Review of Metaphysics* 1, no. 2 (December 1947): 3-36.

————. *Duns Scotus on the Will and Morality: Selected and Translated with an Introduction by Allan B. Wolter, O.F.M.* Washington, D.C.: Catholic University of America Press, 1986.

————. "Native Freedom of the Will as a Key to the Ethics of Scotus." In *The Philosophical Theology of John Duns Scotus,* edited by Marilyn McCord Adams, pp. 148-62. Ithaca and London: Cornell University Press, 1990.

————. "The Realism of Scotus." In *The Philosophical Theology of John Duns Scotus,* edited by Marilyn McCord Adams, pp. 42-53. Ithaca and London: Cornell University Press, 1990.

Wyduckel, Dieter. *Althusius-Bibliographie: Bibliographie zur politischen Ideengeschichte und Staatslehre, zum Staatsrecht und zur Verfassungsgeschichte des 16. bis 18. Jahrhunderts.* 2 vols. Edited by Hans Ulrich Scupin and Ulrich Scheuner. Berlin: Duncker and Humblot, 1973.

Young, M. *The Life and Times of Aonio Paleario: or, A History of the Italian Reformers in the Sixteenth Century Illustrated by Original Letters and Unedited Documents.* 2 vols. London: Bell and Daldy, 1860.

Zahrnt, Heinz. *The Question of God: Protestant Theology in the Twentieth Century.* Translated by R. A. Wilson. New York: Harcourt Brace Jovanovich, Inc., 1969.

Index

Absolute law, 11
Absolute power, 67
Absolutism, 122, 126-27, 183
Absolutist state, 177
Accountability, 71. *See also* Obligation
Acquired knowledge of God, 103-4, 105-6, 116-17, 156, 157
Action and contemplation, 106
Acts 17:27, 80
Actualism, 23, 40-41, 42, 43, 200n.89, 204n.16
Actual knowledge, 156
Adultery, 96. *See also* Ignorance and knowledge of God
Affection for advantage, doctrine of, 49. *See also* justice
Affection for justice, doctrine of, 49
Alberti, Valentin, 180
Aligando (law), 134
Althusius, Johannes: biography, 122-23, 213n.20; natural law, doctrine of, 15-16, 122-50, 237n.4, 247n.102; political theory, 238n.9, 239n.33, 241n.48, 242n.51, 244n.67; Ramist logic, 129-30, 239n.21, 241n.43. *See also Dicaeologica*, Althusius, Johannes; *Politica*, Althusius, Johannes
Althusius-Bibliographie, Johannes Althusius Gesellschaft, 243n.58
Ambrose, Saint, 118-19
American Federalists, 242n.51

Amyraldianism, 152, 173. *See also* Turretin, Francis
Anabaptism, 185-86
Analogia entis, 21, 34, 36, 102. *See also* grace
Anderson, Marvin, 101, 102-3, 236n.118
Animals and doctrine of law, 137, 138, 144, 165
Anknüpfungspunkt (point of contact), 21, 33, 34. *See also* Barth-Brunner debate
Anthropology of faith, 33, 34
Aposkimation, 165
Apostles' Creed, 25, 27
Aquinas, Saint Thomas, 47, 55, 177; Catholic theology, 209n.121, 212n.12; divine will, 50, 60-61, 62, 64, 217n.41; eternal law, 62, 136, 165, 216n.40, 217n.41; knowledge of God, 104, 106; moral law, 90, 172-73; natural law, 57, 59, 92, 114, 137, 239n.33; *Summa Theologica*, 94, 214n.27, 216n.40
Aristotelian Thomism, 9
Aristotle, 105, 106, 110-11, 126, 153, 242n.48, 249n.151; *Ethics, Politics, and Rhetoric*, 102; *Nicomachean Ethics*, 106, 112
Arminius, Jacob, 8-9
Assimilation, 184

298 INDEX

Intellectualism, defined, 74
Intelligence, 71, 162, 178. *See also*
  Goodness of actions
International law, 177-78, 181
Interpretation of law, 173
Isidore, Saint, 137

James, Frank A., III, 101
Janssen, Heinrich, 239n.33
Jeremiah 31, 118
Jesus Christ: natural law, 38, 42; sin,
  knowledge of, 30-31, 32, 41
Jews, 147. *See also* Divine command
  theory
Johannes Althusius Gesellschaft, 129,
  243n.58; *Althusius-Bibliographie,*
  243n.58
John, Gospel of, 75
Judgment: common, 133; divine, 76,
  112, 159; God's, 93-94, 95, 117
Judicial systems. *See Dicaeologica*
Jurieu, Pierre, 183-84
Jus commune (common law), 143,
  237n.4, 247n.102
Jus gentium (law of nations), 144
Jus naturale (natural law), 143-44
Jus rationalis (law of reason), 144
Justice, 10; God's will, 40-41, 42-43,
  166; knowledge of, 95, 117, 119-
  20, 165, 173, 247n.116; loving
  one's neighbor, 135, 140
Justification, 8, 101, 103, 187

Kelly, J. M., 176-77, 178-79, 181
Klauber, Martin, 182
Knowledge (*notitia*), 143
Knowledge of God: acquired, 104-6,
  116-17; Barth-Brunner debate, 24,
  25, 30, 31, 33-34, 37-38; contemplative, 103, 104-16; as Creator, 26,
  70-97, 154-74; effectual, 114-15,
  119-20; frigid, 115, 119-20; moral
  law, 44, 46-47, 71-72, 81, 88, 142,
  144-45; natural revelation, 94, 102,
  111, 113, 140-42; natural theology,
  37-38, 158-63, 206n.42; as Redeemer, 25, 26, 84, 154-55; revealed, 30, 81, 102, 103, 104-6

*The Knowledge of God and the Service
  of God according to the Teaching of
  the Reformation,* Barth, Karl, 24-25
Knowledge of sin, 30, 164

Lane, Anthony, 73
Lapsarian. *See* Post-lapsarian; Pre-
  lapsarian
Law as Christocentric, 41, 42, 178
Law, eternal, 60-61, 62, 136, 165,
  216n.40, 217n.41
Law, etymology of, 164-65
Law, foundation of, 42-43. *See also*
  God as Creator
Law, international, 177-78, 181
Law, knowledge of God, 30. *See also*
  lex naturalis
Law, positive, 165, 181-82
Law, types of, 90-91, 132-50, 216n.40
Law *(lex),* 216n.40
"The Law of God," Turretin, Francis,
  163-73
Law of nations *(jus gentium),* 137,
  144, 166-67
Law of reason *(jus rationalis),* 144
"Law of righteousness," 87-88
Law written on the heart *(lex
  naturalis),* 71-72, 120
Laytham, D. Brent, 27
Ledochowski, Wlodimir, 212n.12
Legal positivism, 66, 220n.75
Legendo, 164
Legere, 164
Legislation, 50, 51, 169
Letter on Toleration, Locke, John, 183
Leviathian, Hobbes, Thomas, 177
Lex (law), 216n.40
Lex aeterna, 31, 41, 50-51, 58, 92-93
Lex communis (common law), 147.
  See also Common law
Lex divina, 50, 51, 73, 130
Lex indicans (declaratory law),
  257n.16
Lex indicative, 60
Lex moralis (moral law), 143, 164. *See
  also* Moral law
Lex naturae (natural law), 31, 144,
  247n.102. *See also* Natural law

Republicanism, federal, 242n.50. *See
also Politica,* Althusius, Johannes
Revealed knowledge of God, 30, 81,
102, 103, 104-6
Revelation, 259n.57; *duplex cognitio
Dei,* 25-26, 37, 80, 82-83; grace,
21-22, 36; knowledge of God, 23,
30, 36, 45, 111-12; Scripture, 31-
32, 82-83, 111, 136, 182, 187
Revelatio specialis, 33
Revocation of the Edict of Nantes,
182-83
Righteousness: God's will, 40-41, 67,
222n.17; knowledge of God, 71,
87, 95, 107, 119-20
Right of nature, 166-67, 173
Right of sovereignty, 123, 176-77, 185
Right reason *(recta ratio),* 58,
217n.40, 223n.22
Rogers, Eugene F., Jr., 114
Roman Catholic theology: critique, 9-
11, 21, 34, 35-36, 39, 187-88; natu-
ral-law tradition, 8, 44-45, 54-55,
127, 212n.12
Romans 1:18-20: knowledge of God,
83, 103, 107-16, 140-41, 143, 157
Romans 2:14: by nature, 41-42, 45,
117-18, 147
Romans 2:14-16: natural law, 94-95,
120, 137-39
Romans 3:20: knowledge of sin, 134
Romans, analysis of Scripture, 67,
102, 103, 107, 113, 116-17
Römerbrief, Barth, Karl, 21
Rommen, Heinrich, 56
Rules, 164, 179, 216n.40, 217n.40.
See also Synderesis (conscience)

Salvation, 24, 81, 84, 108, 119, 159
Scaliger, Joseph Justus, 98, 195n.32
Scholasticism: divine will, 58, 71; me-
dieval, 18, 57-58, 67-69, 245n.77;
theory, 5-6, 44-45, 92, 153,
240n.41
Scholastics, Spanish, 212n.12
Scholia, 102, 103, 233n.45, n.50,
245n.75
Schreiner, Susan, 7, 15

Scientia, 92
Scotism, 67, 72, 249n.146
Scotus, Duns, 54; divine command,
47-49, 55, 90, 92, 164, 170-71; divine will, 57-58, 62, 67, 87, 136,
172
Scripture: foundation of theology, 16-
17, 130; knowledge of God, 26, 70,
76, 81, 83-84; law written on the
heart, 31-32, 137, 145; legislation
(lex divina), 50, 51, 137, 244n.67;
natural law, 126, 182, 185; revelation, 26, 57-58, 77, 82-83, 109,
115, 157; study of, 106-7, 111. *See
also* Romans, analysis of Scripture
Second table precepts, 72
"Secret impulse of nature," 144-45
Security, 138, 176, 179-80
"Seed of religion" *(semen religionis),*
78
Selfishness, 49
Self-preservation, 138, 176, 179-80
Semen religionis ("seed of religion"),
78
Sensus divinitatis (sense of divinity),
71, 77-78, 79, 102, 160, 162-63
Sentences *(Sententiae),* Lombard, Pe-
ter, 65, 90
Sermon on the Mount, 147. *See also*
Decalogue
Simler, Josiah, 99
Sin: conscience, 95, 107, 114, 162,
167; consequences, 30, 32, 33, 41,
56, 81, 93; grace of God, 44, 102,
159; ignorance, 113, 116, 217n.40;
natural knowledge, 30, 79, 81, 83,
134, 164; natural law, 2, 4, 9, 30,
41, 138-39, 248n.125; natural the-
ology, 25, 26, 73, 196n.34,
259n.58; original 56, 183, 188
Skillen, James, 126-27, 240n.41
Skinner, Quentin, 239n.21
Sociableness, 178, 179-80, 184
Social contract, 125, 240n.41
Social relationships, 141, 244n.67
Society, rules of, 10, 29, 72, 86, 130
Society, secular concept of, 238n.9